Undergraduate Topics in Computer Science

Undergraduate Topics in Computer Science' (UTiCS) delivers high-quality instructional content for undergraduates studying in all areas of computing and information science. From core foundational and theoretical material to final-year topics and applications, UTiCS books take a fresh, concise, and modern approach and are ideal for self-study or for a one- or two-semester course. The texts are all authored by established experts in their fields, reviewed by an international advisory board, and contain numerous examples and problems. Many include fully worked solutions.

Also in this series

Iain D. Craig
Object-Oriented Programming Languages: Interpretation
978-1-84628-773-2

Max Bramer
Principles of Data Mining
978-1-84628-765-7

Hanne Riis Nielson and Flemming Nielson
Semantics with Applications: An Appetizer
978-1-84628-691-9

Michael Kifer and Scott A. Smolka
Introduction to Operating System Design and Implementation: The OSP 2 Approcah
978-1-84628-842-5

Phil Brooke and Richard Paige
Practical Distributed Processing
978-1-84628-840-1

Frank Klawonn
Computer Graphics with Java
978-1-84628-847-0

David Salomon

A Concise Introduction to Data Compression

 Springer

Professor David Salomon (emeritus)
Computer Science Department
California State University
Northridge, CA 91330-8281, USA
email: david.salomon@csun.edu

British Library Cataloguing in Publication Data
A catalogue record for this book is available from the British Library

Library of Congress Control Number: 2007939563

Undergraduate Topics in Computer Science ISSN 1863-7310
ISBN 978-1-84800-071-1   e-ISBN 978-1-84800-072-8

This book is dedicated to you, the reader!

Nothing is more impossible than to write
a book that wins every reader's approval.

—Miguel de Cervantes

Preface

It is virtually certain that a reader of this book is both a computer user and an Internet user, and thus the owner of digital data. More and more people all over the world generate, use, own, and enjoy digital data. Digital data is created (by a word processor, a digital camera, a scanner, an audio A/D converter, or other devices), it is edited on a computer, stored (either temporarily, in memory, less temporarily, on a disk, or permanently, on an optical medium), transmitted between computers (on the Internet or in a local-area network), and output (printed, watched, or played, depending on its type).

These steps often apply mathematical methods to modify the representation of the original digital data, because of three factors, time/space limitations, reliability (data robustness), and security (data privacy). These are discussed in some detail here:

The first factor is time/space limitations. It takes time to transfer even a single byte either inside the computer (between the processor and memory) or outside it over a communications channel. It also takes space to store data, and digital images, video, and audio files tend to be large. Time, as we know, is money. Space, either in memory or on our disks, doesn't come free either. More space, in terms of bigger disks and memories, is becoming available all the time, but it remains finite. Thus, decreasing the size of data files saves time, space, and money—three important resources. The process of reducing the size of a data file is popularly referred to as *data compression*, although its formal name is *source coding* (coding done at the source of the data, before it is stored or transmitted).

In addition to being a useful concept, the idea of saving space and time by compression is ingrained in us humans, as illustrated by (1) the rapid development of nanotechnology and (2) the quotation at the end of this Preface.

The second factor is reliability. We often experience noisy telephone conversations (with both cell and landline telephones) because of electrical interference. In general, any type of data, digital or analog, sent over any kind of communications channel may become corrupted as a result of channel noise. When the bits of a data file are sent over a computer bus, a telephone line, a dedicated communications line, or a satellite connection, errors may creep in and corrupt bits. Watching a high-resolution color image or a long video, we may not be able to tell when a few pixels have wrong colors, but other types of data require absolute reliability. Examples are an executable computer program, a legal text document, a medical X-ray image, and genetic information. Change one bit in the executable code of a program, and the program will not run, or worse, it may run and do the wrong thing. Change or omit one word in a contract and it may reverse its meaning. Reliability is therefore important and is achieved by means of error-control codes. The formal name of this mathematical discipline is *channel coding*, because these codes are employed when information is transmitted on a communications channel.

The third factor that affects the storage and transmission of data is security. Generally, we do not want our data transmissions to be intercepted, copied, and read on their way. Even data saved on a disk may be sensitive and should be hidden from prying eyes. This is why digital data can be encrypted with modern, strong encryption algorithms that depend on long, randomly-selected keys. Anyone who doesn't possess the key and wants access to the data may have to resort to a long, tedious process of either trying to break the encryption (by analyzing patterns found in the encrypted file) or trying every possible key. Encryption is especially important for diplomatic communications, messages that deal with money, or data sent by members of secret organizations. A close relative of data encryption is the field of data hiding (steganography). A data file A (a payload) that consists of bits may be hidden in a larger data file B (a cover) by taking advantage of "holes" in B that are the result of redundancies in the way data is represented in B.

Overview and goals

This book is devoted to the first of these factors, namely data compression. It explains why data can be compressed, it outlines the principles of the various approaches to compressing data, and it describes several compression algorithms, some of which are general, while others are designed for a specific type of data.

The goal of the book is to introduce the reader to the chief approaches, methods, and techniques that are currently employed to compress data. The main aim is to start with a clear overview of the principles behind this field, to complement this view with several examples of important compression algorithms, and to present this material to the reader in a coherent manner.

Organization and features

The book is organized in two parts, basic concepts and advanced techniques. The first part consists of the first three chapters. They discuss the basic approaches to data compression and describe a few popular techniques and methods that are commonly used to compress data. Chapter 1 introduces the reader to the important concepts of variable-length codes, prefix codes, statistical distributions, run-length encoding, dictionary compression, transforms, and quantization. Chapter 2 is devoted to the important Huffman algorithm and codes, and Chapter 3 describes some of the many dictionary-based compression methods.

The second part of this book is concerned with advanced techniques. The original and unusual technique of arithmetic coding is the topic of Chapter 4. Chapter 5 is devoted to image compression. It starts with the chief approaches to the compression of images, explains orthogonal transforms, and discusses the JPEG algorithm, perhaps the best example of the use of these transforms. The second part of this chapter is concerned with subband transforms and presents the WSQ method for fingerprint compression as an example of the application of these sophisticated transforms. Chapter 6 is devoted to the compression of audio data and in particular to the technique of linear prediction. Finally, other approaches to compression—such as the Burrows–Wheeler method, symbol ranking, and SCSU and BOCU-1—are given their due in Chapter 7.

The many exercises sprinkled throughout the text serve two purposes, they illuminate subtle points that may seem insignificant to readers and encourage readers to test their knowledge by performing computations and obtaining numerical results.

Other aids to learning are a prelude at the beginning of each chapter and various intermezzi where interesting topics, related to the main theme, are examined. In addition, a short summary and self-assessment exercises follow each chapter. The glossary at the end of the book is comprehensive, and the index is detailed, to allow a reader to easily locate all the points in the text where a given topic, subject, or term appear.

Other features that liven up the text are puzzles (indicated by ✦ with answers at the end of the book) and various boxes with quotations or with biographical information on relevant persons.

Target audience

This book was written with undergraduate students in mind as the chief readership. In general, however, it is aimed at those who have a basic knowledge of computer science; who know something about programming and data structures; who feel comfortable with terms such as *bit*, *mega*, *ASCII*, *file*, *I/O*, and *binary search*; and who want to know how data is compressed. The necessary mathematical background is minimal and is limited to logarithms, matrices, polynomials, calculus, and the concept of probability. This book is not intended as a guide to software implementors and has few programs.

The book's web site, with an errata list, BibTeX information, and auxiliary material, is part of the author's web site, located at `http://www.ecs.csun.edu/~dsalomon/`. Any errors found, comments, and suggestions should be directed to `dsalomon@csun.edu`.

Acknowlegments

I would like to thank Giovanni Motta and John Motil for their help and encouragement. Giovanni also contributed to the text and pointed out numerous errors.

In addition, my editors at Springer Verlag, Wayne Wheeler and Catherine Brett, deserve much praise. They went over the manuscript, made numerous suggestions and improvements, and contributed much to the final appearance of the book.

Lakeside, California   David Salomon
August 2007

> To see a world in a grain of sand
> And a heaven in a wild flower,
> Hold infinity in the palm of your hand
> And eternity in an hour.
>
> —William Blake, *Auguries of Innocence*

Contents

Preface _____ vii

Part I: Basic Concepts   1

Introduction _____ 5

1   **Approaches to Compression** _____ 21

   1.1   Variable-Length Codes   25
   1.2   Run-Length Encoding   41
        Intermezzo: Space-Filling Curves   46
   1.3   Dictionary-Based Methods   47
   1.4   Transforms   50
   1.5   Quantization   51
        Chapter Summary   58

2   **Huffman Coding** _____ 61

   2.1   Huffman Encoding   63
   2.2   Huffman Decoding   67
   2.3   Adaptive Huffman Coding   76
        Intermezzo: History of Fax   83
   2.4   Facsimile Compression   85
        Chapter Summary   90

3   **Dictionary Methods** _____ 93

   3.1   LZ78   95
        Intermezzo: The LZW Trio   98
   3.2   LZW   98
   3.3   Deflate: Zip and Gzip   108
        Chapter Summary   119

Part II: Advanced Techniques 121

4 Arithmetic Coding _____ 123

4.1	The Basic Idea	124
4.2	Implementation Details	130
4.3	Underflow	133
4.4	Final Remarks	134
	Intermezzo: The Real Numbers	135
4.5	Adaptive Arithmetic Coding	137
4.6	Range Encoding	140
	Chapter Summary	141

5 Image Compression _____ 143

5.1	Introduction	144
5.2	Approaches to Image Compression	146
	Intermezzo: History of Gray Codes	151
5.3	Image Transforms	152
5.4	Orthogonal Transforms	156
5.5	The Discrete Cosine Transform	160
	Intermezzo: Statistical Distributions	178
5.6	JPEG	179
	Intermezzo: Human Vision and Color	184
5.7	The Wavelet Transform	198
5.8	Filter Banks	216
5.9	WSQ, Fingerprint Compression	218
	Chapter Summary	225

6 Audio Compression _____ 227

6.1	Companding	230
6.2	The Human Auditory System	231
	Intermezzo: Heinrich Georg Barkhausen	234
6.3	Linear Prediction	235
6.4	μ-Law and A-Law Companding	238
6.5	Shorten	244
	Chapter Summary	245

7 Other Methods _____ 247

7.1	The Burrows–Wheeler Method	248
	Intermezzo: Fibonacci Codes	253
7.2	Symbol Ranking	254
7.3	SCSU: Unicode Compression	258
	Chapter Summary	263

Bibliography _____ 265

Glossary _____ 271

Contents

Solutions to Puzzles ———————————————————— 281

Answers to Exercises ———————————————————— 283

Index ————————————————————————————————— 305

The content of most textbooks is perishable, but the
tools of self-directness serve one well over time.

—Albert Bandura

Part I:
Basic Concepts

Our everyday experience suggests that compression is an option that we naturally select when faced with problems of high cost or restricted space. The following points illustrate how such problems have been solved throughout history by resorting to (often intuitive) compression:

- In ancient Greece, manuscripts were written on papyrus, which was then very expensive. As a result, writers tried to squeeze more text in a given space by eliminating punctuations and interword spaces (Figure 1).

- In ancient Rome, people went around the high cost of tombstone engraving by resorting to acronyms, the most common of which were S.T.L. (Sit Terra Levit, or let the earth rest lightly upon her), D.M. (Dis Manibus, or to the ghosts of the underworld), and B.M. (Bene Merenti, or to one deserving well).

Figure 1: Greek Papyrus and Ancient Coin.

- In the middle ages, praise for the current ruler was often stamped onto coins in the form of acronyms, because of the tight space available (Figure 1).

- In a natural language, common words tend to be shorter than rarely-used words. It is hard to imagine a language where the word for, say, `yes` would be as long as `encyclopedia` or the word for `establishment` would be as short as `me`.

- We are familiar with the term "fine print." This term is often used to hide unfriendly clauses in a contract, or negative aspects of an item being advertised. Sometimes, however, small print is simply used to save space, as is common in newspapers.

- The Arabic numerals that we use are based on weights assigned to positions in the number. Thus, the digit 4 in 24,806 has a weight of $10^3 = 1000$, so its value is 4,000. This numbering system has many advantages, not the least of which is that the numbers are short. They are shorter than Roman numerals and much shorter than stone-age numerals (see the discussion of stone-age binary in Section 1.1.1).

- The well-known Morse code (Section 1.1) assigns short codes to common letters, such as E and T and long codes to rare letters, such as Z and Q. This is an early example of intuitive text compression.

- The six-shutter telecommunication system, used by the British admiralty in the 19th century, could transmit 64 different symbols, more than enough for the letters and digits. The extra symbols were assigned to common words. This system is described in [Holzmann and Pehrson 95] and its application to compression is mentioned in [Bell et al. 90].

- A similar system is the well-known Braille code for the blind. Developed by Louis Braille in the 1820s, this code consists of groups (or cells) of 3×2 dots each, embossed on thick paper. Each of the six dots in a group may be flat or raised, implying that the information content of a group is equivalent to six bits, resulting in 64 possible groups. Once appropriate codes are assigned to the letters, digits, and common punctuation marks, several groups remain and may be used to code common words—such as `and`, `for`, and `of`—and common strings of letters—such as `ound`, `ation`, and `th`.

- Scientists often claim that the chief aim of science is to explain as many known facts as possible by deduction from as few assumptions (or axioms) as possible. This is an example of economy of expression.

- Similarly, Occam's razor (attributed to the 14th-century logician William of Ockham) is a principle which states that the explanation of a phenomenon should make as few assumptions as possible (entia non sunt multiplicanda praeter necessitatem, or entities should not be multiplied beyond necessity).

The first part of this book consists of the first three chapters. They discuss the basic approaches to data compression and describe a few popular techniques and methods that are commonly used to compress data. Chapter 1 introduces the reader to the important concepts of variable-length codes, prefix codes, statistical distributions, run-length encoding, dictionary compression, transforms, and quantization. Chapter 2 is devoted to the important Huffman algorithm and codes, and Chapter 3 describes some of the many dictionary-based compression methods.

> There are four basic food groups: milk chocolate, dark chocolate, white chocolate, and chocolate truffles.
>
> —Anonymous

Introduction

The modern discipline of data compression is concerned with reducing the size of digital binary data. A data compression algorithm inputs a bitstream (a disk file or bits read from a network) and outputs a shorter bitstream. Most of the physical objects surrounding us are difficult or impossible to shrink (or are damaged when forcibly compressed), so shrinking the size of a data file may seem like magic (or perhaps like cheating). Thus, before we try to explain *how* data is compressed, it is important to explain *why* it can be compressed. The key to compressing data is the distinction between data and information. Data is how information is represented; it is the physical embodiment of the information. We know that it is possible to use different amounts of data to convey the same information. A good example is a story. A novel that originally occupies 300 pages can be "digested" and compressed to just 30 pages without losing the main outlines of the plot. The same story may be told by one person in 2000 words and by another in 200 words because the former employs unnecessary (or irrelevant) words, thus introducing redundancy into his narrative, while the latter selects only those words that are strictly needed.

In simple terms, data can be compressed because its original representation is not the shortest possible. We use different digital data structures to represent various types of information in our computers, and we use these particular structures because they make it easy to visualize the information and operate on it. Compression changes the data representation to a shorter one (ideally, the shortest one), but it is difficult or even impossible to visualize and process the information in such a representation.

In technical terms we say that the original representation of data has redundancies and compressing the data reduces or eliminates these redundancies. Random data is just that, random; it has no structure. Any nonrandom data is nonrandom because it has structure in the form of regular patterns, and it is this structure that introduces redundancies into the data. Data that has no redundancy to begin with cannot be compressed. Thus, compression of data is not absolute. Given a data file, we cannot tell whether it is small enough or too large. We have to look for redundancies (in terms of structures or patterns) in the data and compress the data by eliminating them. Compression should always be measured by comparing the size of the compressed data with the size of the original data.

The interpretation of compression as the removal of redundancy also explains why it is impossible to compress data that has already been compressed. When data is compressed, any redundancies in it, in the form of structures or patterns, is removed. The compressed data features no structure and cannot be distinguished from random data; in fact, it is random. Thus, any attempt to compress it again will fail. If it were possible to compress data that is already compressed, then we could start with a data file A, compress it to a smaller file B, compress B in turn to a smaller file C, and continue in this way until a 1-byte (or even a 1-bit) file is reached. A 1-byte file cannot contain all the data of file A (whose size is arbitrary), so recursive compression is impossible.

The following simple argument illustrates the essence of the statement "Data compression is achieved by reducing or removing redundancy in the data." The argument shows that most data files cannot be compressed, no matter what compression method is used. This seems strange at first because we compress our data files all the time. The point is that most files cannot be compressed because they are random or close to random and therefore have no redundancy. The (relatively) few files that can be compressed are the ones that we *want* to compress; they are the files we use all the time. They have redundancy, are nonrandom and are therefore useful and interesting.

Here is the argument. Given two different files A and B that are compressed to files C and D, respectively, it is clear that C and D must be different. If they were identical, there would be no way to decompress them and get back file A or file B.

Suppose that a file of size n bits is given and we want to compress it efficiently. Any compression method that can compress this file to, say, 10 bits would be welcome. Even compressing it to 11 bits or 12 bits would be great. We therefore (somewhat arbitrarily) assume that compressing such a file to half its size or better is considered good compression. There are 2^n n-bit files and they would have to be compressed into 2^n different files of sizes less than or equal to $n/2$. However, the total number of these files is

$$N = 1 + 2 + 4 + \cdots + 2^{n/2} = 2^{1+n/2} - 1 \approx 2^{1+n/2},$$

so only N of the 2^n original files have a chance of being compressed efficiently. The problem is that N is much smaller than 2^n. Here are two examples of the ratio between these two numbers.

For $n = 100$ (files with just 100 bits), the total number of files is 2^{100} and the number of files that can be compressed efficiently is 2^{51}. The ratio of these numbers is the ridiculously small fraction $2^{-49} \approx 1.78 \times 10^{-15}$.

For $n = 1000$ (files with just 1000 bits, about 125 bytes), the total number of files is 2^{1000} and the number of files that can be compressed efficiently is 2^{501}. The ratio of these numbers is the incredibly small fraction $2^{-499} \approx 9.82 \times 10^{-91}$.

Most files of interest are at least some thousands of bytes long. For such files, the percentage of files that can be efficiently compressed is so small that it cannot be computed with floating-point numbers even on a supercomputer (the result comes out as zero).

The 50% figure used here is arbitrary, but even increasing it to 90% isn't going to make a significant difference. Here is why. Assuming that a file of n bits is given and that $0.9n$ is an integer, the number of files of sizes up to $0.9n$ is

$$2^0 + 2^1 + \cdots + 2^{0.9n} = 2^{1+0.9n} - 1 \approx 2^{1+0.9n}.$$

For $n = 100$, there are 2^{100} files and $2^{1+90} = 2^{91}$ can be compressed well. The ratio of these numbers is $2^{91}/2^{100} = 2^{-9} \approx 0.00195$. For $n = 1000$, the corresponding fraction is $2^{901}/2^{1000} = 2^{-99} \approx 1.578 \times 10^{-30}$. These are still extremely small fractions.

It is therefore clear that no compression method can hope to compress all files or even a significant percentage of them. In order to compress a data file, the compression algorithm has to examine the data, find redundancies in it, and try to remove them. The redundancies in data depend on the type of data (text, images, audio, etc.), which is why a new compression method has to be developed for a specific type of data and it performs best on this type. There is no such thing as a universal, efficient data compression algorithm.

In spite of the arguments above, there are always those who claim to have developed a "magic" compression method that can compress any data file to a small fraction of its original size. Reference [incredible 07] lists quite a few such claims.

Multimedia digital data. The first computers were conceived as fast, reliable computing machines, but it did not take computer users long to realize that the computer can also process nonnumeric data. The various compilers for programming languages are one such example, as are also databases, computer games, and computer networks. However, it was not until the 1990s that many *multimedia* applications were developed and came into popular use. The term "multimedia" refers to the ability to digitize, store, and manipulate in the computer all kinds of data, not just numbers. Today (2008), computer users commonly create, edit, store, view, and exchange text, still images, video, and audio data easily and reliably.

Multimedia (noun, plural), the use of different media to convey information; text together with audio, graphics and animation, often packaged on CD-ROM with links to the Internet.

—`wiktionary.com`

Each type of data is represented differently in the computer and features different structures and redundancies. This is why different approaches and techniques are needed to compress it. Following is a discussion of the representations and redundancies of the main data types.

Text is represented in the computer as individual characters, each encoded in binary. The codes are all the same length, because fixed-size codes are easy to store in memory, move about, and operate on. For many years, the ASCII code, developed in the 1960s, was the de facto standard. Each character of text was assigned a 7-bit code (actually, a $(7+1)$-bit code, where the eighth bit serves as a parity, for added reliability). Thus, there are $2^7 = 128$ ASCII codes, for the letters, digits, some punctuation marks, and various control functions. In the 1970s and 1980s, inexpensive, high-resolution printers and display monitors came into being, where virtually any character can be displayed and printed. These developments were the motivation for the Unicode project which started in the early 1990s. Unicode assigns 16-bit codes to text symbols, and can therefore represent $2^{16} = 65,536$ symbols (there are provisions for even longer codes, so the number of possible Unicode symbols is much greater).

The point is that certain letters appear in text more often than others, and the use of fixed-size codes introduces structure (and thus redundancy) into text. It has been known for a long time that the letters E, T, and A are common in English texts, while

J, Z, and Q are rare. Thus, English text can be compressed by assigning variable-length codes to the various letters such that common letters are assigned short codes and rare letters are assigned long codes. Chapter 1 discusses a few variable-length codes and their applications.

Note that text compression must be lossless. It is hard to come up with examples where text data can lose a certain percentage of the text while being compressed, and still be useful after decompression. However, the other types of data discussed here can lose much data while being compressed, and be decompressed later without any noticeable degradation in quality. This is why lossy compression, which often features excellent performance, is so popular.

Images. A digital image is a rectangular array of dots called pixels. A pixel has one attribute, its color, and this attribute is stored in the computer as a fixed-size code. The use of fixed-size codes again introduces redundancy, because adjacent pixels tend to have similar codes (we say that the pixels are correlated). An image where adjacent pixels always have wildly different colors looks random, has no structure, features no redundancy, and therefore cannot be compressed. Images that are of interest, however, are far from random and exhibit structure in the form of pixel correlation. This type of redundancy is termed interpixel redundancy.

Thus, an image can be compressed by, for example, subtracting the values of adjacent pixels. The pixels have similar colors, so their differences are small numbers, which require fewer bits. More sophisticated approaches to image compression are discussed in Chapter 5.

In addition to interpixel redundancy, images often have two more types of redundancy, coding redundancy and psychovisual redundancy, which can be exploited for compression.

Coding redundancy has to do with the distribution of colors in an image. Given a digital image, it is easy to count the number of pixels that have color C. When this is done for every color C, we normally find that a few colors dominate the image. We say that the color distribution (or histogram) is nonuniform. This redundancy suggests a way to compress the image. Replace each pixel with a variable-length code and assign the short codes to the dominant colors.

Psychovisual redundancy has to do with the properties of the human eye. The eye is very sensitive to light and can often detect just a few photons. However, the eye is not a precision device and its sensitivity varies with the type of light that falls on it. It has been known for many years that the eye is very sensitive to variations in the luminance (brightness) of light but is much less sensitive to variations in the chrominance (color) component of the light. Thus, an image can be compressed if the color of each pixel is represented in terms of luminance and chrominance and the latter components are heavily quantized.

Video data consists of a string of images, much as a movie consists of many images (called frames) on a strip of celluloid. There are two sources of redundancy in a video, intraframe redundancy (the correlation of pixels in each frame) and interframe redundancy (the fact that adjacent frames tend to be similar). The former redundancy can be reduced by the same methods employed in image compression, while the latter redundancy is dealt with by methods that compare a frame with its predecessor and encode the differences between them.

Audio data also features redundancy in the form of correlation between consecutive audio samples, but first, a few words about audio and how it is digitized.

Sound is a wave. It can be viewed as a physical disturbance in the air (or some other media) or as a pressure wave propagated by the movement of molecules. A microphone is a device that senses sound and converts it to an electrical wave, i.e., a voltage that varies continuously with time in the same way as the sound. To convert this voltage into a format where it can be input into a computer, stored, edited, and played back, the voltage is sampled many times each second. Each sample is a number whose value is proportional to the voltage at the time of sampling. Figure Intro.1 shows a wave sampled at three points and it is obvious that the first sample is a small number and the third sample is a large number, close to the maximum.

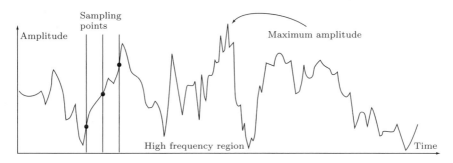

Figure Intro.1: Sound Wave and Three Samples.

Thus, audio sampling (or digitized sound) is a simple concept, but its success in practice depends on one important factor, the sampling rate. How many times should a sound wave be sampled each second? Sampling too often creates too many audio samples, while a very low sampling rate results in low-quality played-back sound. It seems intuitively that the sampling rate should depend on the frequency, but the frequency of a sound wave varies all the time, while the sampling rate should remain constant (a variable sampling rate makes it difficult to edit and play back the digitized sound). The solution was discovered back in the 1920s by H. Nyquist. It states that the optimum sampling frequency should be slightly greater than twice the maximum frequency of the sound. The sound wave of Figure Intro.1 has a region of high frequency at its center. To obtain the optimum sampling rate for this particular wave, we should determine the maximum frequency at this region, double it, and increase the result slightly.

Every sound wave has its own maximum frequency, but digitized sound used in practice is based on the fact that the highest frequency that the human ear can perceive is about 22,000 Hz. The optimum sampling rate that corresponds to this frequency is 44,100 Hz, and this rate is used when sound is digitized and recorded on a CD or DVD.

Now, back to audio compression. Digital audio is a string of audio samples, and it can be compressed because adjacent audio samples tend to be similar; they are correlated, which introduces redundancy into the audio data. With 44,100 samples each second, it is no wonder that adjacent samples are virtually always similar. Audio data where many audio samples are very different from their neighbors would sound harsh and dissonant.

Thus, audio can be compressed by subtracting each audio sample from its predecessor and replacing the differences (which tend to be small integers) by suitable variable-length codes. Practical methods often "predict" the current sample by computing a weighted sum of several previously-input samples, and then subtracting the current sample from the prediction.

Entropy and Redundancy

Understanding data compression and its codes must start with an understanding of information, because the former is based on the latter. This short section introduces the relevant concepts from information theory.

Information theory is the creation, in the late 1940s, of Claude Shannon. Shannon tried to develop means for measuring the amount of information stored in a symbol without considering the meaning of the information. He discovered the connection between the logarithm function and information, and showed that the information content (in bits) of a symbol with probability p is $-\log_2 p$. If the base of the logarithm is e, then the information is measured in units called nats. If the base is 3, the information units are trits, and if the base is 10, the units are referred to as Hartleys.

Information theory is concerned with the transmission of information from a sender (termed a source), through a communications channel, to a receiver. The sender and receiver can be persons or machines and the receiver may, in turn, act as intermediary and send the information it has received to another receiver. The information is sent in units called symbols (normally bits, but in verbal communications the symbols are spoken words) and the set of all possible data symbols is an alphabet.

The most important single factor affecting communications is noise in the communications channel. In verbal communications, this noise is, literally, noise. When trying to talk in a noisy environment, we may lose part of the discussion. In electronic communications, the channel noise is caused by imperfect hardware and by factors such as sudden lightning, voltage fluctuations—old, high-resistance wires—sudden surge in temperature, and interference from machines that generate strong electromagnetic fields.

The presence of noise implies that special codes should be used to increase the reliability of transmitted information. This is referred to as channel coding or, in everyday language, error-control codes.

The second most important factor affecting communications is sheer volume. Any communications channel has a limited capacity. It can transmit only a limited number of symbols per time unit. An obvious way to increase the amount of data transmitted is to compress it before it is sent (in the source). Methods to compress data are therefore known as source coding or, in everyday language, data compression. The feature that makes it possible to compress data is the fact that individual symbols appear in our data files with different probabilities. Thus, data can be compressed by assigning variable-length codes to the individual data symbols such that short codes are assigned to the common symbols.

Two concepts from information theory, namely entropy and redundancy, are needed in order to fully understand the principles behind the various methods for and approaches to data compression.

Roughly speaking, the term "entropy" as defined by Shannon is a real number that is proportional to the minimum number of yes/no questions needed to reach the answer to some question. Another way of looking at entropy is as a quantity that describes how much information is included in a signal or an event.

In order to understand the definition of entropy, we perform a thought experiment where we measure the heights of 10,000 people. Suppose that we find that 1,500 people have a height of h. We can say that the probability of having height h in our sample of 10,000 people is $1,500/10,000 = 0.15$. Statisticians perform such experiments and they talk about random variables. A random variable X is an entity that can have certain values x_i, each with probability P_i. In our experiment, the probability that our random variable will have the value h is 0.15, and it can have other values with different probabilities.

Given a discrete random variable X that can have n values x_i with probabilities P_i, the entropy $H(X)$ of X is defined as

$$H(X) = -\sum_{i=1}^{n} P_i \log_2 P_i.$$

The surprising, unexpected part in this definition is the use of the logarithm. The following paragraphs explain why the familiar logarithm function constitutes such an important part of information theory and plays such an important role in measuring information.

Imagine a source that emits symbols a_i with probabilities p_i. We assume that the source is memoryless, i.e., the probability of a symbol being emitted does not depend on what has been emitted in the past (the parallel in our thought experiment is that the height of a person being measured does not depend on the height of the previous person measured). We want to define a function $I(a_i)$ that will measure the amount of information gained when we discover that the source has emitted symbol a_i. Function I will also measure our uncertainty as to whether the next symbol will be a_i. Alternatively, $I(a_i)$ corresponds to our surprise in finding that the next symbol is a_i. Clearly, our surprise at seeing a_i emitted is inversely proportional to the probability p_i (we are surprised when a low-probability symbol is emitted, but not when we notice a high-probability symbol). Thus, it makes sense to require that function I satisfies the following conditions:

1. $I(a_i)$ is a decreasing function of p_i, and returns 0 when the probability of a symbol is 1. This reflects our feeling that high-probability events convey less information.

2. $I(a_i a_j) = I(a_i) + I(a_j)$. This is a result of the source being memoryless and the probabilities being independent. Discovering that a_i was immediately followed by a_j, provided us with the same information as knowing that a_i and a_j were emitted independently.

Even those with a minimal mathematical background may quickly realize that the logarithm function satisfies the two conditions above. This is the first example of the relation between the logarithm function and the quantitative measure of information. The next few paragraphs illustrate other connections between the two.

Consider the case of person A selecting at random an integer N between 1 and 64 and person B having to guess N. What is the minimum number of yes/no questions that are needed for B to guess N? Those familiar with the technique of binary search know the answer. Using this technique, B should divide the interval 1–64 in two, and should start by asking "is N between 1 and 32?" If the answer is no, then N is in the interval 33 to 64. This interval is then divided by two and B's next question should be "is N between 33 and 48?" This process continues until the interval selected by B shrinks to a single number.

It does not take much to see that exactly six questions are necessary to determine N. This is because 6 is the number of times 64 can be divided in half. Mathematically, this is equivalent to writing $2^6 = 64$ or $6 = \log_2 64$, which is why the logarithm is the mathematical function that quantifies information.

> What we call reality arises in the last analysis from the posing of yes/no questions. All things physical are information-theoretic in origin, and this is a participatory universe.
> —John Wheeler

Another approach to the same problem is to consider a nonnegative integer N and ask how many digits does it take to express it. The answer, of course, depends on N. The greater N, the more digits are needed. The first 100 nonnegative integers (0 through 99) can be expressed by two decimal digits. The first 1,000 such integers can be expressed by three digits. Again it does not take long to see the connection. The number of digits required to represent N equals approximately $\log N$. The base of the logarithm is the same as the base of the digits. For decimal digits, use base 10; for binary digits (bits), use base 2. If we agree that the number of digits it takes to express N is proportional to the information content of N, then again the logarithm is the function that gives us a measure of the information. As an aside, the precise length, in bits, of the binary representation of a positive integer n is $1 + \lfloor \log_2 n \rfloor$, or alternatively, $\lceil \log_2(n+1) \rceil$. When n is represented in any other number base b, its length is given by the same formula, but with the logarithm in base b instead of 2.

Here is another observation that illuminates the relation between the logarithm and information. A 10-bit string can have $2^{10} = 1,024$ values. We say that such a string may contain one of 1,024 messages, or that the length of the string is the logarithm of the number of possible messages the string can convey.

The following example sheds more light on the concept of entropy and will prepare us for the definition of redundancy. Given a set of two symbols a_1 and a_2, with probabilities P_1 and P_2, respectively, we compute the entropy of the set for various values of the probabilities. Since $P_1 + P_2 = 1$, the entropy of the set is $-P_1 \log_2 P_1 - (1-P_1) \log_2(1-P_1)$ and the results are summarized in Table Intro.2.

When $P_1 = P_2$, at least one bit is required to encode each symbol, reflecting the fact that the entropy is at its maximum, the redundancy is zero, and the data cannot be compressed. However, when the probabilities are very different, the minimum number of bits required per symbol drops significantly. We may not be able to conceive of a compression method that expresses each symbol in just 0.08 bits, but we know that when $P_1 = 99\%$, such compression is theoretically possible.

In general, the entropy of a set of n symbols depends on the individual probabilities P_i of the symbols and is largest when all n probabilities are equal. Data representations

P_1	P_2	Entropy
0.99	0.01	0.08
0.90	0.10	0.47
0.80	0.20	0.72
0.70	0.30	0.88
0.60	0.40	0.97
0.50	0.50	1.00

Table Intro.2: Probabilities and Entropies of Two Symbols.

often include redundancies and data can be compressed by reducing or eliminating these redundancies. When the entropy is at its maximum, the data has maximum information content and therefore cannot be further compressed. Thus, it makes sense to define redundancy as a quantity that goes down to zero as the entropy reaches its maximum.

> The fundamental problem of communication is that of reproducing at one point either exactly or approximately a message selected at another point.
> —Claude Shannon (1948)

To understand the definition of redundancy, we start with an alphabet of symbols a_i, where each symbol appears in the data with probability P_i. The data is compressed by replacing each symbol with an l_i-bit-long code. The average code length is the sum $\sum P_i l_i$ and the entropy (the smallest number of bits required to represent the symbols) is $\sum[-P_i \log_2 P_i]$. The redundancy R of the set of symbols is defined as the average code length minus the entropy. Thus,

$$R = \sum_i P_i l_i - \sum_i [-P_i \log_2 P_i].$$

The redundancy is zero when the average code length equals the entropy, i.e., when the codes are the shortest and compression has reached its maximum.

Given a set of symbols (an alphabet), we can assign binary codes to the individual symbols. It is easy to assign long codes to symbols, but most practical applications require the shortest possible codes.

Consider the four symbols a_1, a_2, a_3, and a_4. If they appear in our data strings with equal probabilities ($= 0.25$), then the entropy of the data is $-4(0.25 \log_2 0.25) = 2$. Two is the smallest number of bits needed, on average, to represent each symbol in this case. We can simply assign our symbols the four 2-bit codes 00, 01, 10, and 11. Since the probabilities are equal, the redundancy is zero and the data cannot be compressed below two bits/symbol.

Next, consider the case where the four symbols occur with different probabilities as shown in Table Intro.3, where a_1 appears in the data (on average) about half the time, a_2 and a_3 have equal probabilities, and a_4 is rare. In this case, the data has entropy $-(0.49 \log_2 0.49 + 0.25 \log_2 0.25 + 0.25 \log_2 0.25 + 0.01 \log_2 0.01) \approx -(-0.050 - 0.5 - 0.5 - 0.066) = 1.57$. The smallest number of bits needed, on average, to represent each symbol has dropped to 1.57.

If we again assign our symbols the four 2-bit codes 00, 01, 10, and 11, the redundancy would be $R = -1.57 + \log_2 4 = 0.43$. This suggests assigning variable-length codes to

Symbol	Prob.	Code1	Code2
a_1	0.49	1	1
a_2	0.25	01	01
a_3	0.25	010	000
a_4	0.01	001	001

Table Intro.3: Variable-Length Codes.

the symbols. Code1 of Table Intro.3 is designed such that the most common symbol, a_1, is assigned the shortest code. When long data strings are transmitted using Code1, the average size (the number of bits per symbol) is $1 \times 0.49 + 2 \times 0.25 + 3 \times 0.25 + 3 \times 0.01 = 1.77$, which is very close to the minimum. The redundancy in this case is $R = 1.77 - 1.57 = 0.2$ bits per symbol. An interesting example is the 20-symbol string $a_1a_3a_2a_1a_3a_3a_4a_2a_1a_1a_2a_2a_1a_1a_3a_1a_1a_2a_3a_1$, where the four symbols occur with approximately the right frequencies. Encoding this string with Code1 yields the 37 bits:

$$1|010|01|1|010|010|001|01|1|1|01|01|1|1|010|1|1|01|010|1$$

(without the vertical bars). Using 37 bits to encode 20 symbols yields an average size of 1.85 bits/symbol, not far from the calculated average size. (The reader should bear in mind that our examples are short. To obtain results close to the best that's theoretically possible, an input stream with at least thousands of symbols is needed.)

However, the conscientious reader may have noticed that Code1 is bad because it is not a prefix code. Code2, in contrast, is a prefix code and can be decoded uniquely. Notice how Code2 was constructed. Once the single bit 1 was assigned as the code of a_1, no other codes could start with 1 (they all had to start with 0). Once 01 was assigned as the code of a_2, no other codes could start with 01. This is why the codes of a_3 and a_4 had to start with 00. Naturally, they became 000 and 001.

Several important data compression terms are introduced next.

■ The *compressor* or *encoder* is the program that compresses raw data and generates compressed (low-redundancy) output. The *decompressor* or *decoder* converts in the opposite direction. Note that the term *encoding* is very general and has several meanings, but since this book discusses only data compression, it employs the term *encoder* for compressor. The term *codec* is used to describe both the encoder and the decoder. Similarly, the term *companding* is short for "compressing/expanding."

■ For the original, uncompressed data, we use the terms *unencoded*, *raw*, or *original* data. The compressed data is also termed *encoded*. The term *bitstream* is often used in the literature to indicate the compressed data.

■ A *nonadaptive* compression method is inflexible and does not modify its operations, its parameters, or its tables in response to the particular data being compressed. In contrast, an *adaptive* method examines the raw data and modifies its operations and/or its parameters accordingly. Some compression methods use a 2-pass algorithm, where the first pass reads the input to collect statistics on the data to be compressed, and the second pass does the actual compression using parameters or codes set by the first pass. Such a method may be called *semiadaptive*. A data compression method can also be *locally adaptive*, meaning it adapts itself to local conditions in the input and varies this adaptation as it moves from region to region in the input.

- *Lossy/lossless compression:* Certain compression methods are lossy. They achieve better compression by losing some information. When the compressed data is later decompressed, the result is different from the original. Such a method makes sense especially in image, video, or audio compression. If the loss of data is small, the eye or ear may not perceive any difference. In contrast, text files, especially files containing computer programs, often become meaningless or worthless if even one bit is modified. Such files should be compressed only by a lossless compression method.

- *Perceptive compression:* A lossy encoder must take advantage of the special type of data that is being compressed. It should delete only data whose absence would not be detected by our senses. Such an encoder must therefore employ algorithms based on our understanding of psychoacoustic and psychovisual perception, which is why it is sometimes referred to as a perceptive encoder. Such an encoder can be made to operate at a constant compression ratio, where for each x bits of raw data, it outputs y bits of compressed data. This is convenient in cases where the compressed data has to be transmitted at a constant rate. The trade-off is a variable subjective quality. Parts of the original data that are difficult to compress may, after decompression, look (or sound) bad. Such parts may require more than y bits of output for x bits of input.

- *Symmetric compression* is the case where the decompressor is the reverse of the compressor. Such a method makes sense for general work, where the same number of files is compressed as is decompressed. In an asymmetric compression method, either the compressor or the decompressor may have to work significantly harder. Such methods have their uses and are not necessarily bad. A compression method where the compressor executes a slow, complex algorithm and the decompressor is simple is a natural choice when files are compressed into an archive (a CDs and DVDs are good examples) where they will be decompressed and used very often. The opposite case is useful in environments where files are updated all the time and backups are made. There is only a small chance that a backup file will be used, so the decompressor is rarely used and can be slow.

When you look	kool uoy nehW
into a mirror	rorrim a otni
it is not	ton si ti
yourself you see	ees uoy flesruoy
but a kind	dnik a tub
of apish error	rorre hsipa fo
posed in fearful	lufraef ni desop
symmetry	yrtemmys

John Updike, "Mirror," in *Telephone Poles and Other Poems* (1963)

⋄ **Exercise Intro.1:** Give an example of a compressed file where efficient compression is important but the speed of both compressor and decompressor isn't important.

▪ Many modern compression methods are asymmetric. Often, the formal specification of such a method consists of a description of the decoder and the format of the compressed data, but does not discuss the operation of the encoder. Any encoder that generates a correct compressed file is considered compliant, as is also any decoder that can read and decode such a file. The advantage of such a description is that anyone is free to develop and implement new, sophisticated algorithms for the encoder. The implementor need not even publish the details of the encoder and may consider it proprietary. If a compliant encoder is demonstrably better than competing encoders, it may become a commercial success. In such a scheme, the encoder is considered *algorithmic*, while the decoder, which is normally much simpler, is termed *deterministic*.

▪ A data compression method is called *universal* if the compressor and decompressor do not know the statistics of the input data and do not use it explicitly. A universal method is *optimal* if the compressor can produce compression factors that asymptotically approach the entropy of the input stream for long inputs.

▪ The term *file differencing* refers to any method that locates and compresses the differences between two files. Imagine a file A with two copies that are kept by two users. When a copy is updated by one user, it should be sent to the other user, to keep the two copies identical. Instead of sending a copy of A, which may be big, a much smaller file containing just the differences, in compressed format, can be sent and used at the receiving end to update the copy of A.

▪ Most compression methods operate in the *streaming mode*, where the codec inputs a byte or several bytes, processes them, and continues until an end-of-file is sensed. Some methods, such as Burrows–Wheeler (Section 7.1), work in the *block mode*, where the input is read block by block and each block is encoded separately. The block size in this case should be a user-controlled parameter, because its size may greatly affect the performance of the method.

▪ *Compression performance*: Several measures are commonly used to indicate the performance of a compression method.

1. The *compression ratio* is defined as

$$\text{Compression ratio} = \frac{\text{size of the output stream}}{\text{size of the input stream}}.$$

A value of 0.6 means that the data occupies 60% of its original size after compression. Values greater than 1 imply expansion (negative compression). The compression ratio can also be called bpb (bit per bit), since it equals the number of bits in the compressed data that are needed, on average, to compress one bit in the input data. In modern, efficient text compression methods, it makes sense to talk about bpc (bits per character)—the number of bits it takes, on average, to compress one character in the input.

The term *bitrate* is a general name for bpb and bpc. Thus, the main goal of data compression is to represent any given data at low bitrates.

2. The inverse of the compression ratio is the *compression factor*:

$$\text{Compression factor} = \frac{\text{size of the input stream}}{\text{size of the output stream}}.$$

In this case, values greater than 1 indicate compression and values less than 1 imply expansion. This measure seems natural to many people, since the bigger the factor, the better the compression.

3. The expression $100 \times (1 - \text{compression ratio})$ is also a reasonable measure of compression performance. A value of 60 means that the output occupies 40% of its original size (or that the compression has resulted in savings of 60%).

4. In image compression, the quantity bpp (bits per pixel) is commonly used. It equals the number of bits needed, on average, to compress one pixel of the image. This quantity should always be compared with the bpp before compression.

5. The *compression gain* is defined as

$$100 \log_e \frac{\text{reference size}}{\text{compressed size}},$$

where the reference size is either the size of the input or the size of the compressed data produced by some standard lossless compression method. For small numbers x, it is true that $\log_e(1 + x) \approx x$, so a small change in a small compression gain is very similar to the same change in the compression ratio. Because of the use of the logarithm, two compression gains can be compared simply by subtracting them. The unit of the compression gain is called *percent log ratio* and is denoted by $\frac{\circ}{\circ}$.

6. The speed of compression can be measured in *cycles per byte* (CPB). This is the average number of machine cycles it takes to compress one byte. This measure is important when compression is done by special hardware.

7. Other quantities, such as mean square error (MSE) and peak signal-to-noise ratio (PSNR), are used to measure the distortion caused by lossy compression of still images and video.

■ The *probability model*. This concept is important in statistical data compression methods. In such a method, a model for the data has to be constructed before compression can begin. A typical model may be built by reading the entire input stream, counting the number of times each symbol appears (its frequency of occurrence), and computing the probability of occurrence of each symbol. The data is then input again, symbol by symbol, and is compressed using the information in the probability model.

Reading the entire input twice is slow, which is why practical compression methods use estimates, or adapt themselves to the data as it is being input and compressed. It is easy to scan large quantities of, say, English text and compute the frequencies and probabilities of every character. This information can later serve as an approximate model for English text and can be used by text compression methods to compress any English text. It is also possible to start by assigning equal probabilities to all the symbols in an alphabet, then reading symbols and compressing them, and, while doing that, also counting frequencies and changing the model as compression progresses. This is the principle behind adaptive compression methods.

- The term "baud" is used in this book to mean bits per second, but see a more general definition in `http://en.wikipedia.org/wiki/Baud`.

Data Compression Resources

A vast number of resources on data compression is available. Any Internet search under "data compression," "lossless data compression," "image compression," "audio compression," and similar topics returns at least tens of thousands of results. The following URLs have useful links and pointers to the many data compression resources available on the Internet and elsewhere:

`http://www.hn.is.uec.ac.jp/~arimura/compression_links.html`
`http://cise.edu.mie-u.ac.jp/~okumura/compression.html`
`http://compression.ca/` (mostly comparisons), and `http://datacompression.info/`

The latter URL has a wealth of information on data compression, including tutorials, links to workers in the field, and lists of books. The site was maintained by Mark Nelson but it currently belongs to Visicron Corp.

Traditional (hardcopy) resources range from general texts and texts on specific aspects or particular methods, to survey articles in magazines, to technical reports and research papers in scientific journals. Following is a short list of (mostly general) books, sorted by date of publication.

James Storer, *Proceedings of the IEEE Data Compression Conference*, IEEE Press, published annually since 1991.

Tinku Acharya and Ping-Sing Tsai, *JPEG2000 Standard for Image Compression: Concepts, Algorithms and VLSI Architectures*, John Wiley and Sons (2005).

Ida Mengyi Pu, *Fundamental Data Compression*, Butterworth-Heinemann (2005).

Khalid Sayood, *Introduction to Data Compression*, Morgan Kaufmann, 3rd edition (2005).

Darrel Hankerson, *Introduction to Information Theory and Data Compression*, Chapman & Hall (CRC), 2nd edition (2003).

Peter Symes, *Digital Video Compression*, McGraw-Hill/TAB Electronics (2003).

Charles Poynton, *Digital Video and HDTV Algorithms and Interfaces*, Morgan Kaufmann (2003).

Iain E. G. Richardson, *H.264 and MPEG-4 Video Compression: Video Coding for Next Generation Multimedia*, John Wiley and Sons (2003).

Marina Bosi and Richard E. Goldberg, *Introduction to Digital Audio Coding and Standards*, Springer Verlag (2003).

Khalid Sayood, *Lossless Compression Handbook*, Academic Press (2002).

Touradj Ebrahimi and Fernando Pereira, *The MPEG-4 Book*, Prentice Hall (2002).

Adam Drozdek, *Elements of Data Compression*, Course Technology (2001).

Alistair Moffat and Andrew Turpin, *Compression and Coding Algorithms*, Springer Verlag (2002).

David Taubman and Michael Marcellin (Editors), *JPEG2000: Image Compression Fundamentals, Standards and Practice*, Springer Verlag (2001).

Kamisetty R. Rao, *The Transform and Data Compression Handbook*, CRC (2000).

Ian H. Witten, Alistair Moffat, and Timothy C. Bell, *Managing Gigabytes: Compressing and Indexing Documents and Images*, Morgan Kaufmann, 2nd edition (1999).

Peter Wayner, *Compression Algorithms for Real Programmers*, Morgan Kaufmann (1999).

John Miano, *Compressed Image File Formats: JPEG, PNG, GIF, XBM, BMP*, ACM Press and Addison-Wesley Professional (1999).

Jerry D. Gibson et al. *Digital Compression for Multimedia: Principles & Standards*, Morgan Kaufmann (1998).

Nikil Jayant, *Signal Compression: Coding of Speech, Audio, Text, Image and Video*, World Scientific (1997).

Weidong Kou, *Digital Image Compression: Algorithms and Standards*, Kluwer (1995).

Mark Nelson and Jean-Loup Gailly, *The Data Compression Book*, M&T Books, 2nd edition (1995).

Rafail Krichevsky, *Universal Compression and Retrieval*, Kluwer Academic Publishers, 1994.

William B. Pennebaker and Joan L. Mitchell, *JPEG: Still Image Data Compression Standard*, Springer Verlag (1992).

Timothy C. Bell, John G. Cleary, and Ian H. Witten, *Text Compression*, Prentice Hall (1990).

James A. Storer, *Data Compression: Methods and Theory*, Computer Science Press (1988).

John Woods, ed., *Subband Coding*, Kluwer Academic Press (1990).

The symbol "␣" is used to indicate a blank space in places where spaces may lead to ambiguity.

Comments, suggestions, and corrections are always welcome and should be directed to dsalomon@csun.edu.

History is a kind of introduction to more interesting
people than we can possibly meet in our restricted
lives; let us not neglect the opportunity.

—Dexter Perkins

1
Approaches
to Compression

 Prelude

How can a given a data file be compressed? Compression amounts to eliminating the redundancy in the data, so the first step is to find the source of redundancy in each type of data. Once we understand what causes redundancy in a given type of data, we can propose an approach to eliminating the redundancy.

This chapter covers the basic approaches to the compression of different types of data. The chapter discusses the principles of variable-length codes, run-length encoding, dictionary-based compression, transforms, and quantization. Later chapters illustrate how these approaches are applied in practice.

Variable-length codes. Text is perhaps the simplest example of data with redundancies. A text file consists of individual symbols (characters), each encoded in ASCII or Unicode. These representations are redundant because they employ fixed-length codes, while characters of text appear with different frequencies. Analyzing large quantities of text indicates that certain characters tend to appear in texts more than other characters. In English, for example, the most common letters are E, T, and A, while J, Q, and Z are the rarest. Thus, redundancy can be reduced by the use of variable-length codes, where short codes are assigned to the common symbols and long codes are assigned to the rare symbols. Designing such a set of codes must take into consideration the following points:

■ We have to know the probability (or, equivalently, the frequency of occurrence) of each data symbol. The variable-length codes should be selected according to these probabilities. For example, if a few data symbols are very common (i.e., appear with large probabilities) while the rest are rare, then we should ideally have a set of variable-length codes where a few codes are very short and the rest are long.

■ Once the original data symbols are replaced with variable-length codes, the result (the compressed file) is a long string of bits with no separators between the codes of consecutive symbols. The decoder (decompressor) should be able to read this string and break it up unambiguously into individual codes. We say that such codes have to be uniquely decodable or uniquely decipherable (UD).

Run-length encoding. A digital image is a rectangular array of dots called pixels. There are two sources of redundancy in an image, namely dominant colors and correlation between pixels.

■ A pixel has a single attribute, its color. A pixel is stored in memory or on a file as a color code. A pixel in a monochromatic image (black and white or bi-level) can be either black or white, so a 1-bit code is sufficient to represent it. A pixel in a grayscale image can be a certain shade of gray, so its code should be an integer. Similarly, the code of a pixel in a color image must have three parts, describing the intensities of its three color components. Imagine an image where each pixel is described by a 24-bit code (eight bits for each of the three color components). The total number of colors in such an image can be $2^{24} \approx 16.78$ million, but any particular image may have only a few hundred or a few thousand colors. Thus, one approach to image compression is to replace the original pixel codes with variable-length codes.

■ We know from long experience that the individual pixels of an image tend to be correlated. A pixel will often be identical, or very similar, to its near neighbors. This can easily be verified by looking around. Imagine an outdoor scene with rocks, trees, the sky, the sun, and clouds. As our eye moves across the sky, we see mostly blue. Adjacent points may feature slightly different shades of blue; they are not identical but neither are they completely independent. We say that their colors are correlated. The same is true when we look at points in a cloud. Most points will have a shade of white similar to their near neighbors. At the intersection of a sky and a cloud, some blue points will have immediate white neighbors, but such points constitute a small minority. Pixel correlation is the main source of redundancy in images and most image compression methods exploit this feature to obtain efficient compression.

In a bi-level image, pixels can be only black or white. Thus, a pixel can either be identical to its neighbors or different from them, but not similar. Pixel correlation implies that in such an image, a pixel will tend to be identical to its near neighbors. This suggests another approach to image compression. Given a bi-level image to be compressed, scan it row by row and count the lengths of runs of identical pixels. If a row in such an image starts with 12 white pixels, followed by five black pixels, followed by 36 white pixels, followed by six black pixels, and so on, then only the numbers 12, 5, 36, 6,... need to be output. This is the principle of run-length encoding (RLE), a popular method that is sometimes combined with other techniques to improve compression performance.

◇ **Exercise 1.1:** It seems that in addition to the sequence of run lengths, a practical RLE compression method has to save the color (white or black) of the first pixel of a row, or at least the first pixel of the image. Explain why this is not necessary.

Dictionaries. Returning to text data, we observe that it has another source of redundancy. Given a nonrandom text, we often find that bits and pieces of it—such as words, syllables, and phrases—tend to appear many times, while other pieces are rare or nonexistent. A grammar book, for example, may contain many occurrences of the words `noun`, `pronoun`, `verb`, and `adverb` in one chapter and many occurrences of `conjugation`, `conjunction`, `subject`, and `subjunction` in another chapter. The principle of dictionary-based compression is to read the next data item `D` to be compressed, and search the dictionary for `D`. If `D` is found in the dictionary, it is compressed by emitting a pointer that points to it in the dictionary. If the pointer is shorter than `D`, compression is achieved.

The dictionaries we commonly use consist of lists of words, each with its definition. A dictionary used to compress data is different. It is a list of bits and pieces of data that have already been read from the input. When a data item is input for the first time, it is not found in the dictionary and therefore cannot be compressed. It is written on the output in its original (raw) format, and is also added to the dictionary. When this piece is read again from the data, it is found in the dictionary, and a pointer to it is written on the output.

Many dictionary methods have been developed and implemented. Their details are different, but the principle is the same. Chapter 3 and Section 1.3 describe a few important examples of such methods.

Prediction. The fact that adjacent pixels in an image tend to be correlated implies that the difference between a pixel and any of its near neighbors tends to be a small integer (notice that it can also be negative). The term "prediction" is used in the technical literature to express this useful fact. Some pixels may turn out to be very different from their neighbors, which is why sophisticated prediction compares a pixel to an average (sometimes a weighted average) of several of its nearest neighbors. Once a pixel is predicted, the prediction is subtracted from the pixel to yield a difference. If the pixels are correlated and the prediction is done properly, the differences tend to be small (signed) integers. They are easy to compress by replacing them with variable-length codes. Vast experience with many digital images suggests that the differences tend to be distributed according to the Laplace distribution, a well-known statistical distribution, and this fact helps in selecting the best variable-length codes for the differences.

The technique of prediction is also employed by several audio compression algorithms, because audio samples also tend to be strongly correlated.

Transforms. Sometimes, a mathematical problem can be solved by transforming its constituents (unknowns, coefficients, numbers, vectors, or anything else) to a different format, where they may look familiar or have a simple form and thus make it possible to solve the problem. After the problem is solved in this way, the solution has to be transformed back to the original format. Roman numerals provide a convincing example. The ancient Romans presumably knew how to operate on these numbers, but when we are faced with a problem such as XCVI × XII, we may find it natural to transform the original numbers into modern (Arabic) notation, multiply them, and then transform the result back into a Roman numeral. Here is the result:

$$\text{XCVI} \times \text{XII} \rightarrow 96 \times 12 = 1152 \rightarrow \text{MCLII}.$$

Another example is the integer 65,536. In its original, decimal representation, this number doesn't seem special or interesting, but when transformed to binary it becomes the round number $10,000,000,000,000,000,000_2 = 2^{16}$.

Two types of transforms, orthogonal and subband, are employed by various compression methods. They are described in some detail in Chapter 5. These transforms do not by themselves compress the data and are used only as intermediate steps, transforming the original data to a format where it is easy to compress. Given a list of N correlated numbers, such as adjacent pixels in an image or adjacent audio samples, an orthogonal transform converts them to N transform coefficients, of which the first is large and dominant (it contains much of the information of the original data) and the remaining ones are small and contain the details (i.e., the less important features) of the original data. Compression is achieved in a subsequent step, either by replacing the detail coefficients by variable-length codes or by quantization, RLE, or arithmetic coding. A subband transform (also known as a wavelet transform) also results in coarse and fine transform coefficients, and when applied to an image, it separates the vertical, horizontal, and diagonal constituents of the image, so each can be compressed differently.

Quantization. Text must be compressed without any loss of information, but images, video, and audio can tolerate much loss of data when compressed and later decompressed. The loss, addition, or corruption of one character of text can cause confusion, misunderstanding, or disagreements. Changing `not` to `now`, `want` to `went` or `under the edge` to `under the hedge` may result in a sentence that is syntactically correct but has a different meaning.

◇ **Exercise 1.2:** Change one letter in each of the following phrases to create a syntactically valid phrase with a completely different meaning, "look what the cat dragged in," "my ears are burning," "bad egg," "a real looker," "my brother's keeper," and "put all your eggs in one basket".

Quantization is a simple approach to lossy compression. The idea is to start with a finite list of N symbols S_i and to modify each of the original data symbols to the nearest S_i. For example, if the original data consists of real numbers in a certain interval, then each can be rounded off to the nearest integer. It takes fewer bits to express the integer, so compression is achieved, but it is lossy because it is impossible to retrieve the original real data from the integers. The well-known `mp3` audio compression method is based on quantization of the original audio samples.

> The beauty of code is much more akin to the elegance, efficiency and clean lines of a spiderweb. It is not the chaotic glory of a waterfall, or the pristine simplicity of a flower. It is an aesthetic of structure, design and order.
>
> —Charles Gordon

1.1 Variable-Length Codes

Often, a file of data to be compressed consists of data symbols drawn from an alphabet. At the time of writing (mid-2007) most text files consist of individual ASCII characters. The alphabet in this case is the set of 128 ASCII characters. A grayscale image consists of pixels, each coded as one number indicating a shade of gray. If the image is restricted to 256 shades of gray, then each pixel is represented by eight bits and the alphabet is the set of 256 byte values. Given a data file where the symbols are drawn from an alphabet, it can be compressed by replacing each symbol with a variable-length codeword. The obvious guiding principle is to assign short codewords to the common symbols and long codewords to the rare symbols.

In data compression, the term *code* is often used for the entire set, while the individual codes are referred to as codewords.

Variable-length codes (VLCs for short) are used in several real-life applications, not just in data compression. The following is a short list of applications where such codes play important roles.

■   The Morse code for telegraphy, originated in the 1830s by Samuel Morse and Alfred Vail, employs the same idea. It assigns short codes to commonly-occurring letters (the code of E is a dot and the code of T is a dash) and long codes to rare letters and punctuation marks (--.- to Q, --.. to Z, and --..-- to the comma).

■   Processor design. Part of the architecture of any computer is an instruction set and a processor that fetches instructions from memory and executes them. It is easy to handle fixed-length instructions, but modern computers normally have instructions of different sizes. It is possible to reduce the overall size of programs by designing the instruction set such that commonly-used instructions are short. This also reduces the processor's power consumption and physical size and is especially important in embedded processors, such as processors designed for digital signal processing (DSP).

■   Country calling codes. ITU-T recommendation E.164 is an international standard that assigns variable-length calling codes to many countries such that countries with many telephones are assigned short codes and countries with fewer telephones are assigned long codes. These codes also obey the prefix property (page 28) which means that once a calling code C has been assigned, no other calling code will start with C.

■   The International Standard Book Number (ISBN) is a unique number assigned to a book, to simplify inventory tracking by publishers and bookstores. The ISBN numbers are assigned according to an international standard known as ISO 2108 (1970). One component of an ISBN is a country code, that can be between one and five digits long. This code also obeys the prefix property. Once C has been assigned as a country code, no other country code will start with C.

■   VCR Plus+ (also known as G-Code, VideoPlus+, and ShowView) is a prefix, variable-length code for programming video recorders. A unique number, a VCR Plus+, is computed for each television program by a proprietary algorithm from the date, time, and channel of the program. The number is published in television listings in newspapers and on the Internet. To record a program on a VCR, the number is located in a newspaper and is typed into the video recorder. This programs the recorder to record the correct channel at the right time. This system was developed by Gemstar-TV Guide International [Gemstar 07].

When we consider using VLCs to compress a data file, the first step is to determine which data symbols in this file are common and which ones are rare. More precisely, we need to know the frequency of occurrence (or alternatively, the probability) of each symbol of the alphabet. If, for example, we determine that symbol e appears 205 times in a 1106-symbol data file, then the probability of e is $205/1106 \approx 0.185$ or about 19%. If this is higher than the probabilities of most other alphabet symbols, then e is assigned a short codeword. The list of probabilities (or frequencies of occurrence) is called the statistical distribution of the data symbols. Figure 1.1 displays the distribution of the 256 byte values in a past edition of the book *Data Compression: The Complete Reference* as a histogram. It is easy to see that the most-common symbol is the space, followed by a cr (carriage return at the end of lines) and the lower-case e.

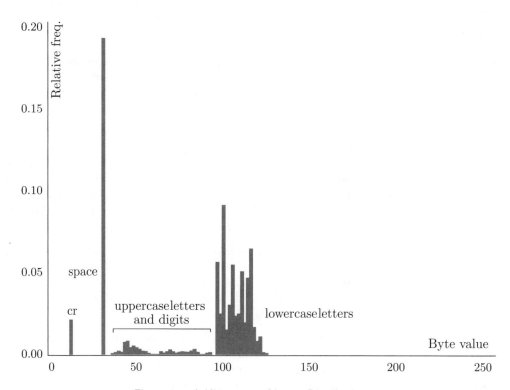

Figure 1.1: A Histogram of Letter Distribution.

The problem of determining the distribution of data symbols in a given file is perhaps the chief consideration in determining the assignment of variable-length codewords to symbols and thus the performance of the compression algorithm. We discuss three approaches to this problem as follows:

■   A two-pass compression job. The compressor (encoder) reads the entire data file and counts the number of times each symbol appears. At the end of this pass, the probabilities of the symbols are computed and are used to determine the set of variable-length codes that will be assigned to the symbols. This set is written on the compressed file and the encoder starts the second pass. In this pass it again reads the entire input file and compresses it by replacing each symbol with its codeword. This method provides very good results because it uses the correct probabilities for each data file. The table of codewords must be included in the output file, but this table is small (typically a few hundred codewords written on the output consecutively, with no separators between codes). The downside of this approach is its low speed. Currently, even the fastest magnetic disks are considerably slower than memory and CPU operations, which is why reading the input file twice normally results in unacceptably-slow execution. Notice that the decoder is simple and fast because it does not need two passes. It starts by reading the code table from the compressed file, following which it reads variable-length codes and replaces each with its original symbol.

■ Use a set of training documents. The first step in implementing fast software for text compression may be to select texts that are judged "typical" and employ them to "train" the algorithm. Training consists of counting symbol frequencies in the training documents, computing the distribution of symbols, and assigning them variable-length codes. The code table is then built into both encoder and decoder and is later used to compress and decompress various texts. An important example of the use of training documents is facsimile compression (page 86). The success of such software depends on how "typical" the training documents are.

It is unlikely that a set of documents will be typical for all kinds of text, but such a set can perhaps be found for certain types of texts. A case in point is facsimile compression. Documents sent on telephone lines between fax machines have to be compressed in order to cut the transmission times from 10–11 minutes per page to about one minute. The compression method must be an international standard because fax machines are made by many manufacturers, and such a standard has been developed (Section 2.4). It is based on a set of eight training documents that have been selected by the developers and include a typed business letter, a circuit diagram, a French technical article with figures and equations, a dense document in Kanji, and a handwritten memo.

Another application of training documents is found in image compression. Researchers trying to develop methods for image compression have long noticed that pixel differences in images tend to be distributed according to the well-known Laplace distribution (by a pixel difference is meant the difference between a pixel and an average of its nearest neighbors).

■ An adaptive algorithm. Such an algorithm does not assume anything about the distribution of the symbols in the data file to be compressed. It starts "with a blank slate" and adapts itself to the statistics of the input file as it reads and compresses more and more symbols. The data symbols are replaced by variable-length codewords, but these codewords are modified all the time as more is known about the input data. The algorithm has to be designed such that the decoder would be able to modify the codewords in precisely the same way as the encoder. We say that the decoder has to work in lockstep with the encoder. The best known example of such a method is the adaptive (or dynamic) Huffman algorithm (Section 2.3).

⋄ **Exercise 1.3:** Compare the three different approaches (two-passes, training, and adaptive compression algorithms) and list some of the pros and cons for each.

Several variable-length codes are listed and described later in this section, and the discussion shows how the average code length can be used to determine the statistical distribution to which the code is best suited.

The second consideration in the design of a variable-length code is unique decodability (UD). We start with a simple example: the code $a_1 = 0$, $a_2 = 10$, $a_3 = 101$, and $a_4 = 111$. Encoding the string $a_1 a_3 a_4 \ldots$ with these codewords results in the bitstring $0101111\ldots$. However, decoding is ambiguous. The same bitstring $0101111\ldots$ can be decoded either as $a_1 a_3 a_4 \ldots$ or $a_1 a_2 a_4 \ldots$. This code is not uniquely decodable. In contrast, the similar code $a_1 = 0$, $a_2 = 10$, $a_3 = 110$, and $a_4 = 111$ (where only the codeword of a_3 is different) is UD. The string $a_1 a_3 a_4 \ldots$ is easily encoded to $0110111\ldots$, and this bitstring can be decoded unambiguously. The first 0 implies a_1, because only the codeword of a_1 starts with 0. The next (second) bit, 1, can be the start of a_2, a_3, or a_4. The next (third) bit is also 1, which reduces the choice to a_3 or a_4. The fourth bit is 0, so the decoder emits a_3.

A little thinking clarifies the difference between the two codes. The first code is ambiguous because 10, the code of a_2, is also the prefix of the code of a_3. When the decoder reads $10\ldots$, it often cannot tell whether this is the codeword of a_2 or the start of the codeword of a_3. The second code is UD because the codeword of a_2 is not the prefix of any other codeword. In fact, none of the codewords of this code is the prefix of any other codeword.

This observation suggests the following rule. To construct a UD code, the codewords should satisfy the following *prefix property*. Once a codeword c is assigned to a symbol, no other codeword should start with the bit pattern c. Prefix codes are also referred to as prefix-free codes, prefix condition codes, or instantaneous codes. Observe, however, that a UD code does not have to be a prefix code. It is possible, for example, to designate the string 111 as a separator (a comma) to separate individual codewords of different lengths, provided that no codeword contains the string 111. There are other ways to construct a set of non-prefix, variable-length codes.

A UD code is said to be instantaneous if it is possible to decode each codeword in a compressed file without knowing the succeeding codewords. Prefix codes are instantaneous.

Constructing a UD code for given finite set of data symbols should start with the probabilities of the symbols. If the probabilities are known (at least approximately), then the best variable-length code for the symbols is obtained by the Huffman algorithm (Chapter 2). There are, however, applications where the set of data symbols is unbounded; its size is either extremely large or is not known in advance. Here are a few practical examples of both cases:

■   Text. There are 128 ASCII codes, so the size of this set of symbols is reasonably small. In contrast, the number of Unicodes is in the tens of thousands, which makes it impractical to use variable-length codes to compress text in Unicode; a different approach is required.

■   A grayscale image. For 8-bit pixels, the number of shades of gray is 256, so a set of 256 codewords is required, large, but not too large.

■   Pixel prediction. If a pixel is represented by 16 or 24 bits, it is impractical to compute probabilities and prepare a huge set of codewords. A better approach is to predict a pixel from several of its near neighbors, subtract the prediction from the pixel value, and encode the resulting difference. If the prediction is done properly, most differences will be small (signed) integers, but some differences may be (positive or negative) large, and a few may be as large as the pixel value itself (typically 16 or 24 bits). In such a case, a code for the integers is the best choice. Each integer has a codeword assigned that can be computed on the fly. The codewords for the small integers should be small, but the lengths should depend on the distribution of the difference values.

■   Audio compression. Audio samples are almost always correlated, which is why many audio compression methods predict an audio sample from its predecessors and encode the difference with a variable-length code for the integers.

Any variable-length code for integers should satisfy the following requirements:

1. Given an integer n, its code should be as short as possible and should be constructed from the magnitude, length, and bit pattern of n, without the need for any table lookups or other mappings.

2. Given a bitstream of variable-length codes, it should be easy to decode the next code and obtain an integer n even if n hasn't been seen before.

Quite a few VLCs for integers are known. Many of them include part of the binary representation of the integer, while the rest of the codeword consists of side information indicating the length or precision of the encoded integer.

The following sections describe popular variable-length codes (the Intermezzo on page 253 describes one more), but first, a few words about notation. It is customary to denote the standard binary representation of the integer n by $\beta(n)$. This representation can be considered a code (the beta code), but this code does not satisfy the prefix property and also has a fixed length. (It is easy to see that the beta code does not satisfy the prefix property because, for example, $2 = 10_2$ is the prefix of $4 = 100_2$.) Given a set of integers between 0 and n, we can represent each in

$$1 + \lfloor \log_2 n \rfloor = \lceil \log_2(n+1) \rceil \tag{1.1}$$

bits, a fixed-length representation. When n is represented in any other number base b, its length is given by the same expression, but with the logarithm in base b instead of 2.

A VLC that can code only positive integers can be extended to encode nonnegative integers by incrementing the integer before it is encoded and decrementing the result produced by decoding. A VLC for arbitrary integers can be obtained by a bijection, a mapping of the form

0	−1	1	−2	2	−3	3	−4	4	−5	5	⋯
1	2	3	4	5	6	7	8	9	10	11	⋯

> A function is bijective if it is one-to-one and onto.

1.1.1 Unary Code

Perhaps the simplest variable-length code for integers is the well-known unary code. The unary code of the positive integer n is constructed from $n-1$ 1's followed by a single 0, or alternatively as $n-1$ zeros followed by a single 1 (the three left columns of Table 1.2). The length of the unary code for the integer n is therefore n bits. The two rightmost columns of Table 1.2 show how the unary code can be extended to encode the nonnegative integers (which makes the codes more useful but also one bit longer). The unary code is simple to construct and is employed in many applications. Stone-age people indicated the integer n by marking n adjacent vertical bars on a stone, which is why the unary code is sometimes known as a stone-age binary and each of its n or $(n-1)$ 1's [or n or $(n-1)$ zeros] is termed a stone-age bit.

Stone Age Binary?

n	Code	Reverse	Alt. code	Alt reverse
0	–	–	0	1
1	0	1	10	01
2	10	01	110	001
3	110	001	1110	0001
4	1110	0001	11110	00001
5	11110	00001	111110	000001

Table 1.2: Some Unary Codes.

It is easy to see that the unary code satisfies the prefix property. Since its length L satisfies $L = n$, we get $2^{-L} = 2^{-n}$, so it makes sense to use this code in cases were the input data consists of integers n with exponential probabilities $P(n) \approx 2^{-n}$. Given data that lends itself to the use of the unary code (i.e., a set of integers that satisfy $P(n) \approx 2^{-n}$), we can assign unary codes to the integers and these codes will be as good as the Huffman codes, with the advantage that the unary codes are trivial to encode and decode. In general, the unary code is used as part of other, more sophisticated, variable-length codes.

Example: Table 1.3 lists the integers 1 through 6 with probabilities $P(n) = 2^{-n}$, except that $P(6)$ is artificially set to $2^{-5} \approx 2^{-6}$ in order for the probabilities to add up to unity. The table lists the unary codes and Huffman codes for the six integers (see Chapter 2 for the Huffman codes), and it is obvious that these codes have the same lengths (except the code of 6, because this symbol does not have the correct probability).

✦(From *The Best Coin Problems*, by Henry E. Dudeney, 1909). It is easy to place 16 pennies in a 4×4 square such that each row, each column, and each of the two main diagonals will have the same number of pennies. Do the same with 20 pennies.

1.1.2 Elias Codes

In his pioneering work [Elias 75], Peter Elias described three useful prefix codes. The main idea of these codes is to prefix the integer being encoded with an encoded representation of its order of magnitude. For example, for any positive integer n there is an integer M such that $2^M \le n < 2^{M+1}$. We can therefore write $n = 2^M + L$ where L is

n	Prob	Unary	Huffman
1	2^{-1}	0	0
2	2^{-2}	10	10
3	2^{-3}	110	110
4	2^{-4}	1110	1110
5	2^{-5}	11110	11110
6	2^{-5}	111110	11111

Table 1.3: Six Unary and Huffman Codes.

at most M bits long, and generate a code that consists of M and L. The problem is to determine the length of M and this is solved in different ways by the various Elias codes. Elias denoted the unary code of n by $\alpha(n)$ and the standard binary representation of n, from its most-significant 1, by $\beta(n)$. His first code was therefore designated γ (gamma).

The Elias gamma code $\gamma(n)$ is designed for positive integers n and is simple to encode and decode.

Encoding. Given a positive integer n, perform the following steps:

1. Denote by M the length of the binary representation $\beta(n)$ of n.
2. Prepend $M - 1$ zeros to it (i.e., the $\alpha(n)$ code without its terminating 1).

Step 2 amounts to prepending the length of the code to the code, in order to ensure unique decodability.

We now show that this code is ideal for applications where the probability of n is $1/(2n^2)$. The length M of the integer n is, from Equation (1.1), $1 + \lfloor \log_2 n \rfloor$, so the length of $\gamma(n)$ is

$$2M - 1 = 2\lfloor \log_2 n \rfloor + 1. \tag{1.2}$$

In general, given a set of symbols a_i, where each symbol occurs in the data with probability P_i and the length of its code is l_i bits, the average code length is the sum $\sum P_i l_i$ and the entropy (the smallest number of bits required to represent the symbols) is $\sum [-P_i \log_2 P_i]$. The difference between the average length and the entropy is $\sum_i P_i l_i - \sum_i [-P_i \log_2 P_i]$ and we are looking for probabilities P_i that will minimize this difference.

For the gamma code, $l_i = 1 + 2 \log_2 i$. If we select symbol probabilities $P_i = 1/(2i^2)$ (a power law distribution of probabilities, where the first 10 values are 0.5, 0.125, 0.0556, 0.03125, 0.02 0.01389, 0.0102, 0.0078, 0.00617, and 0.005), both the average code length and the entropy become the identical sums

$$\sum_i \frac{1 + 2 \log i}{2i^2},$$

indicating that the gamma code is asymptotically optimal for this type of data. A power law distribution of values is dominated by just a few symbols and especially by the first. Such a distribution is very skewed and is therefore handled very well by the gamma code which starts very short. In an exponential distribution, in contrast, the small values have similar probabilities, which is why data with this type of statistical distribution is compressed better by a Rice code (Section 1.1.3).

An alternative construction of the gamma code is as follows:

1. Find the largest integer N such that $2^N \le n < 2^{N+1}$ and write $n = 2^N + L$. Notice that L is at most an N-bit integer.

2. Encode N in unary either as N zeros followed by a 1 or N 1's followed by a 0.

3. Append L as an N-bit number to this representation of N.

Peter Elias

$1 = 2^0 + 0 = 1$	$10 = 2^3 + 2 = 0001010$
$2 = 2^1 + 0 = 010$	$11 = 2^3 + 3 = 0001011$
$3 = 2^1 + 1 = 011$	$12 = 2^3 + 4 = 0001100$
$4 = 2^2 + 0 = 00100$	$13 = 2^3 + 5 = 0001101$
$5 = 2^2 + 1 = 00101$	$14 = 2^3 + 6 = 0001110$
$6 = 2^2 + 2 = 00110$	$15 = 2^3 + 7 = 0001111$
$7 = 2^2 + 3 = 00111$	$16 = 2^4 + 0 = 000010000$
$8 = 2^3 + 0 = 0001000$	$17 = 2^4 + 1 = 000010001$
$9 = 2^3 + 1 = 0001001$	$18 = 2^4 + 2 = 000010010$

Table 1.4: 18 Elias Gamma Codes.

Table 1.4 lists the first 18 gamma codes, where the L part is in italics.

In his 1975 paper, Elias describes two versions of the gamma code. The first version (titled γ) is encoded as follows:

1. Generate the binary representation $\beta(n)$ of n.
2. Denote the length $|\beta(n)|$ of $\beta(n)$ by M.
3. Generate the unary $u(M)$ representation of M as $M - 1$ zeros followed by a 1.
4. Follow each bit of $\beta(n)$ by a bit of $u(M)$.
5. Drop the leftmost bit (the leftmost bit of $\beta(n)$ is always 1).

Thus, for $n = 13$ we prepare $\beta(13) = 1\bar{1}\bar{0}1$, so $M = 4$ and $u(4) = 0001$, resulting in $1\bar{0}1\bar{0}0\bar{0}1\bar{1}$. The final code is $\gamma(13) = 0\bar{1}0\bar{0}0\bar{0}1\bar{1}$.

The second version, dubbed γ', moves the bits of $u(M)$ to the left. Thus $\gamma'(13) = 0001|\bar{1}0\bar{1}$. The gamma codes of Table 1.4 are Elias's γ' codes. Both gamma versions are universal.

Decoding is also simple and is done in two steps:

1. Read zeros from the code until a 1 is encountered. Denote the number of zeros by N.

2. Read the next N bits as an integer L. Compute $n = 2^N + L$.

It is easy to see that this code can be used to encode positive integers even in cases where the largest integer is not known in advance. Also, this code grows slowly (see Figure 1.5), which makes it a good candidate for compressing integer data where small integers are common and large ones are rare.

Elias delta code. In his gamma code, Elias prepends the length of the code in unary (α). In his next code, δ (delta), he prepends the length in binary (β). Thus, the Elias delta code, also for the positive integers, is slightly more complex to construct.

Encoding a positive integer n, is done in the following steps:

1. Write n in binary. The leftmost (most-significant) bit will be a 1.

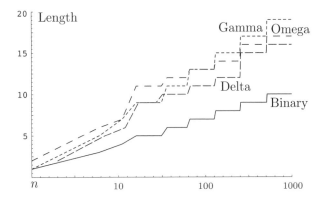

Figure 1.5: Lengths of Three Elias Codes.

```
(* Plot the lengths of four codes
1. staircase plots of binary representation *)
bin[i_] := 1 + Floor[Log[2, i]];
Table[{Log[10, n], bin[n]}, {n, 1, 1000, 5}];
g1 = ListPlot[%, AxesOrigin -> {0, 0}, PlotJoined -> True]
(* 2. staircase plot of Elias Omega code *)
omega[n_] := Module[{l, om},
  l = Length[IntegerDigits[n, 2]];
  om = l + 1;
  While[l > 2,
    l = Length[IntegerDigits[l - 1, 2]]; om = om + l;];
  om]
Table[{Log[10, n], omega[n]}, {n, 1, 1000, 5}];
g2 = ListPlot[%, AxesOrigin -> {0, 0}, PlotJoined -> True,
    PlotStyle -> { AbsoluteDashing[{5, 5}]}]
(* 3. staircase plot of gamma code length*)
gam[i_] := 1 + 2Floor[Log[2, i]];
Table[{Log[10, n], gam[n]}, {n, 1, 1000, 5}];
g3 = ListPlot[%, AxesOrigin -> {0, 0}, PlotJoined -> True,
    PlotStyle -> { AbsoluteDashing[{2, 2}]}]
(* 4. staircase plot of delta code length *)
del[i_] := 1 + Floor[Log[2, i]] + 2Floor[Log[2, Log[2, i]]];
Table[{Log[10, n], del[n]}, {n, 2, 1000, 5}];
g4 = ListPlot[%, AxesOrigin -> {0, 0}, PlotJoined -> True,
    PlotStyle -> { AbsoluteDashing[{6, 2}]}]
Show[g1, g2, g3, g4, PlotRange -> {{0, 3}, {0, 20}}]
```

Code for Figure 1.5

2. Count the bits, remove the leftmost bit of n, and prepend the count, in binary, to what is left of n after its leftmost bit has been removed.

3. Subtract 1 from the count of step 2 and prepend that number of zeros to the code.

When these steps are applied to the integer 17, the results are: $17 = 10001_2$ (five bits). Remove the leftmost 1 and prepend $5 = 101_2$ yields 101|0001. Three bits were added, so we prepend two zeros to obtain the delta code 00|101|0001.

To determine the length of the delta code of n, we notice that step 1 generates [from Equation (1.1)] $M = 1 + \lfloor \log_2 n \rfloor$ bits. For simplicity, we omit the $\lfloor$ and $\rfloor$ and observe that

$$M = 1 + \log_2 n = \log_2 2 + \log_2 n = \log_2(2n).$$

The count of step 2 is M, whose length C is therefore $C = 1 + \log_2 M = 1 + \log_2(\log_2(2n))$

bits. Step 2 therefore prepends C bits and removes the leftmost bit of n. Step 3 prepends $C - 1 = \log_2 M = \log_2(\log_2(2n))$ zeros. The total length of the delta code is therefore the 3-part sum

$$\underbrace{\log_2(2n)}_{\text{step 1}} + \underbrace{[1 + \log_2 \log_2(2n)] - 1}_{\text{step 2}} + \underbrace{\log_2 \log_2(2n)}_{\text{step 3}} = 1 + \lfloor\log_2 n\rfloor + 2\lfloor\log_2 \log_2(2n)\rfloor. \tag{1.3}$$

Figure 1.5 illustrates the length graphically.

It is easy to show that this code is ideal for data where the integer n occurs with probability $1/[2n(\log_2(2n))^2]$. The length of the delta code is $l_i = 1 + \log i + 2\log\log(2i)$. If we select symbol probabilities $P_i = 1/[2i(\log(2i))^2]$ (where the first five values are 0.5, 0.0625, 0.025, 0.0139, and 0.009), both the average code length and the entropy become the identical sums

$$\sum_i \frac{\log 2 + \log i + 2\log\log(2i)}{2i(\log(2i))^2},$$

indicating that the redundancy is zero and the delta code is therefore asymptotically optimal for this type of data.

An equivalent way to construct the delta code employs the gamma code:

1. Find the largest integer N such that $2^N \geq n < 2^{N+1}$ and write $n = 2^N + L$. Notice that L is at most an N-bit integer.

2. Encode $N + 1$ with the Elias gamma code.

3. Append the binary value of L, as an N-bit integer, to the result of step 2.

When these steps are applied to $n = 17$, the results are: $17 = 2^N + L = 2^4 + 1$. The gamma code of $N + 1 = 5$ is 00101, and appending $L = 0001$ to this yields 00101|0001.

Table 1.6 lists the first 18 delta codes, where the L part is in italics.

$1 = 2^0 + 0 \rightarrow \|L\| = 0 \rightarrow 1$	$10 = 2^3 + 2 \rightarrow \|L\| = 3 \rightarrow 00100\textit{010}$
$2 = 2^1 + 0 \rightarrow \|L\| = 1 \rightarrow 010\textit{0}$	$11 = 2^3 + 3 \rightarrow \|L\| = 3 \rightarrow 00100\textit{011}$
$3 = 2^1 + 1 \rightarrow \|L\| = 1 \rightarrow 010\textit{1}$	$12 = 2^3 + 4 \rightarrow \|L\| = 3 \rightarrow 00100\textit{100}$
$4 = 2^2 + 0 \rightarrow \|L\| = 2 \rightarrow 011\textit{00}$	$13 = 2^3 + 5 \rightarrow \|L\| = 3 \rightarrow 00100\textit{101}$
$5 = 2^2 + 1 \rightarrow \|L\| = 2 \rightarrow 011\textit{01}$	$14 = 2^3 + 6 \rightarrow \|L\| = 3 \rightarrow 00100\textit{110}$
$6 = 2^2 + 2 \rightarrow \|L\| = 2 \rightarrow 011\textit{10}$	$15 = 2^3 + 7 \rightarrow \|L\| = 3 \rightarrow 00100\textit{111}$
$7 = 2^2 + 3 \rightarrow \|L\| = 2 \rightarrow 011\textit{11}$	$16 = 2^4 + 0 \rightarrow \|L\| = 4 \rightarrow 00101\textit{0000}$
$8 = 2^3 + 0 \rightarrow \|L\| = 3 \rightarrow 00100\textit{000}$	$17 = 2^4 + 1 \rightarrow \|L\| = 4 \rightarrow 00101\textit{0001}$
$9 = 2^3 + 1 \rightarrow \|L\| = 3 \rightarrow 00100\textit{001}$	$18 = 2^4 + 2 \rightarrow \|L\| = 4 \rightarrow 00101\textit{0010}$

Table 1.6: 18 Elias Delta Codes.

Decoding is done in the following steps:

1. Read bits from the code until you can decode an Elias gamma code. Call the decoded result $M + 1$. This is done in the following substeps:

1.1 Count the leading zeros of the code and denote the count by C.

1.2 Examine the leftmost $2C + 1$ bits (C zeros, followed by a single 1, followed by C more bits). This is the decoded gamma code $M + 1$.

2. Read the next M bits. Call this number L.

3. The decoded integer is $2^M + L$.

In the case of $n = 17$, the delta code is 001010001. We skip two zeros, so $C = 2$. The value of the leftmost $2C + 1 = 5$ bits is $00101 = 5$, so $M + 1 = 5$. We read the next $M = 4$ bits 0001, and end up with the decoded value $2^M + L = 2^4 + 1 = 17$.

Elias omega code. Unlike the previous Elias codes, the omega code uses itself recursively to encode the prefix M, which is why it is sometimes referred to as a recursive Elias code. The main idea is to prepend the length of n to n as a group of bits that starts with a 1, then prepend the length of the length, as another group, to the result, and continue prepending lengths until the last length is 2 or 3 (and therefore fits in two bits). In order to distinguish between a length group and the last, rightmost group (of n itself), the latter is followed by a delimiter of 0, while each length group starts with a 1.

Encoding a positive integer n is done recursively in the following steps:

1. Initialize the code-so-far to 0.

2. If the number to be encoded is 1, stop; otherwise, prepend the binary representation of n to the code-so-far. Assume that we have prepended L bits.

3. Repeat step 2, with the binary representation of $L - 1$ instead of n.

The integer 17 is therefore encoded by (1) a single 0, (2) prepended by the 5-bit binary value 10001, (3) prepended by the 3-bit value of $5 - 1 = 100_2$, and (4) prepended by the 2-bit value of $3 - 1 = 10_2$. The result is $10|100|10001|0$.

Table 1.7 lists the first 18 omega codes. Note that $n = 1$ is handled as a special case.

1	0	10	11 1010 0
2	10 0	11	11 1011 0
3	11 0	12	11 1100 0
4	10 100 0	13	11 1101 0
5	10 101 0	14	11 1110 0
6	10 110 0	15	11 1111 0
7	10 111 0	16	10 100 10000 0
8	11 1000 0	17	10 100 10001 0
9	11 1001 0	18	10 100 10010 0

Table 1.7: 18 Elias Omega Codes.

Decoding is done in several nonrecursive steps where each step reads a group of bits from the code. A group that starts with a zero signals the end of decoding.

1. Initialize n to 1.

2. Read the next bit. If it is 0, stop. Otherwise read n more bits, assign the group of $n + 1$ bits to n, and repeat this step.

Some readers may find it easier to understand these steps rephrased as follows.

1. Read the first group, which will either be a single 0, or a 1 followed by n more digits. If the group is a 0, the value of the integer is 1; if the group starts with a 1, then n becomes the value of the group interpreted as a binary number.

2. Read each successive group; it will either be a single 0, or a 1 followed by n more digits. If the group is a 0, the value of the integer is n; if it starts with a 1, then n becomes the value of the group interpreted as a binary number.

Example. Decode 10|100|10001|0. The decoder initializes $n = 1$ and reads the first bit. It is a 1, so it reads $n = 1$ more bit (0) and assigns $n = 10_2 = 2$. It reads the next bit. It is a 1, so it reads $n = 2$ more bits (00) and assigns the group 100 to n. It reads the next bit. It is a 1, so it reads four more bits (0001) and assigns the group 10001 to n. The next bit read is 0, indicating the end of decoding.

The omega code is constructed recursively, which is why its length $|\omega(n)|$ can also be computed recursively. We define the quantity $l^k(n)$ recursively by $l^1(n) = \lfloor \log_2 n \rfloor$ and $l^{i+1}(n) = l^1(l^i(n))$. Equation (1.1) tells us that $|\beta(n)| = l^1(n) + 1$ (where β is the standard binary representation), and this implies that the length of the omega code is given by the sum

$$|\omega(n)| = \sum_{i=1}^{k} \beta(l^{k-i}(n)) + 1 = 1 + \sum_{i=1}^{k}(l^i(n) + 1),$$

where the sum stops at the k that satisfies $l^k(n) = 1$. From this, Elias concludes that the length satisfies $|\omega(n)| \leq 1 + \frac{5}{2}\lfloor \log_2 n \rfloor$.

A glance at a table of these codes shows that their lengths fluctuate. In general, the length increases slowly as n increases, but when a new length group is added, which happens when $n = 2^{2^k}$ for any positive integer k, the length of the code increases suddenly by several bits. For k values of 1, 2, 3, and 4, this happens when n reaches 4, 16, 256, and 65,536. Because the groups of lengths are of the form "length," "log(length)," "log(log(length))," and so on, the omega code is sometimes referred to as a logarithmic-ramp code.

Table 1.8 compares the length of the gamma, delta, and omega codes. It shows that the delta code is asymptotically best, but if the data consists mostly of small numbers (less than 8) and there are only a few large integers, then the gamma code performs better.

1.1.3 Rice Codes

The Rice code is named after its originator, Robert F. Rice ([Rice 79], [Rice 91], and [Fenwick 96a]). This code is a special case of the Golomb code [Salomon 07], which is why it is sometimes referred to as the Golomb–Rice code.

A Rice code depends on the choice of a base k and is computed in the following steps: (1) Separate the sign bit from the rest of the number. This is optional and the bit becomes the most-significant bit of the Rice code. (2) Separate the k LSBs. They become the LSBs of the Rice code. (3) Code the remaining $j = \lfloor n/2^k \rfloor$ bits as either j zeros followed by a 1 or j 1's followed by a 0 (similar to the unary code). This becomes the middle part of the Rice code. Thus, this code is computed with a few logical

Values	Gamma	Delta	Omega
1	1	1	2
2	3	4	3
3	3	4	4
4	5	5	4
5–7	5	5	5
8–15	7	8	6–7
16–31	9	9	7–8
32–63	11	10	8–10
64–88	13	11	10
100	13	11	11
1000	19	16	16
10^4	27	20	20
10^5	33	25	25
10^5	39	28	30

Table 1.8: Lengths of Three Elias Codes.

operations, which makes it an ideal candidate for applications where speed is important. Table 1.9 shows examples of this code for $k = 2$ (the column labeled "No. of ones" lists the number of 1's in the middle part of the code).

i	Binary	Sign	LSB	No. of ones	Code	i	Code
0	0	0	00	0	0|0|00		
1	1	0	01	0	0|0|01	−1	1|0|01
2	10	0	10	0	0|0|10	−2	1|0|10
3	11	0	11	0	0|0|11	−3	1|0|11
4	100	0	00	1	0|10|00	−4	1|10|00
5	101	0	01	1	0|10|01	−5	1|10|01
6	110	0	10	1	0|10|10	−6	1|10|10
7	111	0	11	1	0|10|11	−7	1|10|11
8	1000	0	00	2	0|110|00	−8	1|110|00
11	1011	0	11	2	0|110|11	−11	1|110|11
12	1100	0	00	3	0|1110|00	−12	1|1110|00
15	1111	0	11	3	0|1110|11	−15	1|1110|11

Table 1.9: Various Positive and Negative Rice Codes.

The length of the (unsigned) Rice code of the integer n with parameter k is $1 + k + \lfloor n/2^k \rfloor$ bits, indicating that these codes are suitable for data where the integer n appears with a probability $P(n)$ that satisfies $\log_2 P(n) = -(1 + k + n/2^k)$ or $P(n) \propto 2^{-n}$, an exponential distribution, such as the Laplace distribution. The Rice code is easy to decode, once the decoder reads the sign bit and skips to the first 0 from the left, it knows how to generate the left and middle parts of the code. The next k bits should be read and appended to that.

There remains the question of what base value n to select for the Rice codes. The base determines how many low-order bits of a data symbol are included directly in the Rice code, and this is linearly related to the variance of the data symbol. Tony Robinson, the developer of the Shorten method for audio compression [Robinson 94], provides the formula $n = \log_2[\log(2)E(|x|)]$, where $E(|x|)$ is the expected value of the data symbols. This value is the sum $\sum |x|p(x)$ taken over all possible symbols x.

Figure 1.10 lists the lengths of various Rice codes and compares them to the length of the standard binary (beta) code.

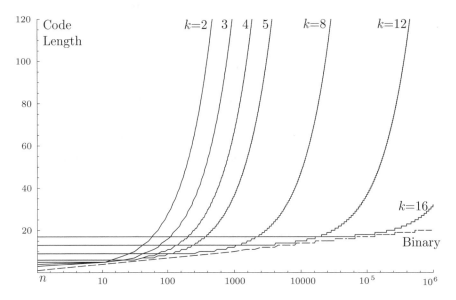

Figure 1.10: Lengths of Various Rice Codes.

```
(* Lengths of binary code and 7 Rice codes *)
bin[i_] := 1 + Floor[Log[2, i]];
Table[{Log[10, n], bin[n]}, {n, 1, 1000000, 500}];
gb = ListPlot[%, AxesOrigin -> {0, 0}, PlotJoined -> True,
    PlotStyle -> { AbsoluteDashing[{6, 2}]}]
rice[k_, n_] := 1 + k + Floor[n/2^k];
k = 2; Table[{Log[10, n], rice[k, n]}, {n, 1, 10000, 10}];
g2 = ListPlot[%, AxesOrigin -> {0, 0}, PlotJoined -> True]
k = 3; Table[{Log[10, n], rice[k, n]}, {n, 1, 10000, 10}];
g3 = ListPlot[%, AxesOrigin -> {0, 0}, PlotJoined -> True]
k = 4; Table[{Log[10, n], rice[k, n]}, {n, 1, 10000, 10}];
g4 = ListPlot[%, AxesOrigin -> {0, 0}, PlotJoined -> True]
k = 5; Table[{Log[10, n], rice[k, n]}, {n, 1, 10000, 10}];
g5 = ListPlot[%, AxesOrigin -> {0, 0}, PlotJoined -> True]
k = 8; Table[{Log[10, n], rice[k, n]}, {n, 1, 100000, 50}];
g8 = ListPlot[%, AxesOrigin -> {0, 0}, PlotJoined -> True]
k = 12; Table[{Log[10, n], rice[k, n]}, {n, 1, 500000, 100}];
g12 = ListPlot[%, AxesOrigin -> {0, 0}, PlotJoined -> True]
k = 16; Table[{Log[10, n], rice[k, n]}, {n, 1, 1000000, 100}];
g16 = ListPlot[%, AxesOrigin -> {0, 0}, PlotJoined -> True]
Show[gb, g2, g3, g4, g5, g8, g12, g16, PlotRange -> {{0, 6}, {0, 120}}]
```

Code for Figure 1.10

1.1.4 The Kraft–McMillan Inequality

The Kraft–McMillan inequality is concerned with the existence of a uniquely decodable (UD) code. It establishes the relation between such a code and the lengths L_i of its codewords.

One part of this inequality, due to [McMillan 56], states that given a UD variable-length code, with n codewords of lengths L_i, the lengths must satisfy the relation

$$\sum_{i=1}^{n} 2^{-L_i} \le 1. \tag{1.4}$$

The other part, due to [Kraft 49], states the opposite. Given a set of n positive integers $(L_1, L_2, \ldots, L_n)$ that satisfy Equation (1.4), there exists an instantaneous variable-length code such that the L_i are the lengths of its individual codewords.

Together, both parts say that there is an instantaneous variable-length code with codeword lengths L_i if and only if there is a UD code with these codeword lengths. The two parts do not say that a variable-length code is instantaneous or UD if and only if the codeword lengths satisfy Equation (1.4). In fact, it is easy to check the three individual code lengths of the code $(0, 01, 011)$ and verify that $2^{-1} + 2^{-2} + 2^{-3} = 7/8$. This code satisfies the Kraft–McMillan inequality and yet it is not instantaneous, because it is not a prefix code. Similarly, the code $(0, 01, 001)$ also satisfies Equation (1.4), but is not UD. A few more comments on this inequality are in order:

■   If a set of lengths L_i satisfies Equation (1.4), then there exist instantaneous and UD variable-length codes with these lengths. For example $(0, 10, 110)$.

■   A UD code is not always instantaneous, but there exists an instantaneous code with the same codeword lengths. For example, code $(0, 01, 11)$ is UD but not instantaneous, while code $(0, 10, 11)$ is instantaneous and has the same lengths.

■   The sum of Equation (1.4) corresponds to the part of the complete code tree that has been used for codeword selection. This is why the sum has to be less than or equal to 1. This intuitive explanation of the Kraft–McMillan relation is explained in the next paragraph.

We can gain a deeper understanding of this useful and important inequality by constructing the following simple prefix code. Given five symbols a_i, suppose that we decide to assign 0 as the code of a_1. Now all the other codes have to start with 1. We therefore assign 10, 110, 1110, and 1111 as the codewords of the four remaining symbols. The lengths of the five codewords are 1, 2, 3, 4, and 4, and it is easy to see that the sum

$$2^{-1} + 2^{-2} + 2^{-3} + 2^{-4} + 2^{-4} = \frac{1}{2} + \frac{1}{4} + \frac{1}{8} + \frac{2}{16} = 1$$

satisfies the Kraft–McMillan inequality. We now consider the possibility of constructing a similar code with lengths 1, 2, 3, 3, and 4. The Kraft–McMillan inequality tells us that this is impossible, because the sum

$$2^{-1} + 2^{-2} + 2^{-3} + 2^{-3} + 2^{-4} = \frac{1}{2} + \frac{1}{4} + \frac{2}{8} + \frac{1}{16}$$

is greater than 1, and this is easy to understand when we consider the code tree. Starting with a complete binary tree of height 4, it is obvious that once 0 was assigned as a codeword, we have "used" one half of the tree and all future codes would have to be selected from the other half of the tree. Once 10 was assigned, we were left with only 1/4 of the tree. Once 110 was assigned as a codeword, only 1/8 of the tree remained available for the selection of future codes. Once 1110 has been assigned, only 1/16 of the tree was left, and that was enough to select and assign code 1111. However, once we select and assign codes of lengths 1, 2, 3, and 3, we have exhausted the entire tree and there is nothing left to select the last (4-bit) code from.

The Kraft–McMillan inequality can be related to the entropy by observing that the lengths L_i can always be written as $L_i = -\log_2 P_i + E_i$, where E_i is simply the amount by which L_i is greater than the entropy (the extra length of code i).

This implies that

$$2^{-L_i} = 2^{(\log_2 P_i - E_i)} = 2^{\log_2 P_i}/2^{E_i} = P_i/2^{E_i}.$$

In the special case where all the extra lengths are the same ($E_i = E$), the Kraft–McMillan inequality says that

$$1 \geq \sum_{i=1}^{n} P_i/2^E = \frac{\sum_{i=1}^{n} P_i}{2^E} = \frac{1}{2^E} \implies 2^E \geq 1 \implies E \geq 0.$$

An unambiguous code has nonnegative extra length, meaning its length is greater than or equal to the length determined by its entropy.

Here is a simple example of the use of this inequality. Consider the simple case of n equal-length binary codewords. The size of each codeword is $L_i = \log_2 n$, and the Kraft–McMillan sum is

$$\sum_{1}^{n} 2^{-L_i} = \sum_{1}^{n} 2^{-\log_2 n} = \sum_{1}^{n} \frac{1}{n} = 1.$$

The inequality is satisfied, so such a code is UD.

A more interesting example is the case of n symbols where the first one is compressed and the second one is expanded. We set $L_1 = \log_2 n - a$, $L_2 = \log_2 n + e$, and $L_3 = L_4 = \cdots = L_n = \log_2 n$, where a and e are positive. We show that $e > a$, which means that compressing a symbol by a factor a requires expanding another symbol by a larger factor. We can benefit from this only if the probability of the compressed symbol is greater than that of the expanded symbol.

$$\sum_{1}^{n} 2^{-L_i} = 2^{-L_1} + 2^{-L_2} + \sum_{3}^{n} 2^{-\log_2 n}$$

$$= 2^{-\log_2 n + a} + 2^{-\log_2 n - e} + \sum_{1}^{n} 2^{-\log_2 n} - 2 \times 2^{-\log_2 n}$$

$$= \frac{2^a}{n} + \frac{2^{-e}}{n} + 1 - \frac{2}{n}.$$

The Kraft–McMillan inequality requires that

$$\frac{2^a}{n} + \frac{2^{-e}}{n} + 1 - \frac{2}{n} \le 1, \quad \text{or} \quad \frac{2^a}{n} + \frac{2^{-e}}{n} - \frac{2}{n} \le 0,$$

or $2^{-e} \le 2 - 2^a$, implying $-e \le \log_2(2 - 2^a)$, or $e \ge -\log_2(2 - 2^a)$.

The inequality above implies $a \le 1$ (otherwise, $2 - 2^a$ is negative) but a is also positive (since we assumed compression of symbol 1). The possible range of values of a is therefore $(0, 1]$, and in this range e is greater than a, proving the statement above. (It is easy to see that $a = 1 \to e \ge -\log_2 0 = \infty$, and $a = 0.1 \to e \ge -\log_2(2 - 2^{0.1}) \approx 0.10745$.)

It can be shown that this is just a special case of a general result that says, given an alphabet of n symbols, if we compress some of them by a certain factor, then the others must be expanded by a greater factor.

1.2 Run-Length Encoding

The technique of run-length encoding (RLE) has been mentioned in the Prelude to this chapter. The idea is that in certain types of data, such as images and audio, adjacent symbols are often correlated, so there may be runs of identical symbols which may be exploited to compress the data. The following are the main considerations that apply to this technique:

■ Text in a natural language (as well as names) may have many doubles and a few triples—as in AAA (an acronym), abbess, Emmanuelle, bookkeeper, arrowwood, freeer (old usage), and hostessship (used by Shakespeare)—but longer runs are limited to consecutive spaces and periods. Thus, RLE is not a good candidate for text compression.

■ In a bi-level image there are two types of symbols, namely black and white pixels, so runs of pixels alternate between these two colors, which implies that RLE can compress such an image by replacing each run with its length.

■ In general, the data to be compressed includes several types of symbols, so RLE compresses a run by replacing it with a pair (length, symbol).

■ If the run is short, such a pair may be longer than the run of symbols, thereby leading to expansion. A reasonable solution is to write such short runs on the output in raw format, so at least they do not cause expansion. However, this raises the question of distinguishing between pairs and raw items, because in the output file both types are binary strings. A practical RLE program must therefore precede each pair and each raw item with a 1-bit indicator. Thus, a pair becomes the triplet (0, length, symbol) and a raw item becomes the pair (1, symbol).

■ Runs have different lengths, which is why the pairs and triplets have different lengths. It therefore makes sense to replace each by a variable-length code and write the codes on the output. Thus, RLE is normally just one step in a multistep compression algorithm that may include a transform, variable-length codes, and perhaps also quantization. The fax compression standard (Section 2.4) and the JPEG image compression method (Section 5.6) employ specially-selected Huffman codes to write the run lengths on the output.

The remainder of this section provides more information on the application of RLE to the compression of bi-level and grayscale images.

The size of the compressed data depends on the complexity of the image. The more detailed the image, the worse the compression. However, given an image with uniform regions, it is easy to estimate the compression ratio of RLE. Figure 1.11 shows how scan lines go through a uniform region. A line enters through one point on the perimeter of the region and exits through another point, and these two points are not part of any other scan lines. It is now clear that the number of scan lines traversing a uniform region is roughly equal to half the length (measured in pixels) of its perimeter. Since the region is uniform, each scan line contributes two runs to the output for each region it crosses. The compression ratio of a uniform region therefore roughly equals the ratio

$$\frac{2\times \text{half the length of the perimeter}}{\text{total number of pixels in the region}} = \frac{\text{perimeter}}{\text{area}}.$$

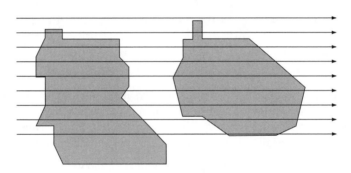

Figure 1.11: Uniform Areas and Scan Lines.

⋄ **Exercise 1.4:** What would be the compressed file in the case of the following 6 × 8 bi-level image?

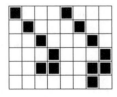

RLE can also be used to compress grayscale images. Each run of pixels of the same intensity (gray level) is encoded as a pair (run length, pixel value). The run length is either emitted as one byte, allowing for runs of up to 255 pixels, or is encoded by a variable-length code. The pixel value is encoded in a short fixed-length code whose length depends on the number of gray levels (typically between 4 and 8 bits).

Example: An 8-bit-deep grayscale bitmap that starts with

$$12, 12, 12, 12, 12, 12, 12, 12, 12, 35, 76, 112, 67, 87, 87, 87, 5, 5, 5, 5, 5, 5, 5, 1, \ldots$$

is compressed into the sequence of bytes $\boxed{9}$,12,35,76,112,67,$\boxed{3}$,87,$\boxed{6}$,5,1,..., where the boxed values indicate counts. The problem is to distinguish between a byte containing a grayscale value (such as 12) and one containing a count (such as $\boxed{9}$). Here are some solutions (although not the only possible ones):

■ If the image is limited to just 128 grayscales, we can devote one bit in each byte to indicate whether the byte contains a grayscale value or a count.

■ If the number of grayscales is 256, it can be reduced to 255 with one value reserved as a flag to precede every byte containing a count. If the flag is, say, 255, then the sequence above becomes 255,9,12,35,76,112,67,255,3,87,255,6,5,1,....

■ Again, one bit is devoted to each byte to indicate whether the byte contains a grayscale value or a count. This time, however, these extra bits are accumulated in groups of 8, and each group is written on the output preceding (or following) the eight bytes it corresponds to.
As an example, the sequence $\boxed{9}$,12,35,76,112,67,$\boxed{3}$,87,$\boxed{6}$,5,1,... becomes

$$\boxed{10000010},9,12,35,76,112,67,3,87,\boxed{100.....},6,5,1,... .$$

The total size of the extra bytes is, of course, 1/8 the size of the output (they contain one bit for each byte of the output), so they increase the size of the output by 12.5%.

■ A group of m pixels that are all different is preceded by a byte with the negative value $-m$. The sequence above is encoded by $9, 12, -4, 35, 76, 112, 67, 3, 87, 6, 5, ?, 1, \ldots$ (the value of the byte with ? is positive or negative depending on what follows the pixel of 1). The worst case is a sequence of pixels (p_1, p_2, p_2) repeated n times throughout the bitmap. It is encoded as $(-1, p_1, 2, p_2)$, four numbers instead of the original three! If each pixel requires one byte, then the original three bytes are expanded into four bytes. If each pixel requires three bytes, then the original three pixels (which constitute nine bytes) are compressed into $1 + 3 + 1 + 3 = 8$ bytes.

Three more points should be mentioned:

■ Since the run length cannot be 0, it makes sense to write the [run length minus one] on the output. Thus the pair $(3, 87)$ denotes a run of *four* pixels with intensity 87. This way, a run can be up to 256 pixels long.

■ In color images it is common to have each pixel stored as three bytes, representing the intensities of the red, green, and blue components of the pixel. In such a case, runs of each color should be encoded separately. Thus, the pixels $(171, 85, 34)$, $(172, 85, 35)$, $(172, 85, 30)$, and $(173, 85, 33)$ should be separated into the three vectors $(171, 172, 172, 173, \ldots)$, $(85, 85, 85, 85, \ldots)$, and $(34, 35, 30, 33, \ldots)$. Each vector should be run-length encoded separately. This means that any method for compressing grayscale images can be applied to color images as well.

■ It is preferable to encode each row of the bitmap individually. Thus, if a row ends with four pixels of intensity 87 and the following row starts with nine such pixels, it is better to write $\dots, 4, 87, 9, 87, \dots$ on the output rather than $\dots, 13, 87, \dots$. It is even better to output the sequence $\dots, 4, 87, \text{eol}, 9, 87, \dots$, where "eol" is a special end-of-line code. The reason is that sometimes the user may decide to accept or reject an image just by examining a rough version of it, without any details. If each line is encoded individually, the decoding algorithm can start by decoding and displaying lines $1, 6, 11, \dots$, follow with lines $2, 7, 12, \dots$, and continue in the same way. The individual rows of the image are interlaced, and the image is displayed on the screen gradually, in steps. This way, it is possible to get an idea of what is in the image at an early stage, when only a small fraction of it has been displayed. Figure 1.12c shows an example of such a scan.

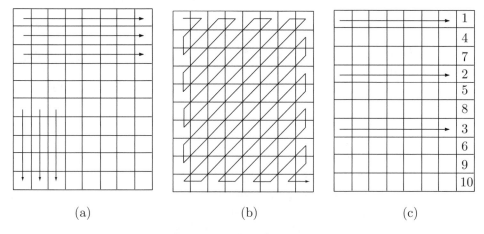

(a)   (b)   (c)

Figure 1.12: RLE Scanning.

Another advantage of individual encoding of rows is to make it possible to extract just part of an encoded image (such as rows k through l). Yet another application is to merge two compressed images without having to decompress them first.

If this idea (encoding each bitmap row individually) is adopted, then the compressed file must contain information on where each bitmap row starts in the file. This can be done by writing, at the start of the file, a header with a group of four bytes (32 bits) for each bitmap row. The kth group contains the offset (in bytes) from the start of the file to the start of the information for image row k. This increases the size of the compressed file but may still offer a good trade-off between space (size of compressed file) and time (time for the user to decide whether to accept or reject the image).

⋄ **Exercise 1.5:** There is another, obvious, reason why each bitmap row should be coded individually. What is it?

⋄ **Exercise 1.6:** In the encoding of a run length, a special symbol has been used to signal the end of a scan line. Is the insertion of the eol always necessary? If we decide to signal the end of a scan line, is it really necessary to allocate a special symbol for it?

```
% Returns the run lengths of
% a matrix of 0s and 1s
function R=runlengths(M)
[c,r]=size(M);
for i=1:c;
 x(r*(i-1)+1:r*i)=M(i,:);
end
N=r*c;
y=x(2:N);
u=x(1:N-1);
z=y+u;
j=find(z==1);
i1=[j N];
i2=[0 j];
R=i1-i2;

the test
M=[0 0 0 1; 1 1 1 0; 1 1 1 0]
runlengths(M)

produces
3    4    1    3    1
```

(a)   (b)

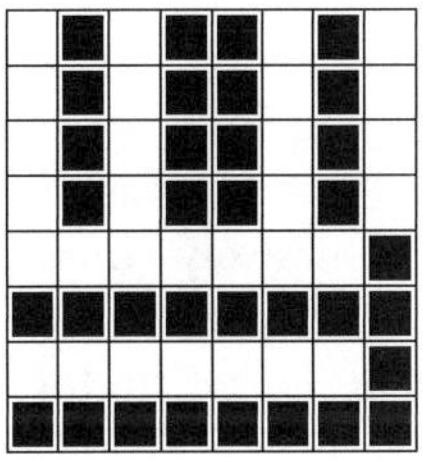

Figure 1.13: (a) Matlab Code To Compute Run Lengths. (b) A Bitmap.

Figure 1.13a lists Matlab code to compute run lengths for a bi-level image. The code is very simple. It starts by flattening the matrix into a one-dimensional vector, so the run lengths continue from row to row.

Image RLE has its downside as well. When the image is modified, the run lengths normally have to be completely redone. The RLE output can sometimes be bigger than pixel-by-pixel storage (i.e., an uncompressed image, a raw dump of the bitmap) for complex pictures. Imagine a picture with many vertical lines. When it is scanned horizontally, it produces very short runs, resulting in very bad compression, or even in expansion. A good, practical RLE image compressor should be able to scan the bitmap by rows, columns, or in a zigzag pattern (Figure 1.12a,b) and it may even try all three ways on every bitmap it compresses to achieve the best compression.

◇ **Exercise 1.7:** Figure 1.12 shows three alternative scannings of an image. What is the advantage of method (b) over (a) and (c)? Does method (b) have any disadvantage?

◇ **Exercise 1.8:** Given the 8×8 bitmap of Figure 1.13b, use RLE to compress it, first row by row, then column by column. Describe the results in detail.

Lossy RLE Image Compression. It is possible to achieve better compression if short runs are ignored. Such a method loses information when compressing an image, but this is sometimes acceptable. (Medical X-rays and images taken by large telescopes are examples of data whose compression must be lossless.)

A lossy run-length encoding algorithm should start by asking the user for the longest run that can be ignored. If the user specifies 3, then the program merges all runs of 1, 2, or 3 identical pixels with their two immediate neighbors. The run lengths "6,8,1,2,4,3,11,2" would be saved, in this case, as "6,8,7,16" where 7 is the sum $1 + 2 + 4$ (three runs merged) and 16 is the sum $3 + 11 + 2$. This makes sense for large, high-resolution images where the loss of some detail may be imperceptible, but may significantly reduce the size of the output file.

Intermezzo

Space-Filling Curves. A space-filling curve is a parametric function $\mathbf{P}(t)$ that passes through every mathematical point in a given two-dimensional region, normally the unit square, when its parameter t varies in the interval $[0, 1]$. For any real t_0 in this interval, $\mathbf{P}(t_0)$ is a point $[x_0, y_0]$ in the unit square. Mathematically, such a curve is a mapping from the interval $[0, 1]$ to the two-dimensional interval $[0, 1] \times [0, 1]$. To understand how such a curve is constructed, it is best to think of it as the limit of an infinite sequence of recursively-constructed curves $\mathbf{P}_1(t), \mathbf{P}_2(t), \ldots$, which are drawn inside the unit square, where each curve is derived from its predecessor by a process of *refinement* which produces longer and longer curves. The details of the refinement depend on the specific curve. The most-well-known space-filling curves are the Peano curve, the Hilbert curve, and the Sierpiński curve. Because the recursive sequence of curves is infinite, it is impossible to compute all its components. In practice, however, we are interested in a curve that passes through every pixel in a finite bitmap, not through every mathematical point in the unit square.

Space-filling curves are useful in data compression, specifically in image compression, because they provide another way of scanning a bitmap. Given an image that we want to compress by RLE, we can scan it by rows, by columns, in a zigzag pattern, or in the order provided by a space-filling curve.

The Hilbert Curve

This discussion is based on the approach taken by [Wirth 76]. The most familiar of the space-filling curves is the Hilbert curve, described by the great mathematician David Hilbert in 1891. The Hilbert curve [Hilbert 91] is the limit of a sequence H_0, H_1, H_2, ... of curves, some of which are shown in Figure 1.14. Each curve H_i is constructed recursively by making four copies of the preceding curve H_{i-1}, shrinking, rotating, and connecting them. The resulting curve H_i ends up covering the same area as its predecessor, but is longer. This is the refinement process for the Hilbert curve.

The curve is defined by the following steps:

0. H_0 is a single point.

1. H_1 consists of four copies of (the point) H_0, connected with three straight segments of length h at right angles to each other. Four orientations of this curve, labeled 1, 2, 3, and 4, are shown in Figure 1.14a.

2. The next curve, H_2, in the sequence is constructed by connecting four copies of different orientations of H_1 with three straight segments of length $h/2$ (shown in bold in Figure 1.14b). Again there are four possible orientations of H_2, and the one shown is #2. It is constructed of orientations 1223 of H_1, connected by segments that go to the right, up, and to the left. The construction of the four orientations of H_2 is summarized in Figure 1.14d.

Curve H_3 is shown in Figure 1.14c. The particular curve shown is orientation 1223 of H_2.

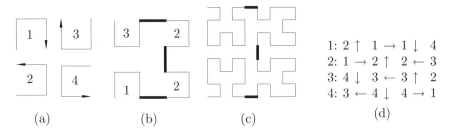

Figure 1.14: Hilbert Curves of Orders 1, 2, and 3 and Construction Rules.

✦A chess board has 64 squares. Given a set of 32 cardboard rectangles, each covering two adjacent squares, we can easily use them to cover the entire board. We now remove two diagonally-opposite squares from the chess board, leaving 62 squares. Can they be covered by 31 cardboard rectangles?

1.3 Dictionary-Based Methods

Dictionary-based compression methods are based on the fact that parts of data tend to appear several times in a given data file. Thus, a text file may contain several occurrences of a word, a phrase, or a syllable. In an image file, the same string of pixels may appear many times, and in an audio file, a string of audio samples may also appear repeatedly. A dictionary-based method maintains a dictionary that contains bits and pieces of the data. As a string of data symbols is read from the input, the algorithm searches the dictionary for the longest match to the string. Once a match is found, the string is compressed by replacing it with a pointer to the dictionary. Quite a few dictionary-based methods are known and the differences between them are in the way they organize and maintain the dictionary, in how they handle strings not found in the dictionary, and in how they write their results (pointers, lengths, raw items, and perhaps flag bits) on the output.

The entire field of dictionary-based compression is based on the pioneering work of two researchers, Jacob Ziv and Abraham Lempel. In 1977 and 1978, they published two papers that laid the foundation of this field and on which later workers based their algorithms. The basic methods developed by Ziv and Lempel have become known as LZ77 and LZ78, and most other dictionary-based algorithms include the digram LZ in their names. The remainder of this section describes LZ77, a simple, albeit not very efficient, dictionary-based method.

1.3.1 LZ77 (Sliding Window)

LZ77 (sometimes also referred to as LZ1) was originally proposed in [Ziv and Lempel 77]. The main idea is to use part of the previously-processed input as the dictionary. The encoder maintains a window to the input data and shifts the input in that window from right to left as strings of symbols are being read and encoded. Thus, the method is based on a *sliding window*. The window shown here is divided into two parts. The part on the left is the *search buffer*. This is the current dictionary, and it includes symbols that have recently been input and encoded. The part on the right is the *look-ahead buffer*, with text yet to be read and encoded. In practical implementations the search buffer is some thousands of bytes long, while the look-ahead buffer is only tens of bytes long. The vertical bar between the t and the e represents the dividing line between the two buffers. It indicates that the text sir␣sid␣eastman␣easily␣t has already been compressed, while the text eases␣sea␣sick␣seals still needs to be compressed.

← coded text... $\boxed{\text{sir␣sid␣eastman␣easily␣t}}$ $\boxed{\text{eases␣sea␣sick␣seals}}$ ... ← text to be read

The encoder scans the search buffer backwards (from right to left) looking for a match for the first symbol e in the look-ahead buffer. It finds one at the e of the word easily. This e is at a distance (offset) of 8 from the end of the search buffer. The encoder then matches as many symbols following the two e's as possible. Three symbols eas match in this case, so the length of the match is 3. The encoder then continues the backward scan, trying to find longer matches. In our case, there is one more match, at the word eastman, with offset 16, and it has the same length. The encoder selects the longest match or, if they are all the same length, the last one found, and prepares the token (16, 3, e).

Selecting the last match, rather than the first one, simplifies the encoder, because it has to keep track of only the last match found. It is interesting to note that selecting the first match, while making the program somewhat more complex, also has an advantage. It selects the smallest offset. It would seem that this is not an advantage, because a token should have room enough for the largest possible offset. However, a sophisticated, multistep compression algorithm may employ LZ77 as a first step, following which the LZ77 tokens may be compressed further by replacing them with variable-length codes.

◇ **Exercise 1.9:** How does the decoder know whether the encoder selects the first match or the last match?

◇ **Exercise 1.10:** Assuming a very long search buffer, what can we say about the distribution of matches? Would there be more matches in the older part (on the left), in the newer part (on the right), or would the distribution of matches be more or less uniform?

In general, an LZ77 token has three parts: offset, length, and next symbol in the look-ahead buffer (which, in our case, is the **second** e of the word teases). This token is written on the output, and the window is shifted to the right (or, alternatively, the input is moved to the left) four positions: three positions for the matched string and one position for the next symbol.

...sir␣$\boxed{\text{sid␣eastman␣easily␣tease}}$ $\boxed{\text{s␣sea␣sick␣seals...}}$...

If the backward search yields no match, an LZ77 token with zero offset and length and with the unmatched symbol is generated and emitted. This is also the reason a token has a third component. Tokens with zero offset and length are common at the beginning of any compression job, when the search buffer is empty or almost empty. The first five steps in encoding our example are the following:

	sir␣sid␣eastman␣	⇒ (0,0,s)
s	ir␣sid␣eastman␣e	⇒ (0,0,i)
si	r␣sid␣eastman␣ea	⇒ (0,0,r)
sir	␣sid␣eastman␣eas	⇒ (0,0,␣)
sir␣	sid␣eastman␣easi	⇒ (4,2,d)

⋄ **Exercise 1.11:** What are the next two steps?

Clearly, a token of the form $(0, 0, \ldots)$, which encodes a single symbol, provides lousy compression and may also cause expansion. It is easy to estimate its length. The size of the offset is $\lceil \log_2 S \rceil$, where S is the length of the search buffer. In practice, the search buffer may be a few thousand bytes long, so the offset size is typically 10–12 bits. The size of the "length" field is similarly $\lceil \log_2(L - 1) \rceil$, where L is the length of the look-ahead buffer (see below for the -1). In practice, the look-ahead buffer is only a few tens of bytes long, so the size of the "length" field is just a few bits. The size of the "symbol" field is typically 8 bits, but in general, it is $\lceil \log_2 A \rceil$, where A is the alphabet size. The total size of the 1-symbol token $(0, 0, \ldots)$ may typically be $11 + 5 + 8 = 24$ bits, much longer than the raw 8-bit size of the (single) symbol it encodes.

Here is an example showing why the "length" field may be longer than the size of the look-ahead buffer:

...Mr.␣ alf␣eastman␣easily␣grows␣alf | alfa␣in␣his␣ | garden... .

The first symbol a in the look-ahead buffer matches the five a's in the search buffer. It seems that the two extreme a's match with a length of 3 and the encoder should select the last (leftmost) of them and create the token (28,3,a). In fact, it creates the token (3,4,␣). The four-symbol string alfa in the look-ahead buffer is matched with the last three symbols alf in the search buffer **and** the first symbol a in the look-ahead buffer. The reason for this is that the decoder can handle such a token naturally, without any modifications. It starts at position 3 of its search buffer and copies the next four symbols, one by one, extending its buffer to the right. The first three symbols are copies of the old buffer contents, and the fourth one is a copy of the first of those three. The next example is even more convincing (and only somewhat contrived):

··· alf␣eastman␣easily␣yells␣A | AAAAAAAAAA | AAAAAH... .

The encoder creates the token (1,9,A), matching the first nine copies of A in the look-ahead buffer and including the tenth A. This is why, in principle, the length of a match can be up to the size of the look-ahead buffer minus 1.

The decoder is much simpler than the encoder (LZ77 is therefore an asymmetric compression method). It has to maintain a buffer, equal in size to the encoder's window. The decoder inputs a token, finds the match in its buffer, writes the match and the third token field on the output, and shifts the matched string and the third field into the buffer. This implies that LZ77, or any of its variants, is useful in cases where a file is compressed once (or just a few times) and is decompressed often. A rarely-used archive of compressed files is a good example.

At first it seems that this method does not make any assumptions about the input data. Specifically, it does not pay attention to any symbol frequencies. A little thinking, however, shows that because of the nature of the sliding window, the LZ77 method always compares the look-ahead buffer to the recently-input text in the search buffer and never to text that was input long ago (which has therefore been flushed out of the search buffer). Thus, the method implicitly assumes that patterns in the input data occur close together. Data that satisfies this assumption compresses well.

The basic LZ77 method was improved in several ways by researchers and programmers during the 1980s and 1990s. One way to improve it is to use variable-size "offset" and "length" fields in the tokens. Another option is to increase the sizes of both buffers. Increasing the size of the search buffer makes it possible to find better matches, but the trade-off is an increased search time. A large search buffer therefore requires a sophisticated data structure that allows for fast search. A third improvement has to do with sliding the window. The simplest approach is to move all the text in the window to the left after each match. A faster method is to replace the linear window with a circular queue, where sliding the window is done by resetting two pointers. Yet another improvement is adding an extra bit (a flag) to each token, thereby eliminating the third field. Of special notice is the hash table employed by the Deflate algorithm [Salomon 07] to search for matches.

1.4 Transforms

A transform is a mathematical operation that changes the appearance or representation of the objects being transformed. A transform by itself does not compress data and is only one step in a multistep compression algorithm. However, transforms play an important role in data compression, especially in the compression of images. A digital image can be compressed mainly because neighboring pixels tend to be similar; the individual pixels are correlated. An image transform takes advantage of this feature and converts correlated pixels to a representation where they are independent.

Two types of transforms are employed in image compression, namely orthogonal and subband. They are described in detail in Chapter 5, while this section only illustrates the power of a transform by an example. Consider the simple mathematical expression

$$(x^*, y^*) = (x, y) \begin{pmatrix} \cos 45° & -\sin 45° \\ \sin 45° & \cos 45° \end{pmatrix} = (x, y) \frac{1}{\sqrt{2}} \begin{pmatrix} 1 & -1 \\ 1 & 1 \end{pmatrix} = (x, y)\mathbf{R}. \qquad (1.5)$$

When applied to a pair (x, y) of consecutive pixels, this expression yields a pair (x^*, y^*) of transform coefficients. As a simple experiment, we apply it to five pairs of correlated (i.e., similar) numbers to obtain $(5, 5) \rightarrow (7.071, 0)$, $(6, 7) \rightarrow (9.19, 0.7071)$, $(12.1, 13.2) \rightarrow (17.9, 0.78)$, $(23, 25) \rightarrow (33.9, 1.41)$, and $(32, 29) \rightarrow (43.13, -2.12)$. A quick glance at these numbers verifies their significance. The y^* transform coefficient of each pair is a small (signed) number, close to zero, while the x^* coefficient is not appreciably different from the corresponding x value.

⋄ **Exercise 1.12:** Why does a 45° rotation decorrelate pairs of consecutive pixels?

If we apply this simple transform to all the pixels of an image, two adjacent pixels at a time, it reduces the sizes of half the pixels without significantly changing the sizes of the other half. In principle, some compression has already been obtained, but in practice we need an algorithm that replaces the transform coefficients with variable-length codes, so they can be output and later input unambiguously. A sophisticated algorithm may extend this transform so that it can be applied to triplets (or even larger n-tuples) of pixels, not just pairs. This will result in two-thirds of the pixels being transformed into small numbers, while the remaining third will not change much in size. In addition, such an algorithm may quantize the small transform coefficients, which results in lossy compression, but also a better compression ratio.

In order to be practical, a transform must have an inverse. A simple check verifies that the inverse of our transform is the expression

$$(x, y) = (x^*, y^*)\mathbf{R}^{-1} = (x^*, y^*)\mathbf{R}^T = (x^*, y^*)\frac{1}{\sqrt{2}}\begin{pmatrix} 1 & 1 \\ -1 & 1 \end{pmatrix}. \tag{1.6}$$

Chapter 5 discusses this transform and its interpretation in some detail. The matrix of Equation (5.1) is a rotation matrix in two dimensions, and the matrix of Equation (5.2) is its inverse.

⋄ **Exercise 1.13:** It seems that this simple transform has produced something for nothing. It has shrunk the sizes of half the numbers without a similar increase in the sizes of the other half. What's the explanation?

1.5 Quantization

The dictionary definition of the term "quantization" is "to restrict a variable quantity to discrete values rather than to a continuous set of values." In the field of data compression, quantization is employed in two contexts as follows:

■ If the data symbols are real numbers, quantization may round each to the nearest integer. If the data symbols are large numbers, quantization may convert them to small numbers. Small numbers take less space than large ones, so quantization generates compression. On the other hand, small numbers convey less information than large ones, which is why quantization produces lossy compression.

■ If the data to be compressed is analog (such as a voltage that varies with time), quantization is employed to digitize it into numbers (normally integers). This is referred to as analog-to-digital (A/D) conversion. If the integers generated by quantization are 8 bits each, then the entire range of the analog signal is divided into 256 intervals and all the signal values within an interval are quantized to the same number. If 16-bit integers are generated, then the range of the analog signal is divided into 65,536 intervals. This relation illustrates the compromise between high resolution (a large number of analog intervals) and high compression (small integers generated). This application of quantization is used by several speech compression methods.

> I would not have the courage to raise this possibility if Academician Arkhangelsky had not come tentatively to the same conclusion. He and I have disagreed about the quantization of quasar red shifts, the explanation of superluminal light sources, the rest mass of the neutrino, quark physics in neutron stars.... We have had many disagreements.
>
> —Carl Sagan, *Contact* (1986)

If the data symbols are numbers, then each is quantized to another number in a process referred to as scalar quantization. Alternatively, if each data symbol is a vector, then vector quantization converts a data symbol to another vector. Both aspects of quantization are discussed here.

1.5.1 Scalar Quantization

We start with an example of naive discrete quantization. Given input data of 8-bit numbers, we can simply delete the least-significant four bits of each data item. This is one of those rare cases where the compression factor ($= 2$) is known in advance and does not depend on the data. The input data consists of 256 different symbols, while the output data consists of just 16 different symbols. This method is simple but not very practical because too much information is lost in order to get the unimpressive compression factor of 2.

The popular JPEG method for image compression (Section 5.6) is based on the discrete cosine transform (DCT) that transforms a square $n \times n$ array of pixel values to a list of n^2 transform coefficients, of which the first is large and the rest are small. A typical output for $n = 4$ may look like 1171, 34.6, 2, 0, 0, 0, -1, 3.8, 0, 1, 0, 0, 7.15, 2, 0, and 0. Scalar quantization may convert this list to 1171, 34, 2, 0, 0, 0, 0, 4, 0, 0, 0, 0, 7, 2, 0, and 0. The latter list can be highly compressed by replacing each nonzero coefficient and each run of zeros by variable-length codes.

A better approach to scalar quantization employs a spacing parameter. We assume that the data consists of 8-bit unsigned integers and we select a spacing parameter s. We compute the sequence of uniform quantized values 0, s, $2s$, ..., ks, such that $ks \leq 255$ but $(k+1)s > 255$. Each input symbol S is quantized by converting it to the nearest value in this sequence. Selecting $s = 3$, for example, produces the uniform sequence 0, 3, 6, 9, 12, ..., 252, 255. Selecting $s = 4$ produces 0, 4, 8, 12, ..., 252, 255 (since the next multiple of 4, after 252, is 256).

A similar approach is to select the quantized values in such a way that any integer in the range $[0, 255]$ will be no more than d units distant from one of the quantized values. This is done by dividing the range $[0, 255]$ into segments of size $2d + 1$. If we select $d = 16$, then the relation $256 = 7(2 \times 16 + 1) + 25$ implies that the range $[0, 255]$ should be partitioned into eight segments, seven of size 33 each and one of size 25. The eight segments cover the subintervals 0–32, 33–65, 66–98, 99–131, 132–164, 165–197, 198–230, and 231–255. We select the middle of each segment as a quantized value and end up with the eight values 16, 49, 82, 115, 148, 181, 214, and 243. Any integer in the range $[0, 255]$ is at most 16 units distant from any of these values.

The quantized values above make sense in cases where each symbol appears in the input data with equal probability (cases where the source is i.i.d.). If the input data is not uniformly distributed, the sequence of quantized values should be distributed in the same way as the data.

(A sequence or any collection of random variables is independent and identically distributed (i.i.d.) if all have the same probability distribution and are mutually independent. All other things being equal, a sequence of die rolls, a sequence of coin flips, and an unbiased random walk are i.i.d., because a step has no effect on the following step.)

bbbbbbbb		bbbbbbbb	
1	1	.	
10	2	.	
11	3	.	
100	4	100|000	32
101	5	101|000	40
110	6	110|000	48
111	7	111|000	56
100|0	8	100|0000	64
101|0	10	101|0000	80
110|0	12	110|0000	96
111|0	14	111|0000	112
100|00	16	100|00000	128
101|00	20	101|00000	160
110|00	24	110|00000	192
111|00	28	111|00000	224

Table 1.15: A Logarithmic Quantization Table.

Imagine, for example, input data of 8-bit unsigned integers of which most are zero or close to zero and only a few are large. A good sequence of quantized values for such data should have the same distribution, i.e., many small values and only a few large ones. One way of computing such a sequence is to select a value for the length parameter l, to construct a "window" of the form

$$1 \underbrace{b \dots bb}_{l}$$

(where each b is a bit), and place it under each of the 8-bit positions of a data item. If the window sticks out to the right, some of the l bits are truncated. As the window is moved to the left, zero bits are appended to it. Table 1.15 illustrates this construction with $l = 2$. It is easy to see how the resulting quantized values start with initial spacing of one unit (i.e., the first eight quantized values are 1 through 8), continue with spacing of two units (the next four quantized values are 8, 10, 12, and 14) and four units, until the last four values are spaced by 32 units (such as 192 and 224). The numbers 0 and 255 should be manually added to such a quasi-logarithmic sequence to make it more general.

Figure 1.16 illustrates another aspect of scalar quantization, namely midtread versus midrise quantization. The figure shows how continuous (real) x input values (also called decision levels) are quantized to discrete y outputs (also called reconstruction levels). The midtread quantization principle is to quantize to y_i all the input values in the subinterval $((x_{i-1} + x_i)/2, (x_i + x_{i+1})/2]$, which is centered on x_i. In contrast, the philosophy behind midrise quantization is to quantize the subinterval $(x_{i-1}, x_i]$ to y_i. Notice that these subintervals are open on the left and closed on the right, but the reverse edge convention can also be used.

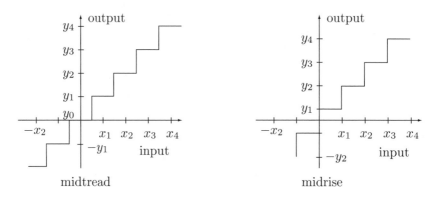

Figure 1.16: Midtread and Midrise Quantization.

It is often convenient to use midrise quantization when the number of quantization values (the y_i) is even and employ midtread quantization when this number is odd. Also, because of its construction, midrise quantization does not have 0 as a quantization value, which is why applications where certain inputs should be quantized to 0 use midtread.

Notice that the input intervals $(x_{i-1}, x_i]$ in Figure 1.16 are uniform (except for the two extreme intervals) and the same is true for the output values. The figure illustrates uniform quantization.

It makes sense to define the quantization error as the difference between an input value and its quantized value, and Figure 1.17 illustrates the behavior of this error as a function of the input. Part (a) of the figure shows a uniform midtread quantizer and part (b) shows how the error behaves as a periodic sawtooth function, rising from -0.5 to 0.5, then dropping back to -0.5.

Nonuniform quantization has to be used in applications where the input is distributed nonuniformly. Table 1.18 (after [Lloyd 82], [Max 60], and [Paez and Glisson 72]) lists input and quantized values for optimal symmetric quantizers for uniform, Gaussian, and Laplace distributions with zero mean and unit variance and for 2, 4, 8, and 16 subintervals of the input.

Scalar quantization produces lossy compression, but makes it is easy to control the trade-off between compression performance and the amount of data loss. However, because it is so simple, applications of scalar quantization are limited to cases where much loss can be tolerated. Many image compression methods are lossy, but scalar quantization is not suitable for image compression because it creates annoying artifacts in the decompressed image. Imagine an image with an almost uniform area where all pixels have values 127 or 128. If 127 is quantized to 111 and 128 is quantized to 144, then the result, after decompression, may resemble a checkerboard where adjacent pixels

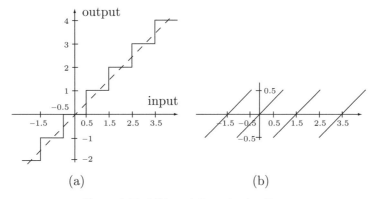

(a)   (b)

Figure 1.17: Midtread Quantization Error.

alternate between 111 and 144. This is why practical algorithms use vector quantization, instead of scalar quantization, for lossy (and sometimes lossless) compression of images and sound.

1.5.2 Vector Quantization

Vector quantization is based on the fact that adjacent data symbols in image and audio files are correlated. The principle is simple and is stated in the following steps:

■   Select a parameter N that will be the size of the vectors and work with groups (called vectors) of N adjacent data symbols (pixels or audio samples).

■   Prepare a set (referred to as a codebook) of vectors V_j. Determining the best vectors for the codebook is the central problem of vector quantization.

■   Scan the input data vector by vector and compress each vector v_i by finding the codebook vector V_j that is "nearest" v_i. The index j is then written on the output.

The left half of Figure 1.19 is a simple example. The original data is a 4×12 image and the codebook consists of five vectors, each a smaller 4×4 image. The arrow indicates that vector 3 is the best match for the center-bottom 4×4 part of the image. Thus, that part is encoded as the single number 3 (in practice, a variable-length code for 3 may be written on the output).

It is obvious that the decoder is very simple. It inputs numbers from the compressed file and interprets each number as an index to the codebook. The corresponding vector is read from the codebook and is appended to the data that's being decompressed. The encoder, on the other hand, is more complex (vector quantization is therefore a highly asymmetric compression method). For each part of the original data, the encoder has to search the entire codebook and determine the best match. There is also the question of selecting the best vectors and constructing the codebook in the first place.

We can gain a deeper understanding of vector quantization by thinking of it as a partitioning of space. The right half of Figure 1.19 is a two-dimensional (approximate) example of space partitioning. Given a number of points in space (nine points in the figure), the space is partitioned into the same number of nonoverlapping regions with one of the given points at the center of each region. The regions are selected such that

	Uniform		Gaussian		Laplacian	
2	−1.000		−∞		−∞	
		−0.500		−0.799		−0.707
	0.000		0.000		0.000	
		0.500		0.799		0.707
	1.000		∞		∞	
4	−1.000		−∞		−∞	
		−0.750		−1.510		−1.834
	−0.500		−0.982		−1.127	
		−0.250		−0.453		−0.420
	0.000		0.000		0.000	
		0.250		0.453		0.420
	0.500		0.982		1.127	
		0.750		1.510		1.834
	1.000		∞		∞	
8	−1.000		−∞		−∞	
		−0.875		−2.152		−3.087
	−0.750		−1.748		−2.377	
		−0.625		−1.344		−1.673
	−0.500		−1.050		−1.253	
		−0.375		−0.756		−0.833
	−0.250		−0.501		−0.533	
		−0.125		−0.245		−0.233
	0.000		0.000		0.000	
		0.125		0.245		0.233
	0.250		0.501		0.533	
		0.375		0.756		0.833
	0.500		1.050		1.253	
		0.625		1.344		1.673
	0.750		1.748		2.377	
		0.875		2.152		3.087
	1.000		∞		∞	
16	−1.000		−∞		−∞	
		−0.938		−2.733		−4.316
	−0.875		−2.401		−3.605	
		−0.813		−2.069		−2.895
	−0.750		−1.844		−2.499	
		−0.688		−1.618		−2.103
	−0.625		−1.437		−1.821	
		−0.563		−1.256		−1.540
	−0.500		−1.099		−1.317	
		−0.438		−0.942		−1.095
	−0.375		−0.800		−0.910	
		−0.313		−0.657		−0.726
	−0.250		−0.522		−0.566	
		−0.188		−0.388		−0.407
	−0.125		−0.258		−0.266	
		−0.063		−0.128		−0.126
	0.000		0.000		0.000	
		0.063		0.128		0.126
	0.125		0.258		0.266	
		0.188		0.388		0.407
	0.250		0.522		0.566	
		0.313		0.657		0.726
	0.375		0.800		0.910	
		0.438		0.942		1.095
	0.500		1.099		1.317	
		0.563		1.256		1.540
	0.625		1.437		1.821	
		0.688		1.618		2.103
	0.750		1.844		2.499	
		0.813		2.069		2.895
	0.875		2.401		3.605	
		0.938		2.733		4.316
	1.000		∞		∞	

Table 1.18: Uniform and Nonuniform Quantizations.

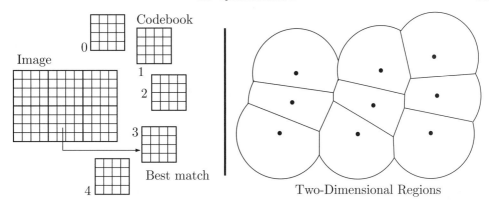

Two-Dimensional Regions

Figure 1.19: Vector Quantization Example.

all the points in a region are closer to the region's center point than to any other center point. Every point in the region is then transformed or projected to the center point.

Voronoi Regions

Imagine a Petri dish ready for growing bacteria. Four bacteria of different types are simultaneously placed in it at different points and immediately start multiplying. We assume that their colonies grow at the same rate. Initially, each colony consists of a growing circle around one of the starting points. After a while, the circles meet and stop growing in the meeting area due to lack of food. The final result is that the entire dish is divided into four areas, one around each of the four starting points, such that all the points within area i are closer to starting point i than to any other start point. Such areas are called Voronoi regions or Dirichlet Tessellations.

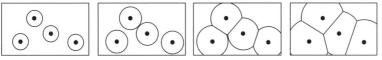

In practice, each vector has N components, so vector quantization becomes the problem of partitioning n-dimensional space into regions and determining a center point for each region. Once this is done, quantization amounts to replacing all the points in a region with the center point.

How is the codebook constructed? This problem is somewhat similar to the problem of determining the distribution of data symbols in a given file (page 26) and can be approached in three ways as follows:

■ A two-pass job, where the first pass analyzes the data to be compressed and constructs the best codebook for that data and the second pass performs the actual compression. In addition to being slow, this approach requires writing the entire codebook on the compressed file.

■ A static codebook that is determined once and for all by means of a set of training documents. The codebook is built into both encoder and decoder, so it doesn't have to be written on the compressed file. Obviously, the performance of this approach depends on how much the data resembles the training documents.

- An adaptive algorithm, where the codebook starts empty and is modified each time new data is input and compressed. Such a method has to be designed carefully to make sure that the decoder can modify the codebook in lockstep with the encoder.

The first two approaches are similar. Both require an algorithm that constructs the best codebook for a given data file (either the data to be compressed or the training documents). An example of such a method is the Linde, Buzo, and Gray (LBG) algorithm [Linde et al. 80]. This algorithm, as well as a method for adaptive vector quantization, are described in [Salomon 07].

Chapter Summary

This chapter introduces the important approaches to data compression. The Prelude discusses variable-length codes, run-length encoding (RLE), the use of dictionaries, the concept of a transform, and the techniques of scalar and vector quantization. Following the Prelude, each approach is described in more detail in a separate section. Here is a short summary of the main concepts involved.

Variable-length codes are a natural choice for simple, effective compression of various types of data. Most types of data (such as text characters, pixels, and audio samples) are encoded with a fixed-length code because this makes it convenient to input, process, and save the individual data symbols. Replacing fixed-length codes with variable-length codes can lead to compression because of the following: (1) Often, certain symbols are more common than others, so replacing them with short codes can greatly save on the total number of bits needed. (2) Data symbols such as pixels and audio samples are correlated. Subtracting adjacent symbols results in differences (or residuals), most of which are small integers and thus can be replaced by short codes.

Run-length encoding is used to compress strings of identical symbols. In principle, a string of n occurrences of symbol S can be replaced by a repetition factor n followed by a single S. RLE is especially useful in combination with quantization, because the latter may often quantize many symbols to zero and thus generate long strings of zeros.

Dictionary-based compression methods exploit the fact that a typical data file is not random; it features patterns and repetitions. At any point during compression, the input file is divided into two parts, data that has been compressed (this is kept in a data structure called the dictionary) and data that still has to be input and compressed. Assume that the latter part starts with the string of symbols abcd.... The encoder searches the dictionary for this string, and locates the longest match. The string is then compressed by replacing it with a pointer to its match in the dictionary. The difference between the various dictionary methods is in how they organize and search the dictionary and how they deal with strings not found in the dictionary.

A transform is a mathematical operation that changes the representation of a data item. Thus, changing the decimal number 12,345 to the binary 11000000111001 is a transform. Correlated data symbols such as the pixels of an image or the audio samples of a sound file, can be transformed to representations where they require fewer bits. This sounds like getting something for nothing, but in fact there is a price to pay. The transformed items (transform coefficients) are decorrelated. Such a transform already achieves some degree of compression, but more can be obtained if lossy compression is an option. The transform coefficients can be quantized, a process that results in small integers (which can be encoded with variable-length codes) and possibly also in runs of zeros (which can be compressed with RLE).

Quantization is the operation of cutting up a number. A real number, for example, can be quantized by converting it to the nearest integer (or the nearest smaller integer). Heavier quantization may convert all the numbers in an interval $[a, b]$ to the integer at the center of the interval. For example, given an input file where the data symbols are 8-bit integers (bytes) we can compress each symbol to four bits as follows. A byte is an integer in the interval $[0, 255]$. We divide this interval to 16 subintervals of width 16 each, and quantize each integer in a subinterval to the integer in the middle (or closest to the middle) of the interval. This is referred to as scalar quantization and is very inefficient. The compression factor is only 2, and the quantization simply discards half the original bits of each data symbol, which may be too much data to lose.

A more efficient form of quantization is the so-called vector quantization, where an array of data symbols is replaced by the index of another array. The replacement arrays are the components of a codebook of arrays and are selected such that (1) for each data array v_i there is a replacement array V_j in the codebook such that v_i and V_j are sufficiently close and (2) the codebook size (the number of replacement arrays) is small enough, such that replacing v_i by the index j result in significant savings of bits.

Self-Assessment Questions

1. Most variable-length codes used in practical compression algorithms are prefix codes, but there are other ways to design UD codes. Consider the following idea for a "taboo" code. The user selects a positive integer n and decides on an n-bit taboo pattern. Each codeword is constructed as a string of n-bit blocks where the last block is the taboo pattern and no other block can have this pattern. Select $n = 3$ and a 3-bit taboo pattern, and then write several taboo codewords with 3, 4, and 5 blocks. Find out how the number of possible values of a b-block codeword depends on b.

2. Section 1.2 mentions mixing run lengths and raw items. Here is the relevant paragraph:

"If the run is short, such a pair may be longer than the run of symbols, thereby leading to expansion. A reasonable solution is to write such short runs on the output in raw format, so at least they do not cause expansion. However, this raises the question of distinguishing between pairs and raw items, because in the output file both types are binary strings. A practical RLE program must therefore precede each pair and each raw item with a 1-bit indicator. Thus, a pair becomes the triplet (0, length, symbol) and a raw item becomes the pair (1, symbol)."

Prepare a data file with many run lengths and write a program that identifies each run and compresses it either as a triplet (0, length, symbol) or as a pair (1, symbol) depending on its length (if the run is long enough to benefit from RLE, it should be converted into a triplet).

3. The last paragraph of Section 1.3.1 mentions several ways to improve the basic LZ77 method. One such technique has to do with a circular queue. Study this interesting data structure in books on data structures and implement a simple version of a circular queue.

4. The matrix of Equation (5.1) is a rotation matrix in two dimensions. Use books on geometric transformations to understand rotations in higher dimensions.

5. Prepare an example of vector quantization similar to that of Figure 1.19.

The best angle from which to approach any problem is the try-angle.

—Unknown

2
Huffman Coding

 Prelude

Huffman coding is a popular method for compressing data with variable-length codes. Given a set of data symbols (an alphabet) and their frequencies of occurrence (or, equivalently, their probabilities), the method constructs a set of variable-length codewords with the shortest average length and assigns them to the symbols. Huffman coding serves as the basis for several applications implemented on popular platforms. Some programs use just the Huffman method, while others use it as one step in a multistep compression process. The Huffman method [Huffman 52] is somewhat similar to the Shannon–Fano method, proposed independently by Claude Shannon and Robert Fano in the late 1940s ([Shannon 48] and [Fano 49]). It generally produces better codes, and like the Shannon–Fano method, it produces the best variable-length codes when the probabilities of the symbols are negative powers of 2. The main difference between the two methods is that Shannon–Fano constructs its codes from top to bottom (and the bits of each codeword are constructed from left to right), while Huffman constructs a code tree from the bottom up (and the bits of each codeword are constructed from right to left).

Since its inception in 1952 by D. Huffman, the method has been the subject of intensive research in data compression. The long discussion in [Gilbert and Moore 59] proves that the Huffman code is a minimum-length code in the sense that no other encoding has a shorter average length. A much shorter proof of the same fact was discovered by Huffman himself [Motil 07]. An algebraic approach to constructing the Huffman code is introduced in [Karp 61]. In [Gallager 78], Robert Gallager shows that the redundancy of Huffman coding is at most $p_1 + 0.086$ where p_1 is the probability of the most-common symbol in the alphabet. The redundancy is the difference between the average Huffman codeword length and the entropy. Given a large alphabet, such as the set of letters, digits and punctuation marks used by a natural language, the largest symbol probability is typically around 15–20%, bringing the value of the quantity $p_1 + 0.086$ to around 0.1. This means that Huffman codes are at most 0.1 bit longer (per symbol) than an ideal entropy encoder, such as arithmetic coding (Chapter 4).

This chapter describes the details of Huffman encoding and decoding and covers related topics such as the height of a Huffman code tree, canonical Huffman codes, and an adaptive Huffman algorithm. Following this, Section 2.4 illustrates an important application of the Huffman method to facsimile compression.

David Huffman (1925–1999)

Being originally from Ohio, it is no wonder that Huffman went to Ohio State University for his BS (in electrical engineering). What is unusual was his age (18) when he earned it in 1944. After serving in the United States Navy, he went back to Ohio State for an MS degree (1949) and then to MIT, for a PhD (1953, electrical engineering).

That same year, Huffman joined the faculty at MIT. In 1967, he made his only career move when he went to the University of California, Santa Cruz as the founding faculty member of the Computer Science Department. During his long tenure at UCSC, Huffman played a major role in the development of the department (he served as chair from 1970 to 1973) and he is known for his motto "my products are my students." Even after his retirement, in 1994, he remained active in the department, teaching information theory and signal analysis courses.

Huffman developed his celebrated algorithm as a term paper that he wrote in lieu of taking a final examination in an information theory class he took at MIT in 1951. The professor, Robert Fano, proposed the problem of constructing the shortest variable-length code for a set of symbols with known probabilities of occurrence.

It should be noted that in the late 1940s, Fano himself (and independently, also Claude Shannon) had developed a similar, but suboptimal, algorithm known today as the Shannon–Fano method ([Shannon 48] and [Fano 49]). The difference between the two algorithms is that the Shannon–Fano code tree is built from the top down, while the Huffman code tree is constructed from the bottom up.

Huffman made significant contributions in several areas, mostly information theory and coding, signal designs for radar and communications, and design procedures for asynchronous logical circuits. Of special interest is the well-known Huffman algorithm for constructing a set of optimal prefix codes for data with known frequencies of occurrence. At a certain point he became interested in the mathematical properties of "zero curvature" surfaces, and developed this interest into techniques for folding paper into unusual sculptured shapes (the so-called computational origami).

2.1 Huffman Encoding

The Huffman encoding algorithm starts by constructing a list of all the alphabet symbols in descending order of their probabilities. It then constructs, from the bottom up, a binary tree with a symbol at every leaf. This is done in steps, where at each step two symbols with the smallest probabilities are selected, added to the top of the partial tree, deleted from the list, and replaced with an auxiliary symbol representing the two original symbols. When the list is reduced to just one auxiliary symbol (representing the entire alphabet), the tree is complete. The tree is then traversed to determine the codewords of the symbols.

This process is best illustrated by an example. Given five symbols with probabilities as shown in Figure 2.1a, they are paired in the following order:

1. a_4 is combined with a_5 and both are replaced by the combined symbol a_{45}, whose probability is 0.2.

2. There are now four symbols left, a_1, with probability 0.4, and a_2, a_3, and a_{45}, with probabilities 0.2 each. We arbitrarily select a_3 and a_{45} as the two symbols with smallest probabilities, combine them, and replace them with the auxiliary symbol a_{345}, whose probability is 0.4.

3. Three symbols are now left, a_1, a_2, and a_{345}, with probabilities 0.4, 0.2, and 0.4, respectively. We arbitrarily select a_2 and a_{345}, combine them, and replace them with the auxiliary symbol a_{2345}, whose probability is 0.6.

4. Finally, we combine the two remaining symbols, a_1 and a_{2345}, and replace them with a_{12345} with probability 1.

The tree is now complete. It is shown in Figure 2.1a "lying on its side" with its root on the right and its five leaves on the left. To assign the codewords, we arbitrarily assign a bit of 1 to the top edge, and a bit of 0 to the bottom edge, of every pair of edges. This results in the codewords 0, 10, 111, 1101, and 1100. The assignments of bits to the edges is arbitrary.

The average size of this code is $0.4 \times 1 + 0.2 \times 2 + 0.2 \times 3 + 0.1 \times 4 + 0.1 \times 4 = 2.2$ bits/symbol, but even more importantly, the Huffman code is not unique. Some of the steps above were chosen arbitrarily, because there were more than two symbols with smallest probabilities. Figure 2.1b shows how the same five symbols can be combined differently to obtain a different Huffman code (11, 01, 00, 101, and 100). The average size of this code is $0.4 \times 2 + 0.2 \times 2 + 0.2 \times 2 + 0.1 \times 3 + 0.1 \times 3 = 2.2$ bits/symbol, the same as the previous code.

⋄ **Exercise 2.1:** Given the eight symbols A, B, C, D, E, F, G, and H with probabilities 1/30, 1/30, 1/30, 2/30, 3/30, 5/30, 5/30, and 12/30, draw three different Huffman trees with heights 5 and 6 for these symbols and compute the average code size for each tree.

⋄ **Exercise 2.2:** Figure Ans.1d shows another Huffman tree, with height 4, for the eight symbols introduced in Exercise 2.1. Explain why this tree is wrong.

It turns out that the arbitrary decisions made in constructing the Huffman tree affect the individual codes but not the average size of the code. Still, we have to answer the obvious question, which of the different Huffman codes for a given set of symbols is best? The answer, while not obvious, is simple: The best code is the one with the

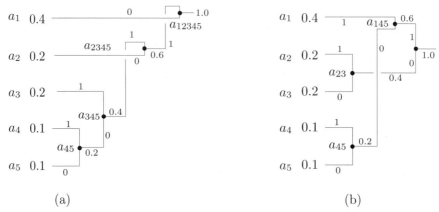

$$(a) \qquad\qquad\qquad\qquad (b)$$

Figure 2.1: Huffman Codes.

smallest variance. The variance of a code measures how much the sizes of the individual codewords deviate from the average size. The variance of the code of Figure 2.1a is

$$0.4(1 - 2.2)^2 + 0.2(2 - 2.2)^2 + 0.2(3 - 2.2)^2 + 0.1(4 - 2.2)^2 + 0.1(4 - 2.2)^2 = 1.36,$$

while the variance of code 2.1b is

$$0.4(2 - 2.2)^2 + 0.2(2 - 2.2)^2 + 0.2(2 - 2.2)^2 + 0.1(3 - 2.2)^2 + 0.1(3 - 2.2)^2 = 0.16.$$

Code 2.1b is therefore preferable (see below). A careful look at the two trees shows how to select the one we want. In the tree of Figure 2.1a, symbol a_{45} is combined with a_3, whereas in the tree of 2.1b a_{45} is combined with a_1. The rule is: When there are more than two smallest-probability nodes, select the ones that are lowest and highest in the tree and combine them. This will combine symbols of low probability with symbols of high probability, thereby reducing the total variance of the code.

If the encoder simply writes the compressed data on a file, the variance of the code makes no difference. A small-variance Huffman code is preferable only in cases where the encoder transmits the compressed data, as it is being generated, over a network. In such a case, a code with large variance causes the encoder to generate bits at a rate that varies all the time. Since the bits have to be transmitted at a constant rate, the encoder has to use a buffer. Bits of the compressed data are entered into the buffer as they are being generated and are moved out of it at a constant rate, to be transmitted. It is easy to see intuitively that a Huffman code with zero variance will enter bits into the buffer at a constant rate, so only a short buffer will be needed. The larger the code variance, the more variable is the rate at which bits enter the buffer, requiring the encoder to use a larger buffer.

The following claim is sometimes found in the literature:

It can be shown that the size of the Huffman code of a symbol a_i with probability P_i is always less than or equal to $\lceil -\log_2 P_i \rceil$.

Even though it is correct in many cases, this claim is not true in general. It seems to be a wrong corollary drawn by some authors from the Kraft–McMillan inequality, Equation (1.4). The author is indebted to Guy Blelloch for pointing this out and also for the example of Table 2.2.

P_i	Code	$-\log_2 P_i$	$\lceil -\log_2 P_i \rceil$
.01	000	6.644	7
*.30	001	1.737	2
.34	01	1.556	2
.35	1	1.515	2

Table 2.2: A Huffman Code Example.

⋄ **Exercise 2.3:** Find an example where the size of the Huffman code of a symbol a_i is greater than $\lceil -\log_2 P_i \rceil$.

⋄ **Exercise 2.4:** It seems that the size of a code must also depend on the number n of symbols (the size of the alphabet). A small alphabet requires just a few codes, so they can all be short; a large alphabet requires many codes, so some must be long. This being so, how can we say that the size of the code of a_i depends just on the probability P_i?

Figure 2.3 shows a Huffman code for the 26 letters.

As a self-exercise, the reader may calculate the average size, entropy, and variance of this code.

⋄ **Exercise 2.5:** Discuss the Huffman codes for equal probabilities.

Exercise 2.5 shows that symbols with equal probabilities don't compress under the Huffman method. This is understandable, since strings of such symbols normally make random text, and random text does not compress. There may be special cases where strings of symbols with equal probabilities are not random and can be compressed. A good example is the string $a_1a_1\ldots a_1a_2a_2\ldots a_2a_3a_3\ldots$ in which each symbol appears in a long run. This string can be compressed with RLE but not with Huffman codes.

Notice that the Huffman method cannot be applied to a two-symbol alphabet. In such an alphabet, one symbol can be assigned the code 0 and the other code 1. The Huffman method cannot assign to any symbol a code shorter than one bit, so it cannot improve on this simple code. If the original data (the source) consists of individual bits, such as in the case of a bi-level (monochromatic) image, it is possible to combine several bits (perhaps four or eight) into a new symbol and pretend that the alphabet consists of these (16 or 256) symbols. The problem with this approach is that the original binary data may have certain statistical correlations between the bits, and some of these correlations would be lost when the bits are combined into symbols. When a typical bi-level image (a painting or a diagram) is digitized by scan lines, a pixel is more likely to be followed by an identical pixel than by the opposite one. We therefore have a file that can start with either a 0 or a 1 (each has 0.5 probability of being the first bit). A zero is more likely to be followed by another 0 and a 1 by another 1. Figure 2.4 is a finite-state machine illustrating this situation. If these bits are combined into, say, groups of eight,

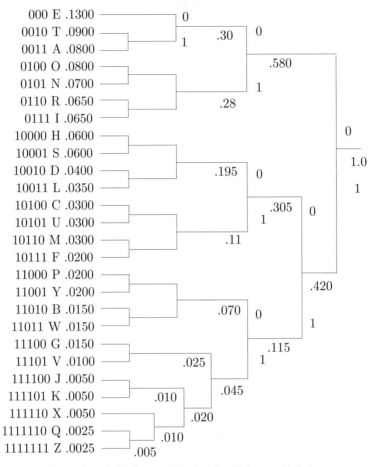

Figure 2.3: A Huffman Code for the 26-Letter Alphabet.

the bits inside a group will still be correlated, but the groups themselves will not be correlated by the original pixel probabilities. If the input data contains, e.g., the two adjacent groups 00011100 and 00001110, they will be encoded independently, ignoring the correlation between the last 0 of the first group and the first 0 of the next group. Selecting larger groups improves this situation but increases the number of groups, which implies more storage for the code table and longer time to calculate the table.

◇ **Exercise 2.6:** How does the number of groups increase when the group size increases from s bits to $s + n$ bits?

A more complex approach to image compression by Huffman coding is to create several complete sets of Huffman codes. If the group size is, e.g., eight bits, then several sets of 256 codes are generated. When a symbol S is to be encoded, one of the sets is selected, and S is encoded using its code in that set. The choice of set depends on the symbol preceding S.

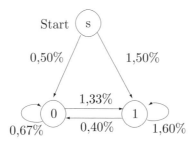

Figure 2.4: A Finite-State Machine.

⋄ **Exercise 2.7:** Imagine an image with 8-bit pixels where half the pixels have values 127 and the other half have values 128. Analyze the performance of RLE on the individual bitplanes of such an image, and compare it with what can be achieved with Huffman coding.

Which two integers come next in the infinite sequence 38, 24, 62, 12, 74, ...?

2.2 Huffman Decoding

Before starting the compression of a data file, the compressor (encoder) has to determine the codes. It does that based on the probabilities (or frequencies of occurrence) of the symbols. The probabilities or frequencies have to be written, as side information, on the output, so that any Huffman decompressor (decoder) will be able to decompress the data. This is easy, because the frequencies are integers and the probabilities can be written as scaled integers. It normally adds just a few hundred bytes to the output. It is also possible to write the variable-length codes themselves on the output, but this may be awkward, because the codes have different sizes. It is also possible to write the Huffman tree on the output, but this may require more space than just the frequencies.

In any case, the decoder must know what is at the start of the compressed file, read it, and construct the Huffman tree for the alphabet. Only then can it read and decode the rest of its input. The algorithm for decoding is simple. Start at the root and read the first bit off the input (the compressed file). If it is zero, follow the bottom edge of the tree; if it is one, follow the top edge. Read the next bit and move another edge toward the leaves of the tree. When the decoder arrives at a leaf, it finds there the original, uncompressed symbol (normally its ASCII code), and that code is emitted by the decoder. The process starts again at the root with the next bit.

This process is illustrated for the five-symbol alphabet of Figure 2.5. The four-symbol input string $a_4a_2a_5a_1$ is encoded into 1001100111. The decoder starts at the root, reads the first bit 1, and goes up. The second bit 0 sends it down, as does the third bit. This brings the decoder to leaf a_4, which it emits. It again returns to the root, reads 110, moves up, up, and down, to reach leaf a_2, and so on.

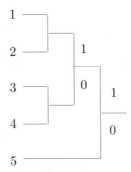

Figure 2.5: Huffman Codes for Equal Probabilities.

2.2.1 Fast Huffman Decoding

Decoding a Huffman-compressed file by sliding down the code tree for each symbol is conceptually simple, but slow. The compressed file has to be read bit by bit and the decoder has to advance a node in the code tree for each bit. The method of this section, originally conceived by [Choueka et al. 85] but later reinvented by others, uses preset partial-decoding tables. These tables depend on the particular Huffman code used, but not on the data to be decoded. The compressed file is read in chunks of k bits each (where k is normally 8 or 16 but can have other values) and the current chunk is used as a pointer to a table. The table entry that is selected in this way can decode several symbols and it also points the decoder to the table to be used for the next chunk.

As an example, consider the Huffman code of Figure 2.1a, where the five codewords are 0, 10, 111, 1101, and 1100. The string of symbols $a_1 a_1 a_2 a_4 a_3 a_1 a_5 \ldots$ is compressed by this code to the string $0|0|10|1101|111|0|1100 \ldots$. We select $k = 3$ and read this string in 3-bit chunks $001|011|011|110|110|0 \ldots$. Examining the first chunk, it is easy to see that it should be decoded into $a_1 a_1$ followed by the single bit 1 which is the prefix of another codeword. The first chunk is $001 = 1_{10}$, so we set entry 1 of the first table (table 0) to the pair $(a_1 a_1, 1)$. When chunk 001 is used as a pointer to table 0, it points to entry 1, which immediately provides the decoder with the two decoded symbols $a_1 a_1$ and also directs it to use table 1 for the next chunk. Table 1 is used when a partially-decoded chunk ends with the single-bit prefix 1. The next chunk is $011 = 3_{10}$, so entry 3 of table 1 corresponds to the encoded bits $1|011$. Again, it is easy to see that these should be decoded to a_2 and there is the prefix 11 left over. Thus, entry 3 of table 1 should be $(a_2, 2)$. It provides the decoder with the single symbol a_2 and also directs it to use table 2 next (the table that corresponds to prefix 11). The next chunk is again $011 = 3_{10}$, so entry 3 of table 2 corresponds to the encoded bits $11|011$. It is again obvious that these should be decoded to a_4 with a prefix of 1 left over. This process continues until the end of the encoded input. Figure 2.6 is the simple decoding algorithm in pseudocode.

Table 2.7 lists the four tables required to decode this code. It is easy to see that they correspond to the prefixes Λ (null), 1, 11, and 110. A quick glance at Figure 2.1a shows that these correspond to the root and the four interior nodes of the Huffman code tree. Thus, each partial-decoding table corresponds to one of the four prefixes of this code. The number m of partial-decoding tables therefore equals the number of interior nodes (plus the root) which is one less than the number N of symbols of the alphabet.

```
i←0; output←null;
repeat
    j←input next chunk;
    (s,i)←Table_i[j];
    append s to output;
until end-of-input
```

Figure 2.6: Fast Huffman Decoding.

$T_0 = \Lambda$			$T_1 = 1$			$T_2 = 11$			$T_3 = 110$		
000	$a_1a_1a_1$	0	1|000	$a_2a_1a_1$	0	11|000	a_5a_1	0	110|000	$a_5a_1a_1$	0
001	a_1a_1	1	1|001	a_2a_1	1	11|001	a_5	1	110|001	a_5a_1	1
010	a_1a_2	0	1|010	a_2a_2	0	11|010	a_4a_1	0	110|010	a_5a_2	0
011	a_1	2	1|011	a_2	2	11|011	a_4	1	110|011	a_5	2
100	a_2a_1	0	1|100	a_5	0	11|100	$a_3a_1a_1$	0	110|100	$a_4a_1a_1$	0
101	a_2	1	1|101	a_4	0	11|101	a_3a_1	1	110|101	a_4a_1	1
110	–	3	1|110	a_3a_1	0	11|110	a_3a_2	0	110|110	a_4a_2	0
111	a_3	0	1|111	a_3	1	11|111	a_3	2	110|111	a_4	2

Table 2.7: Partial-Decoding Tables for a Huffman Code.

Notice that some chunks (such as entry 110 of table 0) simply send the decoder to another table and do not provide any decoded symbols. Also, there is a trade-off between chunk size (and thus table size) and decoding speed. Large chunks speed up decoding, but require large tables. A large alphabet (such as the 128 ASCII characters or the 256 8-bit bytes) also requires a large set of tables. The problem with large tables is that the decoder has to set up the tables after it has read the Huffman codes from the compressed stream and before decoding can start, and this process may preempt any gains in decoding speed provided by the tables.

To set up the first table (table 0, which corresponds to the null prefix Λ), the decoder generates the 2^k bit patterns 0 through $2^k - 1$ (the first column of Table 2.7) and employs the decoding method of Section 2.2 to decode each pattern. This yields the second column of Table 2.7. Any remainders left are prefixes and are converted by the decoder to table numbers. They become the third column of the table. If no remainder is left, the third column is set to 0 (use table 0 for the next chunk). Each of the other partial-decoding tables is set in a similar way. Once the decoder decides that table 1 corresponds to prefix p, it generates the 2^k patterns $p|00\ldots0$ through $p|11\ldots1$ that become the first column of that table. It then decodes that column to generate the remaining two columns.

This method was conceived in 1985, when storage costs were considerably higher than today (early 2007). This prompted the developers of the method to find ways to cut down the number of partial-decoding tables, but these techniques are less important today and are not described here.

2.2.2 Average Code Size

Figure 2.8a shows a set of five symbols with their probabilities and a typical Huffman tree. Symbol A appears 55% of the time and is assigned a 1-bit code, so it contributes $0.55 \cdot 1$ bits to the average code size. Symbol E appears only 2% of the time and is assigned a 4-bit Huffman code, so it contributes $0.02 \cdot 4 = 0.08$ bits to the code size. The average code size is therefore easily computed as

$$0.55 \cdot 1 + 0.25 \cdot 2 + 0.15 \cdot 3 + 0.03 \cdot 4 + 0.02 \cdot 4 = 1.7 \text{ bits per symbol.}$$

Surprisingly, the same result is obtained by adding the values of the four internal nodes of the Huffman code tree $0.05 + 0.2 + 0.45 + 1 = 1.7$. This provides a way to calculate the average code size of a set of Huffman codes without any multiplications. Simply add the values of all the internal nodes of the tree. Table 2.9 illustrates why this works.

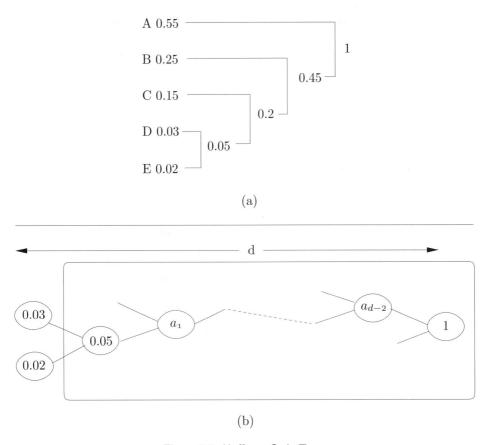

(a)

(b)

Figure 2.8: Huffman Code Trees.

(Internal nodes are shown in italics in this table.) The left column consists of the values of all the internal nodes. The right columns show how each internal node is the sum of

$$
\begin{aligned}
0.05 &= && = 0.02 + 0.03 + \cdots \\
a_1 &= 0.05 &+ \ldots &= 0.02 + 0.03 + \cdots \\
a_2 &= a_1 &+ \ldots &= 0.02 + 0.03 + \cdots \\
&\vdots && = \\
a_{d-2} &= a_{d-3} &+ \ldots &= 0.02 + 0.03 + \cdots \\
1.0 &= a_{d-2} &+ \ldots &= 0.02 + 0.03 + \cdots
\end{aligned}
$$

$$
\begin{aligned}
.05 &= && .02 + .03 \\
.20 &= .05 + .15 &&= .02 + .03 + .15 \\
.45 &= .20 + .25 &&= .02 + .03 + .15 + .25 \\
1.0 &= .45 + .55 &&= .02 + .03 + .15 + .25 + .55
\end{aligned}
$$

Table 2.9: Composition of Nodes.

Table 2.10: Composition of Nodes.

some of the leaf nodes. Summing the values in the left column yields 1.7, and summing the other columns shows that this 1.7 is the sum of the four values 0.02, the four values 0.03, the three values 0.15, the two values 0.25, and the single value 0.55.

This argument can be extended to the general case. It is easy to show that, in a Huffman-like tree (a tree where each node is the sum of its children), the weighted sum of the leaves, where the weights are the distances of the leaves from the root, equals the sum of the internal nodes. (This property has been communicated to the author by J. Motil.)

Figure 2.8b shows such a tree, where we assume that the two leaves 0.02 and 0.03 have d-bit Huffman codes. Inside the tree, these leaves become the children of internal node 0.05, which, in turn, is connected to the root by means of the $d - 2$ internal nodes a_1 through a_{d-2}. Table 2.10 has d rows and shows that the two values 0.02 and 0.03 are included in the various internal nodes exactly d times. Adding the values of all the internal nodes produces a sum that includes the contributions $0.02 \cdot d + 0.03 \cdot d$ from the two leaves. Since these leaves are arbitrary, it is clear that this sum includes similar contributions from all the other leaves, so this sum is the average code size. Since this sum also equals the sum of the left column, which is the sum of the internal nodes, it is clear that the sum of the internal nodes equals the average code size.

Notice that this proof does not assume that the tree is binary. The property illustrated here exists for any tree where a node contains the sum of its children.

2.2.3 Number of Codes

Since the Huffman code is not unique, the natural question is: How many different codes are there? Figure 2.11a shows a Huffman code tree for six symbols, from which we can answer this question in two different ways as follows:

Answer 1. The tree of 2.11a has five interior nodes, and in general, a Huffman code tree for n symbols has $n - 1$ interior nodes. Each interior node has two edges coming out of it, labeled 0 and 1. Swapping the two labels produces a different Huffman code tree, so the total number of different Huffman code trees is 2^{n-1} (in our example, 2^5 or 32). The tree of Figure 2.11b, for example, shows the result of swapping the labels of the two edges of the root. Table 2.12a,b lists the codes generated by the two trees.

Answer 2. The six codes of Table 2.12a can be divided into the four classes $00x$, $10y$, 01, and 11, where x and y are 1-bit each. It is possible to create different Huffman codes by changing the first two bits of each class. Since there are four classes, this is the same as creating all the permutations of four objects, something that can be done in $4! = 24$ ways. In each of the 24 permutations it is also possible to change the values

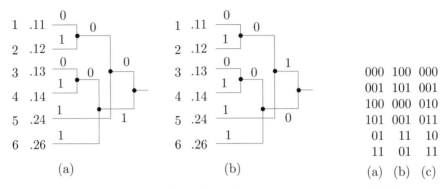

Figure 2.11: Two Huffman Code Trees.   Table 2.12.

of x and y in four different ways (since they are bits) so the total number of different Huffman codes in our six-symbol example is $24 \times 4 = 96$.

The two answers are different because they count different things. Answer 1 counts the number of different Huffman code trees, while answer 2 counts the number of different Huffman codes. It turns out that our example can generate 32 different code trees but only 94 different codes instead of 96. This shows that there are Huffman codes that cannot be generated by the Huffman method! Table 2.12c shows such an example. A look at the trees of Figure 2.11 should convince the reader that the codes of symbols 5 and 6 must start with different bits, but in the code of Table 2.12c they both start with 1. This code is therefore impossible to generate by any relabeling of the nodes of the trees of Figure 2.11.

2.2.4 Ternary Huffman Codes

The Huffman code is not unique. Moreover, it does not have to be binary! The Huffman method can easily be applied to codes based on other number systems. Figure 2.13a shows a Huffman code tree for five symbols with probabilities 0.15, 0.15, 0.2, 0.25, and 0.25. The average code size is

$$2 \times 0.25 + 3 \times 0.15 + 3 \times 0.15 + 2 \times 0.20 + 2 \times 0.25 = 2.3 \, \text{bits/symbol}.$$

Figure 2.13b shows a ternary Huffman code tree for the same five symbols. The tree is constructed by selecting, at each step, three symbols with the smallest probabilities and merging them into one parent symbol, with the combined probability. The average code size of this tree is

$$2 \times 0.15 + 2 \times 0.15 + 2 \times 0.20 + 1 \times 0.25 + 1 \times 0.25 = 1.5 \, \text{trits/symbol}.$$

Notice that the ternary codes use the digits 0, 1, and 2.

⋄ **Exercise 2.8:** Given seven symbols with probabilities 0.02, 0.03, 0.04, 0.04, 0.12, 0.26, and 0.49, construct binary and ternary Huffman code trees for them and calculate the average code size in each case.

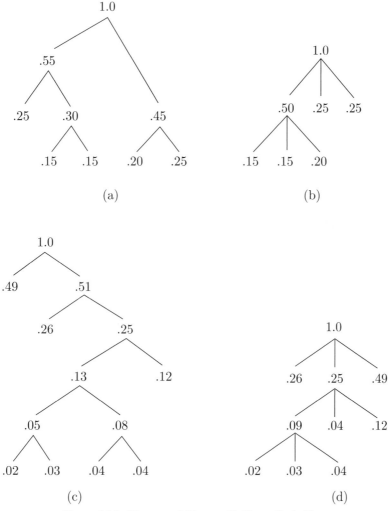

Figure 2.13: Binary and Ternary Huffman Code Trees.

2.2.5 Height of a Huffman Tree

The height of the code tree generated by the Huffman algorithm may sometimes be important because the height is also the length of the longest code in the tree. The Deflate method (Section 3.3), for example, limits the lengths of certain Huffman codes to just three bits.

It is easy to see that the shortest Huffman tree is created when the symbols have equal probabilities. If the symbols are denoted by A, B, C, and so on, then the algorithm combines pairs of symbols, such A and B, C and D, in the lowest level, and the rest of the tree consists of interior nodes as shown in Figure 2.14a. The tree is balanced or close to balanced and its height is $\lceil \log_2 n \rceil$. In the special case where the number of symbols n is a power of 2, the height is exactly $\log_2 n$. In order to generate the tallest tree, we need to assign probabilities to the symbols such that each step in the Huffman method will increase the height of the tree by 1. Recall that each step in the Huffman algorithm combines two symbols. Thus, the tallest tree is obtained when the first step combines two of the n symbols and each subsequent step combines the result of its predecessor with one of the remaining symbols (Figure 2.14b). The height of the complete tree is therefore $n - 1$, and it is referred to as a lopsided or unbalanced tree.

It is easy to see what symbol probabilities result in such a tree. Denote the two smallest probabilities by a and b. They are combined in the first step to form a node whose probability is $a + b$. The second step will combine this node with an original symbol if one of the symbols has probability $a + b$ (or smaller) and all the remaining symbols have greater probabilities. Thus, after the second step, the root of the tree has probability $a + b + (a + b)$ and the third step will combine this root with one of the remaining symbols if its probability is $a + b + (a + b)$ and the probabilities of the remaining $n - 4$ symbols are greater. It does not take much to realize that the symbols have to have probabilities $p_1 = a$, $p_2 = b$, $p_3 = a+b = p_1+p_2$, $p_4 = b+(a+b) = p_2+p_3$, $p_5 = (a + b) + (a + 2b) = p_3 + p_4$, $p_6 = (a + 2b) + (2a + 3b) = p_4 + p_5$, and so on (Figure 2.14c). These probabilities form a Fibonacci sequence whose first two elements are a and b. As an example, we select $a = 5$ and $b = 2$ and generate the 5-number Fibonacci sequence 5, 2, 7, 9, and 16. These five numbers add up to 39, so dividing them by 39 produces the five probabilities 5/39, 2/39, 7/39, 9/39, and 15/39. The Huffman tree generated by them has a maximal height (which is 4).

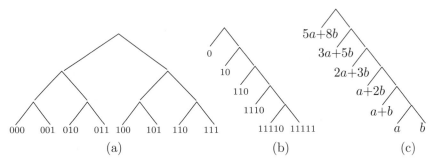

Figure 2.14: Shortest and Tallest Huffman Trees.

In principle, symbols in a set can have any probabilities, but in practice, the probabilities of symbols in an input file are computed by counting the number of occurrences of each symbol. Imagine a text file where only the nine symbols A through I appear. In order for such a file to produce the tallest Huffman tree, where the codes will have lengths from 1 to 8 bits, the frequencies of occurrence of the nine symbols have to form a Fibonacci sequence of probabilities. This happens when the frequencies of the symbols are 1, 1, 2, 3, 5, 8, 13, 21, and 34 (or integer multiples of these). The sum of these frequencies is 88, so our file has to be at least that long in order for a symbol to have 8-bit Huffman codes. Similarly, if we want to limit the sizes of the Huffman codes of a set of n symbols to 16 bits, we need to count frequencies of at least 4,180 symbols. To limit the code sizes to 32 bits, the minimum data size is 9,227,464 symbols.

If a set of symbols happens to have the Fibonacci probabilities and therefore results in a maximal-height Huffman tree with codes that are too long, the tree can be reshaped (and the maximum code length shortened) by slightly modifying the symbol probabilities, so they are not much different from the original, but do not form a Fibonacci sequence.

2.2.6 Canonical Huffman Codes

The code of Table 2.12c has a simple interpretation. It assigns the first four symbols the 3-bit codes 0, 1, 2, and 3, and the last two symbols the 2-bit codes 2 and 3. This is an example of a *canonical Huffman code*. The word "canonical" means that this particular code has been selected from among the several (or even many) possible Huffman codes because its properties make it easy and fast to use.

> Canonical (adjective): Conforming to orthodox or well-established rules or patterns, as of procedure.

Table 2.15 shows a slightly bigger example of a canonical Huffman code. Imagine a set of 16 symbols (whose probabilities are irrelevant and are not shown) such that four symbols are assigned 3-bit codes, five symbols are assigned 5-bit codes, and the remaining seven symbols are assigned 6-bit codes. Table 2.15a shows a set of possible Huffman codes, while Table 2.15b shows a set of canonical Huffman codes. It is easy to see that the seven 6-bit canonical codes are simply the 6-bit integers 0 through 6. The five codes are the 5-bit integers 4 through 8, and the four codes are the 3-bit integers 3 through 6. We first show how these codes are generated and then how they are used.

1:	000	011	9:	10100	01000
2:	001	100	10:	101010	000000
3:	010	101	11:	101011	000001
4:	011	110	12:	101100	000010
5:	10000	00100	13:	101101	000011
6:	10001	00101	14:	101110	000100
7:	10010	00110	15:	101111	000101
8:	10011	00111	16:	110000	000110
	(a)	(b)		(a)	(b)

Table 2.15.

length:	1	2	3	4	5	6
numl:	0	0	4	0	5	7
first:	2	4	3	5	4	0

Table 2.16.

The top row (length) of Table 2.16 lists the possible code lengths, from 1 to 6 bits. The second row (numl) lists the number of codes of each length, and the bottom row (first) lists the first code in each group. This is why the three groups of codes start with values 3, 4, and 0. To obtain the top two rows we need to compute the lengths of all the Huffman codes for the given alphabet (see below). The third row is computed by setting "first[6]:=0;" and iterating

        for l:=5 downto 1 do first[l]:=⌈(first[l+1]+numl[l+1])/2⌉;

This guarantees that all the 3-bit prefixes of codes longer than three bits will be less than first[3] (which is 3), all the 5-bit prefixes of codes longer than five bits will be less than first[5] (which is 4), and so on.

Now for the use of these unusual codes. Canonical Huffman codes are useful in cases where the alphabet is large and where fast decoding is mandatory. Because of the way the codes are constructed, it is easy for the decoder to identify the length of a code by reading and examining input bits one by one. Once the length is known, the symbol can be found in one step. The pseudocode listed here shows the rules for decoding:

```
l:=1; input v;
while v<first[l]
append next input bit to v; l:=l+1;
endwhile
```

As an example, suppose that the next code is 00110. As bits are input and appended to v, it goes through the values 0, 00 = 0, 001 = 1, 0011 = 3, 00110 = 6, while l is incremented from 1 to 5. All steps except the last satisfy v<first[l], so the last step determines the value of l (the code length) as 5. The symbol itself is found by subtracting $v - \texttt{first}[5] = 6 - 4 = 2$, so it is the third symbol (numbering starts at 0) in group $l = 5$ (symbol 7 of the 16 symbols).

The last point to be discussed is the encoder. In order to construct the canonical Huffman code, the encoder needs to know the length of the Huffman code of every symbol. The main problem is the large size of the alphabet, which may make it impractical or even impossible to build the entire Huffman code tree in memory. There is an algorithm—described in [Hirschberg and Lelewer 90], [Sieminski 88], and [Salomon 07]—that solves this problem. It calculates the code sizes for an alphabet of n symbols using just one array of size $2n$.

> Considine's Law. Whenever one word or letter can change the entire meaning of a sentence, the probability of an error being made will be in direct proportion to the embarrassment it will cause.
>
> —Bob Considine

♦One morning I was on my way to the market and met a man with four wives (perfectly legal where we come from). Each wife had four bags, containing four dogs each, and each dog had four puppies. The question is (think carefully) how many were going to the market?

2.3 Adaptive Huffman Coding

The Huffman method assumes that the frequencies of occurrence of all the symbols of the alphabet are known to the compressor. In practice, the frequencies are seldom, if ever, known in advance. One approach to this problem is for the compressor to read the original data twice. The first time, it only counts the frequencies; the second time, it compresses the data. Between the two passes, the compressor constructs the Huffman tree. Such a two-pass method is sometimes called semiadaptive and is normally too slow to be practical. The method that is used in practice is called adaptive (or dynamic) Huffman coding. This method is the basis of the UNIX compact program. The method was originally developed by [Faller 73] and [Gallager 78] with substantial improvements by [Knuth 85].

The main idea is for the compressor and the decompressor to start with an empty Huffman tree and to modify it as symbols are being read and processed (in the case of the compressor, the word "processed" means compressed; in the case of the decompressor, it means decompressed). The compressor and decompressor should modify the tree in the same way, so at any point in the process they should use the same codes, although those codes may change from step to step. We say that the compressor and decompressor are synchronized or that they work in *lockstep* (although they don't necessarily work together; compression and decompression normally take place at different times). The term *mirroring* is perhaps a better choice. The decoder mirrors the operations of the encoder.

Initially, the compressor starts with an empty Huffman tree. No symbols have been assigned codes yet. The first symbol being input is simply written on the output in its uncompressed form. The symbol is then added to the tree and a code assigned to it. The next time this symbol is encountered, its current code is written on the output, and its frequency incremented by 1. Since this modifies the tree, it (the tree) is examined to see whether it is still a Huffman tree (best codes). If not, it is rearranged, an operation that results in modified codes.

The decompressor mirrors the same steps. When it reads the uncompressed form of a symbol, it adds it to the tree and assigns it a code. When it reads a compressed (variable-length) code, it scans the current tree to determine what symbol the code belongs to, and it increments the symbol's frequency and rearranges the tree in the same way as the compressor.

It is immediately clear that the decompressor needs to know whether the item it has just input is an uncompressed symbol (normally, an 8-bit ASCII code, but see Section 2.3.1) or a variable-length code. To remove any ambiguity, each uncompressed symbol is preceded by a special, variable-size *escape code*. When the decompressor reads this code, it knows that the next eight bits are the ASCII code of a symbol that appears in the compressed file for the first time.

> Escape is not his plan. I must face him. Alone.
> —David Prowse as Lord Darth Vader in *Star Wars* (1977)

The trouble is that the escape code should not be any of the variable-length codes used for the symbols. These codes, however, are being modified every time the tree is rearranged, which is why the escape code should also be modified. A natural way to do this is to add an empty leaf to the tree, a leaf with a zero frequency of occurrence, that's always assigned to the 0-branch of the tree. Since the leaf is in the tree, it is assigned a variable-length code. This code is the escape code preceding every uncompressed symbol. As the tree is being rearranged, the position of the empty leaf—and thus its code—change, but this escape code is always used to identify uncompressed symbols in the compressed file. Figure 2.17 shows how the escape code moves and changes as the tree grows.

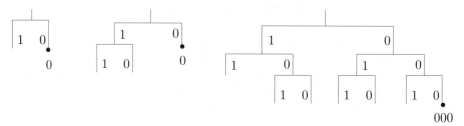

Figure 2.17: The Escape Code.

2.3.1 Uncompressed Codes

If the symbols being compressed are ASCII characters, they may simply be assigned their ASCII codes as uncompressed codes. In the general case where there may be any symbols, uncompressed codes of two different sizes can be assigned by a simple method. Here is an example for the case $n = 24$. The first 16 symbols can be assigned the numbers 0 through 15 as their codes. These numbers require only 4 bits, but we encode them in 5 bits. Symbols 17 through 24 can be assigned the numbers $17 - 16 - 1 = 0$, $18 - 16 - 1 = 1$ through $24 - 16 - 1 = 7$ as 4-bit numbers. We end up with the sixteen 5-bit codes 00000, 00001, ..., 01111, followed by the eight 4-bit codes 0000, 0001, ..., 0111.

In general, we assume an alphabet that consists of the n symbols $a_1, a_2, \ldots, a_n$. We select integers m and r such that $2^m \leq n < 2^{m+1}$ and $r = n - 2^m$. The first 2^m symbols are encoded as the $(m + 1)$-bit numbers 0 through $2^m - 1$. The remaining symbols are encoded as m-bit numbers such that the code of a_k is $k - 2^m - 1$. This code is also called a phased-in binary code (also a minimal binary code).

2.3.2 Modifying the Tree

The chief principle for modifying the tree is to check it each time a symbol is input. If the tree is no longer a Huffman tree, it should be rearranged to become one. A glance at Figure 2.18a shows what it means for a binary tree to be a Huffman tree. The tree in the figure contains five symbols: A, B, C, D, and E. It is shown with the symbols and their frequencies (in parentheses) after 16 symbols have been input and processed. The property that makes it a Huffman tree is that if we scan it level by level, scanning each level from left to right, and going from the bottom (the leaves) to the top (the root), the frequencies will be in sorted, nondescending order. Thus, the bottom-left node (A) has the lowest frequency, and the top-right node (the root) has the highest frequency. This is called the sibling property.

◊ **Exercise 2.9:** Why is this the criterion for a tree to be a Huffman tree?

Here is a summary of the operations needed to update the tree. The loop starts at the current node (the one corresponding to the symbol just input). This node is a leaf that we denote by X, with frequency of occurrence F. Each iteration of the loop involves three steps as follows:

1. Compare X to its successors in the tree (from left to right and bottom to top). If the immediate successor has frequency $F + 1$ or greater, the nodes are still in sorted order and there is no need to change anything. Otherwise, some successors of X have

identical frequencies of F or smaller. In this case, X should be swapped with the last node in this group (except that X should not be swapped with its parent).

2. Increment the frequency of X from F to $F + 1$. Increment the frequencies of all its parents.

3. If X is the root, the loop stops; otherwise, it repeats with the parent of node X.

Figure 2.18b shows the tree after the frequency of node A has been incremented from 1 to 2. It is easy to follow the three rules above to see how incrementing the frequency of A results in incrementing the frequencies of all its parents. No swaps are needed in this simple case because the frequency of A hasn't exceeded the frequency of its immediate successor B. Figure 2.18c shows what happens when A's frequency has been incremented again, from 2 to 3. The three nodes following A, namely, B, C, and D, have frequencies of 2, so A is swapped with the last of them, D. The frequencies of the new parents of A are then incremented, and each is compared with its successor, but no more swaps are needed.

Figure 2.18d shows the tree after the frequency of A has been incremented to 4. Once we decide that A is the current node, its frequency (which is still 3) is compared to that of its successor (4), and the decision is not to swap. A's frequency is incremented, followed by incrementing the frequencies of its parents.

In Figure 2.18e, A is again the current node. Its frequency (4) equals that of its successor, so they should be swapped. This is shown in Figure 2.18f, where A's frequency is 5. The next loop iteration examines the parent of A, with frequency 10. It should be swapped with its successor E (with frequency 9), which leads to the final tree of Figure 2.18g.

2.3.3 Counter Overflow

The frequency counts are accumulated in the Huffman tree in fixed-size fields, and such fields may overflow. A 16-bit unsigned field can accommodate counts of up to $2^{16} - 1 = 65,535$. A simple solution to the counter overflow problem is to watch the count field of the root each time it is incremented, and when it reaches its maximum value, to *rescale* all the frequency counts by dividing them by 2 (integer division). In practice, this is done by dividing the count fields of the leaves, then updating the counts of the interior nodes. Each interior node gets the sum of the counts of its children. The problem is that the counts are integers, and integer division reduces precision. This may change a Huffman tree to one that does not satisfy the sibling property.

A simple example is shown in Figure 2.18h. After the counts of the leaves are halved, the three interior nodes are updated as shown in Figure 2.18i. The latter tree, however, is no longer a Huffman tree, since the counts are no longer in sorted order. The solution is to rebuild the tree each time the counts are rescaled, which does not happen very often. A Huffman data compression program intended for general use should therefore have large count fields that would not overflow very often. A 4-byte count field overflows at $2^{32} - 1 \approx 4.3 \times 10^9$.

It should be noted that after rescaling the counts, the new symbols being read and compressed have more effect on the counts than the old symbols (those counted before the rescaling). This turns out to be fortuitous since it is known from experience that the probability of appearance of a symbol depends more on the symbols immediately preceding it than on symbols that appeared in the distant past.

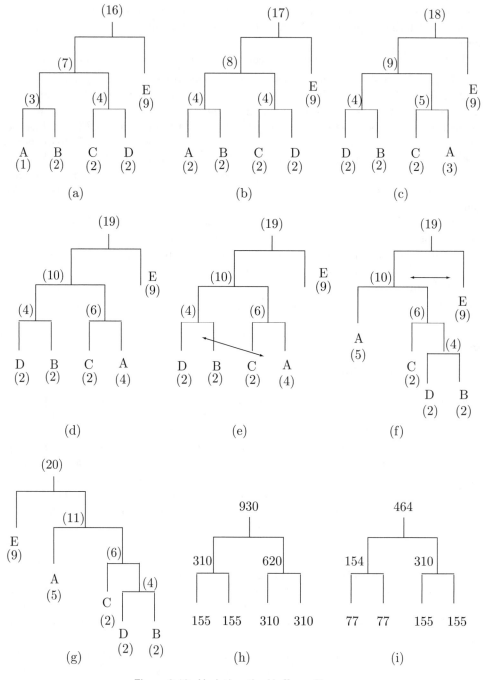

Figure 2.18: Updating the Huffman Tree.

2.3.4 Code Overflow

An even more serious problem is code overflow. This may happen when many symbols are added to the tree, and it becomes tall. The codes themselves are not stored in the tree, since they change all the time, and the compressor has to figure out the code of a symbol X each time X is input. Here are the details of this process:

1. The encoder has to locate symbol X in the tree. The tree has to be implemented as an array of structures, each a node, and the array is searched linearly.

2. If X is not found, the escape code is emitted, followed by the uncompressed code of X. X is then added to the tree.

3. If X is found, the compressor moves from node X back to the root, building the code bit by bit as it goes along. Each time it goes from a left child to a parent, a "1" is appended to the code. Going from a right child to a parent appends a "0" bit to the code (or vice versa, but this should be consistent because it is mirrored by the decoder). Those bits have to be accumulated someplace, since they have to be emitted in the *reverse order* in which they are created. When the tree gets taller, the codes get longer. If they are accumulated in a 16-bit integer, then codes longer than 16 bits would cause a malfunction.

One solution to the code overflow problem is to accumulate the bits of a code in a linked list, where new nodes can be created, limited in number only by the amount of available memory. This is general but slow. Another solution is to accumulate the codes in a large integer variable (perhaps 50 bits wide) and document a maximum code size of 50 bits as one of the limitations of the program.

Fortunately, this problem does not affect the decoding process. The decoder reads the compressed code bit by bit and uses each bit to move one step left or right down the tree until it reaches a leaf node. If the leaf is the escape code, the decoder reads the uncompressed code of the symbol off the compressed data (and adds the symbol to the tree). Otherwise, the uncompressed code is found in the leaf node.

◇ **Exercise 2.10:** Given the 11-symbol string sir␣sid␣is, apply the adaptive Huffman method to it. For each symbol input, show the output, the tree after the symbol has been added to it, the tree after being rearranged (if necessary), and the list of nodes traversed left to right and bottom up.

2.3.5 A Variant

This variant of the adaptive Huffman method is simpler but less efficient. The idea is to calculate a set of n variable-length codes based on equal probabilities, to assign those codes to the n symbols at random, and to change the assignments "on the fly," as symbols are being read and compressed. The method is inefficient because the codes are not based on the actual probabilities of the symbols in the input. However, it is simpler to implement and also faster than the adaptive method described earlier, because it has to swap rows in a table, rather than update a tree, when updating the frequencies of the symbols.

The main data structure is an $n \times 3$ table where the three columns store the names of the n symbols, their frequencies of occurrence so far, and their codes. The table is always kept sorted by the second column. When the frequency counts in the second

Name	Count	Code	Name	Count	Code	Name	Count	Code	Name	Count	Code
a_1	0	0	a_2	1	0	a_2	1	0	a_4	2	0
a_2	0	10	a_1	0	10	a_4	1	10	a_2	1	10
a_3	0	110	a_3	0	110	a_3	0	110	a_3	0	110
a_4	0	111	a_4	0	111	a_1	0	111	a_1	0	111
(a)			(b)			(c)			(d)		

Table 2.19: Four Steps in a Huffman Variant.

column change, rows are swapped, but only columns 1 and 2 are moved. The codes in column 3 never change. Table 2.19 shows an example of four symbols and the behavior of the method when the string a_2, a_4, a_4 is compressed.

Table 2.19a shows the initial state. After the first symbol a_2 is read, its count is incremented, and since it is now the largest count, rows 1 and 2 are swapped (Table 2.19b). After the second symbol a_4 is read, its count is incremented and rows 2 and 4 are swapped (Table 2.19c). Finally, after reading the last symbol a_4, its count is the largest, so rows 1 and 2 are swapped (Table 2.19d).

The only point that can cause a problem with this method is overflow of the count fields. If such a field is k bits wide, its maximum value is $2^k - 1$, so it will overflow when incremented for the 2^kth time. This may happen if the size of the input file is not known in advance, which is very common. Fortunately, we do not really need to know the counts, we just need them in sorted order, which makes it easy to solve this problem.

One solution is to count the input symbols and, after $2^k - 1$ symbols are input and compressed, to (integer) divide all the count fields by 2 (or shift them one position to the right, if this is easier).

Another, similar, solution is to check each count field every time it is incremented, and if it has reached its maximum value (if it consists of all ones), to integer divide all the count fields by 2, as mentioned earlier. This approach requires fewer divisions but more complex tests.

Naturally, whatever solution is adopted should be used by both the compressor and decompressor.

2.3.6 Vitter's Method

An improvement of the original algorithm, due to [Vitter 87], which also includes extensive analysis is based on the following key ideas:

1. A different scheme should be used to number the nodes in the dynamic Huffman tree. It is called *implicit numbering*, and it numbers the nodes from the bottom up and in each level from left to right.

2. The Huffman tree should be updated in such a way that the following will always be satisfied. For each weight w, all leaves of weight w precede (in the sense of implicit numbering) all the internal nodes of the same weight. This is an *invariant*.

These ideas result in the following benefits:

1. In the original algorithm, it is possible that a rearrangement of the tree would move a node down one level. In the improved version, this does not happen.

2. Each time the Huffman tree is updated in the original algorithm, some nodes may be moved up. In the improved version, at most one node has to be moved up.

3. The Huffman tree in the improved version minimizes the sum of distances from the root to the leaves and also has the minimum height.

A special data structure, called a floating tree, is proposed to make it easy to maintain the required invariant. It can be shown that this version performs much better than the original algorithm. Specifically, if a two-pass Huffman method compresses an input file of n symbols to S bits, then the original adaptive Huffman algorithm can compress it to at most $2S + n$ bits, whereas the improved version can compress it down to $S + n$ bits—a significant difference! Notice that these results do not depend on the size of the alphabet, only on the size n of the data being compressed and on its nature (which determines S).

> "I think you're begging the question," said Haydock, "and I can see looming ahead one of those terrible exercises in probability where six men have white hats and six men have black hats and you have to work it out by mathematics how likely it is that the hats will get mixed up and in what proportion. If you start thinking about things like that, you would go round the bend. Let me assure you of that!"
>
> —Agatha Christie, *The Mirror Crack'd*

 **Intermezzo**

History of Fax. Fax machines have been popular since the mid-1980s, so it is natural to assume that this is new technology. In fact, the first fax machine was invented in 1843, by Alexander Bain, a Scottish clock and instrument maker and all-round inventor. Among his many other achievements, Bain also invented the first electrical clock (powered by an electromagnet propelling a pendulum), developed chemical telegraph receivers and punch-tapes for fast telegraph transmissions, and installed the first telegraph line between Edinburgh and Glasgow.

The patent for the fax machine (grandly titled "improvements in producing and regulating electric currents and improvements in timepieces and in electric printing and signal telegraphs") was granted to Bain on May 27, 1843, 33 years before a similar patent (for the telephone) was given to Alexander Graham Bell.

Bain's fax machine transmitter scanned a flat, electrically conductive metal surface with a stylus mounted on a pendulum that was powered by an electromagnet. The stylus picked up writing from the surface and sent it through a wire to the stylus of the receiver, where the image was reproduced on a similar electrically conductive metal surface. Reference [hffax 07] has a figure of this apparatus.

Unfortunately, Bain's invention was not very practical and did not catch on, which is easily proved by the well-known fact that Queen Victoria never actually said "I'll drop you a fax."

In 1850, Frederick Bakewell, a London inventor, made several improvements on Bain's design. He built a device that he called a copying telegraph, and received a patent on it. Bakewell demonstrated his machine at the 1851 Great Exhibition in London.

In 1862, Italian physicist Giovanni Caselli built a fax machine (the pantelegraph), that was based on Bain's invention and also included a synchronizing apparatus. It was more successful than Bain's device and was used by the French Post and Telegraph agency between Paris and Lyon from 1856 to 1870. Even the Emperor of China heard about the pantelegraph and sent officials to Paris to study the device. The Chinese immediately recognized the advantages of facsimile for Chinese text, which was impossible to handle by telegraph because of its thousands of ideograms. Unfortunately, the negotiations between Peking and Caselli failed.

Elisha Gray, arguably the best example of the quintessential loser, invented the telephone, but is virtually unknown today because he was beaten by Alexander Graham Bell, who arrived at the patent office a few hours before Gray on the fateful day of March 7, 1876. Born in Barnesville, Ohio, Gray invented and patented many electrical devices, including a facsimile apparatus. He also founded what later became the Western Electric Company.

Ernest A. Hummel, a watchmaker from St. Paul, Minnesota, invented, in 1895 a device he dubbed a copying telegraph, or telediagraph. This machine was based on synchronized rotating drums, with a platinum stylus as an electrode in the transmitter. It was used by the New York Herald to send pictures via telegraph lines. An improved version (in 1899) was sold to several newspapers (the Chicago Times Herald, the St. Louis Republic, the Boston Herald, and the Philadelphia Inquirer) and it, as well as other, very similar machines, were in use to transmit newsworthy images until the 1970s.

A practical fax machine (perhaps the first practical one) was invented in 1902 by Arthur Korn in Germany. This was a photoelectric device and it was used to transmit photographs in Germany from 1907.

In 1924, Richard H. Ranger, a designer for the Radio Corporation of America (RCA), invented the wireless photoradiogram, or transoceanic radio facsimile. This machine can be considered the true forerunner of today's fax machines. On November 29, 1924, a photograph of the American President Calvin Coolidge that was sent from New York to London became the first image reproduced by transoceanic wireless facsimile.

The next step was the belinograph, invented in 1925 by the French engineer Edouard Belin. An image was placed on a drum and scanned with a powerful beam of light. The reflection was converted to an analog voltage by a photoelectric cell. The voltage was sent to a receiver, where it was converted into mechanical movement of a pen to reproduce the image on a blank sheet of paper on an identical drum rotating at the same speed. The fax machines we all use are still based on the principle of scanning a document with light, but they are controlled by a microprocessor and have a small number of moving parts.

In 1924, the American Telephone & Telegraph Company (AT&T) decided to improve telephone fax technology. The result of this effort was a telephotography machine that was used to send newsworthy photographs long distance for quick newspaper publication.

By 1926, RCA invented the Radiophoto, a fax machine based on radio transmissions.

The Hellschreiber was invented in 1929 by Rudolf Hell, a pioneer in mechanical image scanning and transmission. During WW2, it was sometimes used by the German military in conjunction with the Enigma encryption machine.

In 1947, Alexander Muirhead invented a very successful fax machine.

On March 4, 1955, the first radio fax transmission was sent across the continent.

Fax machines based on optical scanning of a document were developed over the years, but the spark that ignited the fax revolution was the development, in 1983, of the Group 3 CCITT standard for sending faxes at rates of 9,600 bps.

More history and pictures of many early fax and telegraph machines can be found at [hffax 07] and [technikum29 07].

2.4 Facsimile Compression

Data compression is especially important when images are transmitted over a communications line because a person is often waiting at the receiving end, eager to see something quickly. Documents transferred between fax machines are sent as bitmaps, so a standard compression algorithm was needed when those machines became popular. Several methods were developed and proposed by the ITU-T.

The ITU-T is one of four permanent parts of the International Telecommunications Union (ITU), based in Geneva, Switzerland (`http://www.itu.ch/`). It issues recommendations for standards applying to modems, packet switched interfaces, V.24 connectors, and similar devices. Although it has no power of enforcement, the standards it recommends are generally accepted and adopted by industry. Until March 1993, the ITU-T was known as the Consultative Committee for International Telephone and Telegraph (Comité Consultatif International Télégraphique et Téléphonique, or CCITT).

> CCITT: Can't Conceive Intelligent Thoughts Today

The first data compression standards developed by the ITU-T were T2 (also known as Group 1) and T3 (Group 2). These are now obsolete and have been replaced by T4 (Group 3) and T6 (Group 4). Group 3 is currently used by all fax machines designed to operate with the Public Switched Telephone Network (PSTN). These are the machines we have at home, and at the time of writing, they operate at maximum speeds of 9,600 baud. Group 4 is used by fax machines designed to operate on a digital network, such as ISDN. They have typical speeds of 64K bits/sec (baud). Both methods can produce compression factors of 10 or better, reducing the transmission time of a typical page to about a minute with the former, and a few seconds with the latter.

One-dimensional coding. A fax machine scans a document line by line, converting each scan line to many small black and white dots called *pels* (from Picture ELement). The horizontal resolution is always 8.05 pels per millimeter (about 205 pels per inch). An 8.5-inch-wide scan line is therefore converted to 1728 pels. The T4 standard, though, recommends to scan only about 8.2 inches, thereby producing 1664 pels per scan line (these numbers, as well as those in the next paragraph, are all to within $\pm 1\%$ accuracy).

> The word facsimile comes from the Latin *facere* (make) and *similis* (like).

The vertical resolution is either 3.85 scan lines per millimeter (standard mode) or 7.7 lines/mm (fine mode). Many fax machines have also a very-fine mode, where they scan 15.4 lines/mm. Table 2.20 assumes a 10-inch-high page (254 mm), and shows the total number of pels per page, and typical transmission times for the three modes without compression. The times are long, illustrating the importance of compression in fax transmissions.

Scan lines	Pels per line	Pels per page	Time (sec.)	Time (min.)
978	1664	1.670M	170	2.82
1956	1664	3.255M	339	5.65
3912	1664	6.510M	678	11.3

Ten inches equal 254 mm. The number of pels is in the millions, and the transmission times, at 9600 baud without compression, are between 3 and 11 minutes, depending on the mode. However, if the page is shorter than 10 inches, or if most of it is white, the compression factor can be 10 or better, resulting in transmission times of between 17 and 68 seconds.

Table 2.20: Fax Transmission Times.

To derive the Group 3 code, the committee appointed by the ITU-T counted all the run lengths of white and black pels in a set of eight "training" documents that they felt represent typical text and images sent by fax, and then applied the Huffman algorithm to construct a variable-length code and assign codewords to all the run length. (The eight documents are described in Table 2.21 and can be found at [funet 07].) The most common run lengths were found to be 2, 3, and 4 black pixels, so they were assigned the shortest codes (Table 2.22). Next come run lengths of 2–7 white pixels, which were assigned slightly longer codes. Most run lengths were rare and were assigned long, 12-bit codes. Thus, Group 3 uses a combination of RLE and Huffman coding.

Image	Description
1	Typed business letter (English)
2	Circuit diagram (hand drawn)
3	Printed and typed invoice (French)
4	Densely typed report (French)
5	Printed technical article including figures and equations (French)
6	Graph with printed captions (French)
7	Dense document (Kanji)
8	Handwritten memo with very large white-on-black letters (English)

Table 2.21: The Eight CCITT Training Documents.

⋄ **Exercise 2.11:** A run length of 1,664 white pels was assigned the short code 011000. Why is this length so common?

Since run lengths can be long, the Huffman algorithm was modified. Codes were assigned to run lengths of 1 to 63 pels (they are the termination codes in Table 2.22a) and to run lengths that are multiples of 64 pels (the make-up codes in Table 2.22b). Group 3 is therefore a *modified Huffman code* (also called MH). The code of a run length is either a single termination code (if the run length is short) or one or more make-up codes, followed by one termination code (if it is long). Here are some examples:

1. A run length of 12 white pels is coded as 001000.
2. A run length of 76 white pels (= 64 + 12) is coded as 11011|001000.
3. A run length of 140 white pels (= 128 + 12) is coded as 10010|001000.
4. A run length of 64 black pels (= 64 + 0) is coded as 0000001111|0000110111.
5. A run length of 2,561 black pels (2560 + 1) is coded as 000000011111|010.

⋄ **Exercise 2.12:** There are no runs of length zero. Why then were codes assigned to runs of zero black and zero white pels?

⋄ **Exercise 2.13:** An 8.5-inch-wide scan line results in 1,728 pels, so how can there be a run of 2,561 consecutive pels?

Each scan line is coded separately, and its code is terminated by the special 12-bit EOL code 000000000001. Each line also gets one white pel appended to it on the left when it is scanned. This is done to remove any ambiguity when the line is decoded on the receiving end. After reading the EOL for the previous line, the receiver assumes that the new line starts with a run of white pels, and it ignores the first of them. Examples:
1. The 14-pel line ▪▪▪ □ ▪▪ □□□□□□□ is coded as the run lengths 1w 3b 2w 2b 7w EOL, which become 000111|10|0111|11|1111|000000000001. The decoder ignores the single white pel at the start.
2. The line □□ ▪▪▪▪▪ □□□□ ▪▪ is coded as the run lengths 3w 5b 5w 2b EOL, which becomes the binary string 1000|0011|1100|11|000000000001.

⋄ **Exercise 2.14:** The Group 3 code for a run length of five black pels (0011) is also the prefix of the codes for run lengths of 61, 62, and 63 white pels. Explain this.

In computing, a newline (also known as a line break or end-of-line / EOL character) is a special character or sequence of characters signifying the end of a line of text. The name comes from the fact that the next character after the newline will appear on a new line—that is, on the next line below the text immediately preceding the newline. The actual codes representing a newline vary across hardware platforms and operating systems, which can be a problem when exchanging data between systems with different representations.

—From http://en.wikipedia.org/wiki/End-of-line

The Group 3 code has no error correction, but many errors can be detected. Because of the nature of the Huffman code, even one bad bit in the transmission can cause the receiver to get out of synchronization, and to produce a string of wrong pels. This is why each scan line is encoded separately. If the receiver detects an error, it skips

(a)

Run length	White code-word	Black code-word	Run length	White code-word	Black code-word
0	00110101	0000110111	32	00011011	000001101010
1	000111	010	33	00010010	000001101011
2	0111	11	34	00010011	000011010010
3	1000	10	35	00010100	000011010011
4	1011	011	36	00010101	000011010100
5	1100	0011	37	00010110	000011010101
6	1110	0010	38	00010111	000011010110
7	1111	00011	39	00101000	000011010111
8	10011	000101	40	00101001	000001101100
9	10100	000100	41	00101010	000001101101
10	00111	0000100	42	00101011	000011011010
11	01000	0000101	43	00101100	000011011011
12	001000	0000111	44	00101101	000001010100
13	000011	00000100	45	00000100	000001010101
14	110100	00000111	46	00000101	000001010110
15	110101	000011000	47	00001010	000001010111
16	101010	0000010111	48	00001011	000001100100
17	101011	0000011000	49	01010010	000001100101
18	0100111	0000001000	50	01010011	000001010010
19	0001100	00001100111	51	01010100	000001010011
20	0001000	00001101000	52	01010101	000000100100
21	0010111	00001101100	53	00100100	000000110111
22	0000011	00000110111	54	00100101	000000111000
23	0000100	00000101000	55	01011000	000000100111
24	0101000	00000010111	56	01011001	000000101000
25	0101011	00000011000	57	01011010	000001011000
26	0010011	000011001010	58	01011011	000001011001
27	0100100	000011001011	59	01001010	000000101011
28	0011000	000011001100	60	01001011	000000101100
29	00000010	000011001101	61	00110010	000001011010
30	00000011	000001101000	62	00110011	000001100110
31	00011010	000001101001	63	00110100	000001100111

(b)

Run length	White code-word	Black code-word	Run length	White code-word	Black code-word
64	11011	0000001111	1344	011011010	0000001010011
128	10010	000011001000	1408	011011011	0000001010100
192	010111	000011001001	1472	010011000	0000001010101
256	0110111	000001011011	1536	010011001	0000001011010
320	00110110	000000110011	1600	010011010	0000001011011
384	00110111	000000110100	1664	011000	0000001100100
448	01100100	000000110101	1728	010011011	0000001100101
512	01100101	0000001101100	1792	00000001000	same as
576	01101000	0000001101101	1856	00000001100	white
640	01100111	0000001001010	1920	00000001101	from this
704	011001100	0000001001011	1984	000000010010	point
768	011001101	0000001001100	2048	000000010011	
832	011010010	0000001001101	2112	000000010100	
896	011010011	0000001110010	2176	000000010101	
960	011010100	0000001110011	2240	000000010110	
1024	011010101	0000001110100	2304	000000010111	
1088	011010110	0000001110101	2368	000000011100	
1152	011010111	0000001110110	2432	000000011101	
1216	011011000	0000001110111	2496	000000011110	
1280	011011001	0000001010010	2560	000000011111	

Table 2.22: Group 3 and 4 Fax Codes: (a) Termination Codes, (b) Make-Up Codes.

bits, looking for an EOL. This way, one error can cause at most one scan line to be received incorrectly. If the receiver does not see an EOL after a certain number of lines, it assumes a high error rate, and it aborts the process, notifying the transmitter. Since the codes are between two and 12 bits long, the receiver detects an error if it cannot decode a valid code after reading 12 bits.

Each page of the coded document is preceded by one EOL and is followed by six EOL codes. Because each line is coded separately, this method is a *one-dimensional coding* scheme. The compression ratio depends on the image. Images with large contiguous black or white areas (text or black and white images) can be highly compressed. Images with many short runs can sometimes produce negative compression. This is especially true in the case of images with shades of gray (such as scanned photographs). Such shades are produced by halftoning, which covers areas with many alternating black and white pels (runs of length 1).

⋄ **Exercise 2.15:** What is the compression ratio for runs of length one (i.e., strictly alternating pels)?

The T4 standard also allows for fill bits to be inserted between the data bits and the EOL. This is done in cases where a pause is necessary, or where the total number of bits transmitted for a scan line must be a multiple of 8. The fill bits are zeros.

Example: The binary string 000111|10|0111|11|1111|000000000001 becomes 000111|10|0111|11|1111|00|0000000001 after two zeros are added as fill bits, bringing the total length of the string to 32 bits ($= 8 \times 4$). The decoder sees the two zeros of the fill, followed by the 11 zeros of the EOL, followed by the single 1, so it knows that it has encountered a fill followed by an EOL.

Two-dimensional coding. This variant was developed because one-dimensional coding produces poor results for images with gray areas. Two-dimensional coding is optional on fax machines that use Group 3 but is the only method used by machines intended to work in a digital network. When a fax machine using Group 3 supports two-dimensional coding as an option, each EOL is followed by one extra bit, to indicate the compression method used for the next scan line. That bit is 1 if the next line is encoded with one-dimensional coding, and 0 if it is encoded with two-dimensional coding.

The two-dimensional coding method is also called MMR, for *modified modified READ*, where READ stands for *relative element address designate*. The term "modified modified" is used because this is a modification of one-dimensional coding, which itself is a modification of the original Huffman method. The two-dimensional coding method is described in detail in [Salomon 07] and other references, but here are its main principles. The method compares the current scan line (called the *coding line*) to its predecessor (referred to as the *reference line*) and records the differences between them, the assumption being that two consecutive lines in a document will normally differ by just a few pels. The method assumes that there is an all-white line above the page, which is used as the reference line for the first scan line of the page. After coding the first line, it becomes the reference line, and the second scan line is coded. As in one-dimensional coding, each line is assumed to start with a white pel, which is ignored by the receiver.

The two-dimensional coding method is more prone to errors than one-dimensional coding, because any error in decoding a line will cause errors in decoding all its successors and will propagate throughout the entire document. This is why the T.4 (Group 3) standard includes a requirement that after a line is encoded with the one-dimensional method, at most $K - 1$ lines will be encoded with the two-dimensional coding method. For standard resolution $K = 2$, and for fine resolution $K = 4$. The T.6 standard (Group 4) does not have this requirement, and uses two-dimensional coding exclusively.

Chapter Summary

Huffman coding is one of the basic techniques of data compression. It is also fast, conceptually simple, and easy to implement. The Huffman encoding algorithm starts with a set of symbols whose probabilities are known and constructs a code tree. Once the tree is complete, it is used to determine the variable-length, prefix codewords for the individual symbols. Each leaf of the tree corresponds to a data symbol and the prefix code of a symbol S is determined by sliding down the tree from the root to the leaf that corresponds to S. It can be shown that these codewords are the best possible in the sense that they feature the shortest average length. However, the codewords are not unique and there are several (perhaps even many) different sets of codewords that have the same average length. Huffman decoding starts by reading bits from the compressed file and using them to slide down the tree from node to node until a leaf (and thus a data symbol) is reached. Section 2.2.1 describes an interesting method for fast decoding.

The Huffman method requires knowledge of the symbols' probabilities, but in practice, these are not always known in advance. This chapter lists the following methods for handling this problem.

- Use a set of training documents. The implementor of a Huffman codec (compressor/decompressor) selects a set of documents that are judged typical or average. The documents are analyzed once, counting the number of occurrences (and hence also the probability) of each data symbol. Based on these probabilities, the implementor constructs a Huffman code (a set of codewords for all the symbols in the alphabet) and hard-codes this code in both encoder and decoder. Such a code may not conform to the symbols' probabilities of any particular input file that's being compressed, and so does not produce the best compression, but this approach is simple and fast. The compression method used by fax machines (Section 2.4) is based on this approach.

- A two-pass compression job produces the ideal codewords for the input file, but is slow. In this approach, the input file is read twice. In the first pass, the encoder counts symbol occurrences. Between the passes, the encoder uses this information to compute symbol probabilities and constructs a set of Huffman codewords for the particular data being compressed. In the second pass the encoder actually compresses the data by replacing each data symbol with its Huffman codeword.

- An adaptive compression algorithm achieves the best of both worlds, being both effective and fast, but is more difficult to implement. The principle is to start with an empty Huffman code tree and to update the tree as input symbols are read and processed. When a symbol is input, the tree is searched for it. If the symbol is in the tree, its codeword is used; otherwise, it is added to the tree and a new codeword is assigned to it. In either case, the tree is examined and may have to be rearranged to keep it a Huffman code tree. This process has to be designed carefully, to make sure that the decoder can perform it in the same way as the encoder (in lockstep). Such an adaptive algorithm is discussed in Section 2.3.

The Huffman method is simple, fast, and produces excellent results, but is not as effective as arithmetic coding (Chapter 4). The conscientious reader may benefit from the discussion in [Bookstein and Klein 93], where the authors argue in favor of Huffman coding.

Self-Assessment Questions

1. In a programming language of your choice, implement Huffman encoding and test it on the five symbols of Figure 2.1.

2. Complete the decoding example in the second paragraph of Section 2.2.1.

3. The fax compression standard of Section 2.4 is based on eight training documents selected by the CCITT (the predecessor of the ITU-T). Select your own set of eight training documents (black and white images on paper) and scan them at 200 dpi to determine the frequencies of occurrence of all the runs of black and white pels. Sort the runs in ascending order and compare their probabilities to the lengths of the codes of Table 2.22 (your most-common runs should correspond to the shortest codes of this table).

> The novelty of waking up to a fax machine next to your bed going off
> in the middle of the night with an order from Japan wears off.
>
> —Naomi Bradshaw

3
Dictionary Methods

 Prelude

The Huffman algorithm is based on the probabilities of the individual data symbols. These probabilities become a statistical model of the data. As a result, the compression produced by this method depends on how good that model is. Dictionary-based compression methods are different. They do not use a statistical model of the data, nor do they employ variable-length codes. Instead they select strings of symbols from the input and employ a dictionary to encode each string as a *token*. The dictionary holds strings of symbols, and it may be static or dynamic (adaptive). The former is permanent, sometimes allowing the addition of strings but no deletions, whereas the latter holds strings previously found in the input, allowing for additions and deletions of strings as new input is being read.

Given a string of n symbols, a dictionary-based compressor can, in principle, compress it down to nH bits where H is the entropy of the string. Thus, dictionary-based compressors are entropy encoders, but only if the input file is very large. For most files in practical applications, dictionary-based compressors produce results that are good enough to make this type of encoder very popular. Such encoders are also general purpose, performing on images and audio data as well as they perform on text.

The simplest example of a static dictionary is a dictionary of the English language used to compress English text. Imagine a dictionary containing perhaps half a million words (without their definitions). A word (a string of symbols terminated by a space or a punctuation mark) is read from the input and the dictionary is searched. If a match is found, an index to the dictionary is written on the output. Otherwise, the uncompressed word itself is written.

As a result, the output contains indexes and raw words, and it is important to distinguish between them. This can be done by reserving an extra bit in each item written on the output. In principle, a 19-bit index is sufficient to specify an item in a $2^{19} = 524,288$-word dictionary. Thus, when a match is found, we can write a 20-bit token that consists of a flag bit (perhaps a zero) followed by a 19-bit index. When no match is found, a flag of 1 is written on the output, followed by the size of the unmatched word, followed by the word itself.

Example: Assuming that the word `bet` is found in dictionary entry 1025, it is encoded as the 20-bit number 0|0000000010000000001. Assuming that the word `xet` is not found, it is encoded as 1|0000011|01111000|01100101|01110100. This is a 4-byte number where the 7-bit field 0000011 indicates that three more bytes follow.

Assuming that the size is written as a 7-bit number, and that an average word size is five characters, an uncompressed word occupies, on average, six bytes ($= 48$ bits) in the output. Compressing 48 bits into 20 bits is excellent if it happens often enough. Thus, we have to answer the question, how many matches are needed in order to have overall compression? We denote the probability of a match (the case where the word is found in the dictionary) by P. After reading and compressing N words, the size of the output will be $N[20P + 48(1 - P)] = N[48 - 28P]$ bits. The size of the input is (assuming five characters per word) $40N$ bits. Compression is achieved when $N[48-28P] < 40N$, which implies $P > 0.29$. We need a matching rate of 29% or better to achieve compression.

⋄ **Exercise 3.1:** (1) What compression factor do we get with $P = 0.9$? (2) What is the maximum compression possible with this method?

As long as the input consists of English text, most words will be found in a 500,000-word dictionary. Other types of data, however, may not do as well. A file with the source code of a computer program may contain "words" such as `cout`, `xor`, and `malloc` that may not be found in an English dictionary. A binary file normally contains gibberish when viewed in ASCII (Figure 3.1), so very few matches may be found, resulting in considerable expansion instead of compression.

Figure 3.1: An Image and Corresponding Text.

Thus, a static dictionary is not a good choice for a general-purpose compressor. It may, however, be a good choice for a special-purpose dictionary-based encoder. Consider, for example, a chain of hardware stores. Their files may contain words such as `nut`, `bolt`, and `paint` many times, but words such as `peanut`, `lightning`, and `painting` will be rare. Special-purpose compression software for such a company may benefit from a small, specialized dictionary containing, perhaps, just a few hundred words. The computers in each branch would have a copy of the dictionary, making it easy to compress files and send them between stores and offices in the chain.

In general, an adaptive dictionary-based method is preferable. Such a method can start with an empty dictionary or with a small, default dictionary, add words to it as they are found in the input, and delete old words because a big dictionary slows down the search. Such a method consists of a loop where each iteration starts by reading the input and breaking it up (parsing it) into words or phrases. It then should search the dictionary for each word and, if a match is found, write a token on the output. Otherwise, the uncompressed word is output and also added to the dictionary. The last step in each iteration checks whether an old word should be deleted from the dictionary. This may sound complicated, but it has two advantages:

1. It involves string search and match operations, rather than numerical computations. Many programmers prefer that.

2. The decoder is simple (this is an asymmetric compression method). It reads the next input item and determines whether it is a token or raw data. A token is used to obtain data from the dictionary and write it on the output. Raw data is output as is. The decoder does not have to parse the input in a complex way, nor does it have to search the dictionary to find matches. Many programmers like that, too.

> I love the dictionary, Kenny, it's the only book with the words in the right place.
> —Paul Reynolds as Colin Mathews in *Press Gang* (1989)

3.1 LZ78

The LZ78 method (sometimes also referred to as LZ2) [Ziv and Lempel 78] does not employ any search buffer, look-ahead buffer, or sliding window. Instead, there is a dictionary of previously-encountered strings. This dictionary starts empty (or almost empty), and its size is limited only by the amount of available memory. The encoder outputs two-field tokens. The first field is a pointer to the dictionary; the second is the code of a symbol. Tokens do not contain the length of a string, because this is implied in the dictionary. Each token corresponds to a string of input symbols, and that string is added to the dictionary after the token is written on the compressed file. Nothing is ever deleted from the dictionary, which is both an advantage over LZ77 (since future strings can be compressed even by strings seen in the distant past) and a liability (because the dictionary tends to grow rapidly and to fill up the entire available memory).

The dictionary starts with the null string at position zero. As symbols are input and encoded, strings are added to the dictionary at positions 1, 2, and so on. When the next symbol x is read from the input, the dictionary is searched for an entry with the one-symbol string x. If none is found, x is added to the next available position in the dictionary, and the token $(0, x)$ is output. This token indicates the string "null x" (a concatenation of the null string and x). If an entry with x is found (at, say, position 37), the next symbol y is read, and the dictionary is searched for an entry containing the two-symbol string xy. If none is found, then string xy is added to the next available position in the dictionary, and the token $(37, y)$ is output. This token indicates the string xy, since 37 is the dictionary position of string x. The process continues until the end of the input is reached.

In general, the current symbol is read and becomes a one-symbol string. The encoder then tries to find it in the dictionary. If the symbol is found in the dictionary, the next symbol is read and is concatenated with the first to form a two-symbol string that the encoder then tries to locate in the dictionary. As long as those strings are found in the dictionary, more symbols are read and concatenated to the string. At a certain point the string is not found in the dictionary, so the encoder adds it to the dictionary and outputs a token with the last dictionary match as its first field, and the last symbol of the string (the one that caused the search to fail) as its second field. Table 3.2 lists the first 14 steps in encoding the string `sir␣sid␣eastman␣easily␣teases␣sea␣sick␣seals`.

Dictionary	Token		Dictionary	Token
0 null				
1 s	(0,s)		8 a	(0,a)
2 i	(0,i)		9 st	(1,t)
3 r	(0,r)		10 m	(0,m)
4 ␣	(0,␣)		11 an	(8,n)
5 si	(1,i)		12 ␣ea	(7,a)
6 d	(0,d)		13 sil	(5,l)
7 ␣e	(4,e)		14 y	(0,y)

Table 3.2: First 14 Encoding Steps in LZ78.

⋄ **Exercise 3.2:** Complete Table 3.2.

In each step, the string added to the dictionary is the one that is being encoded, minus its last symbol. In a typical compression run, the dictionary starts with short strings, but as more text is being input and processed, longer and longer strings are added to it. The size of the dictionary can either be fixed or may be determined by the size of the available memory each time the LZ78 compression program is executed. A large dictionary may contain more strings and thus allow for longer matches, but the trade-off is longer pointers (which implies longer tokens) and slower dictionary search.

A good data structure for the dictionary is a tree, but not a binary tree. The tree starts with the null string as the root. All the strings that start with the null string (strings for which the token pointer is zero) are added to the tree as children of the root. In the example above those are s, i, r, ␣, d, a, m, y, e, c, and k. Each of them becomes the root of a subtree as shown in Figure 3.3. For example, all the strings that start with s (the four strings si, sil, st, and s(eof)) constitute the subtree of node s.

Assuming an alphabet of 8-bit symbols, there are 256 different symbols, so in principle, each node in the tree could have up to 256 children. The process of adding a child to a tree node should therefore be dynamic. When the node is first created, it has no children and it should not reserve any memory space for them. As a child is added to the node, memory space should be claimed for it. Recall that no nodes are ever deleted, so there is no need to reclaim memory space, which simplifies the memory management task somewhat.

Such a tree makes it easy to search for a string and to add strings. To search for sil, for example, the program looks for the child s of the root, then for the child i of

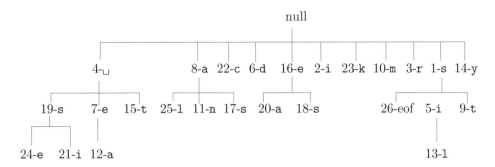

Figure 3.3: An LZ78 Dictionary Tree.

s, and so on, going down the tree. Here are some examples:

1. When the s of sid is input in step 5, the encoder finds node "1-s" in the tree as a child of "null". It then inputs the next symbol i, but node s does not have a child i (in fact, it has no children at all at this point), so the encoder adds node "5-i" as a child of "1-s", which effectively adds the string si to the tree.

2. When the blank space between eastman and easily is input in step 12, a similar situation occurs. The encoder finds node "4-␣", inputs e, finds "7-e", inputs a, but "7-e" does not have "a" as a child, so the encoder adds node "12-a", which effectively adds the string "␣ea" to the tree.

A tree of the type described here is called a *trie* (pronounced try). In general, a trie is a tree in which the branching structure at any level is determined by just part of a data item, not the entire item. In the case of LZ78, each string added to the tree effectively adds just one symbol, and does that by adding a branch.

Since the total size of the tree is limited, it may fill up during compression. This, in fact, happens all the time except when the input is unusually small. The original LZ78 method does not specify what to do in such a case, so we list a few possible solutions.

1. The simplest solution is to freeze the dictionary at that point. No new nodes should be added, the tree becomes a static dictionary, but it can still be used to encode strings.

2. Delete the entire tree once it gets full and start with a new, empty tree. This solution effectively breaks the input into blocks, each with its own dictionary. If the content of the input varies from block to block, this solution will produce good compression, since it will eliminate a dictionary with strings that are unlikely to be used in the future. We can say that this solution implicitly assumes that future symbols will benefit more from new data than from old (the same implicit assumption used by LZ77).

3. The UNIX compress utility uses a more complex solution.

4. When the dictionary is full, delete some of the least-recently-used entries, to make room for new ones. Unfortunately, there is no simple, fast algorithm to decide which entries to delete, and how many.

The LZ78 decoder works by building and maintaining the dictionary in the same way as the encoder. It is therefore more complex than the LZ77 decoder.

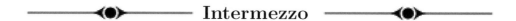

Intermezzo

The LZW Trio. Having one's name attached to a scientific discovery, technique, or phenomenon is considered a special honor in science. Having one's name associated with an entire field of science is even more so. This is what happened to Jacob Ziv and Abraham Lempel. In the 1970s these two researchers developed the first methods, LZ77 and LZ78, for dictionary-based compression. Their ideas have been a source of inspiration to many researchers, who generalized, improved, and combined them with RLE and statistical methods to form many popular lossless compression methods for text, images, and audio. More than a dozen such methods are described in detail in [Salomon 07]. Of special interest is the popular LZW algorithm, partly devised by Terry Welch (Section 3.2), which has extended LZ78 and made it useful in practical applications.

Abraham Lempel and Jacob Ziv.

◆Gamblers like the phrase "heads I win, tails I lose" (if you hear this, make sure you did not hear "heads I win, tails you lose"). Mr G. Ambler, a veteran gambler, decided to try a simple scheme, one where even he could easily figure out his winnings and losses. The principle is to always gamble half the money he has in his pocket. Thus, if he starts with an amount a and wins, he ends up with $1.5a$. If next he loses, he pays out half that and is left with $0.75a$. Assuming that he plays g games and wins half the time, what is his chance of making a net profit?

3.2 LZW

LZW is a popular variant of LZ78, developed by Terry Welch in 1984 ([Welch 84] and [Phillips 92]). Its main feature is eliminating the second field of a token. An LZW token consists of just a pointer to the dictionary. To best understand LZW, we will temporarily forget that the dictionary is a tree, and will think of it as an array of variable-size strings. The LZW method starts by initializing the dictionary to all the symbols in the alphabet. In the common case of 8-bit symbols, the first 256 entries of the dictionary (entries 0 through 255) are occupied before any data is input. Because the dictionary is initialized, the next input character will always be found in the dictionary. This is why an LZW token can consist of just a pointer and does not have to contain a character code as in LZ77 and LZ78.

(LZW was patented and for many years its use required a license. This issue is discussed in [Salomon 07] as well as in many places on the Internet.)

The principle of LZW is that the encoder inputs symbols one by one and accumulates them in a string I. After each symbol is input and is concatenated to I, the dictionary is searched for string I. As long as I is found in the dictionary, the process continues. At a certain point, appending the next symbol x causes the search to fail; string I is in the dictionary but string Ix (symbol x concatenated to I) is not. At this point the encoder (1) outputs the dictionary pointer that points to string I, (2) saves string Ix (which is now called a *phrase*) in the next available dictionary entry, and (3) initializes string I to symbol x. To illustrate this process, we again use the text string sir␣sid␣eastman␣easily␣teases␣sea␣sick␣seals. The steps are as follows:

0. Initialize entries 0–255 of the dictionary to all 256 8-bit bytes.

1. The first symbol s is input and is found in the dictionary (in entry 115, since this is the ASCII code of s). The next symbol i is input, but si is not found in the dictionary. The encoder performs the following: (1) outputs 115, (2) saves string si in the next available dictionary entry (entry 256), and (3) initializes I to the symbol i.

2. The r of sir is input, but string ir is not in the dictionary. The encoder (1) outputs 105 (the ASCII code of i), (2) saves string ir in the next available dictionary entry (entry 257), and (3) initializes I to the symbol r.

Table 3.4 summarizes all the steps of this process. Table 3.5 shows some of the original 256 entries in the LZW dictionary plus the entries added during encoding of the string above. The complete output file is (only the numbers are output, not the strings in parentheses) as follows:

115 (s), 105 (i), 114 (r), 32 (␣), 256 (si), 100 (d), 32 (␣), 101 (e), 97 (a), 115 (s), 116 (t), 109 (m), 97 (a), 110 (n), 262 (␣e), 264 (as), 105 (i), 108 (l), 121 (y), 32 (␣), 116 (t), 263 (ea), 115 (s), 101 (e), 115 (s), 259 (␣s), 263 (ea), 259 (␣s), 105 (i), 99 (c), 107 (k), 280 (␣se), 97 (a), 108 (l), 115 (s), eof.

Figure 3.6 is a pseudo-code listing of the algorithm. We denote by λ the empty string, and by <<a,b>> the concatenation of strings a and b.

The line "append <<di,ch>> to the dictionary" is of special interest. It is clear that in practice, the dictionary may fill up. This line should therefore include a test for a full dictionary, and certain actions for the case where it is full.

Since the first 256 entries of the dictionary are occupied right from the start, pointers to the dictionary have to be longer than 8 bits. A simple implementation would typically use 16-bit pointers, which allow for a 64 K-entry dictionary (where $64\,\mathrm{K} = 2^{16} = 65{,}536$). Naturally, such a dictionary will fill up very quickly in all but the smallest compression jobs. The same problem exists with LZ78, and any solutions used with LZ78 can also be used with LZW. Another interesting fact about LZW is that strings in the dictionary become only one character longer at a time. It therefore takes a long time to end up with long strings in the dictionary, and thus with a chance to achieve really good compression. We say that LZW adapts slowly to its input data.

⋄ **Exercise 3.3:** Use LZW to encode the string alf␣eats␣alfalfa. Show the encoder output and the new entries appended to the dictionary.

I	In dict?	New entry	Output
s	Y		
si	N	256-si	115 (s)
i	Y		
ir	N	257-ir	105 (i)
r	Y		
r	N	258-r	114 (r)
␣	Y		
␣s	N	259-␣s	32 (␣)
s	Y		
si	Y		
sid	N	260-sid	256 (si)
d	Y		
d	N	261-d	100 (d)
␣	Y		
␣e	N	262-␣e	32 (␣)
e	Y		
ea	N	263-ea	101 (e)
a	Y		
as	N	264-as	97 (a)
s	Y		
st	N	265-st	115 (s)
t	Y		
tm	N	266-tm	116 (t)
m	Y		
ma	N	267-ma	109 (m)
a	Y		
an	N	268-an	97 (a)
n	Y		
n	N	269-n	110 (n)
␣	Y		
␣e	Y		
␣ea	N	270-␣ea	262 (␣e)
a	Y		
as	Y		
asi	N	271-asi	264 (as)
i	Y		
il	N	272-il	105 (i)
l	Y		
ly	N	273-ly	108 (l)
y	Y		
y	N	274-y	121 (y)
␣	Y		
␣t	N	275-␣t	32 (␣)
t	Y		
te	N	276-te	116 (t)
e	Y		
ea	Y		
eas	N	277-eas	263 (ea)
s	Y		
se	N	278-se	115 (s)
e	Y		
es	N	279-es	101 (e)
s	Y		
s	N	280-s	115 (s)
␣	Y		
␣s	Y		
␣se	N	281-␣se	259 (␣s)
e	Y		
ea	Y		
ea	N	282-ea	263 (ea)
␣	Y		
␣s	Y		
␣si	N	283-␣si	259 (␣s)
i	Y		
ic	N	284-ic	105 (i)
c	Y		
ck	N	285-ck	99 (c)
k	Y		
k	N	286-k	107 (k)
␣	Y		
␣s	Y		
␣se	Y		
␣sea	N	287-␣sea	281 (␣se)
a	Y		
al	N	288-al	97 (a)
l	Y		
ls	N	289-ls	108 (l)
s	Y		
s,eof	N		115 (s)

Table 3.4: Encoding sir sid eastman easily teases sea sick seals.

0	NULL	110	n	262	⊔e	276	te
1	SOH	...		263	ea	277	eas
...		115	s	264	as	278	se
32	SP	116	t	265	st	279	es
...		...		266	tm	280	s
97	a	121	y	267	ma	281	⊔se
98	b	...		268	an	282	ea
99	c	255	255	269	n	283	⊔si
100	d	256	si	270	⊔ea	284	ic
101	e	257	ir	271	asi	285	ck
...		258	r	272	il	286	k
107	k	259	⊔s	273	ly	287	⊔sea
108	l	260	sid	274	y	288	al
109	m	261	d	275	⊔t	289	ls

Table 3.5: An LZW Dictionary.

```
for i:=0 to 255 do
   append i as a 1-symbol string to the dictionary;
append λ to the dictionary;
di:=dictionary index of λ;
repeat
   read(ch);
   if <<di,ch>> is in the dictionary then
     di:=dictionary index of <<di,ch>>;
   else
     output(di);
     append <<di,ch>> to the dictionary;
     di:=dictionary index of ch;
   endif;
until end-of-input;
```

Figure 3.6: The LZW Algorithm.

⋄ **Exercise 3.4:** Analyze the LZW compression of the string `aaaa...`.

> `A dirty icon` (anagram of "dictionary")

3.2.1 LZW Decoding

To understand how the LZW decoder works, we recall the three steps the encoder performs each time it writes something on the output. They are (1) it outputs the dictionary pointer that points to string `I`, (2) it saves string `Ix` in the next available entry of the dictionary, and (3) it initializes string `I` to symbol `x`.

The decoder starts with the first entries of its dictionary initialized to all the symbols of the alphabet (normally 256 symbols). It then reads its input (which consists of pointers to the dictionary) and uses each pointer to retrieve uncompressed symbols from its dictionary and write them on its output. It also builds its dictionary in the same way as the encoder (this fact is usually expressed by saying that the encoder and decoder are *synchronized*, or that they work in lockstep).

In the first decoding step, the decoder inputs the first pointer and uses it to retrieve a dictionary item `I`. This is a string of symbols, and it is written on the decoder's output. String `Ix` needs to be saved in the dictionary, but symbol `x` is still unknown; it will be the first symbol in the next string retrieved from the dictionary.

In each decoding step after the first, the decoder inputs the next pointer, retrieves the next string `J` from the dictionary, writes it on the output, isolates its first symbol `x`, and saves string `Ix` in the next available dictionary entry (after checking to make sure string `Ix` is not already in the dictionary). The decoder then moves `J` to `I` and is ready for the next step.

In our "`sir sid...`" example, the first pointer that's input by the decoder is 115. This corresponds to the string `s`, which is retrieved from the dictionary, gets stored in `I`, and becomes the first item written on the decoder's output. The next pointer is 105, so string `i` is retrieved into `J` and is also written on the output. `J`'s first symbol is concatenated with `I`, to form string `si`, which does not exist in the dictionary, and is therefore added to it as entry 256. Variable `J` is moved to `I`, so `I` is now the string `i`. The next pointer is 114, so string `r` is retrieved from the dictionary into `J` and is also written on the output. `J`'s first symbol is concatenated with `I`, to form string `ir`, which does not exist in the dictionary, and is added to it as entry 257. Variable `J` is moved to `I`, so `I` is now the string `r`. The next step reads pointer 32, writes ␣ on the output, and saves string `r␣`.

⋄ **Exercise 3.5:** Decode the string `alf␣eats␣alfalfa` by using the encoding results from Exercise 3.3.

⋄ **Exercise 3.6:** Assume a two-symbol alphabet with the symbols `a` and `b`. Show the first few steps for encoding and decoding the string "`ababab...`".

3.2.2 LZW Dictionary Structure

Up until now, we have assumed that the LZW dictionary is an array of variable-size strings. It turns out that a trie is an ideal data structure for a practical implementation of such a dictionary. The first step in understanding such an implementation is to recall how the encoder works. It inputs symbols and concatenates them into a variable I as long as the string in I is found in the dictionary. At a certain point the encoder inputs the first symbol x, which causes the search to fail (string Ix is not in the dictionary). It then adds Ix to the dictionary. This means that each string added to the dictionary effectively adds just one new symbol, x. (Phrased another way; for each dictionary string of more than one symbol, there exists a "parent" string in the dictionary that's one symbol shorter.)

A tree similar to the one used by LZ78 is therefore a good data structure, because adding string Ix to such a tree is done by adding one node with x. The main problem is that each node in the LZW tree may have many children (this is a multiway tree, not a binary tree). Imagine the node for the letter a in entry 97. Initially it has no children, but if the string ab is added to the tree, node 97 receives one child. Later, when, say, the string ae is added, node 97 receives a second child, and so on. The data structure for the tree should therefore be designed such that a node could have any number of children, but without having to reserve any memory for them in advance.

One way of designing such a data structure is to house the tree in an array of nodes, each a structure with two fields: a symbol and a pointer to the parent node. A node has no pointers to any child nodes. Moving down the tree, from a node to one of its children, is done by a hashing process in which the pointer to the node and the symbol of the child are hashed to create a new pointer.

Suppose that string abc has already been input, symbol by symbol, and has been stored in the tree in the three nodes at locations 97, 266, and 284. Following that, the encoder has just input the next symbol d. The encoder now searches for string abcd, or, more specifically, for a node containing the symbol d whose parent is at location 284. The encoder hashes the 284 (the pointer to string abc) and the 100 (ASCII code of d) to create a pointer to some node, say, 299. The encoder then examines node 299. There are three possibilities:

1. The node is unused. This means that abcd is not yet in the dictionary and should be added to it. The encoder adds it to the tree by storing the parent pointer 284 and ASCII code 100 in the node. The result is the following:

Node				
Address :	97	266	284	299
Contents :	(-:a)	(97:b)	(266:c)	(284:d)
Represents:	a	ab	abc	abcd

2. The node contains a parent pointer of 284 and the ASCII code of d. This means that string abcd is already in the tree. The encoder inputs the next symbol, say e, and searches the dictionary tree for string abcde.

3. The node contains something else. This means that another hashing of a pointer and an ASCII code has resulted in 299, and node 299 already contains information from another string. This is called a *collision*, and it can be dealt with in several ways. The simplest way to deal with a collision is to increment pointer 299 and examine nodes 300, 301, ... until an unused node is found, or until a node with (284:d) is found.

In practice, we build nodes that are structures with three fields, a pointer to the parent node, the pointer (or index) created by the hashing process, and the code (nor-

mally ASCII) of the symbol contained in the node. The second field is necessary because
of collisions. A node can therefore be illustrated by

parent
index
symbol

We illustrate this data structure using string `ababab...` of Exercise 3.6. The
dictionary is an array `dict` where each entry is a structure with the three fields `parent`,
`index`, and `symbol`. We refer to a field by, for example, `dict[pointer].parent`, where
`pointer` is an index to the array. The dictionary is initialized to the two entries `a` and
`b`. (To keep the example simple we use no ASCII codes. We assume that `a` has code 1
and `b` has code 2.) The first few steps of the encoder are as follows:

Step 0: Mark all dictionary locations from 3 on as unused.

/	/	/	/	/	
1	2	-	-	-	...
a	b				

Step 1: The first symbol `a` is input into variable `I`. What is actually input is the code
of `a`, which in our example is 1, so $I = 1$. Since this is the first symbol, the encoder
assumes that it is in the dictionary and so does not perform any search.

Step 2: The second symbol `b` is input into `J`, so $J = 2$. The encoder has to search
for string `ab` in the dictionary. It executes `pointer:=hash(I,J)`. Let's assume that
the result is 5. Field `dict[pointer].index` contains "unused", since location 5 is still
empty, so string `ab` is not in the dictionary. It is added by executing

```
dict[pointer].parent:=I;
dict[pointer].index:=pointer;
dict[pointer].symbol:=J;
```

with `pointer` = 5. `J` is moved into `I`, so $I = 2$.

/	/	/	/	1	
1	2	-	-	5	...
a	b			b	

Step 3: The third symbol `a` is input into `J`, so $J = 1$. The encoder has to search for string
`ba` in the dictionary. It executes `pointer:=hash(I,J)`. Let's assume that the result is
8. Field `dict[pointer].index` contains "unused", so string `ba` is not in the dictionary.
It is added as before by executing

```
dict[pointer].parent:=I;
dict[pointer].index:=pointer;
dict[pointer].symbol:=J;
```

with `pointer` = 8. `J` is moved into `I`, so $I = 1$.

/	/	/	/	1	/	/	2	/	
1	2	-	-	5	-	-	8	-	...
a	b			b			a		

Step 4: The fourth symbol `b` is input into `J`, so J=2. The encoder has to search for
string `ab` in the dictionary. It executes `pointer:=hash(I,J)`. We know from step 2 that

the result is 5. Field `dict[pointer].index` contains 5, so string `ab` is in the dictionary. The value of `pointer` is moved into I, so I = 5.

Step 5: The fifth symbol `a` is input into J, so J = 1. The encoder has to search for string `aba` in the dictionary. It executes as usual `pointer:=hash(I,J)`. Let's assume that the result is 8 (a collision). Field `dict[pointer].index` contains 8, which looks good, but field `dict[pointer].parent` contains 2 instead of the expected 5, so the hash function knows that this is a collision and string `aba` is not in dictionary entry 8. It increments `pointer` as many times as necessary until it finds a dictionary entry with `index = 8` and `parent = 5` or until it finds an unused entry. In the former case, string `aba` is in the dictionary, and `pointer` is moved to I. In the latter case `aba` is not in the dictionary, and the encoder saves it in the entry pointed at by `pointer`, and moves J to I.

/	/	/	/	1	/	/	2	5	/	
1	2	-	-	5	-	-	8	8	-	...
a	b			b			a	a		

Example: The 15 hashing steps for encoding the string `alf eats alfalfa` are shown below. The encoding process itself is illustrated in detail in the answer to Exercise 3.3. The results of the hashing are arbitrary; they are not the results produced by a real hash function. The 12 trie nodes constructed for this string are shown in Figure 3.7.

1. Hash(1,97) → 278. Array location 278 is set to (97, 278, 1).
2. Hash(f,108) → 266. Array location 266 is set to (108, 266, f).
3. Hash(␣,102) → 269. Array location 269 is set to (102,269,␣).
4. Hash(e,32) → 267. Array location 267 is set to (32, 267, e).
5. Hash(a,101) → 265. Array location 265 is set to (101, 265, a).
6. Hash(t,97) → 272. Array location 272 is set to (97, 272, t).
7. Hash(s,116) → 265. A collision! Skip to the next available location, 268, and set it to (116, 265, s). This is why the index needs to be stored.
8. Hash(␣,115) → 270. Array location 270 is set to (115, 270, ␣).
9. Hash(a,32) → 268. A collision! Skip to the next available location, 271, and set it to (32, 268, a).
10. Hash(1,97) → 278. Array location 278 already contains index 278 and symbol 1 from step 1, so there is no need to store anything else or to add a new trie entry.
11. Hash(f,278) → 276. Array location 276 is set to (278, 276, f).
12. Hash(a,102) → 274. Array location 274 is set to (102, 274, a).
13. Hash(1,97) → 278. Array location 278 already contains index 278 and symbol 1 from step 1, so there is no need to do anything.
14. Hash(f,278) → 276. Array location 276 already contains index 276 and symbol f from step 11, so there is no need to do anything.
15. Hash(a,276) → 274. A collision! Skip to the next available location, 275, and set it to (276, 274, a).

Readers who have carefully followed the discussion up to this point will be happy to learn that the LZW decoder's use of the dictionary tree-array is simple and no hashing is needed. The decoder starts, like the encoder, by initializing the first 256 array locations. It then reads pointers from its input and uses each to locate a symbol in the dictionary.

In the first decoding step, the decoder inputs the first pointer and uses it to retrieve a dictionary item I. This is a symbol that is now written by the decoder on its output.

265	266	267	268	269	270	271	272	273	274	275	276	277	278
/	/	/	/	/	/	/	/	/	/	/	/	/	97
-	-	-	-	-	-	-	-	-	-	-	-	-	278
													1
/	108	/	/	/	/	/	/	/	/	/	/	/	97
-	266	-	-	-	-	-	-	-	-	-	-	-	278
	f												1
/	108	/	/	102	/	/	/	/	/	/	/	/	97
-	266	-	-	269	-	-	-	-	-	-	-	-	278
	f			␣									1
/	108	32	/	102	/	/	/	/	/	/	/	/	97
-	266	267	-	269	-	-	-	-	-	-	-	-	278
	f	e		␣									1
101	108	32	/	102	/	/	/	/	/	/	/	/	97
265	266	267	-	269	-	-	-	-	-	-	-	-	278
a	f	e		␣									1
101	108	32	/	102	/	/	97	/	/	/	/	/	97
265	266	267	-	269	-	-	272	-	-	-	-	-	278
a	f	e		␣			t						1
101	108	32	116	102	/	/	97	/	/	/	/	/	97
265	266	267	265	269	-	-	272	-	-	-	-	-	278
a	f	e	s	␣			t						1
101	108	32	116	102	115	/	97	/	/	/	/	/	97
265	266	267	265	269	270	-	272	-	-	-	-	-	278
a	f	e	s	␣	␣		t						1
101	108	32	116	102	115	32	97	/	/	/	/	/	97
265	266	267	265	269	270	268	272	-	-	-	-	-	278
a	f	e	s	␣	␣	a	t						1
101	108	32	116	102	115	32	97	/	/	/	278	/	97
265	266	267	265	269	270	268	272	-	-	-	276	-	278
a	f	e	s	␣	␣	a	t				f		1
101	108	32	116	102	115	32	97	/	102	/	278	/	97
265	266	267	265	269	270	268	272	-	274	-	276	-	278
a	f	e	s	␣	␣	a	t		a		f		1
101	108	32	116	102	115	32	97	/	102	276	278	/	97
265	266	267	265	269	270	268	272	-	274	274	276	-	278
a	f	e	s	␣	␣	a	t		a	a	f		1

Figure 3.7: Growing an LZW Trie for alf␣eats␣alfalfa.

String Ix needs to be saved in the dictionary, but symbol x is still unknown; it will be the first symbol in the next string retrieved from the dictionary.

In each decoding step after the first, the decoder inputs the next pointer and uses it to retrieve the next string J from the dictionary and write it on the output. If the pointer is, say 8, the decoder examines field dict[8].index. If this field equals 8, then this is the right node. Otherwise, the decoder examines consecutive array locations until it finds the right one.

Once the right tree node is found, the **parent** field is used to go back up the tree and retrieve the individual symbols of the string *in reverse order*. The symbols are then placed in J in the right order (see below), the decoder isolates the first symbol x of J, and saves string Ix in the next available array location. (String I was found in the previous step, so only one node, with symbol x, needs be added.) The decoder then moves J to I and is ready for the next step.

Retrieving a complete string from the LZW tree therefore involves following the pointers in the **parent** fields. This is equivalent to moving *up* the tree, which is why the hash function is no longer needed.

Example: The previous example describes the 15 hashing steps in the encoding of string alf␣eats␣alfalfa. The last step sets array location 275 to (276,274,a) and writes 275 (a pointer to location 275) on the compressed file. When this file is read by the decoder, pointer 275 is the last item input and processed by the decoder. The decoder finds symbol a in the symbol field of location 275 (indicating that the string stored at 275 ends with an a) and a pointer to location 276 in the **parent** field. The decoder then examines location 276 where it finds symbol f and parent pointer 278. In location 278 the decoder finds symbol l and a pointer to 97. Finally, in location 97 the decoder finds symbol a and a null pointer. The (reversed) string is therefore afla. There is no need for the decoder to do any hashing or to use the **index** fields.

The last point to discuss is string reversal. Two common approaches are outlined here:

1. Use a stack. A stack is a common data structure in modern computers. It is an array in memory that is accessed at one end only. At any time, the item that was last pushed into the stack will be the first one to be popped out (last-in-first-out, or LIFO). Symbols retrieved from the dictionary are pushed into the stack. When the last one has been retrieved and pushed, the stack is popped, symbol by symbol, into variable J. When the stack is empty, the entire string has been reversed. This is a common way to reverse a string.

2. Retrieve symbols from the dictionary and concatenate them into J *from right to left*. When done, the string will be stored in J in the right order. Variable J must be long enough to accommodate the longest possible string, but then it has to be long enough even when a stack is used.

◊ **Exercise 3.7:** What is the longest string that can be retrieved from the LZW dictionary during decoding?

✄ Big Amy lives in London and works in a store on Oxford Street. In order to justify her name, she is married to two men, neither of whom knows about the other. Thus, she has to juggle her marital life carefully. Every day after work, she walks to the Oxford

Circus underground station and takes either the Victoria line (cyan) south, to Brixton, where one husband lives, or the Bakerloo line (brown) north, to Maida Vale, where the other husband lives. Being a loving, impartial, and also a careful wife, she tries to balance her visits so as not to prefer any husband over the other. To this end she gets off work and arrives at the underground station at random times. In spite of this, she finds herself at Maida Vale much more often than at Brixton. What could be a reason for such imbalance?

3.3 Deflate: Zip and Gzip

Deflate is a popular compression method that was originally used in the well-known Zip and Gzip software and has since been adopted by many applications, the most important of which are (1) the HTTP protocol ([RFC1945 96] and [RFC2616 99]), (2) the PPP compression control protocol ([RFC1962 96] and [RFC1979 96]), (3) the PNG (Portable Network Graphics) and MNG (Multiple-Image Network Graphics) graphics file formats ([PNG 03] and [MNG 03]), and (4) Adobe's PDF (Portable Document File) [PDF 01].

Deflate was developed by Philip Katz as a part of the Zip file format and implemented in his PKZIP software [PKWare 03]. Both the ZIP format and the Deflate method are in the public domain, which allowed implementations such as Info-ZIP's Zip and Unzip (essentially, PKZIP and PKUNZIP clones) to appear on a number of platforms. Deflate is described in [RFC1951 96].

Phillip W. Katz was born in 1962. He received a bachelor's degree in computer science from the University of Wisconsin at Madison. Always interested in writing software, he started working in 1984 as a programmer for Allen-Bradley Co. developing programmable logic controllers for the industrial automation industry. He later worked for Graysoft, another software company, in Milwaukee, Wisconsin. At about that time he became interested in data compression and founded PKWare in 1987 to develop, implement, and market software products such as PKarc and PKzip. For a while, the company was very successful selling the programs as shareware.

Always a loner, Katz suffered from personal and legal problems, started drinking heavily, and died on April 14, 2000 from complications related to chronic alcoholism. He was 37 years old.

After his death, PKWare was sold, in March 2001, to a group of investors. They changed its management and the focus of its business. PKWare currently targets the corporate market, and emphasizes compression combined with encryption. Their product line runs on a wide variety of platforms.

The most notable implementation of Deflate is zlib, a portable and free compression library ([zlib 03] and [RFC1950 96]) by Jean-Loup Gailly and Mark Adler who designed and implemented it to be free of patents and licensing requirements. This library (the source code is available at [Deflate 03]) implements the ZLIB and GZIP file formats ([RFC1950 96] and [RFC1952 96]), which are at the core of most Deflate applications, including the popular Gzip software.

Deflate is based on a variation of LZ77 combined with Huffman codes. We start with a simple overview based on [Feldspar 03] and follow with a full description based on [RFC1951 96].

The original LZ77 method (Section 1.3.1) tries to match the text in the look-ahead buffer to strings already in the search buffer. In the example

search buffer   look-ahead

...old␣|..the␣a..then...there...|the␣new...|...more

the look-ahead buffer starts with the string the␣, which can be matched to one of three strings in the search buffer. The longest match has a length of 4. LZ77 writes tokens on the compressed file, where each token is a triplet (offset, length, next symbol). The third component is needed in cases where no string has been matched (imagine having che instead of the in the look-ahead buffer) but it is part of every token, which reduces the performance of LZ77. The LZ77 algorithm variation used in Deflate eliminates the third component and writes a pair (offset, length) on the compressed file. When no match is found, the unmatched character is written on the compressed file instead of a token. Thus, the compressed data consists of three types of entities: literals (unmatched characters), offsets (termed "distances" in the Deflate literature), and lengths. Deflate actually writes Huffman codes on the compressed file for these entities, and it uses two code tables—one for literals and lengths and the other for distances. This makes sense because the literals are normally bytes and are therefore in the interval $[0, 255]$, and the lengths are limited by Deflate to 258. The distances, however, can be large numbers because Deflate allows for a search buffer of up to 32 Kbytes.

◇ **Exercise 3.8:** When no match is found, Deflate writes the unmatched character (in raw format) on the compressed file instead of a token. Suggest an alternative.

When a pair (length, distance) is determined, the encoder searches the table of literal/length codes to find the code for the length. This code (we later use the term "edoc" for it) is then replaced by a Huffman code that's written on the compressed file. The encoder then searches the table of distance codes for the code of the distance and writes that code (a special prefix code with a fixed, 5-bit prefix) on the compressed file. The decoder knows when to expect a distance code, because it always follows a length code.

The LZ77 variant used by Deflate defers the selection of a match in the following way. Suppose that the two buffers contain

search buffer   look-ahead

...old␣|..she␣needs..then...there...|the␣new...|...more input

The longest match is 3. Before selecting this match, the encoder saves the t from the look-ahead buffer and starts a secondary match where it tries to match he␣new... with the search buffer. If it finds a longer match, it outputs t as a literal, followed by the longer match. There is also a 3-valued parameter that controls this secondary match attempt. In the "normal" mode of this parameter, if the primary match was long enough (longer than a preset parameter), the secondary match is reduced (it is up to the implementor to decide how to reduce it). In the "high-compression" mode, the encoder always performs a full secondary match, thereby improving compression but spending more time on selecting a match. In the "fast" mode, the secondary match is omitted.

Deflate compresses an input data file in blocks, where each block is compressed separately. Blocks can have different lengths and the length of a block is determined by the encoder based on the sizes of the various prefix codes used (their lengths are limited to 15 bits) and by the memory available to the encoder (except that blocks in mode 1 are limited to 65,535 bytes of uncompressed data). The Deflate decoder must be able to decode blocks of any size. Deflate offers three modes of compression, and each block can be in any mode. The modes are as follows:

1.   No compression. This mode makes sense for files or parts of files that are incompressible (i.e., random) or already compressed, or for cases where the compression software is asked to segment a file without compression. A typical case is a user who wants to archive an 8 Gb file but has only a DVD "burner." The user may want to segment the file into two 4 Gb segments without compression. Commercial compression software based on Deflate can use this mode of operation to segment the file. This mode uses no code tables. A block written on the compressed file in this mode starts with a special header indicating mode 1, followed by the length LEN of the data, followed by LEN bytes of literal data. Notice that the maximum value of LEN is 65,535.

2. Compression with fixed code tables. Two code tables are built into the Deflate encoder and decoder and are always used. This speeds up both compression and decompression and has the added advantage that the code tables don't have to be written on the compressed file. The compression performance, however, may suffer if the data being compressed is statistically different from the data used to set up the code tables. Literals and match lengths are located in the first table and are replaced by a code (called "edoc") that is, in turn, replaced by a prefix code that's output to the compressed file. Distances are located in the second table and are replaced by special prefix codes that are output to the compressed file. A block written on the compressed file in this mode starts with a special header indicating mode 2, followed by the compressed data in the form of prefix codes for the literals and lengths, and special prefix codes for the distances. The block ends with a single prefix code for end-of-block.

3. Compression with individual code tables generated by the encoder for the particular data that's being compressed. A sophisticated Deflate encoder may gather statistics about the data as it compresses blocks, and may be able to construct improved code tables as it proceeds from block to block. There are two code tables, for literals/lengths and for distances. They again have to be written on the output, and they are written in compressed format. A block output by the encoder in this mode starts with a special header, followed by (1) a compressed Huffman code table and (2) the two code tables, each compressed by the Huffman codes that preceded them. This is followed by the compressed data in the form of prefix codes for the literals, lengths, and distances, and ends with a single code for end-of-block.

✦ What is the next integer in the sequence (12, 6), (6, 3), (10, ?)?

3.3.1 The Details

Each block starts with a 3-bit header where the first bit is 1 for the last block in the file and 0 for all other blocks. The remaining two bits are 00, 01, or 10, indicating modes

1, 2, or 3, respectively. Notice that a block of compressed data does not always end on a byte boundary. The information in the block is sufficient for the decoder to read all the bits of the compressed block and recognize the end of the block. The 3-bit header of the next block immediately follows the current block and may therefore be located at any position in a byte on the compressed file.

The format of a block in mode 1 is as follows:

1. The 3-bit header 000 or 100.

2. The rest of the current byte is skipped, and the next four bytes contain LEN and the one's complement of LEN (as unsigned 16-bit numbers), where LEN is the number of data bytes in the block. This is why the block size in this mode is limited to 65,535 bytes.

3. LEN data bytes.

The format of a block in mode 2 is different:

1. The 3-bit header 001 or 101.

2. This is immediately followed by the fixed prefix codes for literals/lengths and the special prefix codes of the distances.

3. Code 256 (rather, its prefix code) designating the end of the block.

Code	Extra bits	Lengths	Code	Extra bits	Lengths	Code	Extra bits	Lengths
257	0	3	267	1	15,16	277	4	67–82
258	0	4	268	1	17,18	278	4	83–98
259	0	5	269	2	19–22	279	4	99–114
260	0	6	270	2	23–26	280	4	115–130
261	0	7	271	2	27–30	281	5	131–162
262	0	8	272	2	31–34	282	5	163–194
263	0	9	273	3	35–42	283	5	195–226
264	0	10	274	3	43–50	284	5	227–257
265	1	11,12	275	3	51–58	285	0	258
266	1	13,14	276	3	59–66			

Table 3.8: Literal/Length Edocs for Mode 2.

Edoc	Bits	Prefix codes
0–143	8	00110000–10111111
144–255	9	110010000–111111111
256–279	7	0000000–0010111
280–287	8	11000000–11000111

Table 3.9: Huffman Codes for Edocs in Mode 2.

Mode 2 uses two code tables: one for literals and lengths and the other for distances. The codes of the first table are not what is actually written on the compressed file, so in order to remove ambiguity, the term "edoc" is used here to refer to them. Each edoc is converted to a prefix code that's output. The first table allocates edocs 0 through 255 to the literals, edoc 256 to end-of-block, and edocs 257–285 to lengths. The latter 29 edocs are not enough to represent the 256 match lengths of 3 through 258, so extra bits are appended to some of those edocs. Table 3.8 lists the 29 edocs, the extra bits, and the lengths that they represent. What is actually written on the output is prefix codes of the edocs (Table 3.9). Notice that edocs 286 and 287 are never created, so their prefix codes are never used. We show later that Table 3.9 can be represented by the sequence of code lengths

$$\underbrace{8, 8, \ldots, 8,}_{144} \underbrace{9, 9, \ldots, 9,}_{112} \underbrace{7, 7, \ldots, 7,}_{24} \underbrace{8, 8, \ldots, 8,}_{8} \qquad (3.1)$$

but any Deflate encoder and decoder include the entire table instead of just the sequence of code lengths. There are edocs for match lengths of up to 258, so the look-ahead buffer of a Deflate encoder can have a maximum size of 258, but can also be smaller.

Examples. If a string of 10 symbols has been matched by the LZ77 algorithm, Deflate prepares a pair (length, distance) where the match length 10 becomes edoc 264, which is written as the 7-bit prefix code 0001000. A length of 12 becomes edoc 265 followed by the single bit 1. This is written as the 7-bit prefix code 0001010 followed by 1. A length of 20 is converted to edoc 269 followed by the two bits 01. This is written as the nine bits 0001101|01. A length of 256 becomes edoc 284 followed by the five bits 11110. This is written as 11000101|11110. A match length of 258 is indicated by edoc 285 whose 8-bit prefix code is 11000110. The end-of-block edoc of 256 is written as seven zero bits.

The 30 distance codes are listed in Table 3.10. They are special prefix codes with fixed-size 5-bit prefixes that are followed by extra bits in order to represent distances in the interval [1, 32768]. The maximum size of the search buffer is therefore 32,768, but it can be smaller. The table shows that a distance of 6 is represented by 00100|1, a distance of 21 becomes the code 01000|101, and a distance of 8195 corresponds to code 11010|000000000010.

Code	Extra bits	Distance	Code	Extra bits	Distance	Code	Extra bits	Distance
0	0	1	10	4	33–48	20	9	1025–1536
1	0	2	11	4	49–64	21	9	1537–2048
2	0	3	12	5	65–96	22	10	2049–3072
3	0	4	13	5	97–128	23	10	3073–4096
4	1	5,6	14	6	129–192	24	11	4097–6144
5	1	7,8	15	6	193–256	25	11	6145–8192
6	2	9–12	16	7	257–384	26	12	8193–12288
7	2	13–16	17	7	385–512	27	12	12289–16384
8	3	17–24	18	8	513–768	28	13	16385–24576
9	3	25–32	19	8	769–1024	29	13	24577–32768

Table 3.10: Thirty Prefix Distance Codes in Mode 2.

3.3.2 Format of Mode-3 Blocks

In mode 3, the encoder generates two prefix code tables, one for the literals/lengths and the other for the distances. It uses the tables to encode the data that constitutes the block. The encoder can generate the tables in any way. The idea is that a sophisticated Deflate encoder may collect statistics as it inputs the data and compresses blocks. The statistics are used to construct better code tables for later blocks. A naive encoder may use code tables similar to the ones of mode 2 or may even not generate mode 3 blocks at all. The code tables have to be written on the output, and they are written in a highly-compressed format. As a result, an important part of Deflate is the way it compresses the code tables and outputs them. The main steps are (1) Each table starts as a Huffman tree. (2) The tree is rearranged to bring it to a standard format where it can be represented by a sequence of code lengths. (3) The sequence is compressed by run-length encoding to a shorter sequence. (4) The Huffman algorithm is applied to the elements of the shorter sequence to assign them Huffman codes. This creates a Huffman tree that is again rearranged to bring it to the standard format. (5) This standard tree is represented by a sequence of code lengths which are written, after being permuted and possibly truncated, on the output. These steps are described in detail because of the originality of this unusual method.

Recall that the Huffman code tree generated by the basic algorithm of Section 2.1 is not unique. The Deflate encoder applies this algorithm to generate a Huffman code tree, then rearranges the tree and reassigns the codes to bring the tree to a standard form where it can be expressed compactly by a sequence of code lengths. (The result is reminiscent of the canonical Huffman codes of Section 2.2.6.) The new tree satisfies the following two properties:

1. The shorter codes appear on the left, and the longer codes appear on the right of the Huffman code tree.

2. When several symbols have codes of the same length, the (lexicographically) smaller symbols are placed on the left.

The first example employs a set of six symbols A–F with probabilities 0.11, 0.14, 0.12, 0.13, 0.24, and 0.26, respectively. Applying the Huffman algorithm results in a tree similar to the one shown in Figure 3.11a. The Huffman codes of the six symbols are 000, 101, 001, 100, 01, and 11. The tree is then rearranged and the codes reassigned to comply with the two requirements above, resulting in the tree of Figure 3.11b. The new codes of the symbols are 100, 101, 110, 111, 00, and 01. The latter tree has the advantage that it can be fully expressed by the sequence 3, 3, 3, 3, 2, 2 of the lengths of the codes of the six symbols. The task of the encoder in mode 3 is therefore to generate this sequence, compress it, and write it on the output.

The code lengths are limited to at most four bits each. Thus, they are integers in the interval $[0, 15]$, which implies that a code can be at most 15 bits long (this is one factor that affects the Deflate encoder's choice of block lengths in mode 3).

The sequence of code lengths representing a Huffman tree tends to have runs of identical values and can have several runs of the same value. For example, if we assign the probabilities 0.26, 0.11, 0.14, 0.12, 0.24, and 0.13 to the set of six symbols A–F, the Huffman algorithm produces 2-bit codes for A and E and 3-bit codes for the remaining four symbols. The sequence of these code lengths is 2, 3, 3, 3, 2, 3.

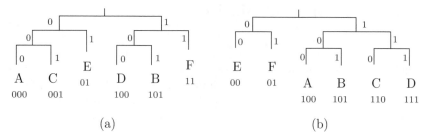

(a)

(b)

Figure 3.11: Two Huffman Trees.

The decoder reads a compressed sequence, decompresses it, and uses it to reproduce the standard Huffman code tree for the symbols. We first show how such a sequence is used by the decoder to generate a code table, then how it is compressed by the encoder.

Given the sequence 3, 3, 3, 3, 2, 2, the Deflate decoder proceeds in three steps as follows:

1. Count the number of codes for each code length in the sequence. In our example, there are no codes of length 1, two codes of length 2, and four codes of length 3.

2. Assign a base value to each code length. There are no codes of length 1, so they are assigned a base value of 0 and don't require any bits. The two codes of length 2 therefore start with the same base value 0. The codes of length 3 are assigned a base value of 4 (twice the number of codes of length 2). The C code shown here (after [RFC1951 96]) was written by Peter Deutsch. It assumes that step 1 leaves the number of codes for each code length n in `bl_count[n]`.

```
code = 0;
bl_count[0] = 0;
for (bits = 1; bits <= MAX_BITS; bits++)
{ code = (code + bl_count[bits-1]) << 1;
  next code[bits] = code;
}
```

3. Use the base value of each length to assign consecutive numerical values to all the codes of that length. The two codes of length 2 start at 0 and are therefore 00 and 01. They are assigned to the fifth and sixth symbols E and F. The four codes of length 3 start at 4 and are therefore 100, 101, 110, and 111. They are assigned to the first four symbols A–D. The C code shown here (by Peter Deutsch) assumes that the code lengths are in `tree[I].Len` and it generates the codes in `tree[I].Codes`.

```
for (n = 0; n <= max code; n++)
{ len = tree[n].Len;
  if (len != 0)
  { tree[n].Code = next_code[len];
    next_code[len]++;
  }
}
```

In the next example, the sequence 3, 3, 3, 3, 3, 2, 4, 4 is given and is used to generate a table of eight prefix codes. Step 1 finds that there are no codes of length 1, one code of length 2, five codes of length 3, and two codes of length 4. The length-1 codes are assigned a base value of 0. There are zero such codes, so the next group is also assigned the base value of 0 (more accurately, twice 0, twice the number of codes of the previous group). This group contains one code, so the next group (length-3 codes) is assigned base value 2 (twice the sum $0 + 1$). This group contains five codes, so the last group is assigned base value of 14 (twice the sum $2 + 5$). Step 3 simply generates the five 3-bit codes 010, 011, 100, 101, and 110 and assigns them to the first five symbols. It then generates the single 2-bit code 00 and assigns it to the sixth symbol. Finally, the two 4-bit codes 1110 and 1111 are generated and assigned to the last two (seventh and eighth) symbols.

Given the sequence of code lengths of Equation (3.1), we apply this method to generate its standard Huffman code tree (listed in Table 3.9).

Step 1 finds that there are no codes of lengths 1 through 6, that there are 24 codes of length 7, 152 codes of length 8, and 112 codes of length 9. The length-7 codes are assigned a base value of 0. There are 24 such codes, so the next group is assigned the base value of $2(0 + 24) = 48$. This group contains 152 codes, so the last group (length-9 codes) is assigned base value $2(48 + 152) = 400$. Step 3 simply generates the 24 7-bit codes 0 through 23, the 152 8-bit codes 48 through 199, and the 112 9-bit codes 400 through 511. The binary values of these codes are listed in Table 3.9.

> How many a dispute could have been deflated into a single paragraph if the disputants had dared to define their terms.
>
> —Aristotle

It is now clear that a Huffman code table can be represented by a short sequence (termed SQ) of code lengths (herein called CLs). This sequence is special in that it tends to have runs of identical elements, so it can be highly compressed by run-length encoding. The Deflate encoder compresses this sequence in a three-step process where the first step employs run-length encoding; the second step computes Huffman codes for the run lengths and generates another sequence of code lengths (to be called CCLs) for those Huffman codes. The third step writes a permuted, possibly truncated sequence of the CCLs on the output.

Step 1. When a CL repeats more than three times, the encoder considers it a run. It appends the CL to a new sequence (termed SSQ), followed by the special flag 16 and by a 2-bit repetition factor that indicates 3–6 repetitions. A flag of 16 is therefore preceded by a CL and followed by a factor that indicates how many times to copy the CL. Thus, for example, if the sequence to be compressed contains six consecutive 7's, it is compressed to 7, 16, 10_2 (the repetition factor 10_2 indicates five consecutive occurrences of the same code length). If the sequence contains 10 consecutive code lengths of 6, it will be compressed to 6, 16, 11_2, 16, 00_2 (the repetition factors 11_2 and 00_2 indicate six and three consecutive occurrences, respectively, of the same code length).

Experience indicates that CLs of zero are very common and tend to have long runs. (Recall that the codes in question are codes of literals/lengths and distances. Any given data file to be compressed may be missing many literals, lengths, and distances.) This is why runs of zeros are assigned the two special flags 17 and 18. A flag of 17 is followed by a 3-bit repetition factor that indicates 3–10 repetitions of CL 0. Flag 18 is followed by a 7-bit repetition factor that indicates 11–138 repetitions of CL 0. Thus, six consecutive zeros in a sequence of CLs are compressed to 17, 11_2, and 12 consecutive zeros in an SQ are compressed to 18, 01_2.

The sequence of CLs is compressed in this way to a shorter sequence (to be termed SSQ) of integers in the interval $[0, 18]$. An example may be the sequence of 28 CLs

$$4, 4, 4, 4, 4, 3, 3, 3, 6, 6, 6, 6, 6, 6, 6, 6, 6, 6, 0, 0, 0, 0, 0, 0, 2, 2, 2, 2$$

that's compressed to the 16-number SSQ

$$4, 16, 01_2, 3, 3, 3, 6, 16, 11_2, 16, 00_2, 17, 11_2, 2, 16, 00_2,$$

or, in decimal, $4, 16, 1, 3, 3, 3, 6, 16, 3, 16, 0, 17, 3, 2, 16, 0.$

Step 2. Prepare Huffman codes for the SSQ in order to compress it further. Our example SSQ contains the following numbers (with their frequencies in parentheses): 0(2), 1(1), 2(1), 3(5), 4(1), 6(1), 16(4), 17(1). Its initial and standard Huffman trees are shown in Figure 3.12a,b. The standard tree can be represented by the SSQ of eight lengths 4, 5, 5, 1, 5, 5, 2, and 4. These are the lengths of the Huffman codes assigned to the eight numbers 0, 1, 2, 3, 4, 6, 16, and 17, respectively.

Step 3. This SSQ of eight lengths is now extended to 19 numbers by inserting zeros in the positions that correspond to unused CCLs.

Position:	0	1	2	3	4	5	6	7	8	9	10	11	12	13	14	15	16	17	18
CCL:	4	5	5	1	5	0	5	0	0	0	0	0	0	0	0	0	2	4	0

Next, the 19 CCLs are permuted according to

Position:	16	17	18	0	8	7	9	6	10	5	11	4	12	3	13	2	14	1	15
CCL:	2	4	0	4	0	0	0	5	0	0	0	5	0	1	0	5	0	5	0

The reason for the permutation is to end up with a sequence of 19 CCLs that's likely to have trailing zeros. The SSQ of 19 CCLs minus its trailing zeros is written on the output, preceded by its actual length, which can be between 4 and 19. Each CCL is written as a 3-bit number. In our example, there is just one trailing zero, so the 18-number sequence 2, 4, 0, 4, 0, 0, 0, 5, 0, 0, 0, 5, 0, 1, 0, 5, 0, 5 is written on the output as the final, compressed code of one prefix-code table. In mode 3, each block of compressed data requires two prefix-code tables, so two such sequences are written on the output.

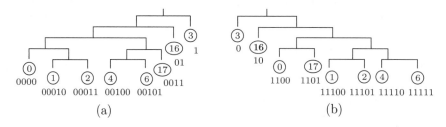

Figure 3.12: Two Huffman Trees for Code Lengths.

A reader finally reaching this point (sweating profusely with such deep concentration on so many details) may respond with the single word "insane." This scheme of Phil

Katz for compressing the two prefix-code tables per block is devilishly complex and hard to follow, but it works!

The format of a block in mode 3 is as follows:

1. The 3-bit header 010 or 110.

2. A 5-bit parameter HLIT indicating the number of codes in the literal/length code table. This table has codes 0–256 for the literals, code 256 for end-of-block, and the 30 codes 257–286 for the lengths. Some of the 30 length codes may be missing, so this parameter indicates how many of the length codes actually exist in the table.

3. A 5-bit parameter HDIST indicating the size of the code table for distances. There are 30 codes in this table, but some may be missing.

4. A 4-bit parameter HCLEN indicating the number of CCLs (there may be between 4 and 19 CCLs).

5. A sequence of HCLEN + 4 CCLs, each a 3-bit number.

6. A sequence SQ of HLIT + 257 CLs for the literal/length code table. This SQ is compressed as explained earlier.

7. A sequence SQ of HDIST + 1 CLs for the distance code table. This SQ is compressed as explained earlier.

8. The compressed data, encoded with the two prefix-code tables.

9. The end-of-block code (the prefix code of edoc 256).

Each CCL is written on the output as a 3-bit number, but the CCLs are Huffman codes of up to 19 symbols. When the Huffman algorithm is applied to a set of 19 symbols, the resulting codes may be up to 18 bits long. It is the responsibility of the encoder to ensure that each CCL is a 3-bit number and none exceeds 7. The formal definition [RFC1951 96] of Deflate does not specify how this restriction on the CCLs is to be achieved.

3.3.3 The Hash Table

This short section discusses the problem of locating a match in the search buffer. The buffer is 32 Kb long, so a linear search is too slow. Searching linearly for a match to any string requires an examination of the entire search buffer. If Deflate is to be able to compress large data files in reasonable time, it should use a sophisticated search method. The method proposed by the Deflate standard is based on a hash table. This method is strongly recommended by the standard, but is not required. An encoder using a different search method is still compliant and can call itself a Deflate encoder. Those unfamiliar with hash tables should consult any text on data structures.

> If it wasn't for faith, there would be no living in this world; we couldn't even eat hash with any safety.
>
> —Josh Billings

Instead of separate look-ahead and search buffers, the encoder should have a single, 32 Kb buffer. The buffer is filled up with input data and initially all of it is a look-ahead buffer. In the original LZ77 method, once symbols have been examined, they are moved into the search buffer. The Deflate encoder, in contrast, does not move the data in its buffer and instead moves a pointer (or a separator) from left to right, to indicate the boundary between the look-ahead and search buffers. Short, 3-symbol strings from the look-ahead buffer are hashed and added to the hash table. After hashing a string, the encoder examines the hash table for matches. Assuming that a symbol occupies n bits, a string of three symbols can have values in the interval $[0, 2^{3n} - 1]$. If $2^{3n} - 1$ isn't too large, the hash function can return values in this interval, which tends to minimize the number of collisions. Otherwise, the hash function can return values in a smaller interval, such as 32 Kb (the size of the Deflate buffer).

We demonstrate the principles of Deflate hashing with the 17-symbol string

abbaabbaabaabaaaa
12345678901234567

Initially, the entire 17-location buffer is the look-ahead buffer and the hash table is empty

0 1 2 3 4 5 6 7 8
|0|0|0|0|0|0|0|0|...

We assume that the first triplet abb hashes to 7. The encoder outputs the raw symbol a, moves this symbol to the search buffer (by moving the separator between the two buffers to the right), and sets cell 7 of the hash table to 1.

a|bbaabbaabaabaaaa   0 1 2 3 4 5 6 7 8
1 2345678901234567 |0|0|0|0|0|0|0|1|...

The next three steps hash the strings bba, baa, and aab to, say, 1, 5, and 0. The encoder outputs the three raw symbols b, b, and a, moves the separator, and updates the hash table as follows:

abba|abbaabaabaaaa   0 1 2 3 4 5 6 7 8
1234 5678901234567 |4|2|0|0|0|3|0|1|...

Next, the triplet abb is hashed, and we already know that it hashes to 7. The encoder finds 1 in cell 7 of the hash table, so it looks for a string that starts with abb at position 1 of its buffer. It finds a match of size 6, so it outputs the pair $(5 - 1, 6)$. The offset (4) is the difference between the start of the current string (5) and the start of the matching string (1). There are now two strings that start with abb, so cell 7 should point to both. It therefore becomes the start of a linked list (or chain) whose data items are 5 and 1. Notice that the 5 precedes the 1 in this chain, so that later searches of the chain will find the 5 first and will therefore tend to find matches with the smallest offset, because those have short Huffman codes.

abbaa|bbaabaabaaaa   0 1 2 3 4 5 6 7 8
12345 678901234567 |4|2|0|0|0|3|0|

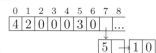

Six symbols have been matched at position 5, so the next position to consider is $6 + 5 = 11$. While moving to position 11, the encoder hashes the five 3-symbol strings it finds along the way (those that start at positions 6 through 10). They are bba, baa, aab, aba, and baa. They hash to 1, 5, 0, 3, and 5 (we arbitrarily assume that aba hashes to 3). Cell 3 of the hash table is set to 9, and cells 0, 1, and 5 become the starts of linked chains.

abbaabbaab|aabaaaa   0 1 2 3 4 5 6 7 8
1234567890 1234567 | | |0|9|0| |0| |...

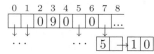

Continuing from position 11, string aab hashes to 0. Following the chain from cell 0, we find matches at positions 4 and 8. The latter match is longer and matches the 5-symbol string aabaa. The encoder outputs the pair $(11 - 8, 5)$ and moves to position

$11 + 5 = 16$. While doing so, it also hashes the 3-symbol strings that start at positions 12, 13, 14, and 15. Each hash value is added to the hash table. (End of example.)

It is clear that the chains can become very long. An example is an image file with large uniform areas where many 3-symbol strings will be identical, will hash to the same value, and will be added to the same cell in the hash table. Since a chain must be searched linearly, a long chain defeats the purpose of a hash table. This is why Deflate has a parameter that limits the size of a chain. If a chain exceeds this size, its oldest elements should be truncated. The Deflate standard does not specify how this should be done and leaves it to the discretion of the implementor. Limiting the size of a chain reduces the compression quality but can reduce the compression time significantly. In situations where compression time is unimportant, the user can specify long chains.

Also, selecting the longest match may not always be the best strategy; the offset should also be taken into account. A 3-symbol match with a small offset may eventually use fewer bits (once the offset is replaced with a variable-length code) than a 4-symbol match with a large offset.

⋄ **Exercise 3.9:** Hashing 3-byte sequences prevents the encoder from finding matches of length 1 and 2 bytes. Is this a serious limitation?

3.3.4 Conclusions

Deflate is a general-purpose lossless compression algorithm that has proved valuable over the years as part of several popular compression programs. The method requires memory for the look-ahead and search buffers and for the two prefix-code tables. However, the memory size needed by the encoder and decoder is independent of the size of the data or the blocks. The implementation is not trivial, but is simpler than that of some modern methods such as JPEG 2000 or MPEG. Compression algorithms that are geared for specific types of data, such as audio or video, may perform better than Deflate on such data, but Deflate normally produces compression factors of 2.5 to 3 on text, slightly smaller for executable files, and somewhat bigger for images. Most important, even in the worst case, Deflate expands the data by only 5 bytes per 32 Kb block. Finally, free implementations that avoid patents are available. Notice that the original method, as designed by Phil Katz, has been patented (United States patent 5,051,745, September 24, 1991) and assigned to PKWARE.

Chapter Summary

The Huffman algorithm is based on the probabilities of the individual data symbols, which is why it is considered a statistical compression method. Dictionary-based compression methods are different. They do not compute or estimate symbol probabilities and they do not use a statistical model of the data. They are based on the fact that the data files that are of interest to us, the files we want to compress and keep for later use, are not random. A typical data file features redundancies in the form of patterns and repetitions of data symbols.

A dictionary-based compression method selects strings of symbols from the input and employs a dictionary to encode each string as a *token*. The dictionary consists of strings of symbols, and it may be static or dynamic (adaptive). The former type is permanent, sometimes allowing the addition of strings but no deletions, whereas the latter type holds strings previously found in the input, thereby allowing for additions and deletions of strings as new input is being read.

If the data features many repetitions, then many input strings will match strings in the dictionary. A matched string is replaced by a token, and compression is achieved if the token is shorter than the matched string. If the next input symbols is not found in the dictionary, then it is output in raw form and is also added to the dictionary. The following points are especially important: (1) Any dictionary-based method must write the raw items and tokens on the output such that the decoder will be able to distinguish them. (2) Also, the capacity of the dictionary is finite and any particular algorithm must have explicit rules specifying what to do when the (adaptive) dictionary fills up. Many dictionary-based methods have been developed over the years, and these two points constitute the main differences between them.

This book describes the following dictionary-based compression methods. The LZ77 algorithm (Section 1.3.1) is simple but not very efficient because its output tokens are triplets and are therefore large. The LZ78 method (Section 3.1) generates tokens that are pairs, and the LZW algorithm (Section 3.2) output single-item tokens. The Deflate algorithm (Section 3.3), which lies at the heart of the various zip implementations, is more sophisticated. It employs several types of blocks and a hash table, for a very effective compression.

Self-Assessment Questions

1. Redo Exercise 3.1 for various values of P (the probability of a match).

2.   Study the topic of patents in data compression. A good starting point is [patents 07].

3. Test your knowledge of the LZW algorithm by manually encoding several short strings, similar to Exercise 3.3.

> Words—so innocent and powerless as they are, as standing in a
> dictionary, how potent for good and evil they become
> in the hands of one who knows how to combine them.
>
> —Nathaniel Hawthorne

Part II:
Advanced Techniques

The second part of this book is concerned with advanced techniques. The original and unusual technique of arithmetic coding is the topic of Chapter 4. Chapter 5 is devoted to image compression. It starts with the chief approaches to the compression of images, explains orthogonal transforms, and discusses the JPEG algorithm, perhaps the best example of the use of these transforms. The second part of this chapter introduces the wavelet transform. It illustrates this transform and its advantages for image compression. It explains the differences between orthogonal and subband transforms, and it presents the WSQ method for fingerprint compression as an example of the application of a wavelet transform. Chapter 6 is devoted to the compression of audio data and in particular to the technique of linear prediction. Finally, other approaches to compression—such as the Burrows–Wheeler method, symbol ranking, and SCSU and BOCU-1—are given their due in Chapter 7.

> Great dancers aren't great because of their technique; they are great because of their passion.
> —Unknown

4
Arithmetic Coding

 Prelude

The Huffman algorithm is simple, efficient, and produces the best codes for the individual data symbols. The discussion in Chapter 2 however, shows that the only case where it produces ideal variable-length codes (codes whose average size equals the entropy) is when the symbols have probabilities of occurrence that are negative powers of 2 (i.e., numbers such as 1/2, 1/4, or 1/8). This is because the Huffman method assigns a code with an integral number of bits to each symbol in the alphabet. Information theory tells us that a symbol with probability 0.4 should ideally be assigned a 1.32-bit code, because $-\log_2 0.4 \approx 1.32$. The Huffman method, however, normally assigns such a symbol a code of one or two bits.

Arithmetic coding overcomes the problem of assigning integer codes to the individual symbols by assigning one (normally long) code to the entire input file. The method starts with a certain interval, it reads the input file symbol by symbol, and employs the probability of each symbol to narrow the interval. Specifying a narrower interval requires more bits, as illustrated in the next paragraph. Thus, the narrow intervals constructed by the algorithm require longer and longer numbers to specify their boundaries. To achieve compression, the algorithm is designed such that a high-probability symbol narrows the interval less than a low-probability symbol, with the result that high-probability symbols contribute fewer bits to the output.

An interval can be specified by its lower and upper limits or by one limit and the width. We use the latter method to illustrate how an interval's specification becomes longer as the interval narrows. The interval $[0, 1]$ can be specified by the two 1-bit numbers 0 and 1. The interval $[0.1, 0.512]$ can be specified by the longer numbers 0.1 and 0.512. The very narrow interval $[0.12575, 0.1257586]$ is specified by the long numbers 0.12575 and 0.0000086.

The output of arithmetic coding is interpreted as a number in the range $[0, 1)$. (The notation $[a, b)$ means the range of real numbers from a to b, including a but not including b. The range is "closed" at a and "open" at b.) Thus, the code 9746509 is interpreted as 0.9746509, although the 0. part is not included in the output file.

Before we plunge into the details, here is a bit of history. The principle of arithmetic coding was first proposed by Peter Elias in the early 1960s. Early practical implementations of this method were developed by several researchers in the 1970s. Of special mention are [Moffat et al. 98] and [Witten et al. 87]. They discuss both the principles and details of practical arithmetic coding and include examples.

4.1 The Basic Idea

The first step is to compute, or at least to estimate, the frequencies of occurrence of each input symbol. For best results, the precise frequencies are computed by reading the entire input file in the first pass of a two-pass compression job. However, if the program can get good estimates of the frequencies from a different source, the first pass may be omitted.

The first example involves the three symbols a_1, a_2, and a_3, with probabilities $P_1 = 0.4$, $P_2 = 0.5$, and $P_3 = 0.1$, respectively. The interval $[0, 1)$ is divided among the three symbols by assigning each a subinterval proportional in size to its probability. The order of the subintervals is unimportant. In our example, the three symbols are assigned the subintervals $[0, 0.4)$, $[0.4, 0.9)$, and $[0.9, 1.0)$. To encode the string $a_2a_2a_2a_3$, we start with the interval $[0, 1)$. The first symbol a_2 reduces this interval to the subinterval from its 40% point to its 90% point. The result is $[0.4, 0.9)$. The second a_2 reduces $[0.4, 0.9)$ in the same way (see note below) to $[0.6, 0.85)$. The third a_2 reduces this to $[0.7, 0.825)$ and the a_3 reduces this to the stretch from the 90% point of $[0.7, 0.825)$ to its 100% point, producing $[0.8125, 0.8250)$. The final code our method produces can be any number in this final range.

Notice that the subinterval $[0.6, 0.85)$ is obtained from the interval $[0.4, 0.9)$ by $0.4 + (0.9 - 0.4) \times 0.4 = 0.6$ and $0.4 + (0.9 - 0.4) \times 0.9 = 0.85$.

With this example in mind, it should be easy to understand the following rules, which summarize the main steps of arithmetic coding:

1. Start by defining the current interval as $[0, 1)$.
2. Repeat the following two steps for each symbol s in the input:
    2.1. Divide the current interval into subintervals whose sizes are proportional to the symbols' probabilities.
    2.2. Select the subinterval for s and define it as the new current interval.
3. When the entire input has been processed in this way, the output should be any number that uniquely identifies the current interval (i.e., any number inside the current interval).

For each symbol processed, the current interval gets smaller, so it takes more bits to express it, but the point is that the final output is a single number and does not consist of codes for the individual symbols. The average code size can be obtained by dividing the size of the output (in bits) by the size of the input (in symbols). Notice also that the probabilities used in step 2.1 may change all the time, since they may be supplied by an adaptive probability model (Section 4.5).

> A theory has only the alternative of being right or wrong. A model has a third possibility: it may be right, but irrelevant.
>
> —Eigen Manfred, *The Physicist's Conception of Nature*

The next example is a bit more complex. We show the compression steps for the short string SWISS␣MISS. Table 4.1 shows the information prepared in the first step (the *statistical model* of the data). The five symbols appearing in the input may be arranged in any order. The number of occurrences of each symbol is counted and is divided by the string size, 10, to determine the symbol's probability. The range $[0, 1)$ is then divided among the symbols, in any order, with each symbol receiving a subinterval equal in size to its probability. Thus, S receives the subinterval $[0.5, 1.0)$ (of size 0.5), whereas the subinterval of I is of size 0.2 $[0.2, 0.4)$. The cumulative frequencies column is used by the decoding algorithm on page 130.

Char	Freq	Prob.	Range	CumFreq
		Total CumFreq=		10
S	5	$5/10 = 0.5$	$[0.5, 1.0)$	5
W	1	$1/10 = 0.1$	$[0.4, 0.5)$	4
I	2	$2/10 = 0.2$	$[0.2, 0.4)$	2
M	1	$1/10 = 0.1$	$[0.1, 0.2)$	1
␣	1	$1/10 = 0.1$	$[0.0, 0.1)$	0

Table 4.1: Frequencies and Probabilities of Five Symbols.

The symbols and frequencies in Table 4.1 are written on the output before any of the bits of the compressed code. This table will be the first thing input by the decoder.

The encoder starts by allocating two variables, Low and High, and setting them to 0 and 1, respectively. They define an interval [Low, High). As symbols are being input and processed, the values of Low and High are moved closer together, to narrow the interval.

After processing the first symbol S, Low and High are updated to 0.5 and 1, respectively. The resulting code for the entire input file will be a number in this range $(0.5 \leq \text{Code} < 1.0)$. The rest of the input will determine precisely where, in the interval $[0.5, 1)$, the final code will lie. A good way to understand the process is to imagine that the new interval $[0.5, 1)$ is divided among the five symbols of our alphabet using the same proportions as for the original interval $[0, 1)$. The result is the five subintervals $[0.5, 0.55)$, $[0.55, 0.60)$, $[0.60, 0.70)$, $[0.70, 0.75)$, and $[0.75, 1.0)$. When the next symbol W is input, the third of those subintervals is selected and is again divided into five subsubintervals.

As more symbols are being input and processed, Low and High are being updated according to

```
NewHigh:=OldLow+Range*HighRange(X);
NewLow:=OldLow+Range*LowRange(X);
```

where $\texttt{Range}=\texttt{OldHigh}-\texttt{OldLow}$ and $\texttt{LowRange(X)}$, $\texttt{HighRange(X)}$ indicate the low and high limits of the range of symbol $\texttt{X}$, respectively. In the example above, the second input symbol is $\texttt{W}$, so we update Low $:= 0.5 + (1.0 - 0.5) \times 0.4 = 0.70$, High $:= 0.5 + (1.0 - 0.5) \times 0.5 = 0.75$. The new interval $[0.70, 0.75)$ covers the stretch $[40\%, 50\%)$ of the subrange of $\texttt{S}$. Table 4.2 shows all the steps of coding the string $\texttt{SWISS\_MISS}$ (the first three steps are illustrated graphically in Figure 4.3). The final code is the final value of $\texttt{Low}$, 0.71753375, of which only the eight digits $\texttt{71753375}$ need be written on the output (but see later for a modification of this statement).

Char.		The computation of low and high
S	L	$0.0 + (1.0 - 0.0) \times 0.5 = 0.5$
	H	$0.0 + (1.0 - 0.0) \times 1.0 = 1.0$
W	L	$0.5 + (1.0 - 0.5) \times 0.4 = 0.70$
	H	$0.5 + (1.0 - 0.5) \times 0.5 = 0.75$
I	L	$0.7 + (0.75 - 0.70) \times 0.2 = 0.71$
	H	$0.7 + (0.75 - 0.70) \times 0.4 = 0.72$
S	L	$0.71 + (0.72 - 0.71) \times 0.5 = 0.715$
	H	$0.71 + (0.72 - 0.71) \times 1.0 = 0.72$
S	L	$0.715 + (0.72 - 0.715) \times 0.5 = 0.7175$
	H	$0.715 + (0.72 - 0.715) \times 1.0 = 0.72$
␣	L	$0.7175 + (0.72 - 0.7175) \times 0.0 = 0.7175$
	H	$0.7175 + (0.72 - 0.7175) \times 0.1 = 0.71775$
M	L	$0.7175 + (0.71775 - 0.7175) \times 0.1 = 0.717525$
	H	$0.7175 + (0.71775 - 0.7175) \times 0.2 = 0.717550$
I	L	$0.717525 + (0.71755 - 0.717525) \times 0.2 = 0.717530$
	H	$0.717525 + (0.71755 - 0.717525) \times 0.4 = 0.717535$
S	L	$0.717530 + (0.717535 - 0.717530) \times 0.5 = 0.7175325$
	H	$0.717530 + (0.717535 - 0.717530) \times 1.0 = 0.717535$
S	L	$0.7175325 + (0.717535 - 0.7175325) \times 0.5 = 0.71753375$
	H	$0.7175325 + (0.717535 - 0.7175325) \times 1.0 = 0.717535$

Table 4.2: The Process of Arithmetic Encoding.

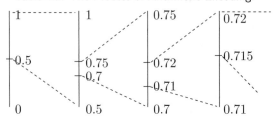

Figure 4.3: Division of the Probability Interval.

The decoder operates in reverse. It starts by inputting the symbols and their ranges, and reconstructing Table 4.1. It then inputs the rest of the code. The first digit is 7, so the decoder immediately knows that the entire code is a number of the form $0.7\ldots$. This number is inside the subrange $[0.5, 1)$ of S, so the first symbol is S. The decoder then eliminates the effect of symbol S from the code by subtracting the lower limit 0.5 of S and dividing by the width of the subrange of S (0.5). The result is 0.4350675, which tells the decoder that the next symbol is W (since the subrange of W is $[0.4, 0.5)$).

To eliminate the effect of symbol X from the code, the decoder performs the operation `Code:=(Code-LowRange(X))/Range`, where `Range` is the width of the subrange of X. Table 4.4 summarizes the steps for decoding our example string (notice that it has two rows per symbol).

The next example is of three symbols with probabilities listed in Table 4.5a. Notice that the probabilities are very different. One is large (97.5%) and the others much smaller. This is an example of skewed probabilities.

Encoding the string $a_2a_2a_1a_3a_3$ produces the strange numbers (accurate to 16 digits) in Table 4.6, where the two rows for each symbol correspond to the `Low` and `High` values, respectively. Figure 4.7 lists the *Mathematica* code that computed the table.

At first glance, it seems that the resulting code is longer than the original string, but Section 4.4 shows how to figure out the true compression produced by arithmetic coding.

The steps of decoding this string are listed in Table 4.8 and illustrate a special problem. After eliminating the effect of a_1, on line 3, the result is 0. Earlier, we implicitly assumed that this means the end of the decoding process, but now we know that there are two more occurrences of a_3 that should be decoded. These are shown on lines 4 and 5 of the table. This problem always occurs when the last symbol in the input is the one whose subrange starts at zero. In order to distinguish between such a symbol and the end of the input, we need to define an additional symbol, the end-of-input (or end-of-file, eof). This symbol should be included in the frequency table (with a very small probability, see Table 4.5b) and it should be encoded once, at the end of the input.

Tables 4.9 and 4.10 show how the string $a_3a_3a_3a_3$eof is encoded into the number 0.000000287808618476417, and then decoded properly. Without the eof symbol, a string of all a_3s would have been encoded into a 0.

Notice how the low value is 0 until the eof is input and processed, and how the high value quickly approaches 0. Now is the time to mention that the final code does not have to be the final low value but can be any number between the final low and high values. In the example of $a_3a_3a_3a_3$eof, the final code can be the much shorter number 0.0000002878086 (or 0.0000002878087 or even 0.0000002878088).

$\diamond$ **Exercise 4.1:** Encode the string $a_2a_2a_2a_2$ and summarize the results in a table similar to Table 4.9. How do the results differ from those of the string $a_3a_3a_3a_3$?

If the size of the input is known, it is possible to do without an eof symbol. The encoder can start by writing this size (unencoded) on the output. The decoder reads the size, starts decoding, and stops when the decoded file reaches this size. If the decoder reads the compressed file byte by byte, the encoder may have to add some zeros at the end, to make sure the compressed file can be read in groups of eight bits.

Char.	Code − low	Range
S	$0.71753375 - 0.5 = 0.21753375$	$/0.5 = 0.4350675$
W	$0.4350675 - 0.4 = 0.0350675$	$/0.1 = 0.350675$
I	$0.350675 - 0.2 = 0.150675$	$/0.2 = 0.753375$
S	$0.753375 - 0.5 = 0.253375$	$/0.5 = 0.50675$
S	$0.50675 - 0.5 = 0.00675$	$/0.5 = 0.0135$
␣	$0.0135 - 0 = 0.0135$	$/0.1 = 0.135$
M	$0.135 - 0.1 = 0.035$	$/0.1 = 0.35$
I	$0.35 - 0.2 = 0.15$	$/0.2 = 0.75$
S	$0.75 - 0.5 = 0.25$	$/0.5 = 0.5$
S	$0.5 - 0.5 = 0$	$/0.5 = 0$

Table 4.4: The Process of Arithmetic Decoding.

Char	Prob.	Range
a_1	0.001838	$[0.998162, \quad 1.0)$
a_2	0.975	$[0.023162, 0.998162)$
a_3	0.023162	$[0.0, \quad 0.023162)$

(a)

Char	Prob.	Range
eof	0.000001	$[0.999999, \quad 1.0)$
a_1	0.001837	$[0.998162, 0.999999)$
a_2	0.975	$[0.023162, 0.998162)$
a_3	0.023162	$[0.0, \quad 0.023162)$

(b)

Table 4.5: (Skewed) Probabilities of Three Symbols.

a_2	$0.0 + (1.0 - 0.0) \times 0.023162 = 0.023162$
	$0.0 + (1.0 - 0.0) \times 0.998162 = 0.998162$
a_2	$0.023162 + .975 \times 0.023162 = 0.04574495$
	$0.023162 + .975 \times 0.998162 = 0.99636995$
a_1	$0.04574495 + 0.950625 \times 0.998162 = 0.99462270125$
	$0.04574495 + 0.950625 \times 1.0 = 0.99636995$
a_3	$0.99462270125 + 0.00174724875 \times 0.0 = 0.99462270125$
	$0.99462270125 + 0.00174724875 \times 0.023162 = 0.994663171025547$
a_3	$0.99462270125 + 0.0000404697755474 9998 \times 0.0 = 0.99462270125$
	$0.99462270125 + 0.00004046977554749998 \times 0.023162 = 0.994623638610941$

Table 4.6: Encoding the String $a_2 a_2 a_1 a_3 a_3$.

```
lowRange={0.998162,0.023162,0.};
highRange={1.,0.998162,0.023162};
low=0.; high=1.;
enc[i_]:=Module[{nlow,nhigh,range},
range=high-low;
nhigh=low+range highRange[[i]];
nlow=low+range lowRange[[i]];
low=nlow; high=nhigh;
Print["r=",N[range,25]," l=",N[low,17]," h=",N[high,17]]]
enc[2]
enc[2]
enc[1]
enc[3]
enc[3]
```

Figure 4.7: *Mathematica* Code for Table 4.6.

Char.	Code − low		Range	
a_2	$0.99462270125 - 0.023162 = 0.97146170125$		$/0.975$	$= 0.99636995$
a_2	$0.99636995 - 0.023162$	$= 0.97320795$	$/0.975$	$= 0.998162$
a_1	$0.998162 - 0.998162$	$= 0.0$	$/0.00138$	$= 0.0$
a_3	$0.0 - 0.0$	$= 0.0$	$/0.023162$	$= 0.0$
a_3	$0.0 - 0.0$	$= 0.0$	$/0.023162$	$= 0.0$

Table 4.8: Decoding the String $a_2a_2a_1a_3a_3$.

a_3	$0.0 + (1.0 - 0.0) \times 0.0 = 0.0$
	$0.0 + (1.0 - 0.0) \times 0.023162 = 0.023162$
a_3	$0.0 + 0.023162 \times 0.0 = 0.0$
	$0.0 + 0.023162 \times 0.023162 = 0.000536478244$
a_3	$0.0 + 0.000536478244 \times 0.0 = 0.0$
	$0.0 + 0.000536478244 \times 0.023162 = 0.000012425909087528$
a_3	$0.0 + 0.000012425909087528 \times 0.0 = 0.0$
	$0.0 + 0.000012425909087528 \times 0.023162 = 0.000000287808906285 3235$
eof	$0.0 + 0.000000287808906285 3235 \times 0.999999 = 0.000000287808618476 4172$
	$0.0 + 0.000000287808906285 3235 \times 1.0 = 0.000000287808906285 3235$

Table 4.9: Encoding the String $a_3a_3a_3a_3$eof.

Char.	Code−low		Range	
a_3	0.000000287808618476 4172-0	=0.000000287808618476 4172	/0.023162	=0.000012425896661618 91247
a_3	0.000012425896661618 91247-0	=0.000012425896661618 91247/0.023162		=0.000536477707521756
a_3	0.000536477707521756-0	=0.000536477707521756	/0.023162	=0.023161976838
a_3	0.023161976838-0.0	=0.023161976838	/0.023162	=0.999999
eof	0.999999-0.999999	=0.0	/0.000001	=0.0

Table 4.10: Decoding the String $a_3a_3a_3a_3$eof.

4.2 Implementation Details

The encoding process described earlier is not practical, because it requires that numbers of unlimited precision be stored in Low and High. The decoding process described on page 127 ("The decoder then eliminates the effect of the S from the code by subtracting...and dividing ...") is simple in principle but also impractical. The code, which is a single number, is normally long and may also be very long. A 1 Mbyte file may be encoded into, say, a 500 Kbyte file that consists of a single number. Dividing a 500 Kbyte number is complex and slow.

Any practical implementation of arithmetic coding should be based on integers, not reals (because floating-point arithmetic is slow and precision is lost), and they should not be very long (preferably just single precision). We describe such an implementation here, using two integer variables Low and High. In our example they are four decimal digits long, but in practice they might be 16 or 32 bits long. These variables hold the low and high limits of the current subinterval, but we don't let them grow too much. A glance at Table 4.2 shows that once the leftmost digits of Low and High become identical, they never change. We therefore shift such digits out of the two variables and write one digit on the output. This way, the two variables don't have to hold the entire code, just the most-recent part of it. As digits are shifted out of the two variables, a zero is shifted into the right end of Low and a 9 into the right end of High. A good way to understand this is to think of each of the two variables as the left ends of two infinitely-long numbers. Low contains $xxxx00\ldots$, and High= $yyyy99\ldots$.

One problem is that High should be initialized to 1, but the contents of Low and High should be interpreted as fractions less than 1. The solution is to initialize High to 9999..., to represent the infinite fraction 0.999..., because this fraction equals 1.

(This is easy to prove. If 0.999... is less than 1, then the average $a = (1+0.999\ldots)/2$ would be a number between 0.999... and 1, but there is no way to write a. It is impossible to give it more digits than to 0.999..., because the latter already has an infinite number of digits. It is impossible to make the digits any bigger, since they are already 9's. This is why the infinite fraction 0.999... must equal 1.)

◇ **Exercise 4.2:** Write the number 0.5 in binary.

Table 4.11 describes the encoding process of the string SWISS␣MISS. Column 1 lists the next input symbol. Column 2 shows the new values of Low and High. Column 3 shows these values as scaled integers, after High has been decremented by 1. Column 4 shows the next digit sent to the output. Column 5 shows the new values of Low and High after being shifted to the left. Notice how the last step sends the four digits 3750 to the output. The final output is 717533750.

Decoding is the opposite of encoding. We start with Low=0000, High=9999, and Code=7175 (the first four digits of the compressed file). These are updated at each step of the decoding loop. Low and High approach each other (and both approach Code) until their most significant digits are the same. They are then shifted to the left, which separates them again, and Code is also shifted at that time. An index is calculated at each step and is used to search the cumulative frequencies column of Table 4.1 to figure out the current symbol.

Each iteration of the loop consists of the following steps:

1	2	3	4	5
S	$L = \quad 0+(1 \quad - \quad 0) \times 0.5 = 0.5$	5000		5000
	$H = \quad 0+(1 \quad - \quad 0) \times 1.0 = 1.0$	9999		9999
W	$L = \quad 0.5+(1 \quad - \quad .5) \times 0.4 = 0.7$	7000	7	0000
	$H = \quad 0.5+(1 \quad - \quad .5) \times 0.5 = 0.75$	7499	7	4999
I	$L = \quad 0+(0.5 \quad - \quad 0) \times 0.2 = 0.1$	1000	1	0000
	$H = \quad 0+(0.5 \quad - \quad 0) \times 0.4 = 0.2$	1999	1	9999
S	$L = \quad 0+(1 \quad - \quad 0) \times 0.5 = 0.5$	5000		5000
	$H = \quad 0+(1 \quad - \quad 0) \times 1.0 = 1.0$	9999		9999
S	$L = \quad 0.5+(1 \quad - \quad 0.5) \times 0.5 = 0.75$	7500		7500
	$H = \quad 0.5+(1 \quad - \quad 0.5) \times 1.0 = 1.0$	9999		9999
␣	$L = 0.75+(1 \quad - \quad 0.75) \times 0.0 = 0.75$	7500	7	5000
	$H = 0.75+(1 \quad - \quad 0.75) \times 0.1 = 0.775$	7749	7	7499
M	$L = \quad 0.5+(0.75 - 0.5) \times 0.1 = 0.525$	5250	5	2500
	$H = \quad 0.5+(0.75 - 0.5) \times 0.2 = 0.55$	5499	5	4999
I	$L = 0.25+(0.5 - 0.25) \times 0.2 = 0.3$	3000	3	0000
	$H = 0.25+(0.5 - 0.25) \times 0.4 = 0.35$	3499	3	4999
S	$L = \quad 0+(0.5 \quad - \quad 0) \times 0.5 = .25$	2500		2500
	$H = \quad 0+(0.5 \quad - \quad 0) \times 1.0 = 0.5$	4999		4999
S	$L = 0.25+(0.5 - 0.25) \times 0.5 = 0.375$	3750	3750	
	$H = 0.25+(0.5 - 0.25) \times 1.0 = 0.5$	4999		4999

Table 4.11: Encoding SWISS␣MISS by Shifting.

1. Compute `index:=((Code-Low+1)x10-1)/(High-Low+1)` and truncate it to the nearest integer. (The number 10 is the total cumulative frequency in our example.)
2. Use `index` to find the next symbol by comparing it to the cumulative frequencies column in Table 4.1. In the example below, the first value of `index` is 7.1759, truncated to 7. Seven is between the 5 and the 10 in the table, so it selects the S.
3. Update `Low` and `High` according to

```
Low:=Low+(High-Low+1)LowCumFreq[X]/10;
High:=Low+(High-Low+1)HighCumFreq[X]/10-1;
```

where `LowCumFreq[X]` and `HighCumFreq[X]` are the cumulative frequencies of symbol `X` and of the symbol above it in Table 4.1.
4. If the leftmost digits of `Low` and `High` are identical, shift `Low`, `High`, and `Code` one position to the left. `Low` gets a 0 entered on the right, `High` gets a 9, and `Code` gets the next input digit from the compressed file.

Here are all the decoding steps for our example:

0. Initialize `Low`=0000, `High`=9999, and `Code`=7175.

1. `index`= $[(7175 - 0 + 1) \times 10 - 1]/(9999 - 0 + 1) = 7.1759 \rightarrow 7$. Symbol S is selected. $Low = 0 + (9999 - 0 + 1) \times 5/10 = 5000$. $High = 0 + (9999 - 0 + 1) \times 10/10 - 1 = 9999$.

2. index= $[(7175 - 5000 + 1) \times 10 - 1]/(9999 - 5000 + 1) = 4.3518 \to 4$. Symbol W is selected.
Low $= 5000 + (9999 - 5000 + 1) \times 4/10 = 7000$. High $= 5000 + (9999 - 5000 + 1) \times 5/10 - 1 = 7499$.
After the 7 is shifted out, we have Low=0000, High=4999, and Code=1753.

3. index= $[(1753 - 0 + 1) \times 10 - 1]/(4999 - 0 + 1) = 3.5078 \to 3$. Symbol I is selected.
Low $= 0 + (4999 - 0 + 1) \times 2/10 = 1000$. High $= 0 + (4999 - 0 + 1) \times 4/10 - 1 = 1999$.
After the 1 is shifted out, we have Low=0000, High=9999, and Code=7533.

4. index= $[(7533 - 0 + 1) \times 10 - 1]/(9999 - 0 + 1) = 7.5339 \to 7$. Symbol S is selected.
Low $= 0 + (9999 - 0 + 1) \times 5/10 = 5000$. High $= 0 + (9999 - 0 + 1) \times 10/10 - 1 = 9999$.

5. index= $[(7533 - 5000 + 1) \times 10 - 1]/(9999 - 5000 + 1) = 5.0678 \to 5$. Symbol S is selected.
Low $= 5000 + (9999 - 5000 + 1) \times 5/10 = 7500$. High $= 5000 + (9999 - 5000 + 1) \times 10/10 - 1 = 9999$.

6. index= $[(7533 - 7500 + 1) \times 10 - 1]/(9999 - 7500 + 1) = 0.1356 \to 0$. Symbol ␣ is selected.
Low $= 7500 + (9999 - 7500 + 1) \times 0/10 = 7500$. High $= 7500 + (9999 - 7500 + 1) \times 1/10 - 1 = 7749$.
After the 7 is shifted out, we have Low=5000, High=7499, and Code=5337.

7. index= $[(5337 - 5000 + 1) \times 10 - 1]/(7499 - 5000 + 1) = 1.3516 \to 1$. Symbol M is selected.
Low $= 5000 + (7499 - 5000 + 1) \times 1/10 = 5250$. High $= 5000 + (7499 - 5000 + 1) \times 2/10 - 1 = 5499$.
After the 5 is shifted out we have Low=2500, High=4999, and Code=3375.

8. index= $[(3375 - 2500 + 1) \times 10 - 1]/(4999 - 2500 + 1) = 3.5036 \to 3$. Symbol I is selected.
Low $= 2500 + (4999 - 2500 + 1) \times 2/10 = 3000$. High $= 2500 + (4999 - 2500 + 1) \times 4/10 - 1 = 3499$.
After the 3 is shifted out we have Low=0000, High=4999, and Code=3750.

9. index= $[(3750 - 0 + 1) \times 10 - 1]/(4999 - 0 + 1) = 7.5018 \to 7$. Symbol S is selected.
Low $= 0 + (4999 - 0 + 1) \times 5/10 = 2500$. High $= 0 + (4999 - 0 + 1) \times 10/10 - 1 = 4999$.

10. index= $[(3750 - 2500 + 1) \times 10 - 1]/(4999 - 2500 + 1) = 5.0036 \to 5$. Symbol S is selected.
Low $= 2500 + (4999 - 2500 + 1) \times 5/10 = 3750$. High $= 2500 + (4999 - 2500 + 1) \times 10/10 - 1 = 4999$.

⋄ **Exercise 4.3:** How does the decoder know to stop the loop at this point?

John's sister (we won't mention her name) wears socks of two different colors, white and gray. She keeps them in the same drawer, completely mixed up. In the drawer she has 20 white socks and 20 gray socks. Assuming that it is dark and she has to find two matching socks. How many socks does she have to take out of the drawer to guarantee that she has a matching pair?

1	2				3	4	5
1	L=0+(1	−	0)×0.0	= 0.0	000000	0	000000
	H=0+(1	−	0)×0.023162	= 0.023162	023162	0	231629
2	L=0+(0.231629 − 0)×0.0			= 0.0	000000	0	000000
	H=0+(0.231629 − 0)×0.023162			= 0.00536478244	005364	0	053649
3	L=0+(0.053649 − 0)×0.0			= 0.0	000000	0	000000
	H=0+(0.053649 − 0)×0.023162			= 0.00124261813	001242	0	012429
4	L=0+(0.012429 − 0)×0.0			= 0.0	000000	0	000000
	H=0+(0.012429 − 0)×0.023162			= 0.00028788049	000287	0	002879
5	L=0+(0.002879 − 0)×0.0			= 0.0	000000	0	000000
	H=0+(0.002879 − 0)×0.023162			= 0.00006668339	000066	0	000669

Table 4.12: Encoding $a_3a_3a_3a_3a_3$ by Shifting.

4.3 Underflow

Table 4.12 shows the steps in encoding the string $a_3a_3a_3a_3a_3$ by shifting. This table is similar to Table 4.11, and it illustrates the problem of underflow. Low and High approach each other, and since Low is always 0 in this example, High loses its significant digits as it approaches Low.

Underflow may happen not just in this case but in any case where Low and High need to converge very closely. Because of the finite size of the Low and High variables, they may reach values of, say, 499996 and 500003, and from there, instead of reaching values where their most significant digits are identical, they reach the values 499999 and 500000. Since the most significant digits are different, the algorithm will not output anything, there will not be any shifts, and the next iteration will only add digits beyond the first six ones. Those digits will be lost, and the first six digits will not change. The algorithm will iterate without generating any output until it reaches the eof.

The solution to this problem is to detect such a case early and rescale both variables. In the example above, rescaling should be done when the two variables reach values of 49xxxx and 50yyyy. Rescaling should squeeze out the second most-significant digits, end up with 4xxxx0 and 5yyyy9, and increment a counter cntr. The algorithm may have to rescale several times before the most-significant digits become equal. At that point, the most-significant digit (which can be either 4 or 5) should be output, followed by cntr zeros (if the two variables converged to 4) or nines (if they converged to 5).

4.4 Final Remarks

All the examples so far have been in decimal, because the required computations are easier to understand in this number base. It turns out that all the algorithms and rules described above apply to the binary case as well and can be used with only one change: every occurrence of 9 (the largest decimal digit) should be replaced with 1 (the largest binary digit).

The examples above don't seem to show any compression at all. It seems that the three example strings SWISS␣MISS, $a_2a_2a_1a_3a_3$, and $a_3a_3a_3a_3$eof are encoded into very long numbers. In fact, it seems that the length of the final code depends on the probabilities involved. The long probabilities of Table 4.5a generate long numbers in the encoding process, whereas the shorter probabilities of Table 4.1 result in the more reasonable Low and High values of Table 4.2. This behavior demands an explanation.

> I am ashamed to tell you to how many figures I carried these computations, having no other business at that time.
>
> —Isaac Newton

To figure out the kind of compression achieved by arithmetic coding, we have to consider two facts: (1) In practice, all the operations are performed on binary numbers, so we have to translate the final results to binary before we can estimate the efficiency of the compression; (2) since the last symbol encoded is the eof, the final code does not have to be the final value of Low; it can be any value between Low and High. This makes it possible to select a shorter number as the final code that's being output.

Table 4.2 encodes string SWISS␣MISS into the final low and high values 0.71753375 and 0.717535. The approximate binary values of these numbers are 0.10110111101100000100101010111 and 0.1011011110110000010111111011, so we can select the number 10110111101100000100 as our final, compressed output. The ten-symbol string has been encoded into a 20-bit number. Does this represent good compression?

The answer is yes. Using the probabilities of Table 4.1, it is easy to calculate the probability of the string SWISS␣MISS. It is $P = 0.5^5 \times 0.1 \times 0.2^2 \times 0.1 \times 0.1 = 1.25 \times 10^{-6}$. The entropy of this string is therefore $-\log_2 P = 19.6096$. Twenty bits are therefore the minimum needed in practice to encode the string.

The symbols in Table 4.5a have probabilities 0.975, 0.001838, and 0.023162. These numbers require quite a few decimal digits, and as a result, the final low and high values in Table 4.6 are the numbers 0.99462270125 and 0.994623638610941. Again it seems that there is no compression, but an analysis similar to the above shows compression that's very close to the entropy.

The probability of the string $a_2a_2a_1a_3a_3$ is $0.975^2 \times 0.001838 \times 0.023162^2 \approx 9.37361 \times 10^{-7}$, and $-\log_2 9.37361 \times 10^{-7} \approx 20.0249$.

The binary representations of the final values of low and high in Table 4.6 are 0.1111111010011111110010111111001 and 0.1111111010011111110100111101. We can select any number between these two, so we select 1111111010011111100, a 19-bit number. (This should have been a 21-bit number, but the numbers in Table 4.6 have limited precision and are not exact.)

⋄ **Exercise 4.4:** Given the three symbols a_1, a_2, and eof, with probabilities $P_1 = 0.4$, $P_2 = 0.5$, and $P_{eof} = 0.1$, encode the string $a_2 a_2 a_2$eof and show that the size of the final code equals the (practical) minimum.

The following argument shows why arithmetic coding can, in principle, be a very efficient compression method. We denote by s a sequence of symbols to be encoded, and by b the number of bits required to encode it. As s gets longer, its probability $P(s)$ gets smaller and b becomes larger. Since the logarithm is the information function, it is easy to see that b should grow at the same rate that $\log_2 P(s)$ shrinks. Their product should therefore be constant, or close to a constant. Information theory shows that b and $P(s)$ satisfy the double inequality

$$2 \le 2^b P(s) < 4,$$

which implies

$$1 - \log_2 P(s) \le b < 2 - \log_2 P(s). \tag{4.1}$$

As s gets longer, its probability $P(s)$ shrinks, the quantity $-\log_2 P(s)$ becomes a large positive number, and the double inequality of Equation (4.1) shows that in the limit, b approaches $-\log_2 P(s)$. This is why arithmetic coding can, in principle, compress a string of symbols to its theoretical limit.

For more information on this topic, see [Moffat et al. 98] and [Witten et al. 87].

Intermezzo

The Real Numbers. We can think of arithmetic coding as a method that compresses a given file by assigning it a real number in the interval $[0, 1)$. Practical implementations of arithmetic coding are based on integers, but in principle we can consider this method as a mapping from the integers (because a data file can be considered a long integer) to the reals. We feel that we understand integers intuitively (because we can count one cow, two cows, etc.), but real numbers have unexpected properties and exhibit unintuitive behavior, a glimpse of which is revealed in this short intermezzo.

The real numbers can be divided into the sets of rational and irrational. A rational number can be represented as the ratio of two integers, whereas an irrational number cannot be represented in this way. The ancient Greeks already knew that $\sqrt{2}$ is irrational. The real numbers can also be divided into algebraic and transcendental numbers. The former is the set of all the reals that are solutions of algebraic equations.

We know many integers (0, 1, 7, 10, and 10^{100} immediately come to mind). We are also familiar with a few irrational numbers ($\sqrt{2}$, e, and π are common examples), so we intuitively feel that most real numbers must be rational and the irrationals are a small minority. Similarly, it is easy to believe that most reals are algebraic and transcendental numbers are rare. However, set theory, the creation, in the 1870s, of Georg Cantor, suggests that there are different kinds of infinities, that the reals constitute a greater infinity than the integers (the integers are said to be countable, while the reals are not), that the rational numbers are countable, while the irrationals are uncountable, and similarly, that the algebraic numbers are countable, while the transcendentals are uncountable; completely counterintuitive notions.

Today, we believe in the existence of atoms. If we start with a chunk of matter, cut it into pieces, cut each piece into smaller pieces, and continue in this way, we will eventually arrive at individual atoms or even their constituents. The real numbers, however, are very different. They can be represented as points along an infinitely long number line, but they are everywhere dense on this line. Thus, any segment on the number line, as short as we can imagine, contains an (uncountable) infinity of real numbers. We cannot arrive at a segment containing just one number by repeatedly segmenting and producing shorter and shorter segments.

We are also familiar with the concepts of successor and predecessor. An integer N has both a successor $N+1$ and a predecessor $N-1$. Cantor has shown that the rational numbers are countable; each can be associated with an integer. Thus, each rational number can be said to have a successor and a predecessor. The real numbers, again, are different. Given a real number a, we cannot point to its successor. If we find another real number b that may be the successor of a, then there is always another number, namely $(a+b)/2$, that is located between a and b and is thus closer to a than b is. We therefore say that a real number does not have a successor or a predecessor; it does not have any immediate neighbors. Yet the real numbers form a continuum, because every point on the number line has a real number that corresponds to it. We cannot imagine any collection of points, numbers, or any other objects that are everywhere (extremely) dense but do not feature a predecessor/successor relation. The real numbers are therefore very counterintuitive.

Pick up two real numbers x and y at random (but with a uniform distribution) in the interval $(0, 1)$, divide them to obtain the real number $R = x/y$, and examine the integer I nearest R. We intuitively feel that I can be even or odd with the same probability, but careful calculations [Weisstein-picking 07] show that the probability of I being even is $0.46460\ldots$ instead of the expected 0.5.

This book contains text, tables, mathematical expressions, and figures, and it can be stored in the computer as a PDF file. Such a file, like any data file, can be considered an integer or a long string B of digits (decimal, binary, or to any other base). A real number is also a (finite or infinite) string of digits. Thus, it is natural to ask, is there a real number that includes B in its string of digits? The answer is yes. Even more, there is a real number that includes in its infinite expansion all the books ever written and all those that will be written. Simply generate all the integers (we will use binary notation) 0, 1, 00, 01, 10, 11, 000, 001, 010, 011, 100, 101, 110, 111, 0000, 0001,... and concatenate them to construct a real number R. From its construction, R includes every possible bitstring and thus every past and future book. (Students pay attention. Both the questions and answers of your next examination are also included in this number. It's just a question of finding this important part of R.)

A Lexicon is a real number that contains in its expansion infinitely many times anything imaginable and unimaginable, everything ever written, or that will ever be written, and any descriptions of every object, process, and phenomenon, real or imaginary. Contrary to any intuitive feelings that we may have, such monsters are not rare. The surprising result, due to [Calude and Zamfirescu 98], is that almost every real number is a Lexicon! This may be easier to comprehend by means of a thought experiment. If we put all the reals in a bag, and pick out one at random, it will almost certainly be a Lexicon.

Gregory Chaitin, the originator of algorithmic information theory, describes in *The Limits of Reason* [Chaitin 07], a real number, denoted by Ω, that is well defined and is a specific number, but is impossible to compute in its entirety.

Unusual, unexpected, counterintuitive, weird!

4.5 Adaptive Arithmetic Coding

The method of arithmetic coding has two features that make it easy to extend:

1. One of the main encoding steps (page 125) updates NewLow and NewHigh. Similarly, one of the main decoding steps (step 3 on page 131) updates Low and High according to

```
Low:=Low+(High-Low+1)LowCumFreq[X]/10;
High:=Low+(High-Low+1)HighCumFreq[X]/10-1;
```

This means that in order to encode symbol X, the encoder should be given the cumulative frequencies of X and of the symbol immediately above it (see Table 4.1 for an example of cumulative frequencies). This also implies that the frequency of X (or, equivalently, its probability) could be modified each time it is encoded, provided that the encoder and the decoder do this in the same way.

2. The order of the symbols in Table 4.1 is unimportant. They can even be swapped in the table during the encoding process as long as the encoder and decoder do it in the same way.

With this in mind, it is easy to understand how adaptive arithmetic coding works. The encoding algorithm has two parts: the probability model and the arithmetic encoder. The model reads the next symbol from the input and invokes the encoder, sending it the symbol and the two required cumulative frequencies. The model then increments the count of the symbol and updates the cumulative frequencies. The point is that the symbol's probability is determined by the model from its *old* count, and the count is incremented only after the symbol has been encoded. This makes it possible for the decoder to mirror the encoder's operations. The encoder knows what the symbol is even before it is encoded, but the decoder has to decode the symbol in order to find out what it is. The decoder can therefore use only the old counts when decoding a symbol. Once the symbol has been decoded, the decoder increments its count and updates the cumulative frequencies in exactly the same way as the encoder.

The model should keep the symbols, their counts (frequencies of occurrence), and their cumulative frequencies in an array. This array should be maintained in sorted order of the counts. Each time a symbol is read and its count is incremented, the model updates the cumulative frequencies, then checks to see whether it is necessary to swap the symbol with another one, to keep the counts in sorted order.

It turns out that there is a simple data structure that allows for both easy search and update. This structure is a balanced binary tree housed in an array. (A balanced binary tree is a complete binary tree where some of the bottom-right nodes may be missing.) The tree should have a node for every symbol in the alphabet, and since it is balanced, its height is $\lceil \log_2 n \rceil$, where n is the size of the alphabet. For $n = 256$, the height of the balanced binary tree is 8, so starting at the root and searching for a node takes at most eight steps. The tree is arranged such that the most probable symbols (the ones with high counts) are located near the root, which speeds up searches. Table 4.13a shows an example of a ten-symbol alphabet with counts. Table 4.13b shows the same symbols sorted by count.

	a_1	a_2	a_3	a_4	a_5	a_6	a_7	a_8	a_9	a_{10}
(a)	11	12	12	2	5	1	2	19	12	8
	a_8	a_2	a_3	a_9	a_1	a_{10}	a_5	a_4	a_7	a_6
(b)	19	12	12	12	11	8	5	2	2	1

Table 4.13: A Ten-Symbol Alphabet With Counts.

The sorted array "houses" the balanced binary tree of Figure 4.15a. This is a simple, elegant way to construct a tree. A balanced binary tree can be housed in an array without the use of any pointers. The rules are (1) the first array location (with index 1) houses the root, (2) the two children of the node at array location i are housed at locations $2i$ and $2i + 1$, and (3) the parent of the node at array location j is housed at location $\lfloor j/2 \rfloor$. It is easy to see how sorting the array has placed the symbols with largest counts at and near the root.

In addition to a symbol and its count, another value is now added to each tree node, the total counts of its left subtree. This will be used to compute cumulative frequencies. The corresponding array is shown in Table 4.14a.

Assume that the next symbol read from the input is a_9. Its count is incremented from 12 to 13. The model keeps the array in sorted order by searching for the farthest array element to the left of a_9 that has a count smaller than that of a_9. This search can be a straight linear search if the array is short enough, or a binary search if the array is long. In our case, symbols a_9 and a_2 should be swapped (Table 4.14b). Figure 4.15b shows the tree after the swap. Notice how the left-subtree counts have been updated.

	a_8	a_2	a_3	a_9	a_1	a_{10}	a_5	a_4	a_7	a_6
(a)	19	12	12	12	11	8	5	2	2	1
	40	16	8	2	1	0	0	0	0	0
	a_8	a_9	a_3	a_2	a_1	a_{10}	a_5	a_4	a_7	a_6
(b)	19	13	12	12	11	8	5	2	2	1
	41	16	8	2	1	0	0	0	0	0

Table 4.14: A Ten-Symbol Alphabet With Counts.

Finally, here is how the cumulative frequencies are computed from this tree. When the cumulative frequency for a symbol X is needed, the model follows the tree branches from the root to the node containing X while adding numbers into an integer `af`. Each time a right branch is taken from an interior node N, `af` is incremented by the two numbers (the count and the left-subtree count) found in that node. When a left branch is taken, `af` is not modified. When the node containing X is reached, the left-subtree count of X is added to `af`, and `af` then contains the quantity `LowCumFreq[X]`.

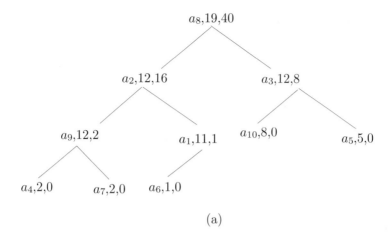

(a)

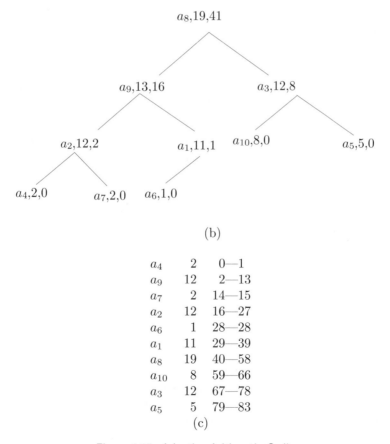

(b)

a_4	2	0—1
a_9	12	2—13
a_7	2	14—15
a_2	12	16—27
a_6	1	28—28
a_1	11	29—39
a_8	19	40—58
a_{10}	8	59—66
a_3	12	67—78
a_5	5	79—83

(c)

Figure 4.15: Adaptive Arithmetic Coding.

As an example, we trace the tree of Figure 4.15a from the root to symbol a_6, whose cumulative frequency is 28. A right branch is taken at node a_2, adding 12 and 16 to `af`. A left branch is taken at node a_1, adding nothing to `af`. When reaching a_6, its left-subtree count, 0, is added to `af`. The result in `af` is $12 + 16 = 28$, as can be verified from Figure 4.15c. The quantity `HighCumFreq[X]` is obtained by adding the count of a_6 (which is 1) to `LowCumFreq[X]`.

To trace the tree and find the path from the root to a_6, the algorithm performs the following steps:

1. Find a_6 in the array housing the tree by means of a binary search. In our example the node with a_6 is found at array location 10.
2. Integer-divide 10 by 2. The remainder is 0, which means that a_6 is the left child of its parent. The quotient is 5, which is the array location of the parent.
3. Location 5 of the array contains a_1. Integer-divide 5 by 2. The remainder is 1, which means that a_1 is the right child of its parent. The quotient is 2, which is the array location of a_1's parent.
4. Location 2 of the array contains a_2. Integer-divide 2 by 2. The remainder is 0, which means that a_2 is the left child of its parent. The quotient is 1, the array location of the root, so the process stops.

The PPM compression method, [Salomon 07], is a good example of a statistical model that invokes an arithmetic encoder in the way described here.

> The driver held out a letter. Boldwood seized it and opened it, expecting another anonymous one—so greatly are people's ideas of probability a mere sense that precedent will repeat itself. "I don't think it is for you, sir," said the man, when he saw Boldwood's action. "Though there is no name I think it is for your shepherd."
>
> —Thomas Hardy, *Far From The Madding Crowd*

4.6 Range Encoding

The use of integers in arithmetic coding is a must in any practical implementation, but it results in slow encoding because of the need for frequent renormalizations. The main steps in any integer-based arithmetic coding implementation are (1) proportional range reduction and (2) range expansion (renormalization).

Range encoding (or range coding) is an improvement of arithmetic coding that reduces the number of renormalizations and thereby speeds up integer-based arithmetic coding by factors of up to 2. The main references are [Schindler 98] and [Campos 06], and the description here is based on the former.

The main idea is to treat the output not as a binary number, but as a number to another base (256 is commonly used as a base, implying that each digit is a byte). This requires fewer renormalizations and no bitwise operations. The following analysis may shed light on this method.

At any point during arithmetic coding, the output consists of four parts as follows:

1. The part already written on the output. This part will not change.

2. One digit (bit, byte, or a digit to another base) that may be modified by at most one carry when adding to the lower end of the interval. (There cannot be two carries because when this digit was originally determined, the range was less than or equal to one unit. Two carries require a range greater than one unit.)

3. A (possibly empty) block of digits that passes on a carry (1 in binary, 9 in decimal, 255 for base-256, etc.) and are represented by a counter counting their number.

4. The low variable of the encoder.

The following states can occur while data is encoded:

- No renormalization is needed because the range is in the desired interval.

- The low end plus the range (this is the upper end of the interval) will not produce any carry. In this case the second and third parts can be output because they will never change.

- The digit produced will become part two, and part three will be empty. The low end has already produced a carry. In this case, the (modified) second and third parts can be output; there will not be another carry. Set the second and third part as before.

- The digit produced will pass on a possible future carry, so it is added to the block of digits of part three.

The difference between conventional integer-based arithmetic coding and range coding is that in the latter, part two, which may be modified by a carry, has to be stored explicitly. With binary output this part is always 0 since the 1's are always added to the carry-passing-block. Implementing that is straightforward.

More information and code can be found in [Campos 06]. Range coding is used in the LZMA dictionary-based method [Salomon 07].

Chapter Summary

An algorithm such as Huffman coding is simple, basic, and has many applications in data compression. However, once we learn it, it does not surprise us. Students exposed to this method tend to say "I could also come up with this algorithm if only I were 10 times more intelligent." Arithmetic coding, however, is different. It is one of those ideas that takes its student by surprise. We tend to say "I would never have thought of that." The main idea is to replace an entire file with a single, short number that can be considered a real number in the interval $[0, 1)$. The number is short because each data symbol input from the file increases the length of the number by an amount inversely proportional to the symbol's probability (whereas in the original file, each symbol increases the length of the file by the same amount).

Given a file with data symbols from an N-symbol alphabet, the principle of arithmetic coding is to divide the interval $[0, 1)$ into N segments, such that the width of the segment for symbol S is proportional to the probability of S. If the first symbol input from the data file is, say, the letter P, then the segment for P is selected and is divided into N segments of the same relative widths.

It is easy to examine two extreme cases of this process. In the first such case, we assume that the input file consists of n copies of the most-common symbol of the alphabet (such as the file EEE...E). The algorithm repeatedly selects the widest segment, divides it into N segments, and again selects the widest of those. The final result, after reading n symbols, is a narrow segment W, but it is the widest possible segment obtainable after n divisions. In the other extreme case, we imagine a file that consists of n copies of the least-common symbol (such as the file QQQ...Q). After reading n such symbols, always selecting the narrowest of N segments, and dividing again, we end up with the narrowest segment R that is possible after n divisions.

Clearly, W is wider than R (although in certain rare cases they may have the same width), and the point is that a narrow segment takes more digits to specify than a wide segment. A segment $[a, b)$ can be fully specified by its left boundary a and its width $b - a$, or by its two boundaries a and b. In either case, the specifications require more digits for a narrow segment. For example, the narrow segment $(0.1234567, 0.1234568)$ can be specified by the two long numbers 0.1234567 and 0.0000001, whereas the wider segment $[0.1, 0.2)$ can be specified by $a = 0.1$ and $b - a = 0.1$.

The Huffman method (Chapter 2) is simple, fast, and produces excellent results, but is not as effective as arithmetic coding. The conscientious reader may benefit from the discussion in [Bookstein and Klein 93], where the authors argue in favor of Huffman coding.

Self-Assessment Questions

1. Arithmetic coding replaces a data file with a real number in the interval $[0, 1)$. The number of possible data files is, of course, infinite, and so is the number of reals in any interval. Discuss these infinities and show that for any data file there is a real number in the interval $[0, 1)$.

2. In a computer, real numbers are represented as floating-point numbers. The chapter mentions that floating-point arithmetic is slow and has limited precision. Search the current literature to find the precision of floating-point numbers on various computing platforms, especially supercomputers, which are designed for fast, high-precision scientific computations.

3. Come up with an argument that shows why arithmetic coding can, in principle, be a very efficient compression method. This argument can be found somewhere in this chapter.

> That arithmetic is the basest of all mental activities is proved by the fact that it is the only one that can be accomplished by a machine.
>
> —Arthur Schopenhauer

5
Image Compression

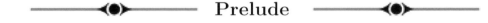

A digital image is a rectangular array of dots, or picture elements, arranged in m rows and n columns. The expression $m \times n$ is called the *resolution* of the image, and the dots are called *pixels* (except in the cases of fax images and video compression, where they are referred to as *pels*). The term "resolution" is often also used to indicate the number of pixels per unit length of the image. Thus, dpi stands for dots per inch. For the purpose of image compression it is useful to distinguish the following types of images:

1. A *bi-level* (or monochromatic) image. This is an image where the pixels can have one of two values, normally referred to as black and white. Each pixel in such an image is represented by one bit, making this the simplest type of image.

2. A *grayscale* image. A pixel in such an image consists of g bits, where g is normally compatible with a byte size; i.e., it is 4, 8, 12, 16, 24, or some other convenient multiple of 4 or of 8. The pixel's value indicates one of 2^g shades of gray (or shades of some other color). The set of the most-significant bits of all the pixels is the most-significant bitplane. Thus, a grayscale image has g bitplanes.

3. A *continuous-tone* image. This type of image can have many similar colors (or grayscales). When adjacent pixels differ by just one unit, it is hard or even impossible for the eye to distinguish their colors. As a result, such an image may contain areas with colors that seem to vary continuously as the eye moves along the area. A pixel in such an image is represented by either a single large number (in the case of many grayscales) or three components (in the case of a color image). A continuous-tone image is normally a natural image (natural as opposed to artificial) and is obtained by taking a photograph with a digital camera, or by scanning a photograph or a painting. Reference [Carpentieri et al. 00] is a general survey of lossless compression of this type of image.

4. A *discrete-tone* image (also called a graphical image or a synthetic image). This is

normally an artificial image. It may have a few colors or many colors, but it does not have the noise and blurring of a natural image. Examples are an artificial object or machine, a page of text, a chart, a cartoon, or the contents of a computer screen. (Not every artificial image is discrete-tone. A computer-generated image that's meant to look natural is a continuous-tone image in spite of its being artificially generated.) Artificial objects, text, and line drawings have sharp, well-defined edges, and are therefore highly contrasted from the rest of the image (the background). Adjacent pixels in a discrete-tone image often are either identical or vary significantly in value. Such an image does not compress well with lossy methods, because the loss of just a few pixels may render a letter illegible, or change a familiar pattern to an unrecognizable one. Compression methods for continuous-tone images often do not handle sharp edges very well, so special methods are needed for efficient compression of these images. Notice that a discrete-tone image may be highly redundant, since the same character or pattern may appear many times in the image.

5. A *cartoon-like* image. This is a color image that consists of uniform areas. Each area has a uniform color but adjacent areas may have very different colors. This feature may be exploited to obtain excellent compression.

> Whether an image is treated as discrete or continuous is usually dictated by the depth of the data. However, it is possible to force an image to be continuous even if it would fit in the discrete category. (From `www.genaware.com`)

It is intuitively clear that each type of image may feature redundancy, but they are redundant in different ways. This is why any given compression method may not perform well for all images, and why different methods are needed to compress the different image types. There are compression methods for bi-level images, for continuous-tone images, and for discrete-tone images. There are also methods that try to break an image up into continuous-tone and discrete-tone parts, and compress each separately.

5.1 Introduction

Modern computers employ graphics extensively. Window-based operating systems display the computer's file directory graphically. The progress of many system operations, such as downloading a file, may also be displayed graphically. Many applications provide a graphical user interface (GUI), which makes it easier to use the program and to interpret displayed results. Computer graphics is used in many areas in everyday life to convert many types of complex information to images. Thus, images are important, but they tend to be big! Modern hardware can display many colors, which is why it is common to have a pixel represented internally as a 24-bit number, where the percentages of red, green, and blue occupy 8 bits each. Such a 24-bit pixel can specify one of $2^{24} \approx 16.78$ million colors. As a result, an image at a resolution of 512×512 that consists of such pixels occupies 786,432 bytes. At a resolution of 1024×1024 it becomes four times as big, requiring 3,145,728 bytes. Videos are also commonly used in computers, making for even bigger images. This is why image compression is so important. An important feature of image compression is that it can be lossy. An image, after all, exists for people to look at, so, when it is compressed, it is acceptable to lose image features to which the eye is not sensitive. This is one of the main ideas behind the many lossy image compression methods that have been developed in recent decades.

In general, information can be compressed if it is redundant. It has been mentioned in the Introduction that data compression amounts to reducing or removing redundancies that exist in the data. With lossy compression, however, we have a new concept, namely compressing by removing *irrelevancy*. An image can be lossy-compressed by removing irrelevant information, even if the original image does not have any redundancy.

⬦ **Exercise 5.1:** It would seem that an image with no redundancy is always random (and therefore uninteresting). It that so?

This chapter discusses methods for image compression. The methods and approaches are all different, but they remove redundancy from an image by using the following principle:

The principle of natural image compression. If we select a pixel in the image at random, there is a good chance that its neighbors will have the same color or very similar colors.

Image compression is therefore based on the fact that neighboring pixels are *highly correlated*. This correlation is also called spatial redundancy.

Here is a simple example that illustrates what can be done with correlated pixels. The following sequence of values gives the intensities of 24 adjacent pixels in a row of a continuous-tone image:

12, 17, 14, 19, 21, 26, 23, 29, 41, 38, 31, 44, 46, 57, 53, 50, 60, 58, 55, 54, 52, 51, 56, 60.

Only two of the 24 pixels are identical. Their average value is 40.3. Subtracting pairs of adjacent pixels results in the sequence

12, 5, −3, 5, 2, 4, −3, 6, 11, −3, −7, 13, 4, 11, −4, −3, 10, −2, −3, 1, −2, −1, 5, 4.

The two sequences are illustrated graphically in Figure 5.1.

Figure 5.1: Values and Differences of 24 Adjacent Pixels.

The sequence of difference values has three properties that illustrate its compression potential: (1) The difference values are smaller than the original pixel values. Their average is 2.58. (2) They repeat. There are just 15 distinct difference values, so in principle they can be coded by four bits each. (3) They are *decorrelated*: adjacent difference values tend to be different. This can be seen by subtracting them, which results in the sequence of 24 second differences

$12, -7, -8, 8, -3, 2, -7, 9, 5, -14, -4, 20, -11, 7, -15, 1, 13, -12, -1, 4, -3, 1, 6, 1,$

which are larger than the differences themselves.

The principle of image compression has another aspect. We know from experience that the *brightness* of neighboring pixels is also correlated. Two adjacent pixels may have different colors. One may be mostly red, and the other may be mostly green. Yet if the red component of the first is bright, the green component of its neighbor will, in most cases, also be bright. This property can be exploited by converting pixel representations from RGB to three other components, one of which is the brightness, and the other two represent color. One such representation (or *color space*) is YCbCr, where Y (the "luminance" component) represents the brightness of a pixel, and Cb and Cr specify its color. This format is discussed in Section 5.6.1 and its advantage is easy to understand. The eye is sensitive to small variations in brightness but not to small changes in color. Thus, losing information in the Cb and Cr components compresses the image while introducing distortions to which the eye is not sensitive. Losing information in the Y component, on the other hand, is very noticeable to the eye.

An extreme example of pixel correlation is the interesting 4096×4096 color image found at [brucelindbloom 07]. Every pair of adjacent pixels in this image differ by one unit of RGB color and therefore they are highly correlated. The following is a quotation from this reference:

"Although the image contains 16 million pixels (a 48 Mb uncompressed image), it compresses very nicely, resulting in a surprisingly small download file. Click here for a ZIP download (53K) or here for a SIT download (36K)."

5.2 Approaches to Image Compression

An image compression method is normally tailored for a specific type of image, and this section lists various approaches to compressing images of different types. Only the general principles are discussed here; specific methods are described in the remainder of this chapter.

Approach 1: This is appropriate for bi-level images. A pixel in such an image is represented by one bit. Applying the principle of image compression to a bi-level image therefore means that the immediate neighbors of a pixel P tend to be *identical* to P. Thus, it makes sense to use run-length encoding (RLE) to compress such an image. A compression method for such an image may scan it in raster order (row by row) and compute the lengths of runs of black and white pixels in each row. The lengths are encoded by variable-length (prefix) codes and are written on the output. An example of such a method is facsimile compression, Section 2.4.

It should be stressed that this is just an approach to bi-level image compression. The details of specific methods vary. For instance, a method may scan the image column by column or in zigzag (Figure 1.12b), it may convert the image to a quadtree, or it may scan it region by region using a space-filling curve.

Approach 2: Also for bi-level images. The principle of image compression tells us that the neighbors of a pixel tend to be similar to the pixel. We can extend this principle and conclude that if the current pixel P has color c (where c is either black or white), then pixels of the same color seen in the past (and also those that will be found in the future) tend to have the same immediate neighbors as P.

This approach looks at n of the near neighbors of the current pixel and considers them as an n-bit number. This number is the *context* of the pixel. In principle there can be 2^n contexts, but because of image redundancy we expect them to be distributed in a nonuniform way. Some contexts should be common, while others will be rare.

The encoder counts how many times each context has already been found for a pixel of color c, and assigns probabilities to the contexts accordingly. If the current pixel has color c and its context has probability p, the encoder can use adaptive arithmetic coding to encode the pixel with that probability. This approach is used by the JBIG compression standard [Salomon 07].

Next, we turn to grayscale images. A pixel in such an image is represented by n bits and can have one of 2^n values. Applying the principle of image compression to a grayscale image implies that the immediate neighbors of a pixel P tend to be similar to P, but are not necessarily identical. Thus, RLE should not be used to compress such an image. Instead, two alternative approaches are discussed.

Approach 3: Separate the grayscale image into n bi-level images and compress each with RLE and prefix codes. The principle of image compression seems to imply intuitively that two adjacent pixels that are similar in the grayscale image will be identical in most of the n bi-level images. This, however, is not true, as the following example makes clear. Imagine a grayscale image with $n = 4$ (i.e., 4-bit pixels, or 16 shades of gray). The image can be separated into four bi-level images. If two adjacent pixels in the original grayscale image have values 0000 and 0001, then they are similar. They are also identical in three of the four bi-level images. However, two adjacent pixels with values 0111 and 1000 are also similar in the grayscale image (their values are 7 and 8, respectively) but differ in all four bi-level images.

This problem occurs because the binary codes of adjacent integers may differ by several bits. The binary codes of 0 and 1 differ by one bit, those of 1 and 2 differ by two bits, and those of 7 and 8 differ by four bits. The solution is to design special binary codes such that the codes of any consecutive integers i and $i + 1$ will differ by one bit only. An example of such a code is the reflected Gray codes of Section 5.2.1.

Approach 4: Use the context of a pixel to *predict* its value. The context of a pixel is the values of some of its near neighbors. We can examine some neighbors of a pixel P, compute an average A of their values, and predict that P will have the value A. The principle of image compression tells us that our prediction will be correct in most cases, almost correct in many cases, and terribly wrong in a few cases. We can say that the predicted value of pixel P represents the redundant information in P. We now calculate the difference

$$\Delta \stackrel{\text{def}}{=} P - A,$$

and assign variable-length (prefix) codes to the different values of Δ such that small values (which we expect to be common) are assigned short codes and large values (which are expected to be rare) are assigned long codes. If P can have the values 0 through

$m - 1$, then values of Δ are in the range $[-(m-1), +(m-1)]$, and the number of codes needed is $2(m-1) + 1$ or $2m - 1$.

Experiments with a large number of images suggest that the values of Δ tend to be distributed according to the well-known Laplace distribution (see the Intermezzo on page 178). A compression method can, therefore, use this distribution to assign a probability to each value of Δ, and use arithmetic coding to encode the Δ values very efficiently. This is the principle of the MLP method [Salomon 07].

The context of a pixel may consist of just one or two of its immediate neighbors. However, better results may be obtained when several neighbor pixels are included in the context. The average A in such a case should be weighted, with near neighbors assigned higher weights (see, for example, Figure 5.2a,b). Another important consideration is the decoder. In order for it to decode the image, it should be able to compute the context of every pixel in the same way as the encoder. This means that the context should employ only pixels that have already been encoded. If the image is scanned in raster order, the context should include only pixels located above the current pixel or on the same row and to its left (Figure 5.2c).

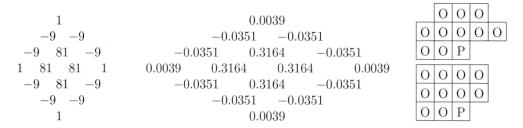

Figure 5.2: (a) Sixteen Integer Weights. (b) Normalized. (c) Contexts.

Approach 5: Transform the values of the pixels and encode the transformed values. The concept of a transform, as well as the most important transforms used in image compression, are discussed in Section 5.3. Section 5.7 is devoted to subband transforms (also referred to as wavelets). Recall that compression is achieved by reducing or removing redundancy. The redundancy of an image is caused by the correlation between pixels, so transforming the pixels to a representation where they are decorrelated eliminates the redundancy. It is also possible to think of a transform in terms of the entropy of the image. In a highly correlated image, the pixels tend to have equiprobable values, which results in maximum entropy. If the transformed pixels are decorrelated, certain pixel values become common, thereby having large probabilities, while others are rare. This results in small entropy. Quantizing the transformed values can result in efficient lossy image compression. We want the transformed values to be independent because coding independent values makes it simpler to construct a statistical model.

We now turn to color images. A pixel in such an image consists of three color components, such as red, green, and blue. Most color images are either continuous-tone or discrete-tone.

Approach 6: The principle of this approach is to separate a continuous-tone color image into three grayscale images and compress each of the three separately, using approaches 3, 4, or 5.

For a continuous-tone image, the principle of image compression implies that adjacent pixels have similar, although perhaps not identical, colors. However, similar colors do not imply similar pixel values. Consider, for example, 12-bit pixel values where each color component is expressed in four bits. Thus, the 12 bits 1000|0100|0000 represent a pixel whose color is a mixture of eight units of red (about 50%, since the maximum is 15 units), four units of green (about 25%), and no blue. Now imagine two adjacent pixels with values 0011|0101|0011 and 0010|0101|0011. They have similar colors, since only their red components differ, and only by one unit. However, when considered as 12-bit numbers, the two numbers 001101010011 and 001001010011 are very different, because they differ in one of their most significant bits.

An important feature of this approach is to use a luminance chrominance color representation instead of the more common RGB. The concepts of luminance and chrominance are discussed in Section 5.6.1 and in [Salomon 99]. The advantage of the luminance chrominance color representation is that the eye is sensitive to small changes in luminance but not in chrominance. This allows the loss of considerable data in the chrominance components, while making it possible to decode the image without a significant visible loss of quality.

Approach 7: A different approach is needed for discrete-tone images. Recall that such an image contains uniform regions, and a region may appear several times in the image. A good example is a screen dump. Such an image consists of text and icons. Each character of text and each icon is a region, and any region may appear several times in the image. A possible way to compress such an image is to scan it, identify regions, and find repeating regions. If a region B is identical to an already-found region A, then B can be compressed by writing a pointer to A on the output. The block decomposition method (FABD [Salomon 07]) is an example of this approach.

Approach 8: Partition the image into parts (overlapping or not) and compress it by processing the parts one by one. Suppose that the next unprocessed image part is part number 15. Try to match it with parts 1–14 that have already been processed. If part 15 can be expressed, for example, as a combination of parts 5 (scaled) and 11 (rotated), then only the few numbers that specify the combination need be saved, and part 15 can be discarded. If part 15 cannot be expressed as a combination of already-processed parts, it is declared processed and is saved in raw format.

This approach is the basis of the various fractal methods for image compression. It applies the principle of image compression to image parts instead of to individual pixels. Applied this way, the principle tells us that "interesting" images (i.e., those that are being compressed in practice) have a certain amount of *self-similarity*. Parts of the image are identical or similar to the entire image or to other parts.

Image compression methods are not limited to these basic approaches. The many image compression methods developed during the last several decades employ many different concepts and techniques such as context trees, Markov models, and wavelets. In addition, the concept of *progressive image compression* [Salomon 07] should be mentioned, because it adds another dimension to the topic of image compression.

5.2.1 Gray Codes

An image compression method that has been developed specifically for a certain image type can sometimes be used for other types. Any method for compressing bi-level images, for example, can be used to compress grayscale images by separating the bitplanes and compressing each individually, as if it were a bi-level image. Imagine, for example, an image with 16 grayscale values. Each pixel is defined by four bits, so the image can be separated into four bi-level images. The trouble with this approach is that it violates the general principle of image compression. Imagine two adjacent 4-bit pixels with values $7 = 0111_2$ and $8 = 1000_2$. These pixels have similar values, but when separated into four bitplanes, the resulting 1-bit pixels are different in every bitplane! This is because the binary representations of the consecutive integers 7 and 8 differ in all four bit positions. In order to apply any bi-level compression method to grayscale images, a binary representation of the integers is needed where consecutive integers have codes differing by one bit only. Such a representation exists and is called reflected Gray code (RGC). This code is easy to generate with the following recursive construction:

Start with the two 1-bit codes $(0, 1)$. Construct two sets of 2-bit codes by duplicating $(0, 1)$ and appending, either on the left or on the right, first a 0, then a 1, to the original set. The result is $(00, 01)$ and $(10, 11)$. Now reverse (reflect) the second set and concatenate the two. The result is the 2-bit RGC $(00, 01, 11, 10)$; a binary code of the integers 0 through 3 where consecutive codes differ by exactly one bit. Applying the rule again produces the two sets $(000, 001, 011, 010)$ and $(110, 111, 101, 100)$, which are concatenated to form the 3-bit RGC. Note that the first and last codes of any RGC also differ by one bit. Here are the first three steps for computing the 4-bit RGC:

$$\text{Add a zero } (0000, 0001, 0011, 0010, 0110, 0111, 0101, 0100),$$
$$\text{add a one } (1000, 1001, 1011, 1010, 1110, 1111, 1101, 1100),$$
$$\text{reflect } (1100, 1101, 1111, 1110, 1010, 1011, 1001, 1000).$$

43210	Gray	43210	Gray	43210	Gray	43210	Gray
00000	00000	01000	10010	10000	00011	11000	10001
00001	00100	01001	10110	10001	00111	11001	10101
00010	01100	01010	11110	10010	01111	11010	11101
00011	01000	01011	11010	10011	01011	11011	11001
00100	11000	01100	01010	10100	11011	11100	01001
00101	11100	01101	01110	10101	11111	11101	01101
00110	10100	01110	00110	10110	10111	11110	00101
00111	10000	01111	00010	10111	10011	11111	00001

```
function b=rgc(a,i)
[r,c]=size(a);
b=[zeros(r,1),a; ones(r,1),flipud(a)];
if i>1, b=rgc(b,i-1); end;
```

Table 5.3: First 32 Binary and Reflected Gray Codes.

Table 5.3 shows how individual bits change when moving through the binary codes of the first 32 integers. The 5-bit binary codes of these integers are listed in the odd-numbered columns of the table, with the bits of integer i that differ from those of $i-1$ shown in boldface. It is easy to see that the least-significant bit (bit b_0) changes all the time, bit b_1 changes for every other number, and, in general, bit b_k changes every k integers. The even-numbered columns list one of the several possible reflected Gray codes for these integers. The table also lists a recursive Matlab function to compute RGC.

⋄ **Exercise 5.2:** It is also possible to generate the reflected Gray code of an integer n with the following nonrecursive rule: Exclusive-OR n with a copy of itself that's logically shifted one position to the right. In the C programming language this is denoted by `n^(n>>1)`. Use this expression to construct a table similar to Table 5.3.

The conclusion is that the most-significant bitplanes of an image obey the principle of image compression more than the least-significant ones. When adjacent pixels have values that differ by one unit (such as p and $p+1$), chances are that the least-significant bits are different and the most-significant ones are identical. Any image compression method that compresses bitplanes individually should therefore treat the least-significant bitplanes differently from the most-significant ones, or should use RGC instead of the binary code to represent pixels.

Intermezzo

History of Gray Codes. Gray codes are named after Frank Gray, who patented their use for shaft encoders in 1953 [Gray 53]. However, the work was performed much earlier, the patent being applied for in 1947. Gray was a researcher at Bell Telephone Laboratories. During the 1930s and 1940s he was awarded numerous patents for work related to television. According to [Heath 72] the code was first, in fact, used by J. M. E. Baudot for telegraphy in the 1870s, though it is only since the advent of computers that the code has become widely known.

The Baudot code uses five bits per symbol. It can represent $32 \times 2 - 2 = 62$ characters (each code can have two meanings, the meaning being indicated by the LS and FS codes). It became popular and, by 1950, was designated the International Telegraph Code No. 1. It was used by many first- and second-generation computers.

The August 1972 issue of *Scientific American* contains two articles of interest, one on the origin of binary codes [Heath 72], and another [Gardner 72] on some entertaining aspects of the Gray codes.

> The binary Gray code is fun,
> For in it strange things can be done.
> Fifteen, as you know,
> Is one, oh, oh, oh,
> And ten is one, one, one, one.
>
> —Anonymous

✪ What do the English words FAST, THROUGH, DOWN, AWAY, WATER and NECK have in common?

5.3 Image Transforms

The mathematical technique of a transform is a powerful tool that is employed in many areas and can also serve as an approach to image compression. The prelude to Chapter 1 discusses this concept and describes a simple transform involving Roman numerals. An image can be compressed by transforming its pixels (which are correlated) to a representation where they are decorrelated. Compression is achieved if the new values are smaller, on average, than the original ones. Lossy compression can be achieved by quantizing the transformed values. The decoder inputs the transformed values from the compressed file and reconstructs the (precise or approximate) original data by applying the inverse transform. The transforms discussed in this section are orthogonal. Section 5.7.1 discusses subband transforms.

The term "decorrelated" implies that the transformed values are independent of one another. As a result, they can be encoded independently, which makes it simpler to construct a statistical model. An image can be compressed if its representation has redundancy. The redundancy in images stems from pixel correlation. If we transform the image to a representation where the pixels are decorrelated, we have eliminated the redundancy and the image has been fully compressed.

We start with a simple example of a transform. Given an image, it is scanned in raster order and pairs of adjacent pixels are prepared. Because the pixels are correlated, the two pixels (x, y) of a pair normally have similar values. We now consider each pair of pixels as a point in two-dimensional space, and we plot the points. We know that all the points of the form (x, x) are located on the $45°$ line $y = x$, so we expect our points to be concentrated around this line. Figure 5.4a shows the results of plotting the pixels of a typical image—where a pixel has values in the interval $[0, 255]$—in such a way. Most points form a cloud around this line, and only a few points are located away from it. We now transform the image by rotating all the points $45°$ clockwise about the origin, such that the $45°$ line now coincides with the x-axis (Figure 5.4b). This is done by the simple transformation

$$(x^*, y^*) = (x, y) \begin{pmatrix} \cos 45° & -\sin 45° \\ \sin 45° & \cos 45° \end{pmatrix} = (x, y) \frac{1}{\sqrt{2}} \begin{pmatrix} 1 & -1 \\ 1 & 1 \end{pmatrix} = (x, y)\mathbf{R}, \qquad (5.1)$$

where the rotation matrix $\mathbf{R}$ is orthonormal (i.e., the dot product of a row with itself is 1, the dot product of different rows is 0, and the same is true for columns). The inverse transformation is

$$(x, y) = (x^*, y^*)\mathbf{R}^{-1} = (x^*, y^*)\mathbf{R}^T = (x^*, y^*)\frac{1}{\sqrt{2}} \begin{pmatrix} 1 & 1 \\ -1 & 1 \end{pmatrix}. \qquad (5.2)$$

(The inverse of an orthonormal matrix is its transpose.)

It is obvious that most points end up with y coordinates that are zero or close to zero, while the x coordinates don't change much. Figure 5.5a,b shows the distributions of the x and y coordinates (i.e., the odd-numbered and even-numbered pixels) of the $128 \times 128 \times 8$ grayscale Lena image before the rotation. It is clear that the two distributions don't differ by much. Figure 5.5c,d shows that the distribution of the x coordinates stays about the same (with greater variance) but the y coordinates are concentrated around

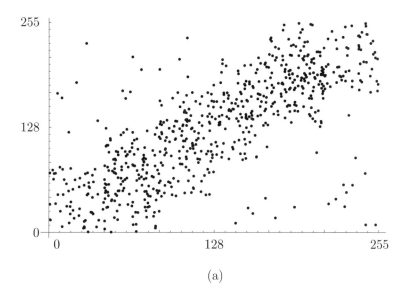

(a)

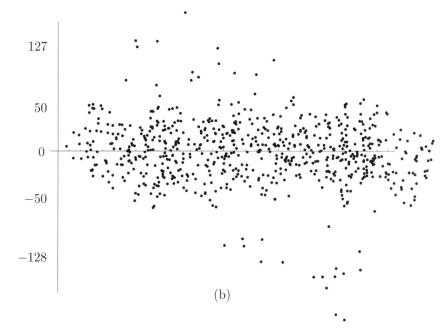

(b)

Figure 5.4: Rotating a Cloud of Points.

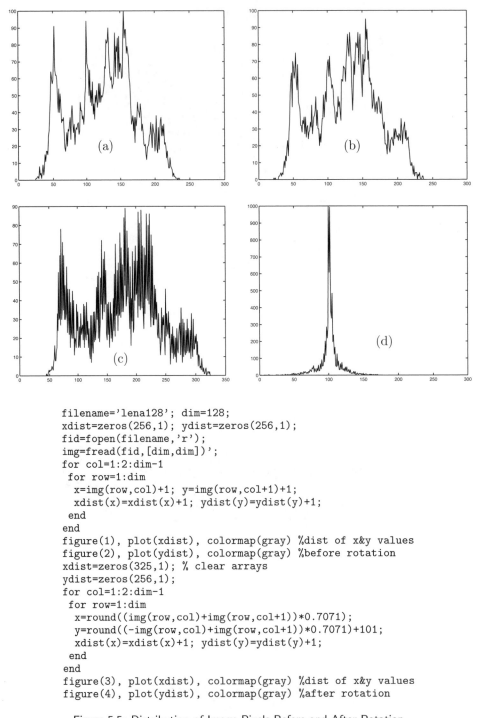

```
filename='lena128'; dim=128;
xdist=zeros(256,1); ydist=zeros(256,1);
fid=fopen(filename,'r');
img=fread(fid,[dim,dim])';
for col=1:2:dim-1
 for row=1:dim
  x=img(row,col)+1; y=img(row,col+1)+1;
  xdist(x)=xdist(x)+1; ydist(y)=ydist(y)+1;
 end
end
figure(1), plot(xdist), colormap(gray) %dist of x&y values
figure(2), plot(ydist), colormap(gray) %before rotation
xdist=zeros(325,1); % clear arrays
ydist=zeros(256,1);
for col=1:2:dim-1
 for row=1:dim
  x=round((img(row,col)+img(row,col+1))*0.7071);
  y=round((-img(row,col)+img(row,col+1))*0.7071)+101;
  xdist(x)=xdist(x)+1; ydist(y)=ydist(y)+1;
 end
end
figure(3), plot(xdist), colormap(gray) %dist of x&y values
figure(4), plot(ydist), colormap(gray) %after rotation
```

Figure 5.5: Distribution of Image Pixels Before and After Rotation.

zero. The Matlab code that generated these results is also shown. (Figure 5.5d shows that the y coordinates are concentrated around 100, but this is because a few were as small as -101, so they had to be scaled by 101 to fit in a Matlab array, which always starts at index 1.)

Once the coordinates of points are known before and after the rotation, it is easy to measure the reduction in correlation. A simple measure is the sum $\sum_i x_i y_i$, also called the cross-correlation of points (x_i, y_i).

$\diamond$ **Exercise 5.3:** Given the five points $(5, 5)$, $(6, 7)$, $(12.1, 13.2)$, $(23, 25)$, and $(32, 29)$, rotate them $45°$ clockwise and calculate their cross-correlations before and after the rotation.

We can now compress the image by simply writing the transformed pixels on the output. If lossy compression is acceptable, then all the pixels can be quantized (Section 1.5), resulting in even smaller numbers. We can also write all the odd-numbered pixels (those that make up the x coordinates of the pairs) on the output, followed by all the even-numbered pixels. These two sequences are called the *coefficient vectors* of the transform. The latter sequence consists of small numbers and may, after quantization, have runs of zeros, resulting in even better compression.

It can be shown that the total variance of the pixels does not change by the rotation, because a rotation matrix is orthonormal. However, since the variance of the new y coordinates is small, most of the variance is now concentrated in the x coordinates. The variance is sometimes called the *energy* of the distribution of pixels, so we can say that the rotation has concentrated (or compacted) the energy in the x coordinate and has created compression in this way.

Concentrating the energy in one coordinate has another advantage. It makes it possible to quantize that coordinate more finely than the other coordinates. This type of quantization results in better (lossy) compression.

The following simple example illustrates the power of this basic transform. We start with the point $(4, 5)$, whose two coordinates are similar. Using Equation (5.1) the point is transformed to $(4, 5)\mathbf{R} = (9, 1)/\sqrt{2} \approx (6.36396, 0.7071)$. The energies of the point and its transform are $4^2 + 5^2 = 41 = (9^2 + 1^2)/2$. If we delete the smaller coordinate (4) of the point, we end up with an error of $4^2/41 = 0.39$. If, on the other hand, we delete the smaller of the two transform coefficients (0.7071), the resulting error is just $0.7071^2/41 = 0.012$. Another way to obtain the same error is to consider the reconstructed point. Passing $\frac{1}{\sqrt{2}}(9, 1)$ through the inverse transform [Equation (5.2)] results in the original point $(4, 5)$. Doing the same with $\frac{1}{\sqrt{2}}(9, 0)$ results in the approximate reconstructed point $(4.5, 4.5)$. The energy difference between the original and reconstructed points is the same small quantity

$$\frac{\left[(4^2 + 5^2) - (4.5^2 + 4.5^2)\right]}{4^2 + 5^2} = \frac{41 - 40.5}{41} = 0.0012.$$

This simple transform can easily be extended to any number of dimensions. Instead of selecting pairs of adjacent pixels we can select triplets. Each triplet becomes a point in three-dimensional space, and these points form a cloud concentrated around the line that forms equal (although not $45°$) angles with the three coordinate axes. When this line is rotated such that it coincides with the x-axis, the y and z coordinates of the transformed points become small numbers. The transformation is done by multiplying each point by a 3×3 rotation matrix, and such a matrix is, of course, orthonormal. The transformed points are then separated into three coefficient vectors, of which the last two consist of small numbers. For maximum compression, each coefficient vector should be quantized separately.

This can be extended to more than three dimensions, with the only difference being that we cannot visualize spaces of dimensions higher than three. However, the mathematics can easily be extended. Some compression methods, such as JPEG, divide an image into blocks of 8×8 pixels each, and rotate first each row then each column of a block by means of Equation (5.6), as shown in Section 5.5. This double rotation produces a set of 64 transformed values, of which the first—termed the "DC coefficient"—is large, and the other 63 (called the "AC coefficients") are normally small. Thus, this transform concentrates the energy in the first of 64 dimensions. The set of DC coefficients and each of the sets of 63 AC coefficients should, in principle, be quantized separately (JPEG does this a little differently, though; see Section 5.6.3).

5.4 Orthogonal Transforms

Image transforms are designed to have two properties: (1) to reduce image redundancy by reducing the sizes of most pixels and (2) to identify the less important parts of the image by isolating the various frequencies of the image. Thus, this section starts with a short discussion of frequencies. We intuitively associate a frequency with a wave. Water waves, sound waves, and electromagnetic waves have frequencies, but pixels in an image can also feature frequencies. Figure 5.6 shows a small, 5×8 bi-level image that illustrates this concept. The top row is uniform, so we can assign it zero frequency. The rows below it have increasing pixel frequencies as measured by the number of color changes along a row. The four waves on the right roughly correspond to the frequencies of the four top rows of the image.

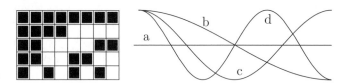

Figure 5.6: Image Frequencies.

An example of a high-frequency image is bright stars on a dark sky. An example of a low-frequency image is a uniform wall, where all the points have identical or similar colors.

Image frequencies are important because of the following basic fact: Low frequencies correspond to the important image features, whereas high frequencies correspond to the details of the image, which are less important. Thus, when a transform isolates the various image frequencies, pixels that correspond to high frequencies can be quantized heavily, whereas pixels that correspond to low frequencies should be quantized lightly or not at all. This is how a transform can compress an image very effectively by losing information, but only information that corresponds to unimportant image details.

Practical image transforms should be fast and preferably also simple to implement. This suggests the use of *linear transforms*. In such a transform, each transformed value (or transform coefficient) c_i is a weighted sum of the data items (the pixels) d_j that are being transformed, where each item is multiplied by a weight w_{ij}. Thus, $c_i = \sum_j d_j w_{ij}$, for $i, j = 1, 2, \ldots, n$. For $n = 4$, this is expressed in matrix notation:

$$\begin{pmatrix} c_1 \\ c_2 \\ c_3 \\ c_4 \end{pmatrix} = \begin{pmatrix} w_{11} & w_{12} & w_{13} & w_{14} \\ w_{21} & w_{22} & w_{23} & w_{24} \\ w_{31} & w_{32} & w_{33} & w_{34} \\ w_{41} & w_{42} & w_{43} & w_{44} \end{pmatrix} \begin{pmatrix} d_1 \\ d_2 \\ d_3 \\ d_4 \end{pmatrix}.$$

In general, we can write $\mathbf{C} = \mathbf{W} \cdot \mathbf{D}$. Each row of $\mathbf{W}$ is called a basis vector.

The only quantities that have to be determined are the weights w_{ij}. The guiding principles are as follows:

1. Reducing redundancy. The first transform coefficient c_1 can be large, but the remaining values $c_2, c_3, \ldots$ should be small.

2. Isolating frequencies. The first transform coefficient c_1 should correspond to zero pixel frequency, and the remaining coefficients should correspond to higher and higher frequencies.

The key to determining the weights w_{ij} is the fact that our data items d_j are not arbitrary numbers but pixel values and therefore nonnegative and correlated.

The basic relation $c_i = \sum_j d_j w_{ij}$ suggests that the first coefficient c_1 will be large if all the weights of the form w_{1j} are positive. To make the other coefficients c_i small, it is enough to make half the weights w_{ij} positive and the other half negative. A simple choice is to assign half the weights the value $+1$ and the other half the value -1. In the extreme case where all the pixels d_j are identical, this will result in $c_i = 0$. When the d_j are similar, c_i will be small (positive or negative).

This choice of w_{ij} satisfies the first requirement: to reduce pixel redundancy by means of a transform. In order to satisfy the second requirement, the weights w_{ij} of row i should feature frequencies that get higher with i. Weights w_{1j} should have zero frequency; they should all be $+1$'s. Weights w_{2j} should have one sign change; i.e., they should be $+1, +1, \ldots, +1, -1, -1, \ldots, -1$. This argument is applied to the other rows with more and more sign changes, until the last row of weights w_{nj} receives the highest frequency $+1, -1, +1, -1, \ldots, +1, -1$. The mathematical discipline of vector spaces employs the term "basis vectors" for our rows of weights.

In addition to isolating the various frequencies of pixels d_j, this choice results in basis vectors that are orthogonal. The basis vectors are the rows of matrix $\mathbf{W}$, which is why this matrix and by implication, the entire transform, are also termed orthogonal.

These considerations are satisfied by the orthogonal matrix

$$\mathbf{W} = \begin{pmatrix} 1 & 1 & 1 & 1 \\ 1 & 1 & -1 & -1 \\ 1 & -1 & -1 & 1 \\ 1 & -1 & 1 & -1 \end{pmatrix}. \tag{5.3}$$

The first basis vector (the top row of $\mathbf{W}$) consists of all 1's, so its frequency is zero. Each of the subsequent vectors has two $+1$'s and two -1's, so they produce small transformed values, and their frequencies (measured as the number of sign changes along the basis vector) become higher.

To illustrate how this matrix identifies the frequencies in a data vector, we multiply it by the following test vectors $(1, 0, 0, 1)$, $(0, 0.33, -0.33, -1)$, $(1, 0, 0, 0)$, and $(1, -0.8, 1, -0.8)$. The results are

$$
\mathbf{W}\cdot\begin{bmatrix}1\\0\\0\\1\end{bmatrix}=\begin{bmatrix}2\\0\\2\\0\end{bmatrix}, \quad
\mathbf{W}\cdot\begin{bmatrix}0\\0.33\\-0.33\\-1\end{bmatrix}=\begin{bmatrix}0\\2.66\\0\\1.33\end{bmatrix}, \quad
\mathbf{W}\cdot\begin{bmatrix}1\\0\\0\\0\end{bmatrix}=\begin{bmatrix}1\\1\\1\\1\end{bmatrix}, \quad
\mathbf{W}\cdot\begin{bmatrix}1\\-0.8\\1\\-0.8\end{bmatrix}=\begin{bmatrix}0.4\\0\\0\\3.6\end{bmatrix}
$$

The results make sense when we discover how the four test vectors were determined

$$
(1, 0, 0, 1) = 0.5(1, 1, 1, 1) + 0.5(1, -1, -1, 1),
$$
$$
(1, 0.33, -0.33, -1) = 0.66(1, 1, -1, -1) + 0.33(1, -1, 1, -1),
$$
$$
(1, 0, 0, 0) = 0.25(1, 1, 1, 1) + 0.25(1, 1, -1, -1) + 0.25(1, -1, -1, 1) + 0.25(1, -1, 1, -1),
$$
$$
(1, -0.8, 1, -0.8) = 0.1(1, 1, 1, 1) + 0.9(1, -1, 1, -1).
$$

The product of $\mathbf{W}$ and the first vector is $(2, 0, 2, 0)$, indicating how that vector consists of equal amounts of the first and the third frequencies. Similarly, the transform $(0.4, 0, 0, 3.6)$ shows that vector $(1, -0.8, 1, -0.8)$ is a mixture of a small amount of the first frequency and nine times the fourth frequency.

It is also possible to modify this transform to conserve the energy of the data vector. All that's needed is to multiply the transformation matrix $\mathbf{W}$ by the scale factor $1/2$. Thus, the product $(\mathbf{W}/2) \times (a, b, c, d)$ has the same energy $a^2 + b^2 + c^2 + d^2$ as the data vector (a, b, c, d). An example is the product of $\mathbf{W}/2$ and the correlated vector $(5, 6, 7, 8)$. It results in the transform coefficients $(13, -2, 0, -1)$, where the first coefficient is large and the remaining ones are smaller than the original data items. The energy of both $(5, 6, 7, 8)$ and $(13, -2, 0, -1)$ is 174, but whereas in the former vector the first component accounts for only 14% of the energy, in the transformed vector the first component accounts for 97% of the energy. This is how our simple orthogonal transform compacts the energy of the data vector.

Another advantage of $\mathbf{W}$ is that it also performs the inverse transform. The product $(\mathbf{W}/2) \cdot (13, -2, 0, -1)^T$ reconstructs the original data $(5, 6, 7, 8)$.

We are now in a position to appreciate the compression potential of this transform. We use matrix $\mathbf{W}/2$ to transform the (not very correlated) data vector $d = (4, 6, 5, 2)$. The result is $t = (8.5, 1.5, -2.5, 0.5)$. It's easy to transform t back to d, but t itself does not provide any compression. In order to achieve compression, we encode the AC coefficients of t by replacing them with variable-length codes, but the real power of an orthogonal transform becomes apparent when we choose lossy compression. In this case, we quantize the components of t before they are encoded, and the point is that even after heavy quantization, it is still possible to get back a vector very similar to the original d.

We first quantize t to the integers $(9, 1, -3, 0)$ and perform the inverse transform to get back $(3.5, 6.5, 5.5, 2.5)$. In a similar experiment, we completely delete the two smallest elements and inverse-transform the coarsely-quantized vector $(8.5, 0, -2.5, 0)$. This produces the reconstructed data $(3, 5.5, 5.5, 3)$, still very close to the original values of d. The conclusion is that even this simple, intuitive transform is a powerful tool for "squeezing out" the redundancy in data. More sophisticated transforms produce results that can be quantized coarsely and still be used to reconstruct the original data to a high degree.

5.4.1 Two-Dimensional Transforms

Given two-dimensional data such as the 4×4 matrix

$$
\mathbf{D} = \begin{pmatrix} 5 & 6 & 7 & 4 \\ 6 & 5 & 7 & 5 \\ 7 & 7 & 6 & 6 \\ 8 & 8 & 8 & 8 \end{pmatrix},
$$

where each of the four columns is highly correlated, we can apply our simple one-dimensional transform to the columns of $\mathbf{D}$. The result is

$$
\mathbf{C}' = \mathbf{W} \cdot \mathbf{D} = \begin{pmatrix} 1 & 1 & 1 & 1 \\ 1 & 1 & -1 & -1 \\ 1 & -1 & -1 & 1 \\ 1 & -1 & 1 & -1 \end{pmatrix} \cdot \mathbf{D} = \begin{pmatrix} 26 & 26 & 28 & 23 \\ -4 & -4 & 0 & -5 \\ 0 & 2 & 2 & 1 \\ -2 & 0 & -2 & -3 \end{pmatrix}.
$$

Each column of $\mathbf{C}'$ is the transform of a column of $\mathbf{D}$. Notice how the top element of each column of $\mathbf{C}'$ is dominant, because the data in the corresponding column of $\mathbf{D}$ is correlated. Notice also that the four components of each row of $\mathbf{C}'$ are still correlated. $\mathbf{C}'$ is the first stage in a two-stage process that produces the two-dimensional transform of matrix $\mathbf{D}$. The second stage should transform each row of $\mathbf{C}'$, and this is done by multiplying $\mathbf{C}'$ by the transpose $\mathbf{W}^T$. Our particular $\mathbf{W}$, however, is symmetric, so we end up with $\mathbf{C} = \mathbf{C}' \cdot \mathbf{W}^T = \mathbf{W} \cdot \mathbf{D} \cdot \mathbf{W}^T = \mathbf{W} \cdot \mathbf{D} \cdot \mathbf{W}$ or

$$
\mathbf{C} = \begin{pmatrix} 26 & 26 & 28 & 23 \\ -4 & -4 & 0 & -5 \\ 0 & 2 & 2 & 1 \\ -2 & 0 & -2 & -3 \end{pmatrix} \begin{pmatrix} 1 & 1 & 1 & 1 \\ 1 & 1 & -1 & -1 \\ 1 & -1 & -1 & 1 \\ 1 & -1 & 1 & -1 \end{pmatrix} = \begin{pmatrix} 103 & 1 & -5 & 5 \\ -13 & -3 & -5 & 5 \\ 5 & -1 & -3 & -1 \\ -7 & 3 & -3 & -1 \end{pmatrix}.
$$

The elements of $\mathbf{C}$ are decorrelated. The top-left element is dominant (it is also the sum of the 16 elements of $\mathbf{D}$). It contains most of the total energy of the original $\mathbf{D}$. The elements in the top row and the leftmost column are somewhat large, while the remaining elements are smaller than the original data items. The double-stage, two-dimensional transformation has reduced the correlation in both the horizontal and vertical dimensions. As in the one-dimensional case, excellent compression can be achieved by quantizing the elements of $\mathbf{C}$, especially those that correspond to higher frequencies (i.e., located toward the bottom-right corner of $\mathbf{C}$).

This is the essence of orthogonal transforms. The next section discusses the discrete cosine transform (DCT), the most popular orthogonal transform, which is the heart of several image and video compression algorithms, most notably JPEG and MPEG-1.

5.5 The Discrete Cosine Transform

This important transform (DCT for short) was first described by [Ahmed et al. 74] and has been used and studied extensively since. Because of its importance for data compression, the DCT is treated here in detail. Section 5.5.1 introduces the mathematical expressions for the DCT in one dimension and two dimensions without any theoretical background or justification. The use of the transform and its advantages for data compression are then demonstrated by several examples. Section 5.5.2 covers the theory of the DCT and discusses its interpretation as a basis of a vector space. More information on this important technique, as well as an alternative interpretation, can be found in [Salomon 07].

> Cosine, the opposite of "stop sign."

5.5.1 Introduction

The DCT in one dimension is defined by

$$G_f = \sqrt{\frac{2}{n}} C_f \sum_{t=0}^{n-1} p_t \cos\left[\frac{(2t+1)f\pi}{2n}\right], \quad \text{for } f = 0, 1, \ldots, n-1, \tag{5.4}$$

where

$$C_f = \begin{cases} \frac{1}{\sqrt{2}}, & f = 0, \\ 1, & f > 0. \end{cases}$$

The input is a set of n data values p_t (pixels, audio samples, or other data), and the output is a set of n DCT transform coefficients (or weights) G_f. The first coefficient G_0 is the DC coefficient, and the rest are the AC coefficients (these terms have been inherited from electrical engineering, where they stand for "direct current" and "alternating current"). Notice that the coefficients are real numbers even if the input data consists of integers. Similarly, the coefficients may be positive or negative even if the input data consists of nonnegative numbers only. This computation is straightforward but slow (reference [Salomon 07] discusses faster versions). Equation (5.4) implies that G_0, the DC coefficient, is given by

$$G_0 = \sqrt{\frac{1}{n}} \sum_{t=0}^{n-1} p_t = \sqrt{n} \frac{1}{n} \sum p_t,$$

and therefore equals $\sqrt{\frac{1}{n}}$ times the average of the n data values.

The decoder inputs the DCT coefficients in sets of n and uses the inverse DCT (IDCT) to reconstruct the original data values (also in groups of n). The IDCT in one dimension is given by

$$p_t = \sqrt{\frac{2}{n}} \sum_{j=0}^{n-1} C_j G_j \cos\left[\frac{(2t+1)j\pi}{2n}\right], \quad \text{for } t = 0, 1, \ldots, n-1. \tag{5.5}$$

The important feature of the DCT, which makes it so useful in data compression, is that it takes correlated input data and concentrates its energy in just the first few transform coefficients. If the input data consists of correlated quantities, then most of the n transform coefficients produced by the DCT are zeros or small numbers, and only a few are large (normally the first ones). We will see that the early coefficients contain the important (low-frequency) image information and the later coefficients contain the less-important (high-frequency) image information. Compressing a set of correlated pixels with the DCT is therefore done by (1) computing the DCT coefficients of the pixels, (2) quantizing the coefficients, and (3) encoding them with variable-length codes or arithmetic coding. The small coefficients are quantized coarsely (possibly all the way to zero), and the large ones can be quantized finely to the nearest integer. After quantization, the coefficients (or variable-length codes assigned to the coefficients) are written on the output. Decompression is done by performing the inverse DCT on the quantized coefficients. This results in data items that are not identical to the original ones but are not much different.

In practical applications, the data to be compressed is partitioned into sets of n items each and each set is DCT-transformed and quantized individually. The value of n is critical. Small values of n such as 3, 4, or 6 result in many small sets of data items. Such a small set is transformed to a small set of coefficients where the energy of the original data is concentrated in a few coefficients, but there are only a few coefficients in such a set! Thus, there are not enough small coefficients to quantize. Large values of n result in a few large sets of data. The problem in this case is that the individual data items of a large set are normally not correlated and therefore result in a set of transform coefficients where all the coefficients are large. Experience indicates that $n = 8$ is a good value, and most data compression methods that employ the DCT use this value of n.

The following experiment illustrates the power of the DCT in one dimension. We start with the set of eight correlated data items $\mathbf{p} = (12, 10, 8, 10, 12, 10, 8, 11)$, apply the DCT in one dimension to them, and find that it results in the eight coefficients

28.6375, 0.571202, 0.46194, 1.757, 3.18198, −1.72956, 0.191342, −0.308709.

(Notice that the DC coefficient equals $\sqrt{8}$ times the average 10.125 of the eight items.) These can be fed to the IDCT and transformed by it to precisely reconstruct the original data (except for small errors caused by limited machine precision). Our goal, however, is to compress (with lossy compression) the data by quantizing the coefficients. We first quantize them to 28.6, 0.6, 0.5, 1.8, 3.2, −1.8, 0.2, −0.3, and apply the IDCT to get back

12.0254, 10.0233, 7.96054, 9.93097, 12.0164, 9.99321, 7.94354, 10.9989.

We then quantize the coefficients even more, to 28, 1, 1, 2, 3, −2, 0, 0, and apply the IDCT to get back

12.1883, 10.2315, 7.74931, 9.20863, 11.7876, 9.54549, 7.82865, 10.6557.

Finally, we quantize the coefficients to 28, 0, 0, 2, 3, −2, 0, 0, and still get back from the IDCT the sequence

11.236, 9.62443, 7.66286, 9.57302, 12.3471, 10.0146, 8.05304, 10.6842, where the largest difference between an original value (12) and a reconstructed one (11.236) is 0.764 (or 6.4% of 12). The code that does all that is listed in Figure 5.7.

```
n=8;
p={12.,10.,8.,10.,12.,10.,8.,11.};
c=Table[If[t==1, 0.7071, 1], {t,1,n}];
dct[i_]:=Sqrt[2/n]c[[i+1]]Sum[p[[t+1]]Cos[(2t+1)i Pi/16],{t,0,n-1}];
q=Table[dct[i],{i,0,n-1}] (* use precise DCT coefficients *)
q={28,0,0,2,3,-2,0,0}; (* or use quantized DCT coefficients *)
idct[t_]:=Sqrt[2/n]Sum[c[[j+1]]q[[j+1]]Cos[(2t+1)j Pi/16],{j,0,n-1}];
ip=Table[idct[t],{t,0,n-1}]
```

Figure 5.7: Experiments with the One-Dimensional DCT.

It seems magical that the eight original data items can be reconstructed to such high precision from just four transform coefficients. The explanation, however, relies on the following arguments instead of on magic: (1) The IDCT is given all eight transform coefficients, so it knows the positions, not just the values, of the nonzero coefficients. (2) The first few coefficients (the large ones) contain the important information of the original data items. The small coefficients, the ones that are quantized heavily, contain less important information (in the case of images, they contain the image details). (3) The original data is correlated.

⋄ **Exercise 5.4:** The quantization error between a vector $X = x_1, x_2, \ldots, x_n$ and its quantized representation $\hat{X} = \hat{x}_1, \hat{x}_2, \ldots, \hat{x}_n$ is defined as $E = \sum_{i=1}^{n} (x_i - \hat{x}_1)^2$.

Use the set of eight correlated data items $\mathbf{p} = (12, 10, 8, 10, 12, 10, 8, 11)$ and the three quantizations of the previous experiment to compute (1) the error between the original items and their quantized DCT coefficients and (2) the error between the original items and the quantized items obtained after the IDCT. Compare the results of (1) and (2). Is there anything surprising about the results? Can this comparison be useful?

The following experiment illustrates the performance of the DCT when applied to decorrelated data items. Given the eight decorrelated data items -12, 24, -181, 209, 57.8, 3, -184, and -250, their DCT produces

$$-117.803, \ 166.823, \ -240.83, \ 126.887, \ 121.198, \ 9.02198, \ -109.496, \ -185.206.$$

When these coefficients are quantized to $(-120, 170, -240, 125, 120, 9, -110, -185)$ and fed into the IDCT, the result is

$$-12.1249, \ 25.4974, \ -179.852, \ 208.237, \ 55.5898, \ 0.364874, \ -185.42, \ -251.701,$$

where the maximum difference (between 3 and 0.364874) is 2.63513 or 88% of 3. Obviously, even with such fine quantization the reconstruction is not as good as with correlated data.

⋄ **Exercise 5.5:** Compute the one-dimensional DCT [Equation (5.4)] of the eight correlated values 11, 22, 33, 44, 55, 66, 77, and 88. Show how to quantize them, and compute their IDCT from Equation (5.5).

The DCT in one dimension can be used to compress one-dimensional data, such as a set of audio samples. This chapter, however, discusses image compression which is based on the two-dimensional correlation of pixels (a pixel tends to resemble all its near neighbors, not just those in its row). This is why practical image compression methods use the DCT in two dimensions. This version of the DCT is applied to small parts (data blocks) of the image. It is computed by applying the DCT in one dimension to each row of a data block, then to each column of the result. Because of the special way the DCT in two dimensions is computed, we say that it is separable in the two dimensions. Because it is applied to blocks of an image, we term it a "blocked transform." It is defined by

$$
G_{ij} = \sqrt{\frac{2}{m}} \sqrt{\frac{2}{n}} C_i C_j \sum_{x=0}^{n-1} \sum_{y=0}^{m-1} p_{xy} \cos\left[\frac{(2y+1)j\pi}{2m}\right] \cos\left[\frac{(2x+1)i\pi}{2n}\right], \tag{5.6}
$$

for $0 \le i \le n-1$ and $0 \le j \le m-1$ and for C_i and C_j defined by Equation (5.4). The first coefficient G_{00} is termed the DC coefficient and is large. The remaining coefficients, which are much smaller, are called the AC coefficients.

The image is broken up into blocks of $n \times m$ pixels p_{xy} (with $n = m = 8$ typically), and Equation (5.6) is used to produce a block of $n \times m$ DCT coefficients G_{ij} for each block of pixels. The top-left coefficient (the DC) is large, and the AC coefficients become smaller as we move from the top-left to the bottom-right corner. The top row and the leftmost column contain the largest AC coefficient, and the remaining coefficients are smaller. This behavior justifies the zigzag sequence illustrated by Figure 1.12b.

The coefficients are then quantized, which results in lossy but highly efficient compression. The decoder reconstructs a block of quantized data values by computing the IDCT whose definition is

$$
p_{xy} = \sqrt{\frac{2}{m}} \sqrt{\frac{2}{n}} \sum_{i=0}^{n-1} \sum_{j=0}^{m-1} C_i C_j G_{ij} \cos\left[\frac{(2x+1)i\pi}{2n}\right] \cos\left[\frac{(2y+1)j\pi}{2m}\right], \tag{5.7}
$$

where

$$
C_f = \begin{cases} \frac{1}{\sqrt{2}}, & f = 0 \\ 1, & f > 0, \end{cases}
$$

for $0 \le x \le n-1$ and $0 \le y \le m-1$. We now show one way to compress an entire image with the DCT in several steps as follows:

1. The image is divided into k blocks of 8×8 pixels each. The pixels are denoted by p_{xy}. If the number of image rows (columns) is not divisible by 8, the bottom row (rightmost column) is duplicated as many times as needed.

2. The DCT in two dimensions [Equation (5.6)] is applied to each block B_i. The result is a block (we'll call it a vector) $W^{(i)}$ of 64 transform coefficients $w_j^{(i)}$ (where

$j = 0, 1, \ldots, 63$). The k vectors $W^{(i)}$ become the rows of matrix $\mathbf{W}$

$$\mathbf{W} = \begin{bmatrix} w_0^{(1)} & w_1^{(1)} & \cdots & w_{63}^{(1)} \\ w_0^{(2)} & w_1^{(2)} & \cdots & w_{63}^{(2)} \\ \vdots & \vdots & & \\ w_0^{(k)} & w_1^{(k)} & \cdots & w_{63}^{(k)} \end{bmatrix}.$$

3. The 64 columns of $\mathbf{W}$ are denoted by $C^{(0)}$, $C^{(1)}$, ..., $C^{(63)}$. The k elements of $C^{(j)}$ are $\left(w_j^{(1)}, w_j^{(2)}, \ldots, w_j^{(k)}\right)$. The first coefficient vector $C^{(0)}$ consists of the k DC coefficients.

4. Each vector $C^{(j)}$ is quantized separately to produce a vector $Q^{(j)}$ of quantized coefficients (JPEG does this differently; see Section 5.6.3). The elements of $Q^{(j)}$ are then written on the output. In practice, variable-length codes are assigned to the elements, and the codes, rather than the elements themselves, are written on the output. Sometimes, as in the case of JPEG, variable-length codes are assigned to runs of zero coefficients, to achieve better compression.

In practice, the DCT is used for lossy compression. For lossless compression (where the DCT coefficients are not quantized) the DCT is inefficient but can still be used, at least theoretically, because (1) most of the coefficients are small numbers and (2) there are often runs of zero coefficients. However, the small coefficients are real numbers, not integers, so it is not clear how to write them in full precision on the output and still achieve compression. Other image compression methods are better suited for lossless image compression.

The decoder reads the 64 quantized coefficient vectors $Q^{(j)}$ of k elements each, saves them as the columns of a matrix, and considers the k rows of the matrix weight vectors $W^{(i)}$ of 64 elements each (notice that these $W^{(i)}$ are not identical to the original $W^{(i)}$ because of the quantization). It then applies the IDCT [Equation (5.7)] to each weight vector, to reconstruct (approximately) the 64 pixels of block B_i. (Again, JPEG does this differently.)

We illustrate the performance of the DCT in two dimensions by applying it to two blocks of 8×8 values. The first block (Table 5.8a) has highly correlated integer values in the range $[8, 12]$, and the second block has random values in the same range. The first block results in a large DC coefficient, followed by small AC coefficients (including 20 zeros, Table 5.8b, where negative numbers are underlined). When the coefficients are quantized (Table 5.8c), the result, shown in Table 5.8d, is very similar to the original values. In contrast, the coefficients for the second block (Table 5.9b) include just one zero. When quantized (Table 5.9c) and transformed back, many of the 64 results are very different from the original values (Table 5.9d).

⋄ **Exercise 5.6:** Explain why the 64 values of Table 5.8a are correlated.

The next example illustrates the difference in the performance of the DCT when applied to a continuous-tone image and to a discrete-tone image. We start with the highly correlated pattern of Table 5.10. This is an idealized example of a continuous-tone image, since adjacent pixels differ by a constant amount except the pixel (underlined) at row 7, column 7. The 64 DCT coefficients of this pattern are listed in Table 5.11. It is

12	10	8	10	12	10	8	11
11	12	10	8	10	12	10	8
8	11	12	10	8	10	12	10
10	8	11	12	10	8	10	12
12	10	8	11	12	10	8	10
10	12	10	8	11	12	10	8
8	10	12	10	8	11	12	10
10	8	10	12	10	8	11	12

(a) Original data

81	0	0	0	0	0	0	0
0	1.57	0.61	1.90	0.38	$\underline{1.81}$	0.20	$\underline{0.32}$
0	$\underline{0.61}$	0.71	0.35	0	0.07	0	0.02
0	$\underline{1.90}$	$\underline{0.35}$	4.76	0.77	$\underline{3.39}$	0.25	$\underline{0.54}$
0	$\underline{0.38}$	0	0.77	8.00	0.51	0	0.07
0	$\underline{1.81}$	0.07	$\underline{3.39}$	$\underline{0.51}$	1.57	0.56	0.25
0	$\underline{0.20}$	0	0.25	0	0.56	$\underline{0.71}$	0.29
0	$\underline{0.32}$	0.02	$\underline{0.54}$	0.07	0.25	$\underline{0.29}$	0.90

(b) DCT coefficients

81	0	0	0	0	0	0	0
0	2	1	2	0	$\underline{2}$	0	0
0	$\underline{1}$	1	0	0	$\overline{0}$	0	0
0	$\overline{2}$	0	5	1	$\underline{3}$	0	$\overline{1}$
0	0	0	1	8	$\overline{1}$	0	0
0	2	0	$\overline{3}$	1	2	1	0
0	0	0	0	0	1	1	0
0	0	0	$\underline{1}$	0	$\overline{0}$	0	1

(c) Quantized

12.29	10.26	7.92	9.93	11.51	9.94	8.18	10.97
10.90	12.06	10.07	7.68	10.30	11.64	10.17	8.18
7.83	11.39	12.19	9.62	8.28	10.10	11.64	9.94
10.15	7.74	11.16	11.96	9.90	8.28	10.30	11.51
12.21	10.08	8.15	11.38	11.96	9.62	7.68	9.93
10.09	12.10	9.30	8.15	11.16	12.19	10.07	7.92
7.87	9.50	12.10	10.08	7.74	11.39	12.06	10.26
9.66	7.87	10.09	12.21	10.15	7.83	10.90	12.29

(d) Reconstructed data (good)

Table 5.8: Two-Dimensional DCT of a Block of Correlated Values.

8	10	9	11	11	9	9	12
11	8	12	8	11	10	11	10
9	11	9	10	12	9	9	8
9	12	10	8	8	9	8	9
12	8	9	9	12	10	8	11
8	11	10	12	9	12	12	10
10	10	12	10	12	10	10	12
12	9	11	11	9	8	8	12

(a) Original data

79.12	0.98	0.64	$\underline{1.51}$	0.62	$\underline{0.86}$	1.22	0.32
0.15	$\underline{1.64}$	0.09	$\underline{1.23}$	0.10	3.29	1.08	$\underline{2.97}$
$\underline{1.26}$	$\overline{0.29}$	$\underline{3.27}$	1.69	$\underline{0.51}$	1.13	1.52	$\overline{1.33}$
$\underline{1.27}$	0.25	$\underline{0.67}$	0.15	$\underline{1.63}$	$\underline{1.94}$	0.47	$\underline{1.30}$
$\overline{2.12}$	$\underline{0.67}$	$\underline{0.07}$	$\underline{0.79}$	0.13	$\underline{1.40}$	0.16	$\underline{0.15}$
$\overline{2.68}$	1.08	$\overline{1.99}$	$\overline{1.93}$	$\overline{1.77}$	$\overline{0.35}$	0	$\underline{0.80}$
$\overline{1.20}$	2.10	$\overline{0.98}$	0.87	$\underline{1.55}$	$\underline{0.59}$	0.98	$\overline{2.76}$
$\overline{2.24}$	0.55	$\overline{0.29}$	0.75	$\underline{2.40}$	$\overline{0.05}$	0.06	1.14

(b) DCT coefficients

79	1	1	$\underline{2}$	1	$\underline{1}$	1	0
0	$\underline{2}$	0	$\underline{1}$	$\overline{0}$	$\overline{3}$	1	$\overline{3}$
$\underline{1}$	$\overline{0}$	3	2	0	1	2	$\overline{1}$
$\underline{1}$	$\overline{0}$	$\underline{1}$	0	2	$\underline{2}$	0	10
$2\overline{0}$	1	$\overline{0}$	1	0	$1\overline{0}$	0	$\overline{0}$
$\overline{3}$	$\overline{1}$	2	$\overline{2}$	$\overline{2}$	$\overline{0}$	0	$\underline{1}$
$\overline{1}$	2	$\overline{1}$	1	$\underline{2}$	1	1	$\overline{3}$
$\underline{2}$	1	$\overline{0}$	1	$\underline{2}$	$\overline{0}$	0	1

(c) Quantized

7.59	9.23	8.33	11.88	7.12	12.47	6.98	8.56
12.09	7.97	9.3	11.52	9.28	11.62	10.98	12.39
11.02	10.06	13.81	6.5	10.82	8.28	13.02	7.54
8.46	10.22	11.16	9.57	8.45	7.77	10.28	11.89
9.71	11.93	8.04	9.59	8.04	9.7	8.59	12.14
10.27	13.58	9.21	11.83	9.99	10.66	7.84	11.27
8.34	10.32	10.53	9.9	8.31	9.34	7.47	8.93
10.61	9.04	13.66	6.04	13.47	7.65	10.97	8.89

(d) Reconstructed data (bad)

Table 5.9: Two-Dimensional DCT of a Block of Random Values.

clear that there are only a few dominant coefficients. Table 5.12 lists the coefficients after they have been coarsely quantized, so that only four nonzero coefficients remain! The results of performing the IDCT on these quantized coefficients are shown in Table 5.13. It is obvious that the four nonzero coefficients have reconstructed the original pattern to a high degree. The only visible difference is in row 7, column 7, which has changed from 12 to 17.55 (marked in both figures). The Matlab code for this computation is listed in Figure 5.18.

Tables 5.14 through 5.17 show the same process applied to a Y-shaped pattern, typical of a discrete-tone image. The quantization, shown in Table 5.16, is light. The coefficients have only been truncated to the nearest integer. It is easy to see that the reconstruction, shown in Table 5.17, isn't as good as before. Quantities that should have been 10 are between 8.96 and 10.11. Quantities that should have been zero are as big as 0.86. The conclusion is that the DCT performs well on continuous-tone images but is less efficient when applied to a discrete-tone image.

00	10	20	30	30	20	10	00
10	20	30	40	40	30	20	10
20	30	40	50	50	40	30	20
30	40	50	60	60	50	40	30
30	40	50	60	60	50	40	30
20	30	40	50	50	40	30	20
10	20	30	40	40	30	12	10
00	10	20	30	30	20	10	00

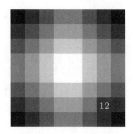

Table 5.10: A Continuous-Tone Pattern.

239	1.19	−89.76	−0.28	1.00	−1.39	−5.03	−0.79
1.18	−1.39	0.64	0.32	−1.18	1.63	−1.54	0.92
−89.76	0.64	−0.29	−0.15	0.54	−0.75	0.71	−0.43
−0.28	0.32	−0.15	−0.08	0.28	−0.38	0.36	−0.22
1.00	−1.18	0.54	0.28	−1.00	1.39	−1.31	0.79
−1.39	1.63	−0.75	−0.38	1.39	−1.92	1.81	−1.09
−5.03	−1.54	0.71	0.36	−1.31	1.81	−1.71	1.03
−0.79	0.92	−0.43	−0.22	0.79	−1.09	1.03	−0.62

Table 5.11: Its DCT Coefficients.

239	1	-90	0	0	0	0	0
0	0	0	0	0	0	0	0
-90	0	0	0	0	0	0	0
0	0	0	0	0	0	0	0
0	0	0	0	0	0	0	0
0	0	0	0	0	0	0	0
0	0	0	0	0	0	0	0
0	0	0	0	0	0	0	0

Table 5.12: Quantized Heavily to Just Four Nonzero Coefficients.

0.65	9.23	21.36	29.91	29.84	21.17	8.94	0.30
9.26	17.85	29.97	38.52	38.45	29.78	17.55	8.91
21.44	30.02	42.15	50.70	50.63	41.95	29.73	21.09
30.05	38.63	50.76	59.31	59.24	50.56	38.34	29.70
30.05	38.63	50.76	59.31	59.24	50.56	38.34	29.70
21.44	30.02	42.15	50.70	50.63	41.95	29.73	21.09
9.26	17.85	29.97	38.52	38.45	29.78	17.55	8.91
0.65	9.23	21.36	29.91	29.84	21.17	8.94	0.30

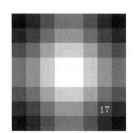

Table 5.13: Results of IDCT.

00	10	00	00	00	00	00	10
00	00	10	00	00	00	10	00
00	00	00	10	00	10	00	00
00	00	00	00	10	00	00	00
00	00	00	00	10	00	00	00
00	00	00	00	10	00	00	00
00	00	00	00	10	00	00	00
00	00	00	00	10	00	00	00

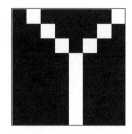

Table 5.14: A Discrete-Tone Image (Y).

13.75	−3.11	−8.17	2.46	3.75	−6.86	−3.38	6.59
4.19	−0.29	6.86	−6.85	−7.13	4.48	1.69	−7.28
1.63	0.19	6.40	−4.81	−2.99	−1.11	−0.88	−0.94
−0.61	0.54	5.12	−2.31	1.30	−6.04	−2.78	3.05
−1.25	0.52	2.99	−0.20	3.75	−7.39	−2.59	1.16
−0.41	0.18	0.65	1.03	3.87	−5.19	−0.71	−4.76
0.68	−0.15	−0.88	1.28	2.59	−1.92	1.10	−9.05
0.83	−0.21	−0.99	0.82	1.13	−0.08	1.31	−7.21

Table 5.15: Its DCT Coefficients.

13.75	−3	−8	2	3	−6	−3	6
4	−0	6	−6	−7	4	1	−7
1	0	6	−4	−2	−1	−0	−0
−0	0	5	−2	1	−6	−2	3
−1	0	2	−0	3	−7	−2	1
−0	0	0	1	3	−5	−0	−4
0	−0	−0	1	2	−1	1	−9
0	−0	−0	0	1	−0	1	−7

Table 5.16: Quantized Lightly by Truncating to Integer.

-0.13	8.96	0.55	-0.27	0.27	0.86	0.15	9.22
0.32	0.22	9.10	0.40	0.84	-0.11	9.36	-0.14
0.00	0.62	-0.20	9.71	-1.30	8.57	0.28	-0.33
-0.58	0.44	0.78	0.71	10.11	1.14	0.44	-0.49
-0.39	0.67	0.07	0.38	8.82	0.09	0.28	0.41
0.34	0.11	0.26	0.18	8.93	0.41	0.47	0.37
0.09	-0.32	0.78	-0.20	9.78	0.05	-0.09	0.49
0.16	-0.83	0.09	0.12	9.15	-0.11	-0.08	0.01

Table 5.17: The IDCT. Bad Results.

```
% 8x8 correlated values
n=8;
p=[00,10,20,30,30,20,10,00; 10,20,30,40,40,30,20,10; 20,30,40,50,50,40,30,20; ...
 30,40,50,60,60,50,40,30; 30,40,50,60,60,50,40,30; 20,30,40,50,50,40,30,20; ...
 10,20,30,40,40,30,12,10; 00,10,20,30,30,20,10,00];
figure(1), imagesc(p), colormap(gray), axis square, axis off
dct=zeros(n,n);
for j=0:7
  for i=0:7
    for x=0:7
      for y=0:7
dct(i+1,j+1)=dct(i+1,j+1)+p(x+1,y+1)*cos((2*y+1)*j*pi/16)*cos((2*x+1)*i*pi/16);
      end;
    end;
  end;
end;
dct=dct/4; dct(1,:)=dct(1,:)*0.7071; dct(:,1)=dct(:,1)*0.7071;
dct
quant=[239,1,-90,0,0,0,0,0; 0,0,0,0,0,0,0,0; -90,0,0,0,0,0,0,0; 0,0,0,0,0,0,0,0; ...
 0,0,0,0,0,0,0,0; 0,0,0,0,0,0,0,0; 0,0,0,0,0,0,0,0; 0,0,0,0,0,0,0,0];
idct=zeros(n,n);
for x=0:7
  for y=0:7
    for i=0:7
if i==0 ci=0.7071; else ci=1; end;
      for j=0:7
  if j==0 cj=0.7071; else cj=1; end;
idct(x+1,y+1)=idct(x+1,y+1)+ ...
            ci*cj*quant(i+1,j+1)*cos((2*y+1)*j*pi/16)*cos((2*x+1)*i*pi/16);
      end;
    end;
  end;
end;
idct=idct/4;
idct
figure(2), imagesc(idct), colormap(gray), axis square, axis off
```

Figure 5.18: Code for Highly Correlated Pattern.

5.5.2 The DCT as a Basis

The discussion so far has concentrated on how to use the DCT for compressing one-dimensional and two-dimensional data. The aim of this section is to show why the DCT works the way it does and how Equations (5.4) and (5.6) were derived. This section interprets the DCT as a special basis of an n-dimensional vector space. We show that transforming a given data vector $\mathbf{p}$ by the DCT is equivalent to representing it by this special basis that isolates the various frequencies contained in the vector. Thus, the DCT coefficients resulting from the DCT transform of vector $\mathbf{p}$ indicate the various frequencies in the vector. The lower frequencies contain the important visual information in $\mathbf{p}$, whereas the higher frequencies correspond to the details of the data in $\mathbf{p}$ and are therefore less important. This is why they can be quantized coarsely. (What visual information is important and what is unimportant is determined by the peculiarities of the human visual system.) We illustrate this interpretation for $n = 3$, because this is the largest number of dimensions where it is possible to visualize geometric transformations.

[Note. It is also possible to interpret the DCT as a rotation, as shown intuitively for $n = 2$ (two-dimensional points) in Figure 5.4. This interpretation [Salomon 07] considers the DCT as a rotation matrix that rotates an n-dimensional point with identical coordinates $(x, x, \ldots, x)$ from its original location to the x-axis, where its coordinates become $(\alpha, \epsilon_2, \ldots, \epsilon_n)$ where the various ϵ_i are small numbers or zeros.]

For the special case $n = 3$, Equation (5.4) reduces to

$$G_f = \sqrt{\frac{2}{3}} C_f \sum_{t=0}^{2} p_t \cos\left[\frac{(2t+1)f\pi}{6}\right], \quad \text{for } f = 0, 1, 2.$$

Temporarily ignoring the normalization factors $\sqrt{2/3}$ and C_f, this can be written in matrix notation as

$$\begin{bmatrix} G_0 \\ G_1 \\ G_2 \end{bmatrix} = \begin{bmatrix} \cos 0 & \cos 0 & \cos 0 \\ \cos\frac{\pi}{6} & \cos\frac{3\pi}{6} & \cos\frac{5\pi}{6} \\ \cos 2\frac{\pi}{6} & \cos 2\frac{3\pi}{6} & \cos 2\frac{5\pi}{6} \end{bmatrix} \begin{bmatrix} p_0 \\ p_1 \\ p_2 \end{bmatrix} = \mathbf{D} \cdot \mathbf{p}.$$

Thus, the DCT of the three data values $\mathbf{p} = (p_0, p_1, p_2)$ is obtained as the product of the DCT matrix $\mathbf{D}$ and the vector $\mathbf{p}$. We can therefore think of the DCT as the product of a DCT matrix and a data vector, where the matrix is constructed as follows: Select the three angles $\pi/6$, $3\pi/6$, and $5\pi/6$ and compute the three basis vectors $\cos(f\theta)$ for $f = 0$, 1, and 2, and for the three angles. The results are listed in Table 5.19 for the benefit of the reader.

θ	0.5236	1.5708	2.618
$\cos 0\theta$	1	1	1
$\cos 1\theta$	0.866	0	−0.866
$\cos 2\theta$	0.5	−1	0.5

Table 5.19: The DCT Matrix for $n = 3$.

Because of the particular choice of the three angles, these vectors are orthogonal but not orthonormal. Their magnitudes are $\sqrt{3}$, $\sqrt{1.5}$, and $\sqrt{1.5}$, respectively. Normalizing them results in the three vectors $\mathbf{v}_1 = (0.5774, 0.5774, 0.5774)$, $\mathbf{v}_2 = (0.7071, 0, -0.7071)$, and $\mathbf{v}_3 = (0.4082, -0.8165, 0.4082)$. When stacked vertically, they produce the following 3×3 matrix

$$\mathbf{M} = \begin{bmatrix} 0.5774 & 0.5774 & 0.5774 \\ 0.7071 & 0 & -0.7071 \\ 0.4082 & -0.8165 & 0.4082 \end{bmatrix}. \tag{5.8}$$

[Equation (5.4) tells us how to normalize these vectors: Multiply each by $\sqrt{2/3}$, and then multiply the first by $1/\sqrt{2}$.] Notice that as a result of the normalization the columns of $\mathbf{M}$ have also become orthonormal, so $\mathbf{M}$ is an orthonormal matrix (such matrices have special properties).

The steps of computing the DCT matrix for an arbitrary n are as follows:

1. Select the n angles $\theta_j = (j+0.5)\pi/n$ for $j = 0, \ldots, n-1$. If we divide the interval $[0, \pi]$ into n equal-size segments, these angles are the centerpoints of the segments.

2. Compute the n vectors $\mathbf{v}_k$ for $k = 0, 1, 2, \ldots, n-1$, each with the n components $\cos(k\theta_j)$.

3. Normalize each of the n vectors and arrange them as the n rows of a matrix.

The angles selected for the DCT are $\theta_j = (j + 0.5)\pi/n$, so the components of each vector $\mathbf{v}_k$ are $\cos[k(j + 0.5)\pi/n]$ or $\cos[k(2j + 1)\pi/(2n)]$. Reference [Salomon 07] covers three other ways to select such angles. This choice of angles has the following useful properties (1) the resulting vectors are orthogonal, and (2) for increasing values of k, the n vectors $\mathbf{v}_k$ contain increasing frequencies (Figure 5.20). For $n = 3$, the top row of $\mathbf{M}$ [Equation (5.8)] corresponds to zero frequency, the middle row (whose elements become monotonically smaller) represents low frequency, and the bottom row (with three elements that first go down, then up) represents high frequency. Given a three-dimensional vector $\mathbf{v} = (v_1, v_2, v_3)$, the product $\mathbf{M} \cdot \mathbf{v}$ is a triplet whose components indicate the magnitudes of the various frequencies included in $\mathbf{v}$; they are *frequency coefficients*. [Strictly speaking, the product is $\mathbf{M} \cdot \mathbf{v}^T$, but we ignore the transpose in cases where the meaning is clear.] The following three extreme examples illustrate the meaning of this statement.

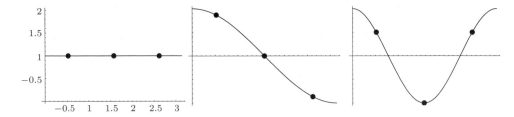

Figure 5.20: Increasing Frequencies.

The first example is $\mathbf{v} = (v, v, v)$. The three components of $\mathbf{v}$ are identical, so they correspond to zero frequency. The product $\mathbf{M} \cdot \mathbf{v}$ produces the frequency coefficients $(1.7322v, 0, 0)$, indicating no high frequencies. The second example is $\mathbf{v} = (v, 0, -v)$. The three components of $\mathbf{v}$ vary slowly from v to $-v$, so this vector contains a low frequency. The product $\mathbf{M} \cdot \mathbf{v}$ produces the coefficients $(0, 1.4142v, 0)$, confirming this result. The third example is $\mathbf{v} = (v, -v, v)$. The three components of $\mathbf{v}$ vary from v to $-v$ to v, so this vector contains a high frequency. The product $\mathbf{M} \cdot \mathbf{v}$ produces $(0, 0, 1.6329v)$, again indicating the correct frequency.

These examples are not very realistic because the vectors being tested are short, simple, and contain a single frequency each. Most vectors are more complex and contain several frequencies, which makes this method useful. A simple example of a vector with two frequencies is $\mathbf{v} = (1, 0.33, -0.34)$. The product $\mathbf{M} \cdot \mathbf{v}$ results in $(0.572, 0.948, 0)$ which indicates a large medium frequency, small zero frequency, and no high frequency. This makes sense once we realize that the vector being tested is the sum $0.33(1, 1, 1) + 0.67(1, 0, -1)$. A similar example is the sum $0.9(-1, 1, -1) + 0.1(1, 1, 1) = (-0.8, 1, -0.8)$, which when multiplied by $\mathbf{M}$ produces $(-0.346, 0, -1.469)$. On the other hand, a vector with random components, such as $(1, 0, 0.33)$, typically contains roughly equal amounts of all three frequencies and produces three large frequency coefficients. The product

$\mathbf{M} \cdot (1, 0, 0.33)$ produces $(0.77, 0.47, 0.54)$ because $(1, 0, 0.33)$ is the sum

$$0.33(1, 1, 1) + 0.33(1, 0, -1) + 0.33(1, -1, 1).$$

Notice that if $\mathbf{M} \cdot \mathbf{v} = \mathbf{c}$, then $\mathbf{M}^T \cdot \mathbf{c} = \mathbf{M}^{-1} \cdot \mathbf{c} = \mathbf{v}$. The original vector $\mathbf{v}$ can therefore be reconstructed from its frequency coefficients (up to small differences due to the limited precision of machine arithmetic). The inverse $\mathbf{M}^{-1}$ of $\mathbf{M}$ is also its transpose $\mathbf{M}^T$ because $\mathbf{M}$ is orthonormal.

A three-dimensional vector can have only three frequencies, namely zero, medium, and high. Similarly, an n-dimensional vector can have n different frequencies, which this method can identify. We concentrate on the case $n = 8$ and start with the DCT in one dimension. Figure 5.21 shows eight cosine waves of the form $\cos(f\theta_j)$, for $0 \le \theta_j \le \pi$, with frequencies $f = 0, 1, \ldots, 7$. Each wave is sampled at the eight points

$$\theta_j = \frac{\pi}{16}, \quad \frac{3\pi}{16}, \quad \frac{5\pi}{16}, \quad \frac{7\pi}{16}, \quad \frac{9\pi}{16}, \quad \frac{11\pi}{16}, \quad \frac{13\pi}{16}, \quad \frac{15\pi}{16} \tag{5.9}$$

to form one basis vector $\mathbf{v}_f$, and the resulting eight vectors $\mathbf{v}_f$, $f = 0, 1, \ldots, 7$ (a total of 64 numbers) are shown in Table 5.22. They serve as the basis matrix of the DCT. Notice the similarity between this table and matrix $\mathbf{W}$ of Equation (5.3).

Because of the particular choice of the eight sample points, the $\mathbf{v}_i$ are orthogonal, which is easy to check directly with appropriate mathematical software. After normalization, the $\mathbf{v}_i$ can be considered either as an 8×8 transformation matrix (specifically, a rotation matrix, since it is orthonormal) or as a set of eight orthogonal vectors that constitute the basis of a vector space. Any vector $\mathbf{p}$ in this space can be expressed as a linear combination of the $\mathbf{v}_i$. As an example, we select the eight (correlated) numbers $\mathbf{p} = (0.6, 0.5, 0.4, 0.5, 0.6, 0.5, 0.4, 0.55)$ as our test data and express $\mathbf{p}$ as a linear combination $\mathbf{p} = \sum w_i \mathbf{v}_i$ of the eight basis vectors $\mathbf{v}_i$. Solving this system of eight equations yields the eight weights

$$w_0 = 0.506, \quad w_1 = 0.0143, \quad w_2 = 0.0115, \quad w_3 = 0.0439,$$
$$w_4 = 0.0795, \quad w_5 = -0.0432, \quad w_6 = 0.00478, \quad w_7 = -0.0077.$$

Weight w_0 is not much different from the elements of $\mathbf{p}$, but the other seven weights are much smaller. This is how the DCT (or any other orthogonal transform) can lead to compression. The eight weights can be quantized and written on the output, where they occupy less space than the eight components of $\mathbf{p}$.

Figure 5.23 illustrates this linear combination graphically. Each of the eight $\mathbf{v}_i$ is shown as a row of eight small, gray rectangles (a basis image) where a value of $+1$ is painted white and -1 is black. The eight elements of vector $\mathbf{p}$ are also displayed as a row of eight grayscale pixels.

To summarize, we interpret the DCT in one dimension as a set of basis images that have higher and higher frequencies. Given a data vector, the DCT separates the frequencies in the data and represents the vector as a linear combination (or a weighted sum) of the basis images. The weights are the DCT coefficients. This interpretation can be extended to the DCT in two dimensions. We apply Equation (5.6) to the case $n = 8$

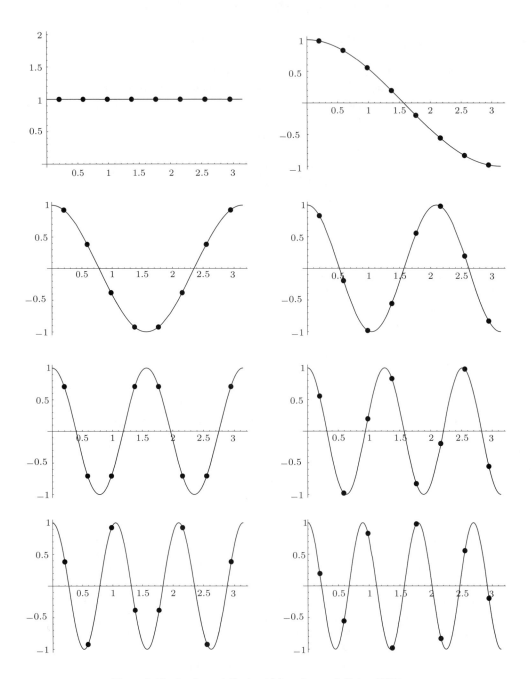

Figure 5.21: Angle and Cosine Values for an 8-Point DCT.

```
dct[pw_]:=Plot[Cos[pw t], {t,0,Pi}, DisplayFunction->Identity,
 AspectRatio->Automatic];
dcdot[pw_]:=ListPlot[Table[{t,Cos[pw t]},{t,Pi/16,15Pi/16,Pi/8}],
 DisplayFunction->Identity]
Show[dct[0],dcdot[0], Prolog->AbsolutePointSize[4],
 DisplayFunction->$DisplayFunction]
...
Show[dct[7],dcdot[7], Prolog->AbsolutePointSize[4],
 DisplayFunction->$DisplayFunction]
```

Code for Figure 5.21.

θ	0.196	0.589	0.982	1.374	1.767	2.160	2.553	2.945
$\cos 0\theta$	1	1	1	1	1	1	1	1
$\cos 1\theta$	0.981	0.831	0.556	0.195	-0.195	-0.556	-0.831	-0.981
$\cos 2\theta$	0.924	0.383	-0.383	-0.924	-0.924	-0.383	0.383	0.924
$\cos 3\theta$	0.831	-0.195	-0.981	-0.556	0.556	0.981	0.195	-0.831
$\cos 4\theta$	0.707	-0.707	-0.707	0.707	0.707	-0.707	-0.707	0.707
$\cos 5\theta$	0.556	-0.981	0.195	0.831	-0.831	-0.195	0.981	-0.556
$\cos 6\theta$	0.383	-0.924	0.924	-0.383	-0.383	0.924	-0.924	0.383
$\cos 7\theta$	0.195	-0.556	0.831	-0.981	0.981	-0.831	0.556	-0.195

Table 5.22: The Unnormalized DCT Matrix in One Dimension for $n = 8$.

```
Table[N[t],{t,Pi/16,15Pi/16,Pi/8}]
dctp[pw_]:=Table[N[Cos[pw t]],{t,Pi/16,15Pi/16,Pi/8}]
dctp[0]
dctp[1]
...
dctp[7]
```

Code for Table 5.22.

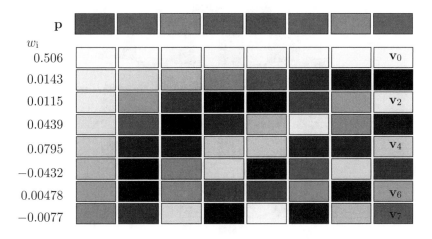

Figure 5.23: A Graphic Representation of the One-Dimensional DCT.

to create 64 small basis images of 8×8 pixels each. The 64 images are then used as a basis of a 64-dimensional vector space. Any image B of 8×8 pixels can be expressed as a linear combination of the basis images, and the 64 weights of this linear combination are the DCT coefficients of B.

Figure 5.24 shows the graphic representation of the 64 basis images of the two-dimensional DCT for $n = 8$. A general element (i, j) in this figure is the 8×8 image obtained by calculating the product $\cos(i \cdot s) \cos(j \cdot t)$, where s and t are varied independently over the values listed in Equation (5.9) and i and j vary from 0 to 7. This figure can easily be generated by the *Mathematica* code shown with it. The alternative code shown is a modification of code in [Watson 94], and it requires the `GraphicsImage.m` package, which is not widely available.

Using appropriate software, it is easy to perform DCT calculations and display the results graphically. Figure 5.25a shows a random 8×8 data unit consisting of zeros and ones. The same unit is shown in Figure 5.25b graphically, with 1 as white and 0 as black. Figure 5.25c shows the weights by which each of the 64 DCT basis images has to be multiplied in order to reproduce the original data unit. In this figure, zero is shown in neutral gray, positive numbers are bright (notice how bright the DC weight is), and negative numbers are shown as dark. Figure 5.25d shows the weights numerically. The *Mathematica* code that does all that is also listed. Figure 5.26 is similar, but for a very regular data unit.

◇ **Exercise 5.7:** Imagine an 8×8 block of values where all the odd-numbered rows consist of 1's and all the even-numbered rows contain zeros. What can we say about the DCT weights of this block?

It must be an even-numbered day. I do so prefer the odd-numbered days when you're kissing my *** for a favor.

—From *Veronica Mars* (a television program)

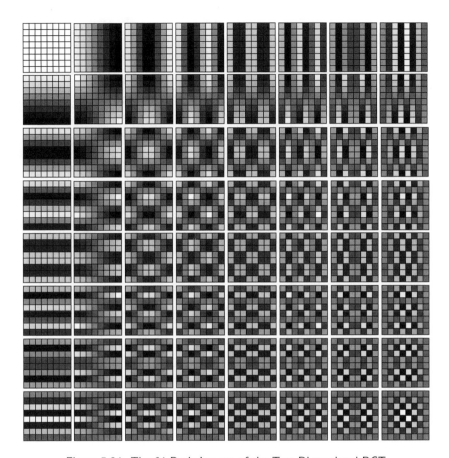

Figure 5.24: The 64 Basis Images of the Two-Dimensional DCT.

```
dctp[fs_,ft_]:=Table[SetAccuracy[N[(1.-Cos[fs s]Cos[ft t])/2],3],
  {s,Pi/16,15Pi/16,Pi/8},{t,Pi/16,15Pi/16,Pi/8}]//TableForm
dctp[0,0]
dctp[0,1]
...
dctp[7,7]
```

Code for Figure 5.24.

```
Needs["GraphicsImage`"] (* Draws 2D DCT Coefficients *)
DCTMatrix=Table[If[k==0,Sqrt[1/8],Sqrt[1/4]Cos[Pi(2j+1)k/16]],
  {k,0,7}, {j,0,7}] //N;
DCTTensor=Array[Outer[Times, DCTMatrix[[#1]],DCTMatrix[[#2]]]&,
  {8,8}];
Show[GraphicsArray[Map[GraphicsImage[#, {-.25,.25}]&, DCTTensor,{2}]]]
```

Alternative Code for Figure 5.24.

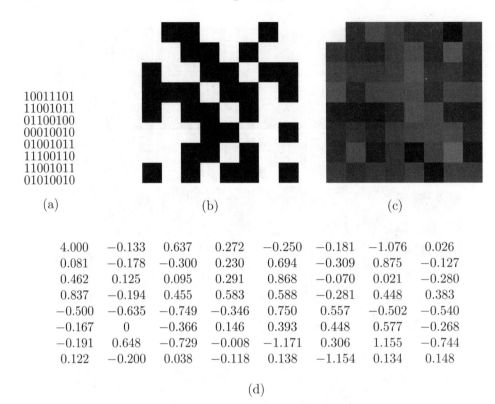

10011101
11001011
01100100
00010010
01001011
11100110
11001011
01010010

(a)   (b)   (c)

4.000	−0.133	0.637	0.272	−0.250	−0.181	−1.076	0.026
0.081	−0.178	−0.300	0.230	0.694	−0.309	0.875	−0.127
0.462	0.125	0.095	0.291	0.868	−0.070	0.021	−0.280
0.837	−0.194	0.455	0.583	0.588	−0.281	0.448	0.383
−0.500	−0.635	−0.749	−0.346	0.750	0.557	−0.502	−0.540
−0.167	0	−0.366	0.146	0.393	0.448	0.577	−0.268
−0.191	0.648	−0.729	−0.008	−1.171	0.306	1.155	−0.744
0.122	−0.200	0.038	−0.118	0.138	−1.154	0.134	0.148

(d)

Figure 5.25: An Example of the DCT in Two Dimensions.

```
DCTMatrix=Table[If[k==0,Sqrt[1/8],Sqrt[1/4]Cos[Pi(2j+1)k/16]],
 {k,0,7}, {j,0,7}] //N;
DCTTensor=Array[Outer[Times, DCTMatrix[[#1]],DCTMatrix[[#2]]]&,
 {8,8}];
img={{1,0,0,1,1,1,0,1},{1,1,0,0,1,0,1,1},
{0,1,1,0,0,1,0,0},{0,0,0,1,0,0,1,0},
{0,1,0,0,1,0,1,1},{1,1,1,0,0,1,1,0},
{1,1,0,0,1,0,1,1},{0,1,0,1,0,0,1,0}};
ShowImage[Reverse[img]]
dctcoeff=Array[(Plus @@ Flatten[DCTTensor[[#1,#2]] img])&,{8,8}];
dctcoeff=SetAccuracy[dctcoeff,4];
dctcoeff=Chop[dctcoeff,.001];
MatrixForm[dctcoeff]
ShowImage[Reverse[dctcoeff]]
```

Code for Figure 5.25.

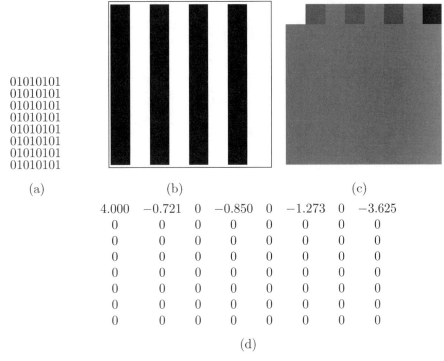

01010101
01010101
01010101
01010101
01010101
01010101
01010101
01010101

     (a)   (b)   (c)

4.000	−0.721	0	−0.850	0	−1.273	0	−3.625
0	0	0	0	0	0	0	0
0	0	0	0	0	0	0	0
0	0	0	0	0	0	0	0
0	0	0	0	0	0	0	0
0	0	0	0	0	0	0	0
0	0	0	0	0	0	0	0
0	0	0	0	0	0	0	0

(d)

Figure 5.26: An Example of the DCT in Two Dimensions.

> Some painters transform the sun into a yellow spot; others transform a yellow spot into the sun.
>
> —Pablo Picasso

```
DCTMatrix=Table[If[k==0,Sqrt[1/8],Sqrt[1/4]Cos[Pi(2j+1)k/16]],
  {k,0,7}, {j,0,7}] //N;
DCTTensor=Array[Outer[Times, DCTMatrix[[#1]],DCTMatrix[[#2]]]&,
  {8,8}];
img={{0,1,0,1,0,1,0,1},{0,1,0,1,0,1,0,1},
  {0,1,0,1,0,1,0,1},{0,1,0,1,0,1,0,1},{0,1,0,1,0,1,0,1},
  {0,1,0,1,0,1,0,1},{0,1,0,1,0,1,0,1},{0,1,0,1,0,1,0,1}};
ShowImage[Reverse[img]]
dctcoeff=Array[(Plus @@ Flatten[DCTTensor[[#1,#2]] img])&,{8,8}];
dctcoeff=SetAccuracy[dctcoeff,4];
dctcoeff=Chop[dctcoeff,.001];
MatrixForm[dctcoeff]
ShowImage[Reverse[dctcoeff]]
```

Code for Figure 5.26.

 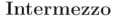 **Intermezzo**

Statistical Distributions.
Most people are of medium height, relatively few are tall or short, and very few are giants or dwarves. Imagine an experiment where we measure the heights of thousands of adults and want to summarize the results graphically. One way to do this is to go over the heights, from the smallest to the largest in steps of, say, 1 cm, and for each height h determine the number p_h of people who have this height. Now consider the pair (h, p_h) as a point, plot the points for all the values of h, and con-

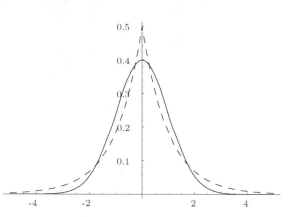

```
<< Statistics'ContinuousDistributions'
g1=Plot[PDF[NormalDistribution[0,1], x], {x,-5,5}]
g2=Plot[PDF[LaplaceDistribution[0,1], x], {x,-5,5},
    PlotStyle->{AbsoluteDashing[{5,5}]}]
Show[g1, g2]
```

nect them with a smooth curve. The result will resemble the solid graph in the figure, except that it will be centered on the average height, not on zero. Such a representation of data is known as a statistical distribution.

The particular distribution of people's heights is centered about the average height, not about zero, and is called a Gaussian (after its originator, Carl F. Gauss) or a normal distribution. The Gaussian distribution with mean m and standard deviation s is defined as

$$f(x) = \frac{1}{s\sqrt{2\pi}} \exp\left\{ -\frac{1}{2}\left(\frac{x-m}{s}\right)^2 \right\}.$$

This function has a maximum for $x = m$ (i.e., at the mean), where its value is $f(m) = 1/(s\sqrt{2\pi})$. It is also symmetric about $x = m$, since it depends on x according to $(x-m)^2$ and has a bell shape. The total area under the normal curve is one unit.

The normal distribution is encountered in many real-life situations and in science. It's easy to convince ourselves that people's heights, weights, and income are distributed in this way. Other examples are the following:

■   The speed of gas molecules. The molecules of a gas are in constant motion. They move randomly, collide with each other and with objects around them, and change their velocities all the time. However, most molecules in a given volume of gas move at about the same speed, and only a few move much faster or much slower than this speed. This speed is related to the temperature of the gas. The higher this average speed, the hotter the gas feels to us. (This example is asymmetric, since the minimum speed is zero, but the maximum speed can be very high.)

■   Château Chambord in the Loire valley of France has a magnificent staircase, designed by Leonardo da Vinci in the form of a double ramp spiral. Worn out by the innumerable footsteps of generations of residents and tourists, the marble tread of this staircase now looks like an inverted normal distribution curve. It is worn mostly in the middle, were the majority of people tend to step, and the wear tapers off to either side from the center. This staircase, and others like it, are physical embodiments of the abstract mathematical concept of probability distribution.

■ Prime numbers are familiar to most people. They are attractive and important to mathematicians because any positive integer can be expressed as a product of prime numbers (its prime factors) in one way only. The prime numbers are thus the building blocks from which all other integers can be constructed. It turns out that the number of distinct prime factors is distributed normally. Few integers have just one or two distinct prime factors, few integers have many distinct prime factors, while most integers have a small number of distinct prime factors. This is known as the Erdős–Kac theorem.

The Laplace probability distribution is similar to the normal distribution, but is narrower and sharply peaked. It is shown dashed in the figure. The general Laplace distribution with variance V and mean m is given by

$$L(V, x) = \frac{1}{\sqrt{2V}} \exp\left(-\sqrt{\frac{2}{V}}|x - m|\right).$$

The factor $1/\sqrt{2V}$ is included in the definition in order to scale the area under the curve to 1.

Some people claim that Canada is a very boring country. There are no great composers, poets, philosophers, scientists, artists, or writers whose names are inextricably associated with Canada. Similarly, no Canadian plays, stories, or traditional legends are as well-known as the Shakespeare plays, Grimm brothers' stories, or Icelandic sagas. However, I once heard that the following simple game may be considered Canada's national game. Two players start with a set of 15 matches (they don't have to be smokers) and take turns. In each turn, a player removes between 1 and 4 matches. The player removing the last match wins. Your task is to devise a winning strategy for this game and publicize it throughout Canada. This winning strategy should not depend on any of the players being Canadian.

5.6 JPEG

JPEG is a sophisticated lossy/lossless compression method for color or grayscale still images (not videos). It does not handle bi-level (black and white) images very well. It also works best on continuous-tone images, where adjacent pixels tend to have similar colors. An important feature of JPEG is its use of many parameters, allowing the user to adjust the amount of the data lost (and thus also the compression ratio) over a very wide range. Often, the eye cannot see any image degradation even at compression factors of 10 or 20. There are two operating modes, lossy (also called baseline) and lossless (which typically produces compression ratios of around 0.5). Most implementations support just the lossy mode. This mode includes progressive and hierarchical coding. A few of the many references to JPEG are [Pennebaker and Mitchell 92], [Wallace 91], and [Zhang 90].

JPEG is a compression method, not a complete standard for image representation. This is why it does not specify image features such as pixel aspect ratio, color space, or interleaving of bitmap rows.

JPEG has been designed as a compression method for continuous-tone images. The main goals of JPEG compression are the following:

1. High compression ratios, especially in cases where image quality is judged as very good to excellent.

2. The use of many parameters, allowing knowledgeable users to experiment and achieve the desired compression/quality trade-off.

3. Obtaining good results with any kind of continuous-tone image, regardless of image dimensions, color spaces, pixel aspect ratios, or other image features.

4. A sophisticated, but not too complex compression method, allowing software and hardware implementations on many platforms.

5. Several modes of operation: (a) sequential mode where each image component (color) is compressed in a single left-to-right, top-to-bottom scan; (b) progressive mode where the image is compressed in multiple blocks (known as "scans") to be viewed from coarse to fine detail; (c) lossless mode that is important in cases where the user decides that no pixels should be lost (the trade-off is low compression ratio compared to the lossy modes); and (d) hierarchical mode where the image is compressed at multiple resolutions allowing lower-resolution blocks to be viewed without first having to decompress the following higher-resolution blocks.

The name JPEG is an acronym that stands for Joint Photographic Experts Group. This was a joint effort by the CCITT and the ISO (the International Standards Organization) that started in June 1987 and produced the first JPEG draft proposal in 1991. The JPEG standard has proved successful and has become widely used for image compression, especially in Web pages.

The main JPEG compression steps are outlined here, and each step is then described in detail in a later section.

1. Color images are transformed from RGB into a luminance/chrominance color space (Section 5.6.1; this step is skipped for grayscale images). The eye is sensitive to small changes in luminance but not in chrominance, so the chrominance part can later lose much data, and thus be highly compressed, without visually impairing the overall image quality much. This step is optional but important because the remainder of the algorithm works on each color component separately. Without transforming the color space, none of the three color components will tolerate much loss, leading to worse compression.

2. Color images are downsampled by creating low-resolution pixels from the original ones (this step is used only when hierarchical compression is selected; it is always skipped for grayscale images). The downsampling is not done for the luminance component. Downsampling is done either at a ratio of 2:1 both horizontally and vertically (the so-called **2h2v** or 4:1:1 sampling) or at ratios of 2:1 horizontally and 1:1 vertically (**2h1v** or 4:2:2 sampling). Since this is done on two of the three color components, **2h2v** reduces the image to $1/3 + (2/3) \times (1/4) = 1/2$ its original size, while **2h1v** reduces it to $1/3 + (2/3) \times (1/2) = 2/3$ its original size. Since the luminance component is not

touched, there is no noticeable loss of image quality. Grayscale images don't go through this step.

3. The pixels of each color component are organized in groups of 8×8 pixels called data units, and each data unit is compressed separately. If the number of image rows or columns is not a multiple of 8, the bottom row or the rightmost column are duplicated as many times as necessary. In the noninterleaved mode, the encoder handles all the data units of the first image component, then the data units of the second component, and finally those of the third component. In the interleaved mode, the encoder processes the three top-left data units of the three image components, then the three data units to their right, and so on. The fact that each data unit is compressed separately is one of the downsides of JPEG. If the user asks for maximum compression, the decompressed image may exhibit blocking artifacts due to differences between blocks. Figure 5.27 is an extreme example of this effect.

Figure 5.27: JPEG Blocking Artifacts.

4. The discrete cosine transform (DCT, Section 5.5) is then applied to each data unit to create an 8×8 map of frequency components (Section 5.6.2). They represent the average pixel value and successive higher-frequency changes within the group. This prepares the image data for the crucial step of losing information. Since DCT involves the transcendental function cosine, it must involve some loss of information due to the limited precision of computer arithmetic. This means that even without the main lossy step (step 5 below), there will be some loss of image quality, but it is normally small.

5. Each of the 64 frequency components in a data unit is divided by a separate number called its *quantization coefficient* (QC), and then rounded to an integer (Section 5.6.3). This is where information is irretrievably lost. Large QCs cause more loss, so the high-frequency components typically have larger QCs. Each of the 64 QCs is a JPEG parameter and can, in principle, be specified by the user. In practice, most JPEG implementations use the QC tables recommended by the JPEG standard for the luminance and chrominance image components (Table 5.30).

6. The 64 quantized frequency coefficients (which are now integers) of each data unit are encoded using a combination of RLE and Huffman coding (Section 5.6.4). An arithmetic coding variant known as the QM coder can optionally be used instead of Huffman coding.

7. The last step adds headers and all the required JPEG parameters, and outputs the result. The compressed file may be in one of three formats (1) the interchange

format, in which the file contains the compressed image and all the tables needed by the decoder (mostly quantization and Huffman codes tables); (2) the abbreviated format for compressed image data, where the file contains the compressed image and either no tables or just a few tables; and (3) the abbreviated format for table-specification data, where the file contains just tables, and no compressed image. The second format makes sense in cases where the same encoder/decoder pair is used, and they have the same tables built in. The third format is used where many images have been compressed by the same encoder, using the same tables. When those images need to be decompressed, they are sent to a decoder preceded by a file with table-specification data.

The JPEG decoder performs the reverse steps (which shows that JPEG is a symmetric compression method).

The progressive mode is a JPEG option. In this mode, higher-frequency DCT coefficients are written on the output in blocks called "scans." Each scan that is read and processed by the decoder results in a sharper image. The idea is to use the first few scans to quickly create a low-quality, blurred preview of the image, and then either input the remaining scans or stop the process and reject the image. The trade-off is that the encoder has to save all the coefficients of all the data units in a memory buffer before they are sent in scans, and also go through all the steps for each scan, slowing down the progressive mode.

Figure 5.28a shows an example of an image with resolution 1024×512. The image is divided into $128 \times 64 = 8192$ data units, and each is transformed by the DCT, becoming a set of 64 8-bit numbers. Figure 5.28b is a block whose depth corresponds to the 8,192 data units, whose height corresponds to the 64 DCT coefficients (the DC coefficient is the top one, numbered 0), and whose width corresponds to the eight bits of each coefficient.

After preparing all the data units in a memory buffer, the encoder writes them on the compressed file in one of two methods, spectral selection or successive approximation (Figure 5.28c,d). The first scan in either method is the set of DC coefficients. If spectral selection is used, each successive scan consists of several consecutive (a band of) AC coefficients. If successive approximation is used, the second scan consists of the four most-significant bits of all AC coefficients, and each of the following four scans, numbers 3 through 6, adds one more significant bit (bits 3 through 0, respectively).

In the hierarchical mode, the encoder stores the image several times in its output file, at several resolutions. However, each high-resolution part uses information from the low-resolution parts of the output file, so the total amount of information is less than that required to store the different resolutions separately. Each hierarchical part may use the progressive mode.

The hierarchical mode is useful in cases where a high-resolution image needs to be output in low resolution. Older dot-matrix printers may be a good example of a low-resolution output device still in use.

The lossless mode of JPEG (Section 5.6.5) calculates a "predicted" value for each pixel, generates the difference between the pixel and its predicted value, and encodes the difference using the same method (i.e., Huffman or arithmetic coding) employed by step 5 above. The predicted value is calculated using values of pixels above and to the left of the current pixel (pixels that have already been input and encoded). The following sections discuss the steps in more detail.

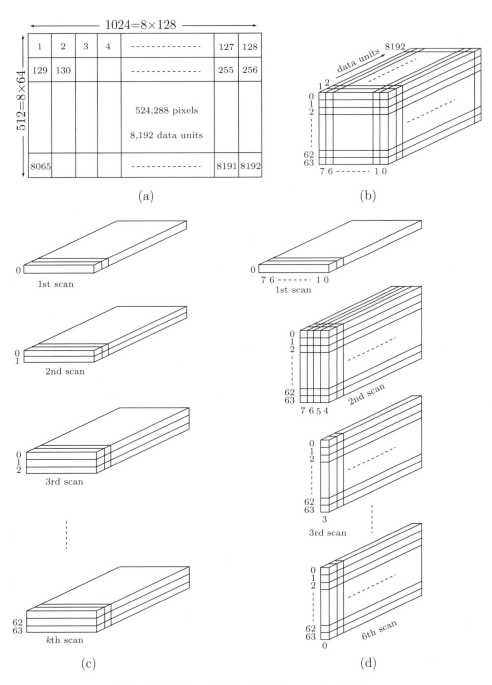

Figure 5.28: Scans in the JPEG Progressive Mode.

5.6.1 Luminance

The main international organization devoted to light and color is the International Committee on Illumination (Commission Internationale de l'Éclairage), abbreviated CIE. It is responsible for developing standards and definitions in this area. One of the early achievements of the CIE was its *chromaticity diagram* [Salomon 99], developed in 1931. It shows that no fewer than three parameters are required to define color. Expressing a certain color by the triplet (x, y, z) is similar to denoting a point in three-dimensional space, hence the term *color space*. The most common color space is RGB, where the three parameters are the intensities of red, green, and blue in a color. When used in computers, these parameters are normally in the range 0–255 (8 bits).

The CIE defines color as the perceptual result of light in the visible region of the spectrum, having wavelengths in the region of 400 nm to 700 nm, incident upon the retina (a nanometer, nm, equals 10^{-9} meter). Physical power (or radiance) is expressed in a spectral power distribution (SPD), often in 31 components each representing a 10-nm band.

The CIE defines brightness as the attribute of a visual sensation according to which an area appears to emit more or less light. The brain's perception of brightness is impossible to define, so the CIE defines a more practical quantity called *luminance*. It is defined as radiant power weighted by a spectral sensitivity function that is characteristic of vision (the eye is very sensitive to green, slightly less sensitive to red, and much less sensitive to blue). The luminous efficiency of the Standard Observer is defined by the CIE as a positive function of the wavelength, which has a maximum at about 555 nm. When a spectral power distribution is integrated using this function as a weighting function, the result is CIE luminance, which is denoted by Y. Luminance is an important quantity in the fields of digital image processing and compression.

Intermezzo

Human Vision and Color. We see light that enters the eye and falls on the retina, where there are two types of photosensitive cells. They contain pigments that absorb visible light and hence give us the sense of vision.

One type of photosensitive cells is the rods, which are numerous, are spread all over the retina, and respond only to light and dark. They are very sensitive and can respond to a single photon of light. There are about 110,000,000 to 125,000,000 rods in the eye [Osterberg 35]. The active substance in the rods is rhodopsin. A single photon can be absorbed by a rhodopsin molecule which changes shape and chemically triggers a signal that is transmitted to the optic nerve. Evolution, however, has protected us from too much sensitivity to light and our brains require at least five to nine photons (arriving within 100 ms) to create the sensation of light.

The other type is the cones, located in one small area of the retina (the fovea). They number about 6,400,000, are sensitive to color, but require more intense light, on the order of hundreds of photons. Incidentally, the cones are very sensitive to red, green, and blue (Figure 5.29), which is one reason why these colors are often used as primaries. In bright light, the cones become active, the rods are less so, and the iris is stopped down. This is called photopic vision.

We know that a dark environment improves our eyes' sensitivity. When we enter a dark place, the rods undergo chemical changes and after about 30 minutes they become 10,000 times more sensitive than the cones. This state is referred to as scotopic vision. It increases our sensitivity to light, but drastically reduces our color vision.

The first accurate experiments that measured human visual sensitivity were performed in 1942 [Hecht et al. 42].

Each of the light sensors (rods and cones) in the eye sends a light sensation to the brain that's essentially a pixel, and the brain combines these pixels to a continuous image. The human eye is therefore similar to a digital camera. Once we realize this, we naturally want to compare the resolution of the eye to that of a modern digital camera. Current digital cameras have from 500,000 sensors (for a cheap camera) to about ten million sensors (for a high-quality one).

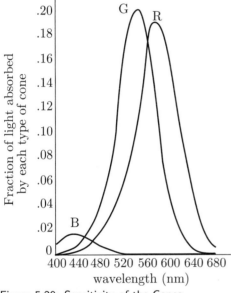

Figure 5.29: Sensitivity of the Cones.

Thus, the eye features a much higher resolution, but its effective resolution is even higher if we consider that the eye can move and refocus itself about three to four times a second. This means that in a single second, the eye can sense and send to the brain about half a billion pixels. Assuming that our camera takes a snapshot once a second, the ratio of the resolutions is about 100.

Certain colors—such as red, orange, and yellow—are psychologically associated with heat. They are considered *warm* and cause a picture to appear larger and closer than it really is. Other colors—such as blue, violet, and green—are associated with cool things (air, sky, water, ice) and are therefore called *cool* colors. They cause a picture to look smaller and farther away.

Luminance is proportional to the power of the light source. It is similar to intensity, but the spectral composition of luminance is related to the brightness sensitivity of human vision.

The eye is very sensitive to small changes in luminance, which is why it is useful to have color spaces that use Y as one of their three parameters. A simple way to do this is to compute Y as a weighted sum of the R, G, and B color components with weights determined by Figure 5.29, and then to subtract Y from the blue and red components and have Y, $B - Y$, and $R - Y$ as the three components of a new color space. The last two components are called chroma. They represent color in terms of the presence or absence of blue (Cb) and red (Cr) for a given luminance intensity.

Various number ranges are used in $B - Y$ and $R - Y$ for different applications. The YPbPr ranges are optimized for component analog video. The YCbCr ranges are appropriate for component digital video such as studio video, JPEG, JPEG 2000, and MPEG.

The YCbCr color space was developed as part of Recommendation ITU-R BT.601 (formerly CCIR 601) during the development of a worldwide digital component video standard. Y is defined to have a range of 16 to 235; Cb and Cr are defined to have a range of 16 to 240, with 128 equal to zero. There are several YCbCr sampling formats, such as 4:4:4, 4:2:2, 4:1:1, and 4:2:0, which are also described in the recommendation.

Conversions between RGB with a 16–235 range and YCbCr are linear and therefore simple. Transforming RGB to YCbCr is done by (note the small weight of blue):

$$Y = (77/256)R + (150/256)G + (29/256)B,$$
$$Cb = -(44/256)R - (87/256)G + (131/256)B + 128,$$
$$Cr = (131/256)R - (110/256)G - (21/256)B + 128;$$

while the opposite transformation is

$$R = Y + 1.371(Cr - 128),$$
$$G = Y - 0.698(Cr - 128) - 0.336(Cb - 128),$$
$$B = Y + 1.732(Cb - 128).$$

When performing YCbCr to RGB conversion, the resulting RGB values have a nominal range of 16–235, with possible occasional values in 0–15 and 236–255.

Other color spaces may be useful in special applications, but each space requires three numbers to describes a color. This interesting and unexpected fact stems from the way the cones in the retina respond to light. There are three types of cones, known as S, L, and M. They are sensitive to wavelengths around 420, 564, and 534 nanometers (corresponding to violet, yellowish-green, and green, respectively). When these cones sense light of wavelength W, each produces a signal whose intensity depends on how close W is to the "personal" wavelength of the cone. The three signals are sent, as a tristimulus, to the brain where they are interpreted as color. Thus, most humans are trichromats and it has been estimated that they can distinguish roughly 10 million different colors. This said, we should also mention that many color blind people can perceive only gray scales (while others may only confuse red and green). Obviously, such a color blind person needs only one number, the intensity of gray, to specify a color. Such a person is therefore a monochromat. A hypothetical creature that can only distinguish black and white (darkness or light) needs only one bit to specify a color, while some persons (or animals or extraterrestrials) may be tetrachromats [Tetrachromat 07]. They may have four types of cones in their eyes, and consequently need four numbers to specify a color.

We therefore conclude that color is only a sensation in our brain; it is not part of the physical world. What actually exists in the world is light of different wavelengths, and we are fortunate that our eyes and brain can interpret mere wavelengths as the rich, vibrant colors that so enrich our lives and that we so much take for granted.

> Colors are only symbols. Reality is to be found in luminance alone.
> —Pablo Picasso

5.6.2 DCT

The general concept of a transform is discussed in Section 5.3. The discrete cosine transform is discussed in some detail in Section 5.5.

The JPEG committee elected to use the DCT because of its good performance, because it does not assume anything about the structure of the data, and because there are ways to speed it up (Section 4.6.5 in [Salomon 07]).

The JPEG standard calls for applying the DCT not to the entire image but to data units (blocks) of 8×8 pixels. The reasons for this are: (1) Applying DCT to large blocks involves many arithmetic operations and is therefore slow. Applying DCT to small data units is faster. (2) Experience shows that, in a continuous-tone image, correlations between pixels are short range. A pixel in such an image has a value (color component or shade of gray) that's close to those of its near neighbors, but has nothing to do with the values of far neighbors. The JPEG DCT is therefore executed by Equation (5.6), duplicated here for $n = 8$

$$
G_{ij} = \frac{1}{4} C_i C_j \sum_{x=0}^{7} \sum_{y=0}^{7} p_{xy} \cos\left(\frac{(2x+1)i\pi}{16}\right) \cos\left(\frac{(2y+1)j\pi}{16}\right),
$$

$$
\text{where } C_f = \begin{cases} \frac{1}{\sqrt{2}}, & f = 0, \\ 1, & f > 0, \end{cases} \quad \text{and } 0 \le i, j \le 7.
$$

(5.6)

The DCT is JPEG's key to lossy compression. The unimportant image information is reduced or removed by quantizing the 64 DCT coefficients, especially the ones located toward the lower-right. If the pixels of the image are correlated, quantization does not degrade the image quality much. For best results, each of the 64 coefficients is quantized by dividing it by a different quantization coefficient (QC). All 64 QCs are parameters that can be controlled, in principle, by the user (Section 5.6.3).

The JPEG decoder works by computing the inverse DCT (IDCT), Equation (5.7), duplicated here for $n = 8$

$$
p_{xy} = \frac{1}{4} \sum_{i=0}^{7} \sum_{j=0}^{7} C_i C_j G_{ij} \cos\left(\frac{(2x+1)i\pi}{16}\right) \cos\left(\frac{(2y+1)j\pi}{16}\right),
$$

$$
\text{where } C_f = \begin{cases} \frac{1}{\sqrt{2}}, & f = 0, \\ 1, & f > 0. \end{cases}
$$

(5.7)

It takes the 64 quantized DCT coefficients and calculates 64 pixels p_{xy}. If the QCs are the right ones, the new 64 pixels will be very similar to the original ones. Mathematically, the DCT is a one-to-one mapping of 64-point vectors from the image domain to the frequency domain. The IDCT is the reverse mapping. If the DCT and IDCT could be calculated with infinite precision and if the DCT coefficients were not quantized, the original 64 pixels would be exactly reconstructed.

5.6.3 Quantization

After each 8×8 data unit of DCT coefficients G_{ij} is computed, it is quantized. This is the step where information is lost (except for some unavoidable loss because of finite precision calculations in other steps). Each number in the DCT coefficients matrix is divided by the corresponding number from the particular "quantization table" used, and the result is rounded to the nearest integer. As has already been mentioned, three such tables are needed, for the three color components. The JPEG standard allows for up to four tables, and the user can select any of the four for quantizing each color component. The 64 numbers that constitute each quantization table are all JPEG parameters. In principle, they can all be specified and fine-tuned by the user for maximum compression. In practice, few users have the patience or expertise to experiment with so many parameters, so JPEG software normally uses the following two approaches:

1. Default quantization tables. Two such tables, for the luminance and the chrominance components, are the result of many experiments performed by the JPEG committee. They are included in the JPEG standard and are reproduced here as Table 5.30. It is easy to see how the QCs in the table generally grow as we move from the upper-left corner to the bottom-right corner. This is how JPEG reduces the DCT coefficients with high spatial frequencies.

2. A simple quantization table Q is computed, based on one parameter R specified by the user. A simple expression such as $Q_{ij} = 1 + (i + j) \times R$ guarantees that QCs start small at the upper-left corner and get bigger toward the lower-right corner. Table 5.31 shows an example of such a table with $R = 2$.

16	11	10	16	24	40	51	61	17	18	24	47	99	99	99	99
12	12	14	19	26	58	60	55	18	21	26	66	99	99	99	99
14	13	16	24	40	57	69	56	24	26	56	99	99	99	99	99
14	17	22	29	51	87	80	62	47	66	99	99	99	99	99	99
18	22	37	56	68	109	103	77	99	99	99	99	99	99	99	99
24	35	55	64	81	104	113	92	99	99	99	99	99	99	99	99
49	64	78	87	103	121	120	101	99	99	99	99	99	99	99	99
72	92	95	98	112	100	103	99	99	99	99	99	99	99	99	99

Luminance   Chrominance

Table 5.30: Recommended Quantization Tables.

1	3	5	7	9	11	13	15
3	5	7	9	11	13	15	17
5	7	9	11	13	15	17	19
7	9	11	13	15	17	19	21
9	11	13	15	17	19	21	23
11	13	15	17	19	21	23	25
13	15	17	19	21	23	25	27
15	17	19	21	23	25	27	29

Table 5.31: The Quantization Table $1 + (i + j) \times 2$.

If the quantization is done correctly, very few nonzero numbers will be left in the DCT coefficients matrix, and they will typically be concentrated in the upper-left region.

These numbers are the output of JPEG, but they are encoded before being written on the output. In the JPEG literature this process is referred to as "entropy coding," and Section 5.6.4 illustrates it in detail. Three techniques are used by entropy coding to compress the 8×8 matrix of integers:

1. The 64 numbers are collected by scanning the matrix in zigzags (Figure 1.12b). This produces a string of 64 numbers that starts with some nonzeros and typically ends with many consecutive zeros. Only the nonzero numbers are output (encoded) and are followed by a special end-of block (EOB) code. This way there is no need to output the trailing zeros (we can say that the EOB is the run-length encoding of all the trailing zeros). The interested reader should also consult [Salomon 07] for other methods to compress binary strings with many consecutive zeros.

⋄ **Exercise 5.8:** Propose a practical way to write a loop that traverses an 8×8 matrix in zigzag.

2. The nonzero numbers are compressed using Huffman coding (Section 5.6.4).
3. The first of those numbers (the DC coefficient, page 156) is treated differently from the others (the AC coefficients).

> She had just succeeded in curving it down into a graceful zigzag, and was going to dive in among the leaves, which she found to be nothing but the tops of the trees under which she had been wandering, when a sharp hiss made her draw back in a hurry.
>
> —Lewis Carroll, *Alice in Wonderland* (1865)

5.6.4 Encoding

We first discuss point 3 above. Each 8×8 matrix of quantized DCT coefficients contains one DC coefficient [at position $(0,0)$, the top left corner] and 63 AC coefficients. The DC coefficient is a measure of the average value of the 64 original pixels, constituting the data unit. Experience shows that in a continuous-tone image, adjacent data units of pixels are normally correlated in the sense that the average values of the pixels in adjacent data units are close. We already know that the DC coefficient of a data unit is a multiple of the average of the 64 pixels that constitute the unit. This implies that the DC coefficients of adjacent data units don't differ much. JPEG outputs the first one (encoded), followed by *differences* (also encoded) of the DC coefficients of consecutive data units.

Example: If the first three 8×8 data units of an image have quantized DC coefficients of 1118, 1114, and 1119, then the JPEG output for the first data unit is 1118 (Huffman encoded, see below) followed by the 63 (encoded) AC coefficients of that data unit. The output for the second data unit will be $1114 - 1118 = -4$ (also Huffman encoded), followed by the 63 (encoded) AC coefficients of that data unit, and the output for the third data unit will be $1119 - 1114 = 5$ (also Huffman encoded), again followed by the 63 (encoded) AC coefficients of that data unit. This way of handling the DC coefficients is worth the extra trouble, because the differences are small.

Coding the DC differences is done with Table 5.32, so first here are a few words about this table. Each row has a row number (on the left), the unary code for the row (on the right), and several columns in between. Each row contains greater numbers (and also more numbers) than its predecessor but not the numbers contained in previous rows. Row i contains the range of integers $[-(2^i-1), +(2^i-1)]$ but is missing the middle range $[-(2^{i-1}-1), +(2^{i-1}-1)]$. Thus, the rows get very long, which means that a simple two-dimensional array is not a good data structure for this table. In fact, there is no need to store these integers in a data structure, since the program can figure out where in the table any given integer x is supposed to reside by analyzing the bits of x.

The first DC coefficient to be encoded in our example is 1118. It resides in row 11 column 930 of the table (column numbering starts at zero), so it is encoded as 111111111110|01110100010 (the unary code for row 11, followed by the 11-bit binary value of 930). The second DC difference is -4. It resides in row 3 column 3 of Table 5.32, so it is encoded as 1110|011 (the unary code for row 3, followed by the 3-bit binary value of 3).

⋄ **Exercise 5.9:** How is the third DC difference, 5, encoded?

Point 2 above has to do with the precise way the 63 AC coefficients of a data unit are compressed. It uses a combination of RLE and either Huffman or arithmetic coding. The idea is that the sequence of AC coefficients normally contains just a few nonzero numbers, with runs of zeros between them, and with a long run of trailing zeros. For each nonzero number x, the encoder (1) finds the number Z of consecutive zeros preceding x; (2) finds x in Table 5.32 and prepares its row and column numbers (R and C); (3) the pair (R, Z) [that's (R, Z), not (R, C)] is used as row and column numbers for Table 5.33; and (4) the Huffman code found in that position in the table is concatenated to C (where C is written as an R-bit number) and the result is (finally) the code emitted by the JPEG encoder for the AC coefficient x and all the consecutive zeros preceding it.

The Huffman codes in Table 5.33 are not the ones recommended by the JPEG standard. The standard recommends the use of Tables 5.34 and 5.35 and says that up to four Huffman code tables can be used by a JPEG codec, except that the baseline mode can use only two such tables. The actual codes in Table 5.33 are thus arbitrary. The reader should notice the EOB code at position $(0,0)$ and the ZRL code at position $(0,15)$. The former indicates end-of-block, and the latter is the code emitted for 15 consecutive zeros when the number of consecutive zeros exceeds 15. These codes are the ones recommended for the luminance AC coefficients of Table 5.34. The EOB and ZRL codes recommended for the chrominance AC coefficients of Table 5.35 are 00 and 1111111010, respectively.

As an example consider the sequence

$$1118, 2, 0, -2, \underbrace{0, \ldots, 0}_{13}, -1, 0, \ldots.$$

The first AC coefficient 2 has no zeros preceding it, so Z = 0. It is found in Table 5.32 in row 2, column 2, so R = 2 and C = 2. The Huffman code in position (R, Z) = (2, 0) of Table 5.33 is 01, so the final code emitted for 2 is 01|10. The next nonzero coefficient, -2, has one zero preceding it, so Z = 1. It is found in Table 5.32 in row 2, column 1, so R = 2 and C = 1. The Huffman code in position (R, Z) = (2, 1) of Table 5.33 is 11011, so the final code emitted for 2 is 11011|01.

0:	0									0
1:	-1	1								10
2:	-3	-2	2	3						110
3:	-7	-6	-5	-4	4	5	6	7		1110
4:	-15	-14	...	-9	-8	8	9	10 ...	15	11110
5:	-31	-30	-29	...	-17	-16	16	17 ...	31	111110
6:	-63	-62	-61	...	-33	-32	32	33 ...	63	1111110
7:	-127	-126	-125	...	-65	-64	64	65 ...	127	11111110
⋮				⋮					
14:	-16383	-16382	-16381	...	-8193	-8192	8192	8193 ...	16383	111111111111110
15:	-32767	-32766	-32765	...	-16385	-16384	16384	16385 ...	32767	1111111111111110
16:	32768									1111111111111111

Table 5.32: Coding the Differences of DC Coefficients.

R Z:	0	1	...	15
0:	1010			11111111001(ZRL)
1:	00	1100	...	1111111111110101
2:	01	11011	...	1111111111110110
3:	100	1111001	...	1111111111110111
4:	1011	111110110	...	1111111111111000
5:	11010	11111110110	...	1111111111111001
⋮	⋮			

Table 5.33: Coding AC Coefficients.

⋄ **Exercise 5.10:** What code is emitted for the last nonzero AC coefficient, −1?

Finally, the sequence of trailing zeros is encoded as 1010 (EOB), so the output for the above sequence of AC coefficients is 0110110111011101010101010. We saw earlier that the DC coefficient is encoded as 111111111110|1110100010, so the final output for the entire 64-pixel data unit is the 46-bit number

1111111111100111010001001101101110111010101010.

These 46 bits encode one color component of the 64 pixels of a data unit. Let's assume that the other two color components are also encoded into 46-bit numbers. If each pixel originally consists of 24 bits, then this corresponds to a compression factor of $64 \times 24/(46 \times 3) \approx 11.13$; very impressive!

(Notice that the DC coefficient of 1118 has contributed 23 of the 46 bits. Subsequent data units encode the differences of their DC coefficient, which may take fewer than 10 bits instead of 23. They may feature much higher compression factors as a result.)

The same tables (Tables 5.32 and 5.33) used by the encoder should, of course, be used by the decoder. The tables may be predefined and used by a JPEG codec as defaults, or they may be specifically calculated for a given image in a special pass preceding the actual compression. The JPEG standard does not specify any code tables, so any JPEG codec must use its own.

Some JPEG variants use a particular version of arithmetic coding, called the QM coder, that is specified in the JPEG standard. This version of arithmetic coding is adaptive, so it does not need Tables 5.32 and 5.33. It adapts its behavior to the image

	R				
Z	1 6	2 7	3 8	4 9	5 A
0	00 1111000	01 11111000	100 1111110110	1011 1111111110000010	11010 1111111110000011
1	1100 1111111110000100	11011 1111111110000101	11110001 1111111110000110	111110110 1111111110000111	1111110110 1111111110001000
2	11100 111111110001010	11111001 111111110001011	1111110111 111111110001100	111111110100 111111110001101	111111110001001 111111110001110
3	111010 1111111110010001	111110111 1111111110010010	111111110101 1111111110010011	1111111110001111 1111111110010100	1111111110010000 1111111110010101
4	111011 1111111110011001	1111111000 1111111110011010	1111111110010110 1111111110011011	1111111110010111 1111111110011100	1111111110011000 1111111110011101
5	1111010 1111111110100001	11111110111 1111111110100010	1111111110011110 1111111110100011	1111111110011111 1111111110100100	1111111110100000 1111111110100101
6	1111011 1111111110101001	111111110110 1111111110101010	1111111110100110 1111111110101011	1111111110100111 1111111110101100	1111111110101000 1111111110101101
7	11111010 1111111110110001	111111110111 1111111110110010	1111111110101110 1111111110110011	1111111110101111 1111111110110100	1111111110110000 1111111110110101
8	111111000 1111111110111001	111111111000000 1111111110111010	1111111110110110 1111111110111011	1111111110110111 1111111110111100	1111111110111000 1111111110111101
9	111111001 1111111111000010	1111111110111110 1111111111000011	1111111110111111 1111111111000100	1111111111000000 1111111111000101	1111111111000001 1111111111000110
A	111111010 1111111111001011	1111111111000111 1111111111001100	1111111111001000 1111111111001101	1111111111001001 1111111111001110	1111111111001010 1111111111001111
B	1111111001 1111111111010100	1111111111010000 1111111111010101	1111111111010001 1111111111010110	1111111111010010 1111111111010111	1111111111010011 1111111111011000
C	1111111010 1111111111011101	1111111111011001 1111111111011110	1111111111011010 1111111111011111	1111111111011011 1111111111100000	1111111111011100 1111111111100001
D	11111111000 1111111111100110	1111111111100010 1111111111100111	1111111111100011 1111111111101000	1111111111100100 1111111111101001	1111111111100101 1111111111101010
E	1111111111101011 1111111111110000	1111111111101100 1111111111110001	1111111111101101 1111111111110010	1111111111101110 1111111111110011	1111111111101111 1111111111110100
F	11111111001 1111111111111001	1111111111110101 1111111111111010	1111111111110110 1111111111111011	1111111111110111 1111111111111101	1111111111111000 1111111111111110

Table 5.34: Recommended Huffman Codes for Luminance AC Coefficients.

	R 1 / 6	R 2 / 7	R 3 / 8	R 4 / 9	R 5 / A
Z					
0	01 111000	100 1111000	1010 111110100	11000 1111110110	11001 111111110100
1	1011 111111110101	111001 111111110001000	11110110 111111110001001	111110101 111111110001010	1111110110 111111110001011
2	11010 1111111110001100	11110111 1111111110001101	1111110111 1111111110001110	111111110110 1111111110001111	111111111000010 1111111110010000
3	11011 1111111110010010	11111000 1111111110010011	1111111000 1111111110010100	111111110111 1111111110010101	1111111110010001 1111111110010110
4	111010 1111111110011010	111110110 1111111110011011	1111111110010111 1111111110011100	1111111110011000 1111111110011101	1111111110011001 1111111110011110
5	111011 1111111110100010	1111111001 1111111110100011	1111111110011111 1111111110100100	1111111110100000 1111111110100101	1111111110100001 1111111110100110
6	1111001 1111111110101010	11111110111 1111111110101011	1111111110100111 1111111110101100	1111111110101000 1111111110101101	1111111110101001 1111111110101110
7	1111010 1111111110110010	11111111000 1111111110110011	1111111110101111 1111111110110100	1111111110110000 1111111110110101	1111111110110001 1111111110110110
8	11111001 1111111110111011	1111111110110111 1111111110111100	1111111110111000 1111111110111101	1111111110111001 1111111110111110	1111111110111010 1111111110111111
9	111110111 1111111111000100	1111111111000000 1111111111000101	1111111111000001 1111111111000110	1111111111000010 1111111111000111	1111111111000011 1111111111001000
A	111111000 1111111111001101	1111111111001001 1111111111001110	1111111111001010 1111111111001111	1111111111001011 1111111111010000	1111111111001100 1111111111010001
B	111111001 1111111111010110	1111111111010010 1111111111010111	1111111111010011 1111111111011000	1111111111010100 1111111111011001	1111111111010101 1111111111011010
C	111111010 1111111111011111	1111111111011011 1111111111100000	1111111111011100 1111111111100001	1111111111011101 1111111111100010	1111111111011110 1111111111100011
D	11111111001 1111111111101000	1111111111100100 1111111111101001	1111111111100101 1111111111101010	1111111111100110 1111111111101011	1111111111100111 1111111111101100
E	11111111100000 1111111111110001	1111111111101101 1111111111110010	1111111111101110 1111111111110011	1111111111101111 1111111111110100	1111111111110000 1111111111110101
F	111111111000011 1111111111111010	1111111111010110 1111111111111011	1111111111110111 1111111111111100	1111111111111110 1111111111111101	1111111111111001 1111111111111110

Table 5.35: Recommended Huffman Codes for Chrominance AC Coefficients.

statistics as it goes along. Using arithmetic coding may produce 5–10% better compression than Huffman for a typical continuous-tone image. However, it is more complex to implement than Huffman coding, so in practice it is rare to find a JPEG codec that uses it.

5.6.5 Lossless Mode

The lossless mode of JPEG uses differencing to reduce the values of pixels before they are compressed. This particular form of differencing is called *predicting*. The values of some near neighbors of a pixel are subtracted from the pixel to get a small number, which is then compressed further using Huffman or arithmetic coding. Figure 5.36a shows a pixel X and three neighbor pixels A, B, and C. Figure 5.36b shows eight possible ways (predictions) to combine the values of the three neighbors. In the lossless mode, the user can select one of these predictions, and the encoder then uses it to combine the three neighbor pixels and subtract the combination from the value of X. The result is normally a small number, which is then entropy-coded in a way very similar to that described for the DC coefficient in Section 5.6.4.

Predictor 0 is used only in the hierarchical mode of JPEG. Predictors 1, 2, and 3 are called one-dimensional. Predictors 4, 5, 6, and 7 are two-dimensional.

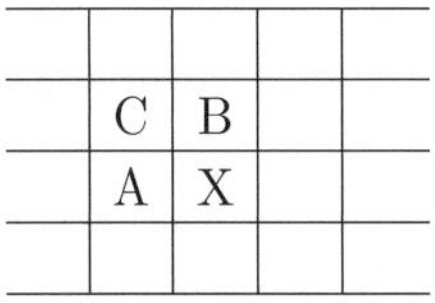

	Selection value	Prediction
	0	no prediction
	1	A
	2	B
	3	C
	4	$A + B - C$
	5	$A + ((B - C)/2)$
	6	$B + ((A - C)/2)$
	7	$(A + B)/2$

C	B	
A	X	

(a)   (b)

Figure 5.36: Pixel Prediction in the Lossless Mode.

It should be noted that the lossless mode of JPEG has never been very successful. It produces typical compression factors of 2, and is therefore inferior to other lossless image compression methods. Because of this, many JPEG implementations do not even implement this mode. Even the lossy (baseline) mode of JPEG does not perform well when asked to limit the amount of loss to a minimum. As a result, some JPEG implementations do not allow parameter settings that result in minimum loss. The strength of JPEG is in its ability to generate highly compressed images that when decompressed are indistinguishable from the original. Recognizing this, the ISO has decided to come up with another standard for lossless compression of continuous-tone images. This standard is now commonly known as JPEG-LS and is described, among other places, in [Salomon 07].

5.6.6 The Compressed File

A JPEG encoder outputs a compressed file that includes parameters, markers, and the compressed data units. The parameters are either four bits (these always come in pairs), one byte, or two bytes long. The markers serve to identify the various parts of the file. Each is two bytes long, where the first byte is X'FF' and the second one is not 0 or X'FF'. A marker may be preceded by a number of bytes with X'FF'. Table 5.38 lists all the JPEG markers (the first four groups are start-of-frame markers). The compressed data units are combined into MCUs (minimal coded unit), where an MCU is either a single data unit (in the noninterleaved mode) or three data units from the three image components (in the interleaved mode).

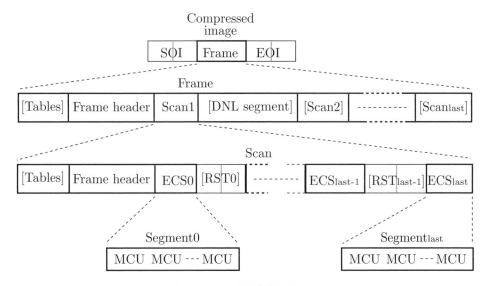

Figure 5.37: JPEG File Format.

Figure 5.37 shows the main parts of the JPEG compressed file (parts in square brackets are optional). The file starts with the SOI marker and ends with the EOI marker. In between these markers, the compressed image is organized in frames. In the hierarchical mode there are several frames, and in all other modes there is only one frame. In each frame the image information is contained in one or more scans, but the frame also contains a header and optional tables (which, in turn, may include markers). The first scan may be followed by an optional DNL segment (define number of lines), which starts with the DNL marker and contains the number of lines in the image that's represented by the frame. A scan starts with optional tables, followed by the scan header, followed by several entropy-coded segments (ECS), which are separated by (optional) restart markers (RST). Each ECS contains one or more MCUs, where an MCU is, as explained earlier, either a single data unit or three such units.

Value	Name	Description
Nondifferential, Huffman coding		
FFC0	SOF_0	Baseline DCT
FFC1	SOF_1	Extended sequential DCT
FFC2	SOF_2	Progressive DCT
FFC3	SOF_3	Lossless (sequential)
Differential, Huffman coding		
FFC5	SOF_5	Differential sequential DCT
FFC6	SOF_6	Differential progressive DCT
FFC7	SOF_7	Differential lossless (sequential)
Nondifferential, arithmetic coding		
FFC8	JPG	Reserved for extensions
FFC9	SOF_9	Extended sequential DCT
FFCA	SOF_{10}	Progressive DCT
FFCB	SOF_{11}	Lossless (sequential)
Differential, arithmetic coding		
FFCD	SOF_{13}	Differential sequential DCT
FFCE	SOF_{14}	Differential progressive DCT
FFCF	SOF_{15}	Differential lossless (sequential)
Huffman table specification		
FFC4	DHT	Define Huffman table
Arithmetic coding conditioning specification		
FFCC	DAC	Define arith coding conditioning(s)
Restart interval termination		
FFD0–FFD7	RST_m	Restart with modulo 8 count m
Other markers		
FFD8	SOI	Start of image
FFD9	EOI	End of image
FFDA	SOS	Start of scan
FFDB	DQT	Define quantization table(s)
FFDC	DNL	Define number of lines
FFDD	DRI	Define restart interval
FFDE	DHP	Define hierarchical progression
FFDF	EXP	Expand reference component(s)
FFE0–FFEF	APP_n	Reserved for application segments
FFF0–FFFD	JPG_n	Reserved for JPEG extensions
FFFE	COM	Comment
Reserved markers		
FF01	TEM	For temporary private use
FF02–FFBF	RES	Reserved

Table 5.38: JPEG Markers.

5.6.7 JFIF

It has been mentioned earlier that JPEG is a compression method, not a graphics file format, which is why it does not specify image features such as pixel aspect ratio, color space, or interleaving of bitmap rows. This is where JFIF comes in.

JFIF (JPEG File Interchange Format) is a graphics file format that makes it possible to exchange JPEG-compressed images between computers. The main features of JFIF are the use of the YCbCr triple-component color space for color images (only one component for grayscale images) and the use of a *marker* to specify features missing from JPEG, such as image resolution, aspect ratio, and features that are application-specific.

The JFIF marker (called the APP0 marker) starts with the zero-terminated string JFIF. Following this, there is pixel information and other specifications (see below). Following this, there may be additional segments specifying JFIF extensions. A JFIF extension contains more platform-specific information about the image.

Each extension starts with the zero-terminated string JFXX, followed by a 1-byte code identifying the extension. An extension may contain application-specific information, in which case it starts with a different string, not JFIF or JFXX but something that identifies the specific application or its maker.

The format of the first segment of an APP0 marker is as follows:

1. APP0 marker (4 bytes): FFD8FFE0.
2. Length (2 bytes): Total length of marker, including the 2 bytes of the "length" field but excluding the APP0 marker itself (field 1).
3. Identifier (5 bytes): $4A46494600_{16}$: This is the JFIF string that identifies the APP0 marker.
4. Version (2 bytes): Example: 0102_{16} specifies version 1.02.
5. Units (1 byte): Units for the X and Y densities. 0 means no units; the Xdensity and Ydensity fields specify the pixel aspect ratio. 1 means that Xdensity and Ydensity are dots per inch, 2, that they are dots per cm.
6. Xdensity (2 bytes), Ydensity (2 bytes): Horizontal and vertical pixel densities (both should be nonzero).
7. Xthumbnail (1 byte), Ythumbnail (1 byte): Thumbnail horizontal and vertical pixel counts.
8. (RGB)n ($3n$ bytes): Packed (24-bit) RGB values for the thumbnail pixels. $n =$ Xthumbnail$\times$Ythumbnail.

The syntax of the JFIF extension APP0 marker segment is as follows:

1. APP0 marker.
2. Length (2 bytes): Total length of marker, including the 2 bytes of the "length" field but excluding the APP0 marker itself (field 1).
3. Identifier (5 bytes): $4A46585800_{16}$ This is the JFXX string identifying an extension.
4. Extension code (1 byte): $10_{16} =$ Thumbnail coded using JPEG. $11_{16} =$ Thumbnail coded using 1 byte/pixel (monochromatic). $13_{16} =$ Thumbnail coded using 3 bytes/pixel (eight colors).
5. Extension data (variable): This field depends on the particular extension.

JFIF is the technical name for the image format better (but inaccurately) known as JPEG. This term is used only when the difference between the Image Format and the Image Compression is crucial. Strictly speaking, however, JPEG does not define an Image Format, and therefore in most cases it would be more precise to speak of JFIF rather than JPEG. Another Image Format for JPEG is SPIFF defined by the JPEG standard itself, but JFIF is much more widespread than SPIFF.

—Erik Wilde, *WWW Online Glossary*

5.7 The Wavelet Transform

The transforms described in Section 5.3 are orthogonal. They transform the original pixels into a few large numbers and many small numbers. In contrast, the wavelet transforms of this section decompose an image into bands (regions or subbands) that correspond to different pixel frequencies and also reflect different geometrical artifacts of the image. The final (lossy) compression of the image can be very efficient, because each band can be independently quantized (by an amount that depends on the pixel frequency it corresponds to) and then encoded. Thus, a wavelet transform may be the key to efficient compression of images with a mixture of high-frequency and low-frequency areas. In contrast, images with large uniform (or almost-uniform) areas may respond better to other compression methods. Reference [Salomon 07] describes several compression methods that are based on wavelet transforms.

Before we start, here are a few words about the origin of the term wavelet. In the early 1800s, the French mathematician Joseph Fourier discovered that any periodic function f can be expressed as a (possibly infinite) sum of sines and cosines. These functions are represented graphically as waves, which is why the Fourier expansion of a function f is associated with waves and reveals the frequencies "hidden" in f. Fourier expansion has many applications in engineering, mainly in the analysis of signals. It can isolate the various frequencies that underlie a signal and thereby enable the user to study the signal and also edit it by deleting or adding frequencies. The downside of Fourier expansion is that it does not tell us when (at which point or points in time) each frequency is active in a given signal. We therefore say that Fourier expansion offers frequency resolution but no time resolution.

Wavelet analysis (or the wavelet transform) is a successful approach to the problem of analyzing a signal both in time and in frequency. Given a signal that varies with time, we select a time interval, and use the wavelet transform to identify and isolate the frequencies that constitute the signal in that interval. The interval can be wide, in which case we say that the signal is analyzed on a large scale. As the time interval gets narrower, the scale of analysis is said to become smaller and smaller. A large-scale analysis illustrates the global behavior of the signal, while each small-scale analysis illuminates the way the signal behaves in a short interval of time; it is like zooming in the signal in time, instead of in space. Thus, the fundamental idea behind wavelets is to analyze a function or a signal according to scale.

The continuous wavelet transform [Salomon 07] illustrates the connection between (1) the time-frequency analysis of continuous functions and (2) waves that are concentrated in a small area. This analysis therefore justifies the diminutive "wavelet" instead of "wave." In practical applications, the raw data is normally collected as sets of numbers, not as a continuous function, and is therefore discrete. Thus, the discrete, and not the continuous, wavelet transform is the tool used in practice to analyze digital data and compress it.

> The wavelet transform is a tool that cuts up data or functions or operators into different frequency components, and then studies each component with a resolution matched to its scale.
> —Ingrid Daubechies (approximate pronunciation "Dobe-uh-shee"),
> *Ten Lectures on Wavelets* (1992)

We start with the Haar transform, originated in work done by Alfred Haar in 1910–1912 on systems of orthogonal functions [Haar 10]. The Haar transform is the simplest wavelet transform, and we illustrate it in one dimension. Given an array of n pixels, where n is a power of 2 (if it is not, we extend the array by appending copies of the last pixels), we divide it into $n/2$ pairs of consecutive pixels, compute the average and the difference of each pair, and end up with $n/2$ averages followed by $n/2$ differences. We then repeat this process on the $n/2$ averages to obtain $n/4$ averages followed by $n/4$ differences. This is repeated until we end up with one average followed by $n-1$ differences.

As an example, consider the eight correlated values 31, 32, 33.5, 33.5, 31.5, 34.5, 32, and 28. We compute the four averages $(31 + 32)/2 = 31.5$, $(33.5 + 33.5)/2 = 33.5$, $(31.5 + 34.5)/2 = 33$, and $(32 + 28)/2 = 30$ and the four differences $31 - 32 = -1$, $33.5 - 33.5 = 0$, $31.5 - 34.5 = -3$, and $32 - 28 = 4$. The differences are called *detail coefficients*, and in this section the terms "difference" and "detail" are used interchangeably. We can think of the averages as a coarse resolution representation of the original values, and of the details as the extra data needed to reconstruct the original image from this coarse resolution. The four averages and four differences are sufficient to reconstruct the original eight values, but because these values are correlated, the averages and differences feature additional properties. The averages are a coarse representation of the original values and the differences are small.

We repeat the process on the four averages and transform them into two averages and two differences. The results are $(31.5 + 33.5)/2 = 32.5$, $(33 + 30)/2 = 31.5$, $31.5 + 33.5 = -2$, and $33 - 30 = 3$. The last iteration of this process transforms the two new averages into one average $(32.5 + 31.5)/2 = 32$ (the average of all eight components of the original array) and one difference $32.5 - 31.5 = 1$. The eight numbers 32, 1, -2, 3, -1, 0, -3, and 4 constitute the *Haar wavelet transform* of the original correlated values.

In general, the one-dimensional Haar transform converts n correlated values to n transform coefficients of which the first is the average of the original values and the remaining are small numbers. Compression is lossy and is achieved by quantizing the differences (at least to the nearest integers and perhaps even coarser) and encoding them with Huffman or other variable-length codes.

Alfréd Haar (1885–1933)

Alfréd Haar was born in Budapest and received his higher mathematical training in Göttingen, where he later became a privatdozent. In 1912, he returned to Hungary and became a professor of mathematics first in Kolozsvár and then in Szeged, where he and his colleagues created a major mathematical center.

Haar is best remembered for his work on analysis on groups. In 1932 he introduced an invariant measure on locally compact groups, now called the Haar measure, which allows an analog of Lebesgue integrals to be defined on locally compact topological groups. Mathematical lore has it that John von Neumann tried to discourage Haar in this work because he felt certain that no such measure could exist. The following limerick celebrates Haar's achievement.

> Said a mathematician named Haar,
> "Von Neumann can't see very far.
> He missed a great treasure—
> They call it Haar measure—
> Poor Johnny's just not up to par."

Before we continue, it is important (and also interesting) to estimate the computational complexity of this transform, i.e., the number of arithmetic operations needed to transform N data values. In our example we needed $8+4+2 = 14$ operations (additions and subtractions, the divisions by 2 are ignored since they can be done with shifts), a number that can also be expressed as $14 = 2(8-1)$. In the general case, assume that we start with $N = 2^n$ data items. The first iteration requires 2^n operations, the second iteration requires 2^{n-1} operations, and so on, until the last iteration, where $2^{n-(n-1)} = 2^1$ operations are needed. The total number of operations is therefore

$$\sum_{i=1}^{n} 2^i = \sum_{i=0}^{n} 2^i - 1 = \frac{1 - 2^{n+1}}{1 - 2} - 1 = 2^{n+1} - 2 = 2(2^n - 1) = 2(N - 1).$$

The Haar transform of N values can therefore be performed with $2(N-1)$ operations, so its complexity is $\mathcal{O}(N)$, an excellent result.

It is useful to associate with each iteration a quantity called *resolution*, which is defined as the number of remaining averages at the end of the iteration. The resolutions after each of the three iterations above are $4(= 2^2)$, $2(= 2^1)$, and $1(= 2^0)$. Section 5.7.3 shows that each component of the wavelet transform should be normalized by dividing it by the square root of the resolution. (This is the *normalized Haar transform*, also discussed in Section 5.7.3.) Thus, our example wavelet transform becomes

$$\left(\frac{32}{\sqrt{2^0}}, \frac{1}{\sqrt{2^0}}, \frac{-2}{\sqrt{2^1}}, \frac{3}{\sqrt{2^1}}, \frac{-1}{\sqrt{2^2}}, \frac{0}{\sqrt{2^2}}, \frac{-3}{\sqrt{2^2}}, \frac{4}{\sqrt{2^2}} \right).$$

If the normalized wavelet transform is used, it can be shown that ignoring the smallest differences is the best choice for lossy wavelet compression, since it causes the smallest loss of image information.

The two procedures of Figure 5.39 illustrate how the normalized wavelet transform of an array of n components (where n is a power of 2) can be computed. Reconstructing the original array from the normalized wavelet transform is illustrated by the pair of procedures of Figure 5.40.

These procedures seem at first to be different from the averages and differences discussed earlier. They don't compute averages, because they divide by $\sqrt{2}$ instead of by 2; the first procedure starts by dividing the entire array by $\sqrt{n}$, and the second one ends by doing the reverse. The final result, however, is the same.

We believe that the future of wavelet theory will continue to be marked by the synthesis of traditionally distinct disciplines in mathematics, engineering, and the sciences. This will require adjustments by all parties, including an increased willingness to address applications on the part of mathematicians, and an increased attention to mathematical rigor on the part of the engineering community. We hope that this book will contribute toward this future.

—J. Benedetto and M. Frazier, *Wavelets: Mathematics and Applications* (1994)

5.7.1 Applying the Haar Transform

Once the concept of a wavelet transform is grasped, it's easy to generalize it to a complete two-dimensional image. This can be done in quite a few ways which are discussed in [Salomon 07]. Here we describe only two such approaches, called the *standard decomposition* and the *pyramid decomposition*.

The former (Figure 5.41) starts by computing the wavelet transform of every row of the image. This results in a transformed image where the first column contains averages and all the other columns contain differences. The standard algorithm then computes the wavelet transform of every column. This results in one average value at the top-left corner, with the rest of the top row containing averages of differences, and with all other pixel values transformed into differences.

The latter method computes the wavelet transform of the image by alternating between rows and columns. The first step is to calculate averages and differences for all the rows (just one iteration, not the entire wavelet transform). This creates averages in the left half of the image and differences in the right half. The second step is to calculate averages and differences (just one iteration) for all the columns, which results in averages in the top-left quadrant of the image and differences elsewhere. Steps 3 and 4 operate on the rows and columns of that quadrant, resulting in averages concentrated in the top-left subquadrant. Pairs of steps are executed repeatedly on smaller and smaller subsquares, until only one average is left, at the top-left corner of the image, and all other pixel values have been reduced to differences. This process is summarized in Figure 5.42.

Armed with these decompositions, it is easy to understand why the wavelet transform is the key to efficient lossy image compression. The transforms described in Section 5.3 are orthogonal. They transform the original pixels into a few large numbers and many small numbers. In contrast, wavelet transforms, such as the Haar transform, are *subband* transforms. They partition the image into regions (also called subbands) such that one region contains large numbers (averages in the case of the Haar transform) and the other regions contain small numbers (differences). However, the subbands are more than just sets of large and small numbers. They reveal different geometrical artifacts

```
procedure NWTcalc(a:array of real, n:int);
 comment n is the array size (a power of 2)
 a:=a/√n comment divide entire array
 j:=n;
 while j≥ 2 do
  NWTstep(a, j);
  j:=j/2;
 endwhile;
end;


procedure NWTstep(a:array of real, j:int);
 for i=1 to j/2 do
  b[i]:=(a[2i-1]+a[2i])/√2;
  b[j/2+i]:=(a[2i-1]-a[2i])/√2;
 endfor;
 a:=b; comment move entire array
end;
```

Figure 5.39: Computing the Normalized Wavelet Transform.

```
procedure NWTreconst(a:array of real, n:int);
 j:=2;
 while j≤n do
  NWTRstep(a, j);
  j:=2j;
 endwhile
 a:=a√n; comment multiply entire array
end;

procedure NWTRstep(a:array of real, j:int);
 for i=1 to j/2 do
  b[2i-1]:=(a[i]+a[j/2+i])/√2;
  b[2i]:=(a[i]-a[j/2+i])/√2;
 endfor;
 a:=b; comment move entire array
end;
```

Figure 5.40: Restoring From a Normalized Wavelet Transform.

```
procedure StdCalc(a:array of real, n:int);
 comment array size is nxn (n = power of 2)
 for r=1 to n do NWTcalc(row r of a, n);
 endfor;
 for c=n to 1 do comment loop backwards
  NWTcalc(col c of a, n);
 endfor;
end;
procedure StdReconst(a:array of real, n:int);
 for c=n to 1 do comment loop backwards
  NWTreconst(col c of a, n);
 endfor;
 for r=1 to n do
  NWTreconst(row r of a, n);
 endfor;
end;
```

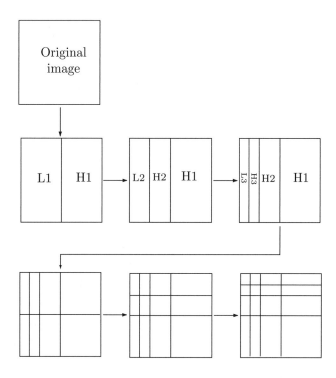

Figure 5.41: The Standard Image Wavelet Transform and Decomposition.

```
procedure NStdCalc(a:array of real, n:int);
 a:=a/√n̄ comment divide entire array
 j:=n;
 while j≥2 do
  for r=1 to j do NWTstep(row r of a, j);
  endfor;
  for c=j to 1 do comment loop backwards
   NWTstep(col c of a, j);
  endfor;
  j:=j/2;
 endwhile;
end;
procedure NStdReconst(a:array of real, n:int);
 j:=2;
 while j≤n do
  for c=j to 1 do comment loop backwards
   NWTRstep(col c of a, j);
  endfor;
  for r=1 to j do
   NWTRstep(row r of a, j);
  endfor;
  j:=2j;
 endwhile
 a:=a√n̄; comment multiply entire array
end;
```

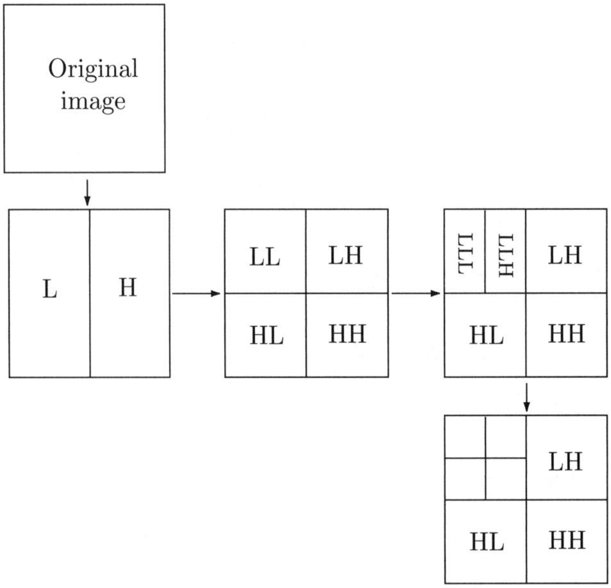

Figure 5.42: The Pyramid Image Wavelet Transform.

of the image. To illustrate this important feature, we examine a small, mostly-uniform image with one vertical line and one horizontal line. Figure 5.43a shows an 8×8 image with pixel values of 12, except for a vertical line with pixel values of 14 and a horizontal line with pixel values of 16.

```
12 12 12 12 14 12 12 12     12 12 13 12│0 0 2 0      12 12 13 12│0 0 2 0
12 12 12 12 14 12 12 12     12 12 13 12│0 0 2 0      12 12 13 12│0 0 2 0
12 12 12 12 14 12 12 12     12 12 13 12│0 0 2 0      14 14 14 14│0 0 0 0
12 12 12 12 14 12 12 12     12 12 13 12│0 0 2 0      12 12 13 12│0 0 2 0
12 12 12 12 14 12 12 12     12 12 13 12│0 0 2 0       0  0  0  0 0 0 0 0
16 16 16 16 14 16 16 16     16 16 15 16│0 0 2 0       0  0  0  0 0 0 0 0
12 12 12 12 14 12 12 12     12 12 13 12│0 0 2 0       4  4  2  4 0 0 4 0
12 12 12 12 14 12 12 12     12 12 13 12│0 0 2 0       0  0  0  0 0 0 0 0
         (a)                        (b)                       (c)
```

Figure 5.43: An 8×8 Image and Its Subband Decomposition.

Figure 5.43b shows the results of applying the Haar transform once to the rows of the image. The right half of this figure (the differences) is mostly zeros, reflecting the uniform nature of the image. However, traces of the vertical line can easily be seen (the notation $\underline{2}$ indicates a negative difference). Figure 5.43c shows the results of applying the Haar transform once to the columns of Figure 5.43b. The upper-right subband now features traces of the vertical line, whereas the lower-left subband shows traces of the horizontal line. These subbands are denoted by HL and LH, respectively (Figures 5.42 and 5.44, although there is inconsistency in the use of this notation by various authors). The lower-right subband, denoted by HH, reflects diagonal image artifacts (which our example image lacks). Most interesting is the upper-left subband, denoted by LL, that consists entirely of averages. This subband is a one-quarter version of the entire image, containing traces of both the vertical and the horizontal lines.

⋄ **Exercise 5.11:** Construct a diagram similar to Figure 5.43 to show how subband HH reveals diagonal artifacts of the image.

(Artifact: A feature not naturally present, introduced during preparation or investigation.)

Figure 5.44 shows four levels of subbands, where level 1 contains the detailed features of the image (also referred to as the high-frequency or fine-resolution wavelet coefficients) and the top level, level 4, contains the coarse image features (low-frequency or coarse-resolution coefficients). It is clear that the lower levels can be quantized coarsely without much loss of important image information, while the higher levels should be quantized only finely. The subband structure is the basis of all the image compression methods that employ the wavelet transform.

Figure 5.45 shows typical results of the pyramid wavelet transform. The original image is shown in Figure 5.45a, and Figure 5.45c is a general pyramid decomposition. In order to illustrate how the pyramid transform works, this image consists only of horizontal, vertical, and slanted lines. The four quadrants of Figure 5.45b show smaller

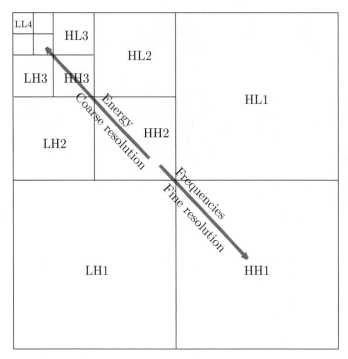

Figure 5.44: Subbands and Levels in Wavelet Decomposition.

versions of the image. The top-left subband, containing the averages, is similar to the entire image, while each of the other three subbands shows image details. Because of the way the pyramid transform is constructed, the top-right subband contains vertical details, the bottom-left subband contains horizontal details, and the bottom-right subband contains the details of slanted lines. Figure 5.45c shows the results of repeatedly applying this transform. The image is transformed into subbands of horizontal, vertical, and diagonal details, while the top-left subsquare, containing the averages, is shrunk to a single pixel. Figure 5.46 lists simple Matlab code to compute the pyramid transform of a raw (uncompressed) image.

Either method, standard or uniform, results in a transformed, although not yet compressed, image that has one average at the top-left corner and smaller numbers, differences or averages of differences, everywhere else. These numbers are now compressed (lossy compression) by quantizing them to integers which are then encoded by replacing them with variable-length codes. Coarse quantization often results in runs of zeros, which can be compressed by RLE (each run of zeros is replaced by a single variable-length code).

Color Images. So far, we have assumed that each pixel is a single number (i.e., we have a single-component image, in which all pixels are shades of the same color, normally gray). Any compression method for single-component images can be extended to color (three-component) images by separating the three components, then transforming and compressing each individually. If the compression method is lossy, it makes sense

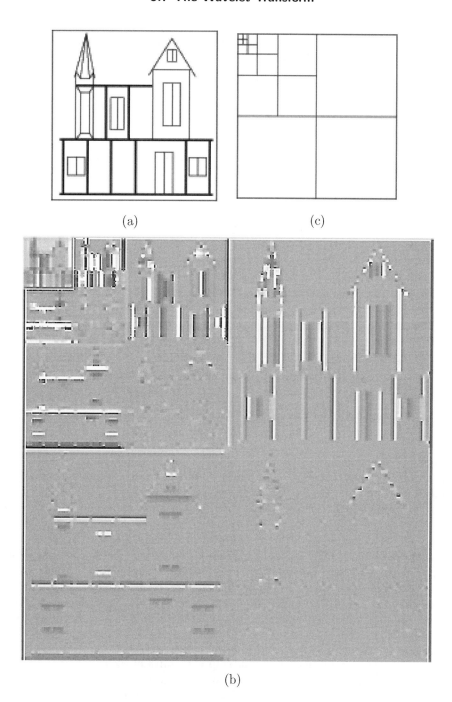

Figure 5.45: An Example of the Pyramid Image Wavelet Transform.

```
clear; % main program, file pyramid.m
filename='house128'; global dim; dim=128;
fid=fopen(filename,'r');
if fid==-1 disp('file not found')
else img=fread(fid,[dim,dim])'; fclose(fid);
end
figure(1), image(img), colormap(gray), axis square
global timg; timg=zeros(dim,dim);
stp(img);
img=timg;
figure(2), image(img), colormap(gray), axis square
dim=64;
stp(img);
img=timg;
figure(3), image(img), colormap(gray), axis square

function x=stp(img) % file stp.m
global dim; global timg
for r = 1:dim
  for c=1:2:dim-1;
    timg(r,c)=(img(r,c)+img(r,c+1))/2;
    timg(r,c+c)=img(r,c)-img(r,c+1);
  end;
end
for c=1:dim;
  for r=1:2:dim-1;
    timg(r,c)=(img(r,c)+img(r+1,c))/2;
    timg(r+r,c)=img(r,c)-img(r+1,c);
  end;
end;
```

Figure 5.46: Matlab Code for a Pyramid Image Wavelet Transform.

to convert the three image components from their original color representation (often RGB) to the YIQ color representation. The Y component of this representation is called *luminance*, and the I and Q (the chrominance) components are responsible for the color information [Salomon 99]. The advantage of this color representation is that the human eye is most sensitive to Y and least sensitive to Q. A lossy compression method for color images in YIQ should therefore: (1) apply a wavelet transform to each of the three components separately; (2) quantize the transform coefficients of the Y component lightly (perhaps only to the nearest integer), perform medium quantization on the coefficients of the I component, and coarse quantization on the coefficients of the Q component; and finally (3) encode all the quantized transform coefficients. Such a process results in excellent compression, while losing only image data to which the eye is not sensitive.

> Man's life was spacious in the early world:
> It paused, like some slow ship with sail unfurled
> Waiting in seas by scarce a wavelet curled;
> —George Eliot, *Poems* (1895)

It is interesting to note that United States color television transmission also takes advantage of the YIQ representation. Signals are broadcast with bandwidths of 4 MHz for Y, 1.5 MHz for I, and only 0.6 MHz for Q.

✜Make two squares and four right-angled triangles by drawing only seven straight lines.

5.7.2 Properties of the Haar Transform

The examples in this section illustrate some properties of the Haar transform, and of the discrete wavelet transform in general. Figure 5.47 shows a highly correlated 8×8 image and its Haar wavelet transform. Both the grayscale and numeric values of the pixels and of the transform coefficients are shown. Because the original pixels are highly correlated, the wavelet coefficients are small and there are many zeros.

◇ **Exercise 5.12:** A glance at Figure 5.47 suggests that the last sentence is wrong. The wavelet transform coefficients listed in the figure are very large compared with the pixel values of the original image. In fact, we know that the top-left Haar transform coefficient should be the average of all the image pixels. Since the pixels of our image have values that are (more or less) uniformly distributed in the interval $[0, 255]$, this average should be around 128, yet the top-left transform coefficient is 1051. Explain this!

In a discrete wavelet transform, most of the wavelet coefficients are details (or differences). The details in the lower levels represent the fine details of the image. As we move higher in the subband level, we find details that correspond to coarser image features. Figure 5.48a illustrates this concept. It shows an image that is smooth on the left and has "activity" (i.e., adjacent pixels that tend to be different) on the right. Part (b) shows the wavelet transform of the image. Low levels (corresponding to fine details) have transform coefficients on the right, since this is where the image activity is located. High levels (coarse details) look similar but also have coefficients on the left side, because the image is not completely blank on the left.

The Haar transform is the simplest wavelet transform, but even this simple method illustrates the power of this type of transform. It has been mentioned earlier that the low levels of the discrete wavelet transform contain the unimportant image features, so quantizing these coefficients (even all the way to zero) can lead to lossy compression that is both efficient and of high quality. Often, the image can be reconstructed from very few transform coefficients without any noticeable loss of quality. Figure 5.49a–c shows three reconstructions of the simple 8×8 image of Figure 5.47. They were obtained from only 32, 13, and 5 wavelet coefficients, respectively.

Figure 5.50 is a similar example. It shows a bi-level image fully reconstructed from just 4% of its transform coefficients (653 coefficients out of 128×128).

Experimenting is the key to understanding these concepts. Proper mathematical software makes it easy to input images and experiment with various features of the discrete wavelet transform. In order to help the interested reader, Figure 5.51 lists a Matlab program that inputs a grayscale image (in raw format, just rows of pixel values), computes its Haar wavelet transform, discards a given percentage of the smallest transform coefficients, and then computes the inverse transform to reconstruct the image.

Lossy wavelet image compression involves the discarding of coefficients (quantizing them to zero), so the concept of *sparseness ratio* is defined to measure the amount of coefficients discarded. Sparseness is defined as the number of nonzero wavelet coefficients divided by the number of coefficients left after some are discarded. The higher

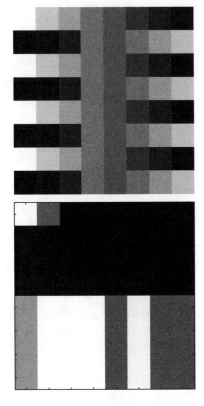

255	224	192	159	127	95	63	32
0	32	64	159	127	159	191	223
255	224	192	159	127	95	63	32
0	32	64	159	127	159	191	223
255	224	192	159	127	95	63	32
0	32	64	159	127	159	191	223
255	224	192	159	127	95	63	32
0	32	64	159	127	159	191	223

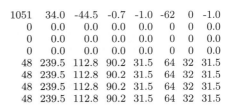

1051	34.0	-44.5	-0.7	-1.0	-62	0	-1.0
0	0.0	0.0	0.0	0.0	0	0	0.0
0	0.0	0.0	0.0	0.0	0	0	0.0
0	0.0	0.0	0.0	0.0	0	0	0.0
48	239.5	112.8	90.2	31.5	64	32	31.5
48	239.5	112.8	90.2	31.5	64	32	31.5
48	239.5	112.8	90.2	31.5	64	32	31.5
48	239.5	112.8	90.2	31.5	64	32	31.5

Figure 5.47: An 8×8 Image (top) and its Haar Transform (below).

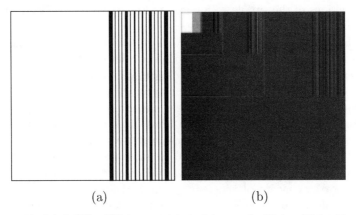

(a)   (b)

Figure 5.48: (a) A 128×128 Image with Activity on the Right. (b) Its Transform.

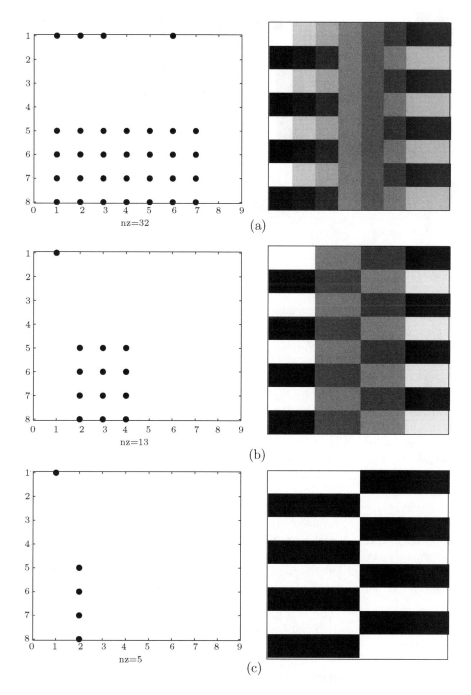

Figure 5.49: Three Lossy Reconstructions of the Image of Figure 5.47.

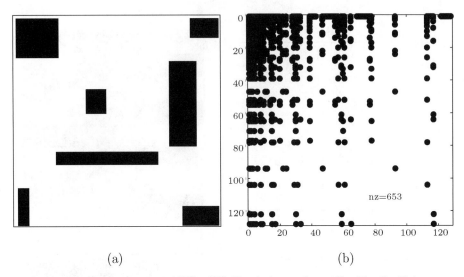

(a)　　　　　　　　　　　　　　　　　　(b)

Figure 5.50: Reconstructing a 128×128 Simple Image from 4% of its Coefficients.

the sparseness ratio, the fewer coefficients are left. Higher sparseness ratios lead to better compression but may result in poorly reconstructed images. The sparseness ratio is distantly related to the compression factor, a compression measure defined in the Introduction.

The line "`filename='lena128'; dim=128;`" contains the image file name and the dimension of the image. The image files used by the author were in raw form and contained just the grayscale values, each as a single byte. There is no header, and not even the image resolution (number of rows and columns) is included in the file. However, Matlab can read other types of files. The image is assumed to be square, and parameter "`dim`" should be a power of 2. The assignment "`thresh=`" specifies the percentage of transform coefficients to be deleted. This provides an easy way to experiment with lossy wavelet image compression.

File `harmatt.m` contains two functions that compute the Haar wavelet coefficients in a matrix form (Section 5.7.3).

(A technical note: A Matlab `m` file may include commands or a function but not both. It may, however, contain more than one function, provided that only the top function is invoked from outside the file. All the other functions must be called from within the file. In our case, function `harmatt(dim)` calls function `individ(n)`.)

⋄ **Exercise 5.13:** Use the code of Figure 5.51 (or similar code) to compute the Haar transform of the well-known *Lena* image and reconstruct it three times by discarding more and more detail coefficients.

5.7.3 A Matrix Approach

The principle of the Haar transform is to compute averages and differences. It turns out that this can be done by means of matrix multiplication ([Mulcahy 96] and [Mulcahy 97]). We use the top row of the 8×8 image of Figure 5.47 as an example. Anyone

```
clear; % main program
filename='lena128'; dim=128;
fid=fopen(filename,'r');
if fid==-1 disp('file not found')
else img=fread(fid,[dim,dim])'; fclose(fid);
end
thresh=0.0;          % percent of transform coefficients deleted
figure(1), imagesc(img), colormap(gray), axis off, axis square
w=harmatt(dim);  % compute the Haar dim x dim transform matrix
timg=w*img*w';    % forward Haar transform
tsort=sort(abs(timg(:)));
tthresh=tsort(floor(max(thresh*dim*dim,1)));
cim=timg.*(abs(timg) > tthresh);
[i,j,s]=find(cim);
dimg=sparse(i,j,s,dim,dim);
% figure(2) displays the remaining transform coefficients
%figure(2), spy(dimg), colormap(gray), axis square
figure(2), image(dimg), colormap(gray), axis square
cimg=full(w'*sparse(dimg)*w);        % inverse Haar transform
density = nnz(dimg);
disp([num2str(100*thresh) '% of smallest coefficients deleted.'])
disp([num2str(density) ' coefficients remain out of ' ...
 num2str(dim) 'x' num2str(dim) '.'])
figure(3), imagesc(cimg), colormap(gray), axis off, axis square

File harmatt.m with two functions

function x = harmatt(dim)
num=log2(dim);
p = sparse(eye(dim)); q = p;
i=1;
while i<=dim/2;
 q(1:2*i,1:2*i) = sparse(individ(2*i));
 p=p*q; i=2*i;
end
x=sparse(p);

function f=individ(n)
x=[1, 1]/sqrt(2);
y=[1,-1]/sqrt(2);
while min(size(x)) < n/2
 x=[x, zeros(min(size(x)),max(size(x)));...
   zeros(min(size(x)),max(size(x))), x];
end
while min(size(y)) < n/2
 y=[y, zeros(min(size(y)),max(size(y)));...
   zeros(min(size(y)),max(size(y))), y];
end
f=[x;y];
```

Figure 5.51: Matlab Code for the Haar Transform of an Image.

with a little experience with matrices can construct a matrix that when multiplied by this vector results in a vector with four averages and four differences. Matrix A_1 of Equation (5.10) does that and, when multiplied by the top row of pixels of Figure 5.47, generates $(239.5, 175.5, 111.0, 47.5, 15.5, 16.5, 16.0, 15.5)$. Similarly, matrices A_2 and A_3 perform the second and third steps of the transform, respectively. The results are shown in Equation (5.11):

$$
A_1 = \begin{pmatrix}
\frac{1}{2} & \frac{1}{2} & 0 & 0 & 0 & 0 & 0 & 0 \\
0 & 0 & \frac{1}{2} & \frac{1}{2} & 0 & 0 & 0 & 0 \\
0 & 0 & 0 & 0 & \frac{1}{2} & \frac{1}{2} & 0 & 0 \\
0 & 0 & 0 & 0 & 0 & 0 & \frac{1}{2} & \frac{1}{2} \\
\frac{1}{2} & -\frac{1}{2} & 0 & 0 & 0 & 0 & 0 & 0 \\
0 & 0 & \frac{1}{2} & -\frac{1}{2} & 0 & 0 & 0 & 0 \\
0 & 0 & 0 & 0 & \frac{1}{2} & -\frac{1}{2} & 0 & 0 \\
0 & 0 & 0 & 0 & 0 & 0 & \frac{1}{2} & -\frac{1}{2}
\end{pmatrix}, \quad
A_1 \begin{pmatrix} 255 \\ 224 \\ 192 \\ 159 \\ 127 \\ 95 \\ 63 \\ 32 \end{pmatrix} = \begin{pmatrix} 239.5 \\ 175.5 \\ 111.0 \\ 47.5 \\ 15.5 \\ 16.5 \\ 16.0 \\ 15.5 \end{pmatrix}, \quad (5.10)
$$

$$
A_2 = \begin{pmatrix}
\frac{1}{2} & \frac{1}{2} & 0 & 0 & 0 & 0 & 0 & 0 \\
0 & 0 & \frac{1}{2} & \frac{1}{2} & 0 & 0 & 0 & 0 \\
\frac{1}{2} & -\frac{1}{2} & 0 & 0 & 0 & 0 & 0 & 0 \\
0 & 0 & \frac{1}{2} & -\frac{1}{2} & 0 & 0 & 0 & 0 \\
0 & 0 & 0 & 0 & 1 & 0 & 0 & 0 \\
0 & 0 & 0 & 0 & 0 & 1 & 0 & 0 \\
0 & 0 & 0 & 0 & 0 & 0 & 1 & 0 \\
0 & 0 & 0 & 0 & 0 & 0 & 0 & 1
\end{pmatrix}, \quad
A_3 = \begin{pmatrix}
\frac{1}{2} & \frac{1}{2} & 0 & 0 & 0 & 0 & 0 & 0 \\
\frac{1}{2} & -\frac{1}{2} & 0 & 0 & 0 & 0 & 0 & 0 \\
0 & 0 & 1 & 0 & 0 & 0 & 0 & 0 \\
0 & 0 & 0 & 1 & 0 & 0 & 0 & 0 \\
0 & 0 & 0 & 0 & 1 & 0 & 0 & 0 \\
0 & 0 & 0 & 0 & 0 & 1 & 0 & 0 \\
0 & 0 & 0 & 0 & 0 & 0 & 1 & 0 \\
0 & 0 & 0 & 0 & 0 & 0 & 0 & 1
\end{pmatrix},
$$

$$
A_2 \begin{pmatrix} 239.5 \\ 175.5 \\ 111.0 \\ 47.5 \\ 15.5 \\ 16.5 \\ 16.0 \\ 15.5 \end{pmatrix} = \begin{pmatrix} 207.5 \\ 79.25 \\ 32.0 \\ 31.75 \\ 15.5 \\ 16.5 \\ 16.0 \\ 15.5 \end{pmatrix}, \quad
A_3 \begin{pmatrix} 207.5 \\ 79.25 \\ 32.0 \\ 31.75 \\ 15.5 \\ 16.5 \\ 16.0 \\ 15.5 \end{pmatrix} = \begin{pmatrix} 143.375 \\ 64.125 \\ 32. \\ 31.75 \\ 15.5 \\ 16.5 \\ 16. \\ 15.5 \end{pmatrix}. \quad (5.11)
$$

Instead of calculating averages and differences, all we have to do is construct matrices A_1, A_2, and A_3, multiply them to get $W = A_1 A_2 A_3$, and apply W to all the columns of an image I by multiplying $W \cdot I$:

$$
W \begin{pmatrix} 255 \\ 224 \\ 192 \\ 159 \\ 127 \\ 95 \\ 63 \\ 32 \end{pmatrix} = \begin{pmatrix}
\frac{1}{8} & \frac{1}{8} & \frac{1}{8} & \frac{1}{8} & \frac{1}{8} & \frac{1}{8} & \frac{1}{8} & \frac{1}{8} \\
\frac{1}{8} & \frac{1}{8} & \frac{1}{8} & \frac{1}{8} & \frac{-1}{8} & \frac{-1}{8} & \frac{-1}{8} & \frac{-1}{8} \\
\frac{1}{4} & \frac{1}{4} & \frac{-1}{4} & \frac{-1}{4} & 0 & 0 & 0 & 0 \\
0 & 0 & 0 & 0 & \frac{1}{4} & \frac{1}{4} & \frac{-1}{4} & \frac{-1}{4} \\
\frac{1}{2} & \frac{-1}{2} & 0 & 0 & 0 & 0 & 0 & 0 \\
0 & 0 & \frac{1}{2} & \frac{-1}{2} & 0 & 0 & 0 & 0 \\
0 & 0 & 0 & 0 & \frac{1}{2} & \frac{-1}{2} & 0 & 0 \\
0 & 0 & 0 & 0 & 0 & 0 & \frac{1}{2} & \frac{-1}{2}
\end{pmatrix} \begin{pmatrix} 255 \\ 224 \\ 192 \\ 159 \\ 127 \\ 95 \\ 63 \\ 32 \end{pmatrix} = \begin{pmatrix} 143.375 \\ 64.125 \\ 32 \\ 31.75 \\ 15.5 \\ 16.5 \\ 16 \\ 15.5 \end{pmatrix}.
$$

This, of course, is only half the job. In order to compute the complete transform, we still have to apply W to the rows of the product $W \cdot I$, and we do this by applying it to the columns of the transpose $(W \cdot I)^T$, then transposing the result. Thus, the complete transform is (see line `timg=w*img*w'` in Figure 5.51)

$$I_{\text{tr}} = \left(W(W \cdot I)^T\right)^T = W \cdot I \cdot W^T.$$

The inverse transform is performed by

$$W^{-1}(W^{-1} \cdot I_{\text{tr}}^T)^T = W^{-1}\left(I_{\text{tr}} \cdot (W^{-1})^T\right),$$

and this is where the normalized Haar transform (mentioned on page 200) becomes important. Instead of calculating averages [quantities of the form $(d_i + d_{i+1})/2$] and differences [quantities of the form $(d_i - d_{i+1})$], it is better to compute the quantities $(d_i + d_{i+1})/\sqrt{2}$ and $(d_i - d_{i+1})/\sqrt{2}$. This results is an orthonormal matrix W, and it is well known that the inverse of such a matrix is simply its transpose. Thus, we can write the inverse transform in the simple form $W^T \cdot I_{\text{tr}} \cdot W$ [see line `cimg=full(w'*sparse(dimg)*w)` in Figure 5.51].

In between the forward and inverse transforms, some transform coefficients may be quantized or deleted. Alternatively, matrix I_{tr} may be compressed by means of run length encoding and/or Huffman codes.

Function `individ(n)` of Figure 5.51 starts with a 2×2 Haar transform matrix (notice that it uses $\sqrt{2}$ instead of 2) and then uses it to construct as many individual matrices A_i as necessary. Function `harmatt(dim)` combines those individual matrices to form the final Haar matrix for an image of `dim` rows and `dim` columns.

⋄ **Exercise 5.14:** Perform the calculation $W \cdot I \cdot W^T$ for the 8×8 image of Figure 5.47.

The past decade has witnessed the development of wavelet analysis, a new tool which emerged from mathematics and was quickly adopted by diverse fields of science and engineering. In the brief period since its creation in 1987–88, it has reached a certain level of maturity as a well-defined mathematical discipline, with its own conferences, journals, research monographs, and textbooks proliferating at a rapid rate.

—Howard L. Resnikoff and Raymond O'Neil Wells,
Wavelet Analysis: The Scalable Structure of Information (1998)

5.8 Filter Banks

So far, we have worked with the Haar transform, the simplest wavelet (and subband) transform. We are now ready for the general subband transform. As a preparation for the material in this section, we again examine the two main types of image transforms, orthogonal and subband. An orthogonal linear transform is performed by computing the *inner product* of the data (pixel values or audio samples) with a set of *basis functions*. The result is a set of transform coefficients that can later be quantized and encoded. In contrast, a subband transform is performed by computing a *convolution* of the data with a set of bandpass filters. Each of the resulting subbands encodes a particular portion of the frequency content of the data.

Note. The discrete inner product of the two vectors f_i and g_i is defined as the following sum of products

$$\langle f, g \rangle = \sum_i f_i \, g_i.$$

The discrete convolution h is denoted by $f \star g$ and is defined as

$$h_i = f \star g = \sum_j f_j \, g_{i-j}. \tag{5.12}$$

(Each element h_i of the discrete convolution h is the sum of products. It depends on i in the special way shown in Equation (5.12).)

This section employs the matrix approach to the Haar transform to introduce the reader to the idea of filter banks. We show how the Haar transform can be interpreted as a bank of two filters, a lowpass and a highpass. We explain the terms "filter," "lowpass," and "highpass" and show how the idea of filter banks leads naturally to the concept of subband transform. The Haar transform, of course, is the simplest wavelet transform, which is why it was used earlier to illustrate wavelet concepts. However, employing it as a filter bank is not the most efficient. Most practical applications of wavelet filters employ more sophisticated sets of filter coefficients, but they are all based on the concept of filters and filter banks [Strang and Nguyen 96].

The simplest way to describe the discrete wavelet transform (DWT) is by means of matrix multiplication, along the lines developed in Section 5.7.3. The Haar transform depends on two *filter coefficients* c_0 and c_1, both with a value of $1/\sqrt{2} \approx 0.7071$. The smallest transform matrix that can be constructed in this case is $\left(\begin{smallmatrix} 1 & 1 \\ 1 & -1 \end{smallmatrix} \right)/\sqrt{2}$. It is a 2×2 matrix, and it generates two transform coefficients, an average and a difference. (Notice that these are not exactly an average and a difference, because $\sqrt{2}$ is used instead of 2. Better names for them are *coarse detail* and *fine detail*, respectively.) In general, the DWT can use any set of wavelet filters, but it is computed in the same way regardless of the particular filter used.

We start with one of the most popular wavelets, the Daubechies D4. As its name implies, it is based on four filter coefficients c_0, c_1, c_2, and c_3, whose values are listed in

Equation (5.13). The transform matrix W is [compare with matrix A_1, Equation (5.10)]

$$W = \begin{pmatrix} c_0 & c_1 & c_2 & c_3 & 0 & 0 & \cdots & 0 \\ c_3 & -c_2 & c_1 & -c_0 & 0 & 0 & \cdots & 0 \\ 0 & 0 & c_0 & c_1 & c_2 & c_3 & \cdots & 0 \\ 0 & 0 & c_3 & -c_2 & c_1 & -c_0 & \cdots & 0 \\ \vdots & \vdots & & & & \ddots & & \\ 0 & 0 & \cdots & 0 & c_0 & c_1 & c_2 & c_3 \\ 0 & 0 & \cdots & 0 & c_3 & -c_2 & c_1 & -c_0 \\ c_2 & c_3 & 0 & \cdots & 0 & 0 & c_0 & c_1 \\ c_1 & -c_0 & 0 & \cdots & 0 & 0 & c_3 & -c_2 \end{pmatrix}.$$

When this matrix is applied to a column vector of data items $(x_1, x_2, \ldots, x_n)$, its top row generates the weighted sum $s_1 = c_0 x_1 + c_1 x_2 + c_2 x_3 + c_3 x_4$, its third row generates the weighted sum $s_2 = c_0 x_3 + c_1 x_4 + c_2 x_5 + c_3 x_6$, and the other odd-numbered rows generate similar weighted sums s_i. Such sums are *convolutions* of the data vector x_i with the four filter coefficients. In the language of wavelets, each of them is called a *smooth coefficient*, and together they are termed an H smoothing filter.

In a similar way, the second row of the matrix generates the quantity $d_1 = c_3 x_1 - c_2 x_2 + c_1 x_3 - c_0 x_4$, and the other even-numbered rows generate similar convolutions. Each d_i is called a *detail coefficient*, and together they are referred to as a G filter. G is not a smoothing filter. In fact, the filter coefficients are chosen such that the G filter generates small values when the data items x_i are correlated. Together, H and G are called *quadrature mirror filters* (QMF).

The discrete wavelet transform of an image can therefore be viewed as passing the original image through a QMF that consists of a pair of lowpass (H) and highpass (G) filters.

If W is an $n \times n$ matrix, it generates $n/2$ smooth coefficients s_i and $n/2$ detail coefficients d_i. The transposed matrix is

$$W^T = \begin{pmatrix} c_0 & c_3 & 0 & 0 & \cdots & & & c_2 & c_1 \\ c_1 & -c_2 & 0 & 0 & \cdots & & & c_3 & -c_0 \\ c_2 & c_1 & c_0 & c_3 & \cdots & & & 0 & 0 \\ c_3 & -c_0 & c_1 & -c_2 & \cdots & & & 0 & 0 \\ & & & & \ddots & & & & \\ & & & & c_2 & c_1 & c_0 & c_3 & 0 & 0 \\ & & & & c_3 & -c_0 & c_1 & -c_2 & 0 & 0 \\ & & & & & & c_2 & c_1 & c_0 & c_3 \\ & & & & & & c_3 & -c_0 & c_1 & -c_2 \end{pmatrix}.$$

It can be shown that in order for W to be orthonormal, the four coefficients have to satisfy the two relations $c_0^2 + c_1^2 + c_2^2 + c_3^2 = 1$ and $c_2 c_0 + c_3 c_1 = 0$. The other two equations used to determine the four filter coefficients are $c_3 - c_2 + c_1 - c_0 = 0$ and $0c_3 - 1c_2 + 2c_1 - 3c_0 = 0$. They represent the vanishing of the first two moments of the sequence $(c_3, -c_2, c_1, -c_0)$. The solutions are

$$c_0 = (1 + \sqrt{3})/(4\sqrt{2}) \approx 0.48296, \quad c_1 = (3 + \sqrt{3})/(4\sqrt{2}) \approx 0.8365,$$

$$c_2 = (3 - \sqrt{3})/(4\sqrt{2}) \approx 0.2241, \quad c_3 = (1 - \sqrt{3})/(4\sqrt{2}) \approx -0.1294. \tag{5.13}$$

Using a transform matrix W is conceptually simple, but not very practical, since W should be of the same size as the image, which can be large. However, a look at W shows that it is very regular, so there is really no need to construct the full matrix. It is enough to have just the top row of W. In fact, it is enough to have just an array with the filter coefficients. Figure 5.52 lists Matlab code that performs this computation. Function `fwt1(dat,coarse,filter)` takes a row vector `dat` of 2^n data items, and another array, `filter`, with filter coefficients. It then calculates the first `coarse` levels of the discrete wavelet transform.

◇ **Exercise 5.15:** Write similar code for the inverse one-dimensional discrete wavelet transform.

5.9 WSQ, Fingerprint Compression

This section presents WSQ, a wavelet-based image compression method that was specifically developed to compress fingerprint images. Other compression methods that employ the wavelet transform can be found in [Salomon 07].

Most of us may not realize it, but fingerprints are "big business." The FBI started collecting fingerprints in the form of inked impressions on paper cards back in 1924, and today they have about 200 million cards, occupying an acre of filing cabinets in the J. Edgar Hoover building in Washington, D.C. (The FBI, like many of us, never throws anything away. They also have many "repeat customers," which is why "only" about 29 million out of the 200 million cards are distinct; these are the ones used for running background checks.) What's more, these cards keep accumulating at a rate of 30,000–50,000 new cards per day (this is per day, not per year)! There's clearly a need to digitize this collection, so it will occupy less space and will lend itself to automatic search and classification. The main problem is size (in bits). When a typical fingerprint card is scanned at 500 dpi, with eight bits/pixel, it results in about 10 Mb of data. Thus, the total size of the digitized collection would be more than 2,000 terabytes (a terabyte is 2^{40} bytes); huge even by current (2008) standards.

◇ **Exercise 5.16:** Apply these numbers to estimate the size of a fingerprint card.

Compression is therefore a must. At first, it seems that fingerprint compression must be lossless because of the small but important details involved. However, lossless image compression methods produce typical compression ratios of 0.5, whereas in order to make a serious dent in the huge amount of data in this collection, compressions of about 1 bpp or better are needed. What is needed is a lossy compression method that results in graceful degradation of image details, and does not introduce any artifacts into the reconstructed image. Most lossy image compression methods involve the loss of small details and are therefore unacceptable, since small fingerprint details, such as sweat pores, are admissible points of identification in court. This is where wavelets come into the picture. Lossy wavelet compression, if carefully designed, can satisfy the criteria above and result in efficient compression where important small details are preserved or

```
function wc1=fwt1(dat,coarse,filter)
%  The 1D Forward Wavelet Transform
%  dat must be a 1D row vector of size 2^n,
%  coarse is the coarsest level of the transform
%  (note that coarse should be <<n)
%  filter is an orthonormal quadrature mirror filter
%  whose length should be <2^(coarse+1)
n=length(dat); j=log2(n); wc1=zeros(1,n);
beta=dat;
for i=j-1:-1:coarse
  alfa=HiPass(beta,filter);
  wc1((2^(i)+1):(2^(i+1)))=alfa;
  beta=LoPass(beta,filter) ;
end
wc1(1:(2^coarse))=beta;

function d=HiPass(dt,filter) % highpass downsampling
d=iconv(mirror(filter),lshift(dt));
% iconv is matlab convolution tool
n=length(d);
d=d(1:2:(n-1));

function d=LoPass(dt,filter) % lowpass downsampling
d=aconv(filter,dt);
% aconv is matlab convolution tool with time-
% reversal of filter
n=length(d);
d=d(1:2:(n-1));

function sgn=mirror(filt)
% return filter coefficients with alternating signs
sgn=-((-1).^(1:length(filt))).*filt;
```

A simple test of fwt1 is

```
n=16; t=(1:n)./n;
dat=sin(2*pi*t)
filt=[0.4830 0.8365 0.2241 -0.1294];
wc=fwt1(dat,1,filt)
```

which outputs

```
dat=
0.3827  0.7071  0.9239 1.0000 0.9239 0.7071 0.3827 0
-0.3827 -0.7071 -0.9239 -1.0000 -0.9239 -0.7071 -0.3827 0
wc=
1.1365 -1.1365 -1.5685 1.5685 -0.2271 -0.4239 0.2271 0.4239
-0.0281 -0.0818 -0.0876 -0.0421 0.0281 0.0818 0.0876 0.0421
```

Figure 5.52: Code for the One-Dimensional Forward Discrete Wavelet Transform.

are at least identifiable. Figure 5.53a,b (obtained, with permission, from Christopher M. Brislawn), shows two examples of fingerprints and one detail, where ridges and sweat pores can clearly be seen.

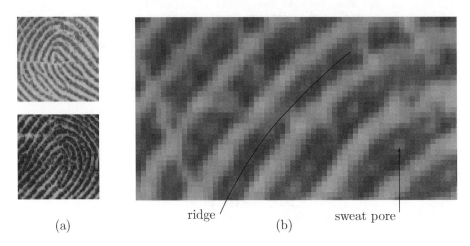

ridge   (b)   sweat pore

(a)

Figure 5.53: Examples of Scanned Fingerprints (courtesy Christopher Brislawn).

Compression is also necessary, because fingerprint images are routinely sent between law enforcement agencies. Overnight delivery of the actual card is too slow and risky (there are no backup cards), and sending 10 Mb of data through a 9,600 baud modem takes about three hours.

The method described here [Bradley et al. 93] has been adopted by the FBI as its standard for fingerprint compression [Federal Bureau of Investigations 93]. It involves three steps: (1) a discrete wavelet transform, (2) adaptive scalar quantization of the wavelet transform coefficients, and (3) a two-pass Huffman coding of the quantization indices. This is the reason for the name *wavelet/scalar quantization*, or WSQ. The method typically produces compression factors of about 20. Decoding is the reverse of encoding, so WSQ is a symmetric compression method.

The first step is a symmetric discrete wavelet transform (SWT) using the symmetric filter coefficients listed in Table 5.54 (where $\mathcal{R}$ indicates the real part of a complex number). They are symmetric filters with seven and nine impulse response taps, and they depend on the two numbers x_1 (real) and x_2 (complex). The final standard adopted by the FBI uses the values

$$x_1 = A + B - \frac{1}{6}, \quad x_2 = \frac{-(A+B)}{2} - \frac{1}{6} + \frac{i\sqrt{3}(A-B)}{2},$$

where

$$A = \left(\frac{-14\sqrt{15} + 63}{1080\sqrt{15}}\right)^{1/3}, \quad \text{and } B = \left(\frac{-14\sqrt{15} - 63}{1080\sqrt{15}}\right)^{1/3}.$$

This wavelet image decomposition can be called symmetric. It is shown in Figure 5.55. The SWT is first applied to the image rows and columns, resulting in $4 \times 4 = 16$

Tap	Exact value	Approximate value
$h_0(0)$	$-5\sqrt{2}x_1(48|x_2|^2 - 16\mathcal{R}x_2 + 3)/32$	0.852698790094000
$h_0(\pm 1)$	$-5\sqrt{2}x_1(8|x_2|^2 - \mathcal{R}x_2)/8$	0.377402855612650
$h_0(\pm 2)$	$-5\sqrt{2}x_1(4|x_2|^2 + 4\mathcal{R}x_2 - 1)/16$	-0.110624404418420
$h_0(\pm 3)$	$-5\sqrt{2}x_1(\mathcal{R}x_2)/8$	-0.023849465019380
$h_0(\pm 4)$	$-5\sqrt{2}x_1/64$	0.037828455506995
$h_1(-1)$	$\sqrt{2}(6x_1 - 1)/16x_1$	0.788485616405660
$h_1(-2,0)$	$-\sqrt{2}(16x_1 - 1)/64x_1$	-0.418092273222210
$h_1(-3,1)$	$\sqrt{2}(2x_1 + 1)/32x_1$	-0.040689417609558
$h_1(-4,2)$	$-\sqrt{2}/64x_1$	0.064538882628938

Table 5.54: Symmetric Wavelet Filter Coefficients for WSQ.

subbands. The SWT is then applied in the same manner to three of the 16 subbands, decomposing each into 16 smaller subbands. The last step is to decompose the top-left subband into four smaller ones.

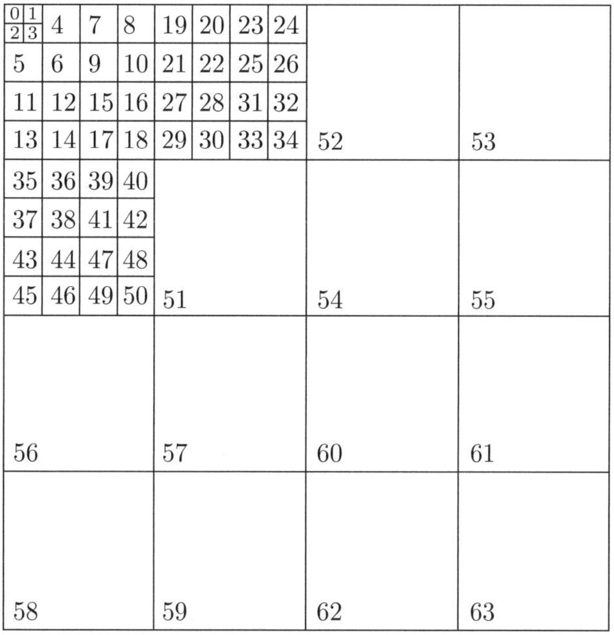

Figure 5.55: Symmetric Image Wavelet Decomposition.

The larger subbands (51–63) contain the fine-detail, high-frequency information of the image. They can later be heavily quantized without loss of any important information (i.e., information needed to classify and identify fingerprints). In fact, subbands

60–63 are completely discarded. Subbands 7–18 are important. They contain that portion of the image frequencies that corresponds to the ridges in a fingerprint. This information is important and should be quantized lightly.

The transform coefficients in the 64 subbands are floating-point numbers to be denoted by a. They are quantized to a finite number of floating-point numbers that are denoted by $\hat{a}$. The WSQ encoder maps a transform coefficient a to a quantization index p (an integer that is later mapped to a code that is itself Huffman encoded). The index p can be considered a pointer to the quantization bin where a lies. The WSQ decoder receives an index p and maps it to a value $\hat{a}$ that is close, but not identical, to a. This is how WSQ loses image information. The set of $\hat{a}$ values is a discrete set of floating-point numbers called the *quantized wavelet coefficients*. The quantization depends on parameters that may vary from subband to subband, since different subbands have different quantization requirements.

Figure 5.56 shows the setup of quantization bins for subband k. Parameter Z_k is the width of the zero bin, and parameter Q_k is the width of the other bins. Parameter C is in the range $[0, 1]$. It determines the reconstructed value $\hat{a}$. For $C = 0.5$, for example, the reconstructed value for each quantization bin is the center of the bin. Equation (5.14) shows how parameters Z_k and Q_k are used by the WSQ encoder to quantize a transform coefficient $a_k(m, n)$ (i.e., a coefficient in position (m, n) in subband k) to an index $p_k(m, n)$ (an integer), and how the WSQ decoder computes a quantized coefficient $\hat{a}_k(m, n)$ from that index:

$$
p_k(m, n) = \begin{cases} \left\lfloor \frac{a_k(m,n) - Z_k/2}{Q_k} \right\rfloor + 1, & a_k(m, n) > Z_k/2, \\ 0, & -Z_k/2 \le a_k(m, n) \le Z_k/2, \\ \left\lceil \frac{a_k(m,n) + Z_k/2}{Q_k} \right\rceil + 1, & a_k(m, n) < -Z_k/2, \end{cases}
$$

$$(5.14)$$

$$
\hat{a}_k(m, n) = \begin{cases} \big(p_k(m, n) - C\big)Q_k + Z_k/2, & p_k(m, n) > 0, \\ 0, & p_k(m, n) = 0, \\ \big(p_k(m, n) + C\big)Q_k - Z_k/2, & p_k(m, n) < 0. \end{cases}
$$

The final standard adopted by the FBI uses the value $C = 0.44$ and determines the bin widths Q_k and Z_k from the variances of the coefficients in the different subbands in the following steps:

Step 1: Let the width and height of subband k be denoted by X_k and Y_k, respectively. We compute the six quantities

$$
W_k = \left\lfloor \frac{3X_k}{4} \right\rfloor, \quad H_k = \left\lfloor \frac{7Y_k}{16} \right\rfloor,
$$

$$
x_{0k} = \left\lfloor \frac{X_k}{8} \right\rfloor, \quad x_{1k} = x_{0k} + W_k - 1,
$$

$$
y_{0k} = \left\lfloor \frac{9Y_k}{32} \right\rfloor, \quad y_{1k} = y_{0k} + H_k - 1.
$$

Step 2: Assuming that position $(0,0)$ is the top-left corner of the subband, we use the subband region from position (x_{0k}, y_{0k}) to position (x_{1k}, y_{1k}) to estimate the variance σ_k^2 of the subband by

$$\sigma_k^2 = \frac{1}{W \cdot H - 1} \sum_{n=x_{0k}}^{x_{1k}} \sum_{m=y_{0k}}^{y_{1k}} \bigl(a_k(m,n) - \mu_k\bigr)^2,$$

where μ_k denotes the mean of $a_k(m,n)$ in the region.

Step 3: Parameter Q_k is computed by

$$q\,Q_k = \begin{cases} 1, & 0 \le k \le 3, \\ \dfrac{10}{A_k \log_e(\sigma_k^2)}, & 4 \le k \le 59, \text{ and } \sigma_k^2 \ge 1.01, \\ 0, & 60 \le k \le 63, \text{ or } \sigma_k^2 < 1.01, \end{cases}$$

where q is a proportionality constant that controls the bin widths Q_k and thereby the overall level of compression. The procedure for computing q is complex and will not be described here. The values of the constants A_k are

$$A_k = \begin{cases} 1.32, & k = 52, 56, \\ 1.08, & k = 53, 58, \\ 1.42, & k = 54, 57, \\ 1.08, & k = 55, 59, \\ 1, & \text{otherwise.} \end{cases}$$

Notice that the bin widths for subbands 60–63 are zero. As a result, these subbands, containing the finest detail coefficients, are simply discarded.

Step 4: The width of the zero bin is set to $Z_k = 1.2Q_k$.

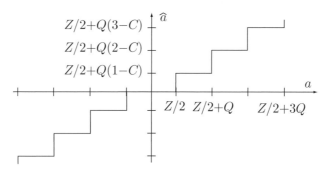

Figure 5.56: WSQ Scalar Quantization.

The WSQ encoder computes the quantization indices $p_k(m,n)$ as shown, then maps them to the 254 codes shown in Table 5.57. These values are encoded with Huffman codes (using a two-pass process), and the Huffman codes are then written on the compressed file. A quantization index $p_k(m,n)$ can be any integer, but most are small and there are many zeros. Thus, the codes of Table 5.57 are divided into three groups. The first group consists of 100 codes (codes 1 through 100) for run lengths of 1 to 100 zero indices. The second group is codes 107 through 254. They specify small indices, in the range $[-73, +74]$. The third group consists of the six *escape* codes 101 through 106. They indicate large indices or run lengths of more than 100 zero indices. Code 180 (which corresponds to an index $p_k(m, n) = 0$) is not used, because this case is really a run length of a single zero. An escape code is followed by the (8-bit or 16-bit) raw value of the index (or size of the run length). Here are some examples:

An index $p_k(m, n) = -71$ is coded as 109. An index $p_k(m, n) = -1$ is coded as 179. An index $p_k(m, n) = 75$ is coded as 101 (escape for positive 8-bit indices) followed by 75 (in eight bits). An index $p_k(m, n) = -259$ is coded as 104 (escape for negative large indices) followed by 259 (the absolute value of the index, in 16 bits). An isolated index of zero is coded as 1, and a run length of 260 zeros is coded as 106 (escape for large run lengths) followed by 260 (in 16 bits). Indices or run lengths that require more than 16 bits cannot be encoded, but the particular choices of the quantization parameters and the wavelet transform virtually guarantee that large indices will never be generated.

Code	Index or run length
1	run length of 1 zeros
2	run length of 2 zeros
3	run length of 3 zeros
⋮	
100	run length of 100 zeros
101	escape code for positive 8-bit index
102	escape code for negative 8-bit index
103	escape code for positive 16-bit index
104	escape code for negative 16-bit index
105	escape code for zero run, 8-bit
106	escape code for zero run, 16-bit
107	index value -73
108	index value -72
109	index value -71
⋮	
179	index value -1
180	unused
181	index value 1
⋮	
253	index value 73
254	index value 74

Table 5.57: WSQ Codes for Quantization Indices and Run Lengths.

The last step is to prepare the Huffman code tables. They depend on the image, so they have to be written on the compressed file. The standard adopted by the FBI specifies that subbands be grouped into three blocks and all the subbands in a group use the same Huffman code table. This facilitates progressive transmission of the image.

The first block consists of the low- and mid-frequency subbands 0–18. The second and third blocks contain the highpass detail subbands 19–51 and 52–59, respectively (recall that subbands 60–63 are completely discarded). Two Huffman code tables are prepared, one for the first block and the other for the second and third blocks.

A Huffman code table for a block of subbands is prepared by counting the number of times each of the 254 codes of Table 5.57 appears in the block. The counts are used to determine the length of each code and to construct the Huffman code tree. This is a two-pass job (one pass to determine the code tables and another pass to encode), and it is done in a way similar to the use of the Huffman code by JPEG (Section 5.6.4).

O'Day figured that that was more than he'd had the right to expect under the circumstances. A fingerprint identification ordinarily required ten individual points—the irregularities that constituted the art of fingerprint identification—but that number had always been arbitrary. The inspector was certain that Cutter had handled this computer disk, even if a jury might not be completely sure, if that time ever came.

—Tom Clancy, *Clear and Present Danger*

Chapter Summary

Images are an important type of digital multimedia data. Images are popular, they are easy to create (by a digital camera, scanning a document, or by creating a drawing or an illustration), and they feature several types of redundancies, which makes it easy to come up with methods for compressing them. In addition, the human visual system can perceive the general form and many details of an image, but it cannot register the precise color of every pixel. We therefore say that a typical image has much noise, and this feature allows for much loss of original image information when the image is compressed and then decompressed.

The chapter starts by discussing the various types of images, bi-level, grayscale, continuous-tone, discrete-tone, and cartoon-like. It then states the main principle of image compression, a principle that stems from the correlation of pixels. Eight approaches to image compression are briefly discussed, all of them based on the main principle.

The remainder of the chapter concentrates on image transforms (Section 5.3) and in particular on orthogonal and wavelet transforms. The popular JPEG method is based on the discrete cosine transform (DCT), one of the important orthogonal transforms, and is explained in detail (Section 5.6).

The last part of the chapter, starting at Section 5.7, is devoted to the wavelet transform. This type of transform is introduced by the Haar transform, which serves to illustrate the concept of subbands and their importance. Finally, Section 5.9 discusses WSQ, a sophisticated wavelet-based image compression method that was developed specifically for the compression of fingerprint images.

Self-Assessment Questions

1. Explain why this is the longest chapter in this book.

2. The zigzag sequence employed by JPEG starts at the top-left corner of an 8×8 unit and works its way to the bottom-right corner in zigzag. This way, the sequence proceeds from large to small transform coefficients and may therefore contain runs of zero coefficients. Propose other (perhaps more sophisticated) ways to scan such a unit from large coefficients to small ones.

3. Section 5.7.1 discusses the standard and pyramid subband transforms. Check the data compression literature for other ways to apply a two-dimensional subband transform to the entire image.

4. Figure 5.27 illustrates the blocking artifacts caused by JPEG when it is asked to quantize the DCT transform coefficients too much. Locate a JPEG implementation that allows the user to select the degree of compression (which it does by quantizing the DCT coefficients more or quantizing them less) and run it repeatedly, asking for better and better compression, until the decompressed image clearly shows these artifacts.

5. Figure 5.52 lists Matlab code for performing a one-dimensional discrete wavelet transform with the four filter coefficients 0.4830, 0.8365, 0.2241, and -0.1294. Copy this code from the book's web site and run it with other sets of filter coefficients (reference [Salomon 07] has examples of other sets). Even better, rewrite this code in a programming language of your choice.

A picture of many colors proclaims images of many thoughts.

—Donna A. Favors

6
Audio Compression

 Prelude

In the Introduction, it is mentioned that the electronic digital computer was originally conceived as a fast, reliable calculating machine. It did not take computer users long to realize that a computer can also store and process nonnumeric data. The term "multimedia," which became popular in the 1990s, refers to the ability to digitize, store, and manipulate in the computer all kinds of data, not just numbers. Previous chapters discussed digital images and methods for their compression, and this chapter concentrates on audio data.

An important fact about audio compression is that decoding must be fast. Given a compressed text file, we don't mind waiting until it is fully decompressed before we can read it. However, given a compressed audio file, we often want to listen to it while it is decompressed (in fact, we decompress it only in order to listen to it). This is why audio compression methods tend to be asymmetric. The encoder can be sophisticated, complex, and slow, but the decoder must be fast.

First, a few words about audio and how it is digitized. The term audio refers to the recording and reproduction of sound. Sound is a wave. It can be viewed as a physical disturbance in the air (or some other medium) or as a pressure wave propagated by the vibrations of molecules. A microphone is a device that senses sound and converts it to an electrical wave, a voltage that varies continuously with time in the same way as the sound. To convert this voltage into a format where it can be input into a computer, stored, edited, and played back, the voltage is sampled many times each second. Each audio sample is a number whose value is proportional to the voltage at the time of sampling. Figure Intro.1, duplicated here, shows a wave sampled at three points in time. It is obvious that the first sample is a small number and the third sample is a large number, close to the maximum.

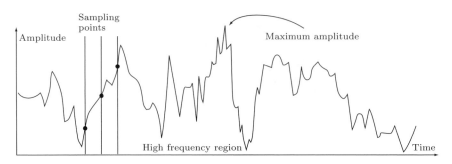

Figure Intro.1. Sound Wave and Three Samples.

Thus, audio sampling (or digitized sound) is a simple concept, but its success in practice depends on two important factors, the sampling rate and the sample size. How many times should a sound wave be sampled each second and how large (how many bits) should each sample be? Sampling too often creates too many audio samples, while a very low sampling rate results in low-quality played-back sound. It seems intuitively that the sampling rate should depend on the frequency, but the frequency of a sound wave varies all the time, whereas the sampling rate should remain constant (a variable sampling rate makes it difficult to edit and play back the digitized sound). The solution was discovered back in the 1920s by H. Nyquist. It states that the optimum sampling frequency should be slightly greater than twice the maximum frequency of the sound. The sound wave of Figure Intro.1 has a region of high frequency at its center. To obtain the optimum sampling rate for this particular wave, we should determine the maximum frequency at this region, double it, and increase the result slightly. The process of audio sampling is also known as analog-to-digital conversion (ADC).

Every sound wave has its own maximum frequency, but the digitized sound used in practical applications is based on the fact that the highest frequency that the human ear can perceive is about 22,000 Hz. The optimum sampling rate that corresponds to this frequency is 44,100 Hz, and this rate is used when sound is digitized and recorded on a CD or DVD.

Modern computers are based on 8-bit storage units called bytes, which is why many quantities, including audio samples, are stored in a computer in a byte or several bytes. If each audio sample is a byte, there can be 256 sample sizes, so the digitized audio can have up to 256 different amplitudes. If the highest voltage produced by a microphone is 1 volt, then 8-bit audio samples can distinguish voltages as low as $1/256 \approx 0.004$ volt or 4 millivolts (mv). Any quiet sound that is converted by the microphone to a lower voltage would result in audio samples of zero and played back as silence. This is why most ADC converters create 16-bit audio samples. Such a sample can have $2^{16} = 65,536$ values, so it can distinguish sounds as low as $1/65,536$ volt ≈ 15 microvolt (μv). Thus, the sample size can be considered quantization of the original, analog, audio signal. Eight-bit samples correspond to coarse quantization, while 16-bit samples lead to fine quantization and thus to better quality of the played-back sound.

Audio sampling (or ADC) is also known as pulse-code-modulation (PCM), a term often found in the professional literature.

Armed with this information, we can estimate the sizes of various audio files and thereby show why audio compression is so important. A typical 3-minute song lasts 180 sec and results in $180 \times 44{,}100 = 7{,}938{,}000$ audio samples when it is digitized (for stereo sound, the number of samples is double that). For 16-bit samples, this translates to close to 16 Mb, bigger than most still images. A 30-minute symphony is ten times longer, so it results in a 160 Mb file when digitized. Thus, audio files are much bigger than text files and can easily be bigger than (raw) image files. Another point to consider is that audio compression, similar to image compression, can be lossy and thus feature large compression factors.

◇ **Exercise 6.1:** It is a handy rule of thumb that an average book occupies about a million bytes. Explain why this makes sense.

Approaches to audio compression. The problem of compressing an audio file can be approached from various directions, because audio data has several sources of redundancy. The discussion that follows concentrates on three common approaches.

■ The main source of redundancy in digital audio is the fact that adjacent audio samples tend to be similar; they are correlated. With 44,100 samples each second, it is no wonder that adjacent samples are virtually always similar. Audio data where many audio samples are very different from their immediate neighbors would sound harsh and dissonant.

Thus, a simple approach to audio compression is to subtract each audio sample from its predecessor and encode the differences (which are termed errors or residuals and tend to be small integers) with suitable variable-length codes. Experience suggests that the Rice codes (Section 1.1.3) are a good choice for this task. Practical methods often "predict" the current sample by computing a weighted sum of several of its immediate neighbors, and then subtracting the current sample from the prediction. When done carefully, linear prediction (Section 6.3) produces very small residuals (smaller than those produced by simple subtraction). Because the residuals are integers, smaller residuals implies few residual values and therefore efficient encoding (for example, if the residuals are in the interval $[-6, 5]$, then there are only 12 residual values and only 12 variable-length codes are needed, making it possible to choose very short codes). The MLP and FLAC lossless compression methods [Salomon 07] are examples of this approach.

◇ **Exercise 6.2:** The first audio sample has no predecessor, so how can it be encoded?

■ Companding is an approach to lossy audio compression (companding is short for compressing/expanding). It is based on the experimental fact that the human ear is more sensitive to low sound amplitudes and less sensitive to high amplitudes. The idea is to quantize each audio sample by a different amount according to its size (recall that the size of a sample is proportional to the sound amplitude). Large samples, which correspond to high amplitudes, are quantized more than small samples. Thus, companding is based on nonlinear quantization. Section 6.1 says more about companding. The μ-law and A-law compression methods (Section 6.4) are examples of this approach.

■ Another source of redundancy in audio is the limitations of the ear–brain system. The human ear is very sensitive to sound, but its sensitivity is not uniform (Section 6.2) and it depends on the frequency. Also, a loud sound may severely affect the sensitivity of the ear for a short period of time. Scientific experiments conducted over many years have taught us much about how the ear–brain system responds to sound in various situations, and this knowledge can be exploited to achieve very efficient lossy audio compression. The idea is to analyze the raw audio second by second, to identify those parts of the audio to which the ear is not sensitive, and to heavily quantize the audio samples in those parts.

This approach is the principle of the popular lossy mp3 method [Brandenburg and Stoll 94]. The mp3 encoder is complex, because (1) it has to identify the frequencies contained in the input sound at each point in time and (2) it has to decide which parts of the original audio will not be heard by the ear. Recall that the input to the encoder is a set of audio samples, not a sound wave. Thus, the encoder has to prepare overlapping subsets of the samples and apply a Fourier transform to each subset to determine the frequencies of the sound contained in it. The encoder also has to include a psychoacoustic model in order to decide which sounds will not be heard by the ear. The decoder, in contrast, is very simple.

This chapter starts with a detailed discussion of companding (Section 6.1), the human auditory system (Section 6.2), and linear prediction (Section 6.3). This material is followed by descriptions of three audio compression algorithms, μ-law and A-law companding (Section 6.4) and Shorten (Section 6.5).

6.1 Companding

Companding (short for "compressing/expanding") is a simple nonlinear technique based on the experimental fact that the ear requires more precise samples at low amplitudes (soft sounds), but is more forgiving at higher amplitudes. The typical ADC found in many personal computers converts voltages to numbers linearly. If an amplitude a is converted to the number n, then amplitude $2a$ will be converted to the number $2n$. A compression method based on companding, however, is nonlinear. It examines every audio sample in the sound file, and employs a nonlinear relation to reduce the number of bits devoted to it. For 16-bit samples, for example, a companding encoder may use a formula as simple as

$$\text{mapped} = 32{,}767 \left(2^{\frac{\text{sample}}{65535}} - 1 \right) \tag{6.1}$$

to reduce each sample. This formula maps the 16-bit samples nonlinearly to 15-bit numbers (i.e., numbers in the range $[0, 32{,}767]$) such that small samples are less affected than large ones. Table 6.1 illustrates the nonlinearity of this mapping. It shows eight pairs of samples, where the two samples in each pair differ by 100. The two samples of the first pair are mapped to numbers that differ by 34, whereas the two samples of the last pair are mapped to numbers that differ by 65. The mapped 15-bit numbers can be decoded back into the original 16-bit samples by the inverse formula

$$\text{Sample} = 65{,}535 \log_2 \left(1 + \frac{\text{mapped}}{32{,}767} \right). \tag{6.2}$$

Sample	Mapped	Diff	Sample	Mapped	Diff
100 →	35	34	30,000 →	12,236	47
200 →	69		30,100 →	12,283	
1,000 →	348	35	40,000 →	17,256	53
1,100 →	383		40,100 →	17,309	
10,000 →	3,656	38	50,000 →	22,837	59
10,100 →	3,694		50,100 →	22,896	
20,000 →	7,719	43	60,000 →	29,040	65
20,100 →	7,762		60,100 →	29,105	

Table 6.1: 16-Bit Samples Mapped to 15-Bit Numbers.

Reducing 16-bit numbers to 15 bits doesn't produce much compression. Better results can be achieved by substituting a smaller number for 32,767 in equations (6.1) and (6.2). A value of 127, for example, would map each 16-bit sample into an 8-bit integer, yielding a compression ratio of 0.5. However, decoding would be less accurate. A 16-bit sample of 60,100, for example, would be mapped into the 8-bit number 113, but this number would produce 60,172 when decoded by Equation (6.2). Even worse, the small 16-bit sample 1,000 would be mapped into 1.35, which has to be rounded to 1. When Equation (6.2) is used to decode a 1, it produces 742, significantly different from the original sample. The amount of compression should therefore be a user-controlled parameter, and this is an interesting example of a compression method where the compression ratio is known in advance!

In practice, there is no need to go through Equations (6.1) and (6.2), since the mapping of all the samples can be prepared in advance in a table. Both encoding and decoding are therefore fast.

Companding is not limited to Equations (6.1) and (6.2). More sophisticated methods, such as μ-law and A-law, are commonly used and have been designated international standards.

What do the integers 3, 7, 10, 11, 12 have in common?

6.2 The Human Auditory System

The frequency range of the human ear is from about 20 Hz to about 20,000 Hz, but the ear's sensitivity to sound is not uniform. It depends on the frequency, and experiments indicate that in a quiet environment the ear's sensitivity is maximal for frequencies in the range 2 kHz to 4 kHz. Figure 6.2a shows the *hearing threshold* for a quiet environment. Any sound whose amplitude is below the curve will not be heard by the ear. The threshold curve makes it clear that the ear's sensitivity is minimal at very low and very high frequencies and reaches a maximum for sound frequencies around 5 kHz.

⋄ **Exercise 6.3:** Propose an appropriate way to conduct such experiments.

It should also be noted that the range of the human voice is much more limited. It is only from about 500 Hz to about 2 kHz.

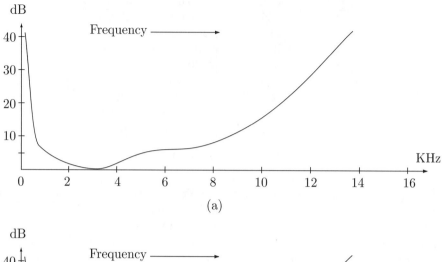

(a)

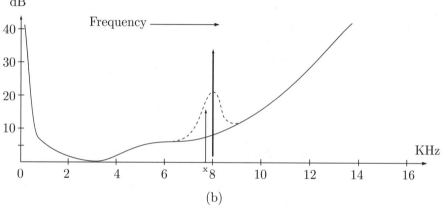

(b)

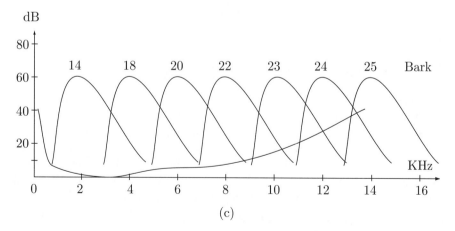

(c)

Figure 6.2: Threshold and Masking of Sound.

The existence of the hearing threshold suggests an approach to lossy audio compression. Apply a Fourier transform to determine the frequency of the sound at any point, associate each audio sample with a frequency, and delete any sample whose corresponding amplitude is below this threshold. Since the threshold depends on the frequency, the encoder needs to know the frequency spectrum of the sound being compressed at any time. The encoder therefore has to save several of the previously-input audio samples at any time ($n-1$ samples, where n is either a constant or a user-controlled parameter). When the current sample is input, the first step is to compute the Fourier transform of the most-recent n samples in order to reveal the frequencies contained in this part of the audio. The result is a number m of values (called *signals*) that indicate the strength of the sound at m different frequencies. If a sample for frequency f is smaller than the hearing threshold at f, it (the sample) should be deleted.

In addition, two more properties of the human hearing system are exploited for effective lossy audio compression. They are *frequency masking* and *temporal masking*.

Frequency masking (also known as *auditory masking*) occurs when a soft sound that we can normally hear (because it is not too soft) is masked by another sound at a nearby frequency. The thick arrow in Figure 6.2b represents a strong sound source at 800 kHz. This source temporarily raises the normal threshold in its vicinity (the dashed curve), with the result that the nearby sound represented by the arrow at "x", a sound that would normally be audible because it is above the threshold, is now masked, and is inaudible. A good lossy audio compression method should identify this case and delete the audio samples that correspond to sound "x", because it cannot be heard anyway. This is a complex but very effective technique for the lossy compression of sound.

The frequency masking (the width of the dashed curve of Figure 6.2b) depends on the frequency. It varies from about 100 Hz for the lowest audible frequencies to more than 4 kHz for the highest. The range of audible frequencies can therefore be partitioned into a number of *critical bands* that indicate the declining sensitivity of the ear (more accurately, its declining resolving power) for higher frequencies. We can think of the critical bands as a measure similar to frequency. However, in contrast to frequency, which is absolute and independent of human hearing, the critical bands are determined according to the sound perception of the ear. Thus, they constitute a perceptually uniform measure of frequency. Table 6.3 lists 27 approximate critical bands.

Another way to describe critical bands is to say that because of the ear's limited perception of frequencies, the threshold at a frequency f is raised by a nearby sound only if that sound is within the critical band of f. This also points the way to developing a practical lossy compression algorithm. The audio signal should first be transformed into its frequency domain, and the resulting values (the frequency spectrum) should be divided into subbands that resemble the critical bands as much as possible. Once this is done, the signals in each subband should be quantized such that the quantization noise (the difference between the original audio sample and its quantized value) should be inaudible.

Yet another way to look at the concept of critical bands is to consider the human auditory system as a filter that lets through only frequencies in the range (bandpass) of 20 Hz to 20,000 Hz. We visualize the ear–brain system as a collection of filters, each with a different bandpass. The bandpasses are called critical bands. They overlap and they have different widths. They are narrow (about 100 Hz) at low frequencies and

band	range	band	range	band	range
0	0–50	9	800–940	18	3280–3840
1	50–95	10	940–1125	19	3840–4690
2	95–140	11	1125–1265	20	4690–5440
3	140–235	12	1265–1500	21	5440–6375
4	235–330	13	1500–1735	22	6375–7690
5	330–420	14	1735–1970	23	7690–9375
6	420–560	15	1970–2340	24	9375–11625
7	560–660	16	2340–2720	25	11625–15375
8	660–800	17	2720–3280	26	15375–20250

Table 6.3: Twenty-Seven Approximate Critical Bands.

become wider (to about 4–5 kHz) at high frequencies.

The width of a critical band is called its size. The widths of the critical bands introduce a new unit, the *Bark* (after H. G. Barkhausen) such that one Bark is the width (in Hz) of one critical band. The Bark is defined as

$$
1 \text{ Bark} = \begin{cases} \frac{f}{100}, & \text{for frequencies } f < 500 \text{ Hz,} \\ 9 + 4\log_2\left(\frac{f}{1000}\right), & \text{for frequencies } f \geq 500 \text{ Hz.} \end{cases}
$$

Figure 6.2c shows some critical bands, with Barks between 14 and 25, positioned above the threshold.

Intermezzo

Heinrich Georg Barkhausen was born on December 2, 1881, in Bremen, Germany. He spent his entire career as a professor of electrical engineering at the Technische Hochschule in Dresden, where he concentrated on developing electron tubes. He also discovered the so-called "Barkhausen effect," where acoustical waves are generated in a solid by the movement of domain walls when the material is magnetized. He also coined the term "phon" as a unit of sound loudness. The institute in Dresden was destroyed, as was most of the city, in the famous fire bombing in February 1945. After the war, Barkhausen helped rebuild the institute. He died on February 20, 1956.

The dashed masking curve of Figure 6.2b is temporary and it disappears quickly. It illustrates temporal masking. This type of masking may occur when a strong sound A of frequency f is preceded or followed in time by a weaker sound B at a nearby (or identical) frequency. If the time interval between A and B is short, sound B may not be audible. Figure 6.4 illustrates an example of temporal masking. The threshold of temporal masking due to a loud sound at time 0 goes down, first sharply and then slowly.

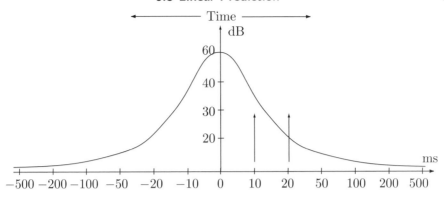

Figure 6.4: Threshold and Masking of Sound.

A weaker sound of 30 dB will not be audible if it occurs 10 ms before or after the loud sound, but will be audible if the time interval between the sounds is 20 ms.

6.3 Linear Prediction

In a stream of correlated audio samples $s(t)$, almost every sample $s(t)$ is similar to its predecessor $s(t-1)$ and its successor $s(t+1)$. Thus, a simple subtraction $s(t) - s(t-1)$ normally produces a small difference. Sound, however, is a wave, and this is reflected in the audio samples. Consecutive audio samples may become larger and larger and be followed by smaller and smaller samples. It therefore makes sense to assume that an audio sample is related in a simple way to several of its immediate predecessors and several of its successors. This assumption is the basis of the technique of linear prediction. A predicted value $\hat{s}(t)$ for the current sample $s(t)$ is computed from the p immediately-preceding samples by a linear combination

$$\hat{s}(t) = \sum_{i=1}^{p} a_i s(t-i).$$

Notice that only the samples preceding $s(t)$ can be used to predict it. The encoder cannot use any of the successors of $s(t)$ because the decoder must be able to compute the same prediction as the encoder, but it (the decoder) is decoding $s(t)$ so it hasn't yet decoded any of its successors.

If linear prediction is done properly, the resulting differences (also termed errors or residuals) $e(t) = s(t) - \hat{s}(t)$ will almost always be a small (positive or negative) integers. The simplest type of wave is stationary. In such a wave, a single set of coefficients a_i always produces the best prediction. Naturally, most waves are not stationary and should select a different set of a_i coefficients to predict each sample. Such selection can be done in different ways, involving more and more neighbor samples, and this results in predictors of different orders. A few such predictors are described here.

A zeroth-order predictor simply predicts each sample $s(t)$ as zero. A first-order predictor (Figure 6.5a) predicts each $s(t)$ as equal to its predecessor $s(t-1)$. Similarly, a second-order predictor (Figure 6.5b) computes a straight segment (a linear function or a degree-1 polynomial) from $s(t-2)$ to $s(t-1)$ and continues it to predict $s(t)$. Extending this idea to one more point, a third-order predictor (Figure 6.5c) computes a degree-2 polynomial (a conic section) that passes through the three points $s(t-3)$, $s(t-2)$, and $s(t-1)$ and extrapolates it to predict $s(t)$. In general, an nth-order predictor computes a degree-$(n-1)$ polynomial that passes through the n points $s(t-n)$ through $s(t-1)$ and extrapolates it to predict $s(t)$. This section shows how to compute several such predictors.

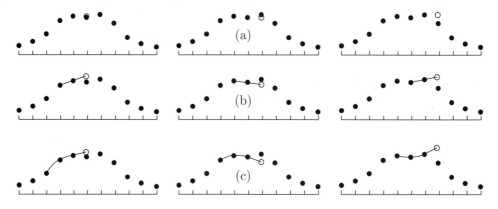

Figure 6.5: Predictors of Orders 1, 2, and 3.

Given the two points $P_2 = (t-2, s_2)$ and $P_1 = (t-1, s_1)$, we can write the parametric equation of the straight segment connecting them as

$$L(u) = (1-u)P_2 + u\,P_1 = (1-u)(t-2, s_2) + u(t-1, s_1) = (u+t-2, (1-u)s_2 + u\,s_1).$$

It's easy to see that $L(0) = P_2$ and $L(1) = P_1$. Extrapolating to the next point, at $u = 2$, yields $L(2) = (t, 2s_1 - s_2)$. Using our notation, we conclude that the second-order predictor predicts sample $s(t)$ as the linear combination $2s(t-1) - s(t-2)$.

For the third-order predictor, we start with the three points $P_3 = (t-3, s_3)$, $P_2 = (t-2, s_2)$, and $P_1 = (t-1, s_1)$. The degree-2 polynomial that passes through those points is given by the uniform quadratic Lagrange interpolation polynomial (see, for example, [Salomon 06] p. 78, Equation 3.12).

$$L(u) = [u^2, u, 1] \begin{bmatrix} \frac{1}{2} & -1 & \frac{1}{2} \\ -\frac{3}{2} & 2 & -\frac{1}{2} \\ 1 & 0 & 0 \end{bmatrix} \begin{bmatrix} P_3 \\ P_2 \\ P_1 \end{bmatrix}$$

$$= \left[\frac{u^2}{2} - \frac{3u}{2} + 1 \right] P_3 + (-u^2 + 2u)P_2 + \left[\frac{u^2}{2} - \frac{u}{2} \right] P_1.$$

It is easy to verify that $L(0) = P_3$, $L(1) = P_2$, and $L(2) = P_1$. Extrapolating to $u = 3$ yields $L(3) = 3P_1 - 3P_2 + P_3$. When this is translated to our samples, the result is

$\hat{s}(t) = 3s(t-1) - 3s(t-2) + s(t-3)$. The first four predictors are summarized as

$$
\begin{aligned}
\hat{s}_0(t) &= 0, \\
\hat{s}_1(t) &= s(t-1), \\
\hat{s}_2(t) &= 2s(t-1) - s(t-2), \\
\hat{s}_3(t) &= 3s(t-1) - 3s(t-2) + s(t-3).
\end{aligned}
\tag{6.3}
$$

These predictors can now be used to compute the error (or difference) values for the first four orders:

$$
\begin{aligned}
e_0(t) &= s(t) - \hat{s}_0(t) = s(t), \\
e_1(t) &= s(t) - \hat{s}_1(t) = s(t) - s(t-1) = e_0(t) - e_0(t-1), \\
e_2(t) &= s(t) - \hat{s}_2(t) = s(t) - 2s(t-1) + s(t-2) \\
&= [s(t) - s(t-1)] - [s(t-1) - s(t-2)] = e_1(t) - e_1(t-1), \\
e_3(t) &= s(t) - \hat{s}_3(t) = s(t) - 3s(t-1) + 3s(t-2) - s(t-3) \\
&= [s(t) - 2s(t-1) + s(t-2)] - [s(t-1) - 2s(t-2) + s(t-3)] \\
&= e_2(t) - e_2(t-1).
\end{aligned}
\tag{6.4}
$$

This computation is recursive but it involves only three steps, it is arithmetically simple, and does not require any multiplications (see also Equation (6.6)).

For even better compression, it is possible to compute all four predictors and their errors and select the smallest error. However, experience gained with practical implementations of this technique indicates that even a zeroth-order predictor results in typical compression of 48%, and going all the way to third-order prediction improves this only to 58%. For most cases, there is therefore no need to use higher-order predictors, and the precise predictor used should be determined by compression quality versus run-time considerations. The Shorten method (Section 6.5) uses linear (second-order) prediction as a default.

Extending these concepts to a fourth-order linear predictor is straightforward. We start with the four points $P_4 = (t-4, s_4)$, $P_3 = (t-3, s_3)$, $P_2 = (t-2, s_2)$, and $P_1 = (t-1, s_1)$ and construct a degree-3 polynomial that passes through those points (the points are selected such that their x coordinates correspond to time and their y coordinates are audio samples). A natural choice is the nonuniform cubic Lagrange interpolation polynomial $Q_{3nu}(t) = \sum_{i=0}^{3} P_{i+1} L_i^3(t)$ whose coefficients are given by (see, for example, [Salomon 99] p. 204, Equations 4.17 and 4.18)

$$
L_i^3(t) = \frac{\prod_{j \neq i}^3 (t - t_j)}{\prod_{j \neq i}^3 (t_i - t_j)}, \quad \text{for} \quad 0 \leq i \leq 3.
$$

The *Mathematica* code of Figure 6.6 performs the computations and produces

$$
Q(t) = -\frac{1}{6}(t-1)(t-2)(t-3)P_4 + \frac{1}{2}t(t-2)(t-3)P_3 - \frac{1}{2}t(t-1)(t-3)P_2 + \frac{1}{6}t(t-1)(t-2)P_1.
$$

It is easy to verify that $Q(0) = P_4$, $Q(1) = P_3$, $Q(2) = P_2$, and $Q(3) = P_1$. Extrapolating to $t = 4$ yields $Q(4) = 4P_1 - 6P_2 + 4P_3 - P_4$, and when this is translated to audio samples the result is

$$\hat{s}_4(t) = 4s(t-1) - 6s(t-2) + 4s(t-3) - s(t-4) \tag{6.5}$$

[compare with Equation (6.3)]. When this prediction is subtracted from the current audio sample $s(t)$, the residue is

$$e_4(t) = s(t) - \hat{s}_4(t) = s(t) - 4s(t-1) + 6s(t-2) - 4s(t-3) + s(t-4). \tag{6.6}$$

This is a simple arithmetic expression that involves only four additions and subtractions.

```
(* Uniform Cubic Lagrange polynomial for 4th-order prediction in FLAC *)
Clear[Q,t]; t0=0; t1=1; t2=2; t3=3;
Q[t_] := Plus @@ {
((t-t1)(t-t2)(t-t3))/((t0-t1)(t0-t2)(t0-t3))P4,
((t-t0)(t-t2)(t-t3))/((t1-t0)(t1-t2)(t1-t3))P3,
((t-t0)(t-t1)(t-t3))/((t2-t0)(t2-t1)(t2-t3))P2,
((t-t0)(t-t1)(t-t2))/((t3-t0)(t3-t1)(t3-t2))P1}
```

Figure 6.6: Code for a Lagrange Polynomial.

◇ **Exercise 6.4:** Check the performance of the fourth-order prediction developed here. Select four correlated items and compare the prediction of Equation (6.5) to the actual value of the next correlated item.

Given six matches, arrange them so as to end up with nothing.

6.4 μ-Law and A-Law Companding

These two international standards, formally known as recommendation G.711, are documented in [ITU-T 89]. They employ logarithm-based functions to encode audio samples for ISDN (integrated services digital network) digital telephony services, by means of nonlinear quantization (companding). The ISDN hardware samples the voice signal from the telephone 8,000 times per second, and generates 14-bit samples (13 for A-law). The method of μ-law companding is used in North America and Japan, and A-law is used elsewhere. The two methods are similar; they differ mostly in their quantizations (midtread vs. midriser).

Experiments (documented in [Shenoi 95]) indicate that low amplitudes of speech signals contain more information than high amplitudes. This is why nonlinear quantization makes sense. Imagine an audio signal sent on a telephone line and digitized to 14-bit samples. The louder the conversation, the higher the amplitude, and the bigger the value of the sample. Since high amplitudes are less important, they can be coarsely quantized. If the largest sample, which is $2^{14} - 1 = 16{,}383$, is quantized to 255 (the largest 8-bit number), then the compression factor is $14/8 = 1.75$. When decoded, a code of 255 will become very different from the original 16,383. We say that because of the coarse quantization, large samples end up with high quantization noise. Smaller samples should be finely quantized, so they end up with low quantization noise.

The μ-law encoder inputs 14-bit samples and outputs 8-bit codewords. The A-law inputs 13-bit samples and also outputs 8-bit codewords. The telephone signals are sampled at 8 kHz (8,000 times per second), so the μ-law encoder receives $8{,}000 \times 14 = 112{,}000$ bits/sec. At a compression factor of 1.75, the encoder outputs 64,000 bits/sec. The G.711 standard [G.711 72] also specifies output rates of 48 Kbps and 56 Kbps.

The μ-law encoder receives a 14-bit *signed* input sample x. Thus, the input is in the range $[-8{,}192, +8{,}191]$. The sample is normalized to the interval $[-1, +1]$, and the encoder uses the logarithmic expression

$$\mathrm{sgn}(x)\frac{\ln(1 + \mu|x|)}{\ln(1 + \mu)}, \text{ where } \mathrm{sgn}(x) = \begin{cases} +1, & x > 0, \\ 0, & x = 0, \\ -1, & x < 0 \end{cases}$$

(and μ is a positive integer), to compute and output an 8-bit code in the same interval $[-1, +1]$. The output is then scaled to the range $[-256, +255]$. Figure 6.7 shows this output as a function of the input for the three μ values 25, 255, and 2555. It is clear that large values of μ cause coarser quantization for larger amplitudes. Such values allocate more bits to the smaller, more important, amplitudes. The G.711 standard recommends the use of $\mu = 255$. The diagram shows only the nonnegative values of the input (i.e., from 0 to 8191). The negative side of the diagram has the same shape but with negative inputs and outputs.

The A-law encoder uses the similar expression

$$\begin{cases} \mathrm{sgn}(x)\dfrac{A|x|}{1 + \ln(A)}, & \text{for } 0 \le |x| < \frac{1}{A}, \\ \mathrm{sgn}(x)\dfrac{1 + \ln(A|x|)}{1 + \ln(A)}, & \text{for } \frac{1}{A} \le |x| < 1. \end{cases}$$

The G.711 standard recommends the use of $A = 87.6$.

The following simple examples illustrate the nonlinear nature of the μ-law. The two (normalized) input samples 0.15 and 0.16 are transformed by μ-law to outputs 0.6618 and 0.6732. The difference between the outputs is 0.0114. On the other hand, the two input samples 0.95 and 0.96 (bigger inputs but with the same difference) are transformed to 0.9908 and 0.9927. The difference between these two outputs is 0.0019; much smaller.

Bigger samples are decoded with more noise, and smaller samples are decoded with less noise. However, the signal-to-noise ratio (SNR) is constant because both it and the μ-law are based on logarithmic expressions.

Logarithms are slow to compute, so the μ-law encoder performs much simpler calculations that produce an approximation. The output specified by the G.711 standard is an 8-bit codeword whose format is shown in Figure 6.8.

Bit P in Figure 6.8 is the sign bit of the output (same as the sign bit of the 14-bit signed input sample). Bits S2, S1, and S0 are the segment code, and bits Q3 through Q0 are the quantization code. The encoder determines the segment code by (1) adding

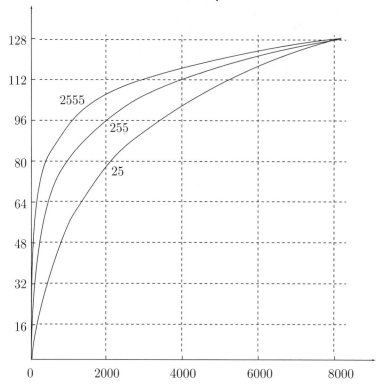

Figure 6.7: The μ-Law for μ Values of 25, 255, and 2555.

```
dat=linspace(0,1,1000);
mu=255;
plot(dat*8159,128*log(1+mu*dat)/log(1+mu));
```

Matlab code for Figure 6.7. Notice how the input is normalized to the range $[0,1]$ before the calculations, and how the output is scaled from the interval $[0,1]$ to $[0,128]$.

Figure 6.8: G.711 μ-Law Codeword.

Figure 6.9: Encoding Input Sample -656.

a bias of 33 to the absolute value of the input sample, (2) determining the bit position of the most significant 1-bit among bits 5 through 12 of the input, and (3) subtracting 5 from that position. The 4-bit quantization code is set to the four bits following the bit position determined in step 2. The encoder ignores the remaining bits of the input sample, and it inverts (1's complements) the codeword before it is output.

We use the input sample -656 as an example. The sample is negative, so bit P becomes 1. Adding 33 to the absolute value of the input yields $689 = 0001010110001_2$ (Figure 6.9). The most significant 1-bit in positions 5 through 12 is found at position 9. The segment code is thus $9 - 5 = 4$. The quantization code is the four bits 0101 at positions 8–5, and the remaining five bits 10001 are ignored. The 8-bit codeword (which is later inverted) becomes

P	S2	S1	S0	Q3	Q2	Q1	Q0
1	1	0	0	0	1	0	1

The μ-law decoder inputs an 8-bit codeword and inverts it. It then decodes it as follows:

1. Multiply the quantization code by 2 and add 33 (the bias) to the result.
2. Multiply the result by 2 raised to the power of the segment code.
3. Decrement the result by the bias.
4. Use bit P to determine the sign of the result.

Applying these steps to our example produces

1. The quantization code is $101_2 = 5$, so $5 \times 2 + 33 = 43$.
2. The segment code is $100_2 = 4$, so $43 \times 2^4 = 688$.
3. Decrement by the bias $688 - 33 = 655$.
4. Bit P is 1, so the final result is -655. Thus, the quantization error (the noise) is 1; very small.

Figure 6.10a illustrates the nature of the μ-law midtread quantization. Zero is one of the valid output values, and the quantization steps are centered at the input value of 0. The steps are organized in eight segments of 16 steps each. The steps within each segment have the same width, but they double in width from one segment to the next. If we denote the segment number by i (where $i = 0, 1, \ldots, 7$) and the width of a segment by k (where $k = 1, 2, \ldots, 16$), then the middle of the tread of each step in Figure 6.10a (i.e., the points labeled x_j) is given by

$$x(16i + k) = T(i) + k \times D(i), \qquad (6.7)$$

where the constants $T(i)$ and $D(i)$ are the initial value and the step size for segment i, respectively. They are given by

i	0	1	2	3	4	5	6	7
$T(i)$	1	35	103	239	511	1055	2143	4319
$D(i)$	2	4	8	16	32	64	128	256

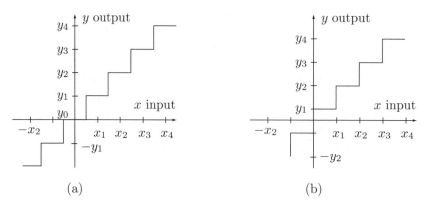

Figure 6.10: (a) μ-Law Midtread Quantization. (b) A-Law Midriser Quantization.

Segment 0		Segment 1		$\cdots$	Segment 7	
Break points	Output values	Break points	Output values		Break points	Output values
	$y_0 = 0$		$y_{16} = 33$	$\cdots$		$y_{112} = 4191$
$x_1 = 1$		$x_{17} = 35$			$x_{113} = 4319$	
	$y_1 = 2$		$y_{17} = 37$	$\cdots$		$y_{113} = 4447$
$x_2 = 3$		$x_{18} = 39$			$x_{114} = 4575$	
	$y_2 = 4$		$y_{18} = 41$	$\cdots$		$y_{114} = 4703$
$x_3 = 5$		$x_{19} = 43$			$x_{115} = 4831$	
	$y_3 = 6$		$y_{19} = 45$	$\cdots$		$y_{115} = 4959$
$x_4 = 7$		$x_{20} = 47$			$x_{116} = 5087$	
$\cdots$						
$\cdots$				$\cdots$		
$x_{15} = 29$		$x_{31} = 91$			$x_{127} = 7903$	
	$y_{15} = 28$		$y_{31} = 93$	$\cdots$		$y_{127} = 8031$
$x_{16} = 31$		$x_{32} = 95$			$x_{128} = 8159$	

Table 6.11: Specification of the μ-Law Quantizer.

Table 6.11 lists some values of the breakpoints (points x_j) and outputs (points y_j) shown in Figure 6.10a.

The operation of the A-law encoder is similar, except that the quantization (Figure 6.10b) is of the midriser variety. The breakpoints x_j are given by Equation (6.7), but the initial value $T(i)$ and the step size $D(i)$ for segment i are different from those used by the μ-law encoder and are given by

i	0	1	2	3	4	5	6	7
$T(i)$	0	32	64	128	256	512	1024	2048
$D(i)$	2	2	4	8	16	32	64	128

Table 6.12 lists some values of the breakpoints (points x_j) and outputs (points y_j) shown in Figure 6.10b.

Segment 0		Segment 1		$\cdots$	Segment 7	
Break points	Output values	Break points	Output values		Break points	Output values
$x_0 = 0$		$x_{16} = 32$			$x_{112} = 2048$	
	$y_1 = 1$		$y_{17} = 33$	$\cdots$		$y_{113} = 2112$
$x_1 = 2$		$x_{17} = 34$			$x_{113} = 2176$	
	$y_2 = 3$		$y_{18} = 35$	$\cdots$		$y_{114} = 2240$
$x_2 = 4$		$x_{18} = 36$			$x_{114} = 2304$	
	$y_3 = 5$		$y_{19} = 37$	$\cdots$		$y_{115} = 2368$
$x_3 = 6$		$x_{19} = 38$			$x_{115} = 2432$	
	$y_4 = 7$		$y_{20} = 39$	$\cdots$		$y_{116} = 2496$
$\cdots$				$\cdots$		
$\cdots$				$\cdots$		
$x_{15} = 30$		$x_{31} = 62$			$x_{128} = 4096$	
	$y_{16} = 31$		$y_{32} = 63$	$\cdots$		$y_{127} = 4032$

Table 6.12: Specification of the A-Law Quantizer.

The A-law encoder generates an 8-bit codeword with the same format as the μ-law encoder. It sets the P bit to the sign of the input sample. It then determines the segment code in the following steps:

1. Determine the bit position of the most significant 1-bit among the seven most significant bits of the input.
2. If such a 1-bit is found, the segment code becomes that position minus 4. Otherwise, the segment code becomes zero.

The 4-bit quantization code is set to the four bits following the bit position determined in step 1, or to half the input value if the segment code is zero. The encoder ignores the remaining bits of the input sample, and it inverts bit P and the even-numbered bits of the codeword before it is output.

The A-law decoder decodes an 8-bit codeword into a 13-bit audio sample as follows:

1. It inverts bit P and the even-numbered bits of the codeword.
2. If the segment code is nonzero, the decoder multiplies the quantization code by 2 and increments this by the bias (33). The result is then multiplied by 2 and raised to the power of the (segment code minus 1). If the segment code is 0, the decoder outputs twice the quantization code, plus 1.
3. Bit P is then used to determine the sign of the output.

Normally, the output codewords are generated by the encoder at the rate of 64 Kbps. The G.711 standard [G.711 72] also provides for two other rates, as follows:

1. To achieve an output rate of 48 Kbps, the encoder masks out the two least-significant bits of each codeword. This works because $6/8 = 48/64$.

2. To achieve an output rate of 56 Kpbs, the encoder masks out the least-significant bit of each codeword. This works because $7/8 = 56/64 = 0.875$.

This applies to both the μ-law and the A-law. The decoder typically fills up the masked bit positions with zeros before decoding a codeword.

6.5 Shorten

Shorten is a simple, special-purpose, lossless compressor for waveform files. Any file whose data items (which are referred to as *samples*) go up and down as in a wave can be efficiently compressed by this method. Its developer [Robinson 94] had in mind applications to speech compression (where audio files with speech are distributed on a CD-ROM), but any other waveform files can be similarly compressed. The compression performance of Shorten isn't as good as that of mp3, but Shorten is lossless. Shorten performs best on files with low-amplitude and low-frequency samples, where it yields compression factors of 2 or better. It has been implemented on UNIX and on MS-DOS and is freely available at [Softsound 07].

Shorten encodes the individual samples of the input file by partitioning the file into blocks, predicting each sample from some of its predecessors, subtracting the prediction from the sample, and encoding the difference with a special variable-length code. It also has a lossy mode, where samples are quantized before being compressed. The algorithm has been implemented by its developer and can input files in the audio formats ulaw, s8, u8, s16 (this is the default input format), u16, s16x, u16x, s16hl, u16hl, s16lh, and u16lh, where "s" and "u" stand for "signed" and "unsigned," respectively, a trailing "x" specifies byte-mapped data, "hl" implies that the high-order byte of a sample is followed in the file by the low-order byte, and "lh" signifies the reverse.

An entire file is encoded in blocks, where the block size (typically 128 or 256 samples) is specified by the user and has a default value of 256. (At a sampling rate of 16 kHz, this is equivalent to 16 ms of sound.) The samples in the block are first converted to integers with an expected mean of 0. The idea is that the samples within each block have the same spectral characteristic and can therefore be predicted accurately. Some audio files consist of several interleaved channels, so Shorten starts by separating the channels in each block. Thus, if the file has two channels and the samples are interleaved as L_1, R_1, L_2, R_2, and so on up to L_b, R_b, the first step creates the two blocks $(L_1, L_2, \ldots, L_b)$ and $(R_1, R_2, \ldots, R_b)$ and each block is then compressed separately. In practice, blocks that correspond to audio channels are often highly correlated, so sophisticated methods, such as MLP [Salomon 07], try to remove interblock correlations before tackling the samples within a block.

Once the channels have been separated, the audio samples in each channel are predicted and the resulting differences are losslessly encoded by Rice codes (Section 1.1.3). These steps result in lossless coding of the audio samples. Sometimes, a certain loss in the samples is acceptable if it results in significantly better compression. Shorten offers two options of lossy compression by quantizing the original audio samples before they are compressed. The quantization is done separately for each segment. One lossy option encodes every segment at the same bitrate (the user specifies the maximum bitrate), and the other option maintains a user-specified signal-to-noise ratio in each segment (the user specifies the minimum acceptable signal-to-noise ratio in dB).

Tests of Shorten indicate that it generally performs better and faster than UNIX compress and gzip, but that its lossy options are slow.

Chapter Summary

Audio data is one of the important members of the family of multimedia digital data. It has become even more important and popular with the advent of popular mp3 players. Standards organizations as well as researchers have long felt the need for high-performance audio compression algorithms that offer fast, simple decompression. The best-known example of such an algorithm, mp3, started its life in 1988, when a group of audio experts first met to discuss this topic, and became an approved international standard in 1992. Since then, many different algorithms, both lossy and lossless, have been proposed, developed, and implemented. Reference [Salomon 07] describes about a dozen different methods, based on different principles, that have been specifically developed to compress audio data.

This chapter starts with general discussion of companding (Section 6.1), the human auditory system (Section 6.2), and linear prediction (Section 6.3). It follows with descriptions of two audio compression algorithms, μ-law and A-law companding (Section 6.4) and Shorten (Section 6.5).

Companding (also termed nonlinear quantization) exploits the fact that the human ear is sensitive to low sound amplitudes (quiet sound) and loses sensitivity as the sound becomes louder. The principle of companding is to quantize each audio sample by a different amount according to its size (recall that the size of a sample is proportional to the sound amplitude). Large samples, which correspond to high amplitudes, are quantized more than small samples. This is the reason for the term nonlinear quantization. Section 6.1 says more about companding. The μ-law and A-law compression methods (Section 6.4) are examples of this approach.

The ear receives sound waves and converts them to signals that are sent to the brain to create the sensation of sound. The ear–brain system is very sensitive and can perceive very quiet sounds, but its sensitivity depends on the frequency of the sound. Also, a loud sound drastically reduces the sensitivity of the ear over a short period. These properties of the human auditory system can be exploited to achieve effective lossy audio compression. The principle is to develop a psychoacoustic model to identify those parts of the input audio that will not be perceived by the ear and brain because of the limitations of these organs. These parts can either be completely omitted or at least coarsely quantized, thereby resulting in substantial savings and effective compression. This is how mp3 works.

The term "correlation" dominates this book. Images can be tightly compressed because the pixels of an image tend to be correlated. Similarly, audio can be compressed because its smallest units, the audio samples, are correlated. Thus, a simple approach to audio compression may be to subtract each audio sample from its predecessor and encode the resulting differences. The audio samples are unsigned integers, but the differences (also termed errors or residuals) are signed. The point is that the residuals tend to be small numbers and therefore can be encoded very efficiently. This simple approach can be improved when we subtract from the current sample $s(t)$ not just its predecessor $s(t-1)$ (which is usually similar to $s(t)$ but may sometimes be different) but a linear combination of several past samples $s(t-1)$, $s(t-2)$, down to $s(t-p)$ for some integer p. This process of *predicting* the current sample from p of its predecessors, smoothes out any unexpected differences between consecutive audio samples and results in smaller residuals and thus better compression.

Self-Assessment Questions

1. The term "audio sample" is central to digital audio and its processing, compression, and playback. The audio samples are generated when a sound wave is sampled many times per second. The question is, can audio samples be created solely by software, or is there a need for a special piece of hardware to do the sampling?

2. The term "pulse modulation" refers to techniques for converting a continuous wave to a stream of binary numbers (audio samples). The term pulse code modulation (PCM) has been mentioned in this chapter. Search the professional literature and the Internet for other modulation techniques, such as pulse amplitude modulation (PAM), pulse position modulation (PPM), pulse width modulation (PWM), and pulse number modulation (PNM).

3. Discuss the possible applications of RLE and dictionary-based methods for audio compression. Does it make sense to adapt such approaches to the compression of audio samples, and if so, can they be as efficient as the methods discussed here?

4. Audio is a physical entity that varies in a very wide range. The interval from the quietest sound (the threshold of hearing) to the loudest sound that we can hear is spread over 12 orders of magnitude. As a result, sound intensity is measured by a quantity called the decibel (dB) that is based on a logarithmic scale. Anyone interested in sound, its measurement, and its applications should be familiar with decibels and their properties.

The sweetest sound of all is praise.

—Xenophon

7
Other Methods

 Prelude

The discipline of data compression is vast. It is based on many approaches and techniques and it borrows many tools, ideas, and concepts from diverse scientific, engineering, and mathematical fields. The following are just a few examples:

Fourier transform, finite automata, Markov processes, the human visual and auditory systems, statistical terms, distributions, and concepts, Unicode, XML, convolution, space-filling curves, Voronoi diagrams, interpolating polynomials, Fibonacci numbers, polygonal surfaces, data structures, error-correcting codes, fractals, fingerprint identification, and analog and digital video. The Intermezzo on page 253 discusses one of these topics.

This book is relatively short and concentrates on the most important approaches and ideas used in data compression. It discusses sources of data redundancies, correlation of data items, variable-length codes, the use of dictionaries, and the power of transforms. About a dozen specific compression methods are described in order to illustrate these concepts and approaches.

This chapter is an attempt to extend the scope of the book somewhat. It tries to convince the reader that useful, practical compression algorithms can be based on other techniques, and it illustrates this point by discussing the following: the Burrows–Wheeler method (Section 7.1), symbol ranking (Section 7.2), and SCSU and BOCU-1, two algorithms (Sections 7.3 and 7.3.1) for the compression of Unicode-based documents.

7.1 The Burrows–Wheeler Method

Most compression methods operate in the streaming mode, where the codec inputs a byte or several bytes, processes them, and continues until an end-of-file is sensed. The Burrows–Wheeler (BW) method, described in this section [Burrows and Wheeler 94], works in a block mode, where the input is read block by block and each block is encoded separately as one string. The method is therefore referred to as block sorting. The BW method is general purpose, it works well on images, sound, and text, and can achieve very high compression ratios (1 bit per byte or even better).

The main idea of the BW method is to start with a string S of n symbols and to scramble them into another string L that satisfies two conditions:

1. Any region of L will tend to have a concentration of just a few symbols. Another way of saying this is, if a symbol s is found at a certain position in L, then other occurrences of s are likely to be found nearby. This property means that L can easily and efficiently be compressed with the move-to-front method [Salomon 07], perhaps in combination with RLE. This also means that the BW method will work well only if n is large (at least several thousand symbols per string).

2. It is possible to reconstruct the original string S from L (a little more data may be needed for the reconstruction, in addition to L, but not much).

The mathematical term for scrambling symbols is permutation, and it is easy to show that a string of n symbols has $n!$ (pronounced "n factorial") permutations. This is a large number even for relatively small values of n, so the particular permutation used by BW has to be carefully selected. The BW codec proceeds in the following steps:

1. String L is created, by the encoder, as a permutation of S. Some more information, denoted by I, is also created, to be used later by the decoder in step 3.

2. The encoder compresses L and I and writes the results on the output. This step typically starts with RLE, continues with move-to-front coding, and finally applies Huffman coding.

3. The decoder reads the output and decodes it by applying the same methods as in step 2 but in reverse order. The result is string L and variable I.

4. Both L and I are used by the decoder to reconstruct the original string S.

I do hate sums. There is no greater mistake than to call arithmetic an exact science. There are permutations and aberrations discernible to minds entirely noble like mine; subtle variations which ordinary accountants fail to discover; hidden laws of number which it requires a mind like mine to perceive. For instance, if you add a sum from the bottom up, and then from the top down, the result is always different.

—Mrs. La Touche, *Mathematical Gazette*, v. 12 (1924)

The first step is to understand how string L is created from S, and what information needs to be stored in I for later reconstruction. We use the familiar string swiss⎵miss to illustrate this process.

			$\underline{F}$	$\underline{T}$	$\underline{L}$
		0:	␣	4 ——— s	
swiss␣miss	␣missswiss	1:	i	9	w
wiss␣misss	iss␣misssw	2:	i	3	m
iss␣misssw	issswiss␣m	3:	m	0 ——— ␣	
ss␣missswi	missswiss␣	4:	s	5 ——— s	
s␣missswis	s␣missswis	5:	s	1	i
␣missswiss	ss␣missswi	6:	s	2 ——— i	
missswiss␣	ssswiss␣mi	7:	s	6 ——— s	
issswiss␣m	sswiss␣mis	8:	s	7	s
ssswiss␣mi	swiss␣miss	9:	w	8 ——— s	
sswiss␣mis	wiss␣misss				

(a)	(b)	(c)

Figure 7.1: Principles of BW Compression.

Given an input string of n symbols, the encoder constructs an $n \times n$ matrix where it stores string S in the top row, followed by $n-1$ copies of S, each cyclically shifted (rotated) one symbol to the left (Figure 7.1a). The matrix is then sorted lexicographically by rows, producing the sorted matrix of Figure 7.1b. Notice that every row and every column of each of the two matrices is a permutation of S and thus contains all n symbols of S. The permutation L selected by the encoder is the **last column** of the sorted matrix. In our example this is the string swm␣siisss. The only other information needed to eventually reconstruct S from L is the row number of the original string in the sorted matrix, which in our example is 8 (row and column numbering starts from 0). This number is stored in I.

It is easy to see why L contains concentrations of identical symbols. Assume that the words bail, fail, hail, jail, mail, nail, pail, rail, sail, tail, and wail appear somewhere in S. After sorting, all the permutations that start with il will appear together. All of them contribute an a to L, so L will have a concentration of a's. Also, all the permutations starting with ail will end up together, contributing to a concentration of the letters bfhjmnprstw in one region of L.

We can now characterize the BW method by saying that it uses sorting to group together symbols based on their contexts. However, the method considers context on only one side of each symbol.

◇ **Exercise 7.1:** The last column, L, of the sorted matrix contains concentrations of identical characters, which is why L is easy to compress. However, the first column, F, of the same matrix is even easier to compress, since it contains runs, not just concentrations, of identical characters. Why select column L and not column F?

Notice also that the encoder does not actually have to construct the two $n \times n$ matrices (or even one of them) in memory. The practical details of the encoder are discussed in Section 7.1.2, as well as the compression of L and I, but let's first see how the decoder works.

The decoder reads a compressed file, decompresses it using Huffman, move-to-front, and perhaps also RLE (see [Salomon 07] for the move-to-front method), and then reconstructs string S from the decompressed L in three steps:

1. The first column of the sorted matrix (column F in Figure 7.1c) is constructed from L. This is a straightforward process, since F and L contain the same symbols (both are permutations of S) and F is sorted. The decoder simply sorts string L to obtain F.

2. While sorting L, the decoder prepares an auxiliary array T that shows the relations between elements of L and F (Figure 7.1c). The first element of T is 4, implying that the first symbol of L (the letter "s") is located in position 4 of F. The second element of T is 9, implying that the second symbol of L (the letter "w") is located in position 9 of F, and so on. The contents of T in our example are $(4, 9, 3, 0, 5, 1, 2, 6, 7, 8)$.

3. String F is no longer needed. The decoder uses L, I, and T to reconstruct S according to

$$S[n - 1 - i] \leftarrow L[T^i[I]], \quad \text{for } i = 0, 1, \ldots, n - 1,$$

$$\text{where } T^0[j] = j, \text{ and } T^{i+1}[j] = T[T^i[j]]. \tag{7.1}$$

Here are the first two steps in this reconstruction:

```
S[10-1-0]=L[T⁰[I]]=L[T⁰[8]]=L[8]=s,
S[10-1-1]=L[T¹[I]]=L[T[T⁰[I]]]=L[T[8]]=L[7]=s.
```

⋄ **Exercise 7.2:** Complete this reconstruction.

Before getting to the details of the compression, it may be interesting to understand why Equation (7.1) reconstructs S from L. The following arguments explain why this process works:

1. T is constructed such that $F[T[i]] = L[i]$ for $i = 0, \ldots, n$.

2. A look at the sorted matrix of Figure 7.1b shows that in each row i, symbol L[i] precedes symbol F[i] in the original string S (the word *precedes* has to be understood as *precedes cyclically*). Specifically, in row I (8 in our example), L[I] cyclically precedes F[I], but F[I] is the first symbol of S, so L[I] is the *last* symbol of S. The reconstruction starts with L[I] and reconstructs S from right to left.

3. L[i] precedes F[i] in S for $i = 0, \ldots, n - 1$. Therefore L[T[i]] precedes F[T[i]], but F[T[i]] = L[i]. The conclusion is that L[T[i]] precedes L[i] in S.

4. The reconstruction therefore starts with L[I] = L[8] = s (the last symbol of S) and proceeds with L[T[I]] = L[T[8]] = L[7] = s (the next-to-last symbol of S). This is why Equation (7.1) correctly describes the reconstruction.

7.1.1 Compressing L

Compressing L is based on its main attribute, namely, it contains concentrations (although not necessarily runs) of identical symbols. Using RLE makes sense, but only as a first step in a multistep compression process. The main step in compressing L should use the move-to-front method [Salomon 07]. This method is applied to our example L=swm⊔siisss as follows:

1. Initialize A to a list containing our alphabet A=(⊔, i, m, s, w).
2. For $i := 0, \ldots, n - 1$, encode symbol L_i as the number of symbols preceding it in A, and then move symbol L_i to the beginning of A.

3. Combine the codes of step 2 in a list C, which will be further compressed with Huffman or arithmetic coding.

The results are summarized in Figure 7.2a. The final list of codes is the 10-element array C = $(3, 4, 4, 3, 3, 4, 0, 1, 0, 0)$, illustrating how any concentration of identical symbols produces small codes. The first occurrence of i is assigned code 4 but the second occurrence is assigned code 0. The first two occurrences of s get code 3, but the next one gets code 1.

L	A	Code	C	A	L
s	⊔imsw	3	3	⊔imsw	s
w	s imw	4	4	s imw	w
m	ws im	4	4	ws im	m
⊔	mws i	3	3	mws i	⊔
s	⊔mwsi	3	3	⊔mwsi	s
i	s mwi	4	4	s mwi	i
i	is mw	0	0	is mw	i
s	is mw	1	1	is mw	s
s	si mw	0	0	si mw	s
s	si mw	0	0	si mw	s
	(a)			(b)	

Figure 7.2: Encoding/Decoding L by Move-to-Front.

It is interesting to compare the codes in C, which are integers in the range $[0, n-1]$, with the codes obtained without the extra step of "moving to front." It is easy to encode L using the three steps above but without moving symbol L_i to the beginning of A. The result is C' = $(3, 4, 2, 0, 3, 1, 1, 3, 3, 3)$, a list of integers *in the same range* $[0, n-1]$. This is why applying move-to-front is not enough. Lists C and C' contain elements in the same range, but the elements of C are smaller on average. They should therefore be further encoded using Huffman coding or some other statistical method. Huffman codes for C can be assigned assuming that code 0 has the highest probability and code $n-1$, the smallest probability.

In our example, a possible set of Huffman codes is 0—0, 1—10, 2—110, 3—1110, 4—1111. Applying this set to C yields "1110|1111|1111|1110|1110|1111|0|10|0|0"; 29 bits. (Applying it to C' yields "1110|1111|110|0|1110|10|10|1110|1110|1110"; 32 bits.) Our original 10-character string swiss miss has thus been coded using 2.9 bits/character, a very good result. It should be noted that the Burrows–Wheeler method can easily achieve better compression than that when applied to longer strings (thousands of symbols).

⋄ **Exercise 7.3:** Given the string S=sssssssssh, calculate string L and its move-to-front compression.

Decoding C is done with the inverse of move-to-front. We assume that the alphabet list A is available to the decoder (it is either the list of all possible bytes or it is written by the encoder on the output). Figure 7.2b shows the details of decoding

C = $(3, 4, 4, 3, 3, 4, 0, 1, 0, 0)$. The first code is 3, so the first symbol in the newly constructed L is the *fourth* one in A, or "s". This symbol is then moved to the front of A, and the process continues.

7.1.2 Implementation Hints

Since the Burrows–Wheeler method is efficient only for long strings (at least thousands of symbols), any practical implementation should allow for large values of n. The maximum value of n should be so large that two $n \times n$ matrices would not fit in the available memory (at least not comfortably), and all the encoder operations (preparing the permutations and sorting them) should be done with one-dimensional arrays of size n. In principle, it is enough to have just the original string S and the auxiliary array T in memory. [Manber and Myers 93] and [McCreight 76] discuss the data structures used in this implementation.

String S contains the original data, but surprisingly, it also contains all the necessary permutations. Since the only permutations we need to generate are rotations, we can generate permutation i of matrix 7.1a by scanning S from position i to the end, then continuing cyclically from the start of S to position $i - 1$. Permutation 5, for example, can be generated by scanning substring $(5, 9)$ of S (␣miss), followed by substring $(0, 4)$ of S (swiss). The result is ␣missswiss. The first step in a practical implementation would thus be to write a procedure that takes a parameter i and scans the corresponding permutation.

Any method used to sort the permutations has to compare them. Comparing two permutations can be done by scanning them in S, without having to move symbols or create new arrays.

Once the sorting algorithm determines that permutation i should be in position j in the sorted matrix (Figure 7.1b), it sets $T[i]$ to j. In our example, the sort ends up with $T = (5, 2, 7, 6, 4, 3, 8, 9, 0, 1)$.

⋄ **Exercise 7.4:** Show how how T is used to create the encoder's main output, L and I.

Implementing the decoder is straightforward, because there is no need to create $n \times n$ matrices. The decoder inputs bits that are Huffman codes. It uses them to create the codes of C, decompressing each as it is created, with inverse move-to-front, into the next symbol of L. When L is ready, the decoder sorts it into F, generating array T in the process. Following that, it reconstructs S from L, T, and I. Thus, the decoder needs at most three structures at any time, the two strings L and F (having typically one byte per symbol), and the array T (with at least two bytes per pointer, to allow for large values of n).

> We describe a block-sorting,lossless data compression algorithm, and our implementation of that algorithm. We compare the performance of our implementation with widely available data compressors running on the same hardware.
>
> M. Burrows and D. J. Wheeler, May 10, 1994

What is the next integer in the sequence 5, 25, 61, 113, 181?

Intermezzo

Fibonacci Codes. This short intermezzo explain how the well-known Fibonacci numbers can be harnessed and employed to compress data. First, a few words about this important sequence. The Fibonacci numbers, as their name implies, are named after Leonardo Fibonacci and have many interesting and beautiful properties and many useful applications. The first two Fibonacci numbers are 1, and any other Fibonacci number is simply the sum of its two immediate predecessors. Thus, the sequence starts with 1, 1, 3, 5, 8, 13, 21, ... and can also can serve as a number system; any integer can be expressed as a weighted sum of the Fibonacci numbers. Thus,  $15 = 12 + 3$ can be written as $1 \times 12 + 0 \times 8 + 0 \times 5 + 1 \times 3 + 0 \times 1$ or 10010.

A little thinking should convince the reader that the Fibonacci representation of an integer cannot have two consecutive 1's. The number 110, for example, equals $1 \times 5 + 1 \times 3 + 0 \times 1 = 8$, so it should be written 1000. This property was exploited in [Fraenkel and Klein 96] to construct a variable-length Fibonacci code (in fact, several codes) for the integers, a code that has a short average length and that is also easy to encode and decode. Given an integer n, the idea is to construct its Fibonacci representation, reverse the resulting string of bits, and append a 1 to it. Thus, the codeword of the integer 8 starts as 1000, reversed to 0001, to become 0001|1. Table 7.3 lists the first 12 Fibonacci codewords and it is clear that this code can be uniquely decoded because the only pair of successive 1's occurs at the end of a codeword.

1	11	7	01011
2	011	8	000011
3	0011	9	100011
4	1011	10	010011
5	00011	11	001011
6	10011	12	101011

Table 7.3: Twelve Fibonacci Codes.

To decode a given Fibonacci codeword, skip bits of the codeword until a pair 11 is reached. Replace this 11 by 1. Multiply the skipped bits by the values ..., 13, 8, 5, 3, 2, 1 (the Fibonacci numbers), and add the products. Obviously, it is not necessary to actually multiply. Simply use the 1 bits to select the proper Fibonacci numbers and add.

7.2 Symbol Ranking

Like so many other ideas in the realm of information and data, the idea of text compression by symbol ranking is due to Claude Shannon, the creator of information theory. In his classic paper on the information content of English text [Shannon 51] he describes a method for experimentally determining the entropy of such texts. In a typical experiment, a passage of text has to be predicted, character by character, by a person (the examinee). In one version of the method the examinee predicts the next character and is then told by the examiner whether the prediction was correct or, if it was not, what the next character is. In another version, the examinee has to continue predicting until he obtains the right answer. The examiner then uses the number of wrong answers to estimate the entropy of the text.

As it turned out, in the latter version of the test, the human examinees were able to predict the next character in one guess about 79% of the time and rarely needed more than 3–4 guesses. Table 7.4 shows the distribution of guesses as published by Shannon.

# of guesses	1	2	3	4	5	> 5
Probability	79%	8%	3%	2%	2%	5%

Table 7.4: Probabilities of Guesses of English Text.

The fact that this probability is so skewed implies low entropy (Shannon's conclusion was that the entropy of English text is in the range of 0.6–1.3 bits per letter), which in turn implies the possibility of very good compression.

The symbol ranking method of this section [Fenwick 96b] is based on the latter version of the Shannon test. The method uses the context C of the current symbol S (the N symbols preceding S) to prepare a list of symbols that are likely to follow C. The list is arranged from most likely to least likely. The position of S in this list (position numbering starts from 0) is then written by the encoder on the output after being suitably encoded. If the program performs as well as a human examinee, we can expect 79% of the symbols being encoded to result in 0 (first position in the ranking list), creating runs of zeros, which can easily be compressed by RLE.

The various context-based methods (most notably PPM) described in the data compression literature use context to estimate symbol probabilities. They have to generate and output escape symbols when switching contexts. In contrast, symbol ranking does not estimate probabilities and does not use escape symbols. The absence of escapes seems to be the main feature contributing to the excellent performance of the method. Following is an outline of the main steps of the encoding algorithm.

Step 0: The *ranking index* (an integer counting the position of S in the ranked list) is set to 0.

Step 1: An LZ77-type dictionary is used, with a search buffer containing text that has already been input and encoded, and with a look-ahead buffer containing new, unprocessed text. The most-recent text in the search buffer becomes the *current context* C. The leftmost symbol, R, in the look-ahead buffer (immediately to the right of C) is the *current symbol*. The search buffer is scanned from right to left (from recent to older text) for strings matching C. The longest match is selected (if there are several longest matches, the most recent one is selected). The match length, N, becomes the *current order*. The symbol P following the matched string (i.e., immediately to the right of it) is examined. This is the symbol ranked first by the algorithm. If P is identical to R, the search is over and the algorithm outputs the ranking index (which is currently 0).

Step 2: If P is different from R, the ranking index is incremented by 1, P is declared *excluded*, and the other order-N matches, if any, are examined in the same way. Assume that Q is the symbol following such a match. If Q is in the list of excluded symbols, then it is pointless to examine it, and the search continues with the next match. If Q has not been excluded, it is compared with R. If they are identical, the search is over, and the encoding algorithm outputs the ranking index. Otherwise the ranking index is incremented by 1, and Q is excluded.

Step 3: If none of the order-N matches is followed by a symbol identical to R, the order of the match is decremented by 1, and the search buffer is again scanned from right to left (from more recent text to older text) for strings of size $N - 1$ that match C. For each failure in this scan, the ranking index is incremented by 1, and Q is excluded.

Step 4: When the match order gets all the way down to 0, symbol R is compared with symbols in a list containing the entire alphabet, again using exclusions and incrementing the ranking index. If the algorithm gets to this step, it will find R in this list, and will output the current value of the ranking index (which will then normally be a large number).

Some implementation details are discussed here.

1. Implementing exclusion. When a string S that matches C is found, the symbol P immediately to the right of S is compared with R. If P and R are different, P should be declared excluded. This means that any future occurrences of P should be ignored. The first implementation of exclusion that comes to mind is a list to which excluded symbols are appended. Searching such a list, however, is time consuming, and it is possible to do much better.

The method described here uses an array `excl` indexed by the alphabet symbols. If the alphabet consists, for example, of just the 26 letters, the array will have 26 locations indexed `a` through `z`. Figure 7.5 shows a simple implementation that requires just one step to determine whether a given symbol is excluded. Assume that the current context C is the string "...abc". We know that the c will remain in the context even if the algorithm has to go down all the way to order-1. The algorithm therefore prepares a pointer to c (to be called the *context index*). Assume that the scan finds another string `abc`, followed by a `y`, and compares it to the current context. They match, but they are followed by different symbols. The decision is to exclude y, and this is done by setting array element `excl[y]` to the context index (i.e., to point to c). As long as the algorithm scans for matches to the same context C, the context index will stay the same. If another matching string `abc` is later found, also followed by `y`, the algorithm compares `excl[y]` to the context index, finds that they are equal, so it knows that y has already been excluded. When switching to the next current context there is no need to initialize or modify the pointers in array `excl`.

2. Recall that N (the order) is initially unknown. The algorithm has to scan the search buffer and find the longest match to the current context. Once this is done, the length N of the match becomes the current order. The process therefore starts by hashing the two rightmost symbols of the current context C and using them to locate a possible

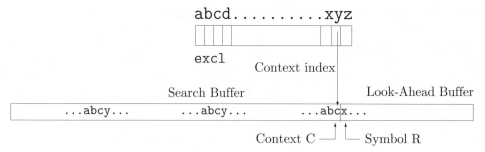

Figure 7.5: Exclusion Mechanism.

match.

Figure 7.6 shows the current context "...amcde". We assume that it has already been matched to some string of length 3 (i.e., a string "...cde"), and we try to match it to a longer string. The two symbols "de" are hashed and produce a pointer to string "lmcde". The problem is to compare the current context to "lmcde" and find whether and by how much they match. This is done by the following three rules.

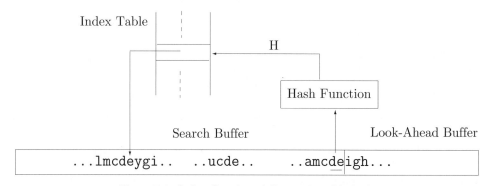

Figure 7.6: String Search and Comparison Method.

1. Compare the symbols preceding (i.e., to the left of) cde in the two strings. In our example they are both m, so the match is now of size 4. Repeat this rule until it fails. It determines the order N of the match. Once the order is known, the algorithm may have to decrement it later and compare shorter strings. In such a case, this rule has to be modified. Instead of comparing the symbols *preceding* the strings, it should compare the leftmost symbols of the two strings.

2. (We are still not sure whether the two strings are identical.) Compare the middle symbols of the two strings. In our case, since the strings have a length of 4, this would be either the c or the d. If the comparison fails, the strings are different. Otherwise, Rule 3 is used.

3. Compare the strings symbol by symbol to finally determine whether they are identical.

It seems unnecessarily cumbersome to go through three rules when only the third one is really necessary. However, the first two rules are simple, and they identify 90%

of the cases where the two strings are different. Rule 3, which is slow, has to be applied only if the first two rules have not identified the strings as different.

3. If the encoding algorithm has to decrement the order all the way down to 1, it faces a special problem. It can no longer hash two symbols. Searching for order-1 matching strings (i.e., single symbols) therefore requires a different method which is illustrated by Figure 7.7. Two linked lists are shown, one linking occurrences of s and the other linking occurrences of i. Notice how only certain occurrences of s are linked, while others are skipped. The rule is to skip an occurrence of s which is followed by a symbol that has already been seen. Thus, the first occurrences of si, ss, s␣, and sw are linked, whereas other occurrences of s are skipped.

The list linking these occurrences of s starts empty and is built gradually, as more text is input and is moved into the search buffer. When a new context is created with s as its rightmost symbol, the list is updated. This is done by finding the symbol to the right of the new s, say a, scanning the list for a link sa, deleting it if found (not more than one may exist), and linking the current s to the list.

Figure 7.7: Context Searching for Order-1.

This list makes it easy to search and find all occurrences of the order-1 context s that are followed by different symbols (i.e., with exclusions).

Such a list should be constructed and updated for each symbol in the alphabet. If the algorithm is implemented to handle 8-bit symbols, then 256 such lists are needed and have to be updated.

The implementation details above show how complex this method is. It is slow, but it produces excellent compression.

✄Doublets (also known as word ladders or word chains) is a popular word game invented by Lewis Carroll. A source word is transformed into a target word of the same length in steps, by changing a single letter in each step, so that each link in the chain is a valid word. For example, the ladder LEAD, LOAD, GOAD, GOLD can make you rich if performed literally. Your task is to transform FLOUR into BREAD.

7.3 SCSU: Unicode Compression

The ASCII code is old, having been designed in the early 1960s. With the advent of inexpensive laser and inkjet printers and high-resolution displays, it has become possible to display and print characters of any size and shape. As a result, the ASCII code, with its 128 characters, no longer satisfies the needs of modern computing. Starting in 1991, the Unicode consortium (whose members include major computer corporations, software producers, database vendors, research institutions, international agencies, various user groups, and interested individuals) has proposed and designed a new character coding scheme that satisfies the demands of current hardware and software. Information about Unicode is available at [Unicode 07].

The Unicode Standard assigns a number, called a code point, to each character (code element). A code point is listed in hexadecimal with a "U+" preceding it. Thus, the code point U+0041 is the number $0041_{16} = 65_{10}$. It represents the character "A" in the Unicode Standard.

The Unicode Standard also assigns a unique name to each character. Code element U+0041, for example, is assigned the name "LATIN CAPITAL LETTER A" and U+0A1B is assigned the name "GURMUKHI LETTER CHA."

An important feature of the Unicode Standard is the way it groups related codes. A group of related characters is referred to as a script, and such characters are assigned consecutive codes; they become a contiguous area or a region of Unicode. If the characters are ordered in the original script (such as A–Z and α through ω), then their Unicodes reflect that order. Region sizes vary greatly, depending on the script.

Most Unicode code points are 16-bit (2-byte) numbers. There are 64K (or 65,536) such codes, but Unicode reserves 2,048 of the 16-bit codes to extend this set to 32-bit codes (thereby adding about 1.4 million surrogate code pairs). Most of the characters in common use fit into the first 64K code points, a region of the codespace that's called the basic multilingual plane (BMP). There are about 6,700 unassigned code points for future expansion in the BMP, plus over 870,000 unused supplementary code points in the other regions of the codespace. More characters are under consideration for inclusion in future versions of the standard.

Unicode starts with the set of 128 ASCII codes U+0000 through U+007F and continues with Greek, Cyrillic, Hebrew, Arabic, Indic, and other scripts. These are followed by symbols and punctuation marks, diacritics, mathematical symbols, technical symbols, arrows, dingbats, and so forth. The codespace continues with Hiragana, Katakana, and Bopomofo. The unified Han ideographs are followed by the complete set of modern Hangul. Toward the end of the BMP is a range of code points reserved for private use, followed by a range of compatibility characters. The compatibility characters are character variants that are encoded only to enable transcoding to earlier standards and old implementations that happen to use them.

The Unicode Standard also reserves code points for private use. Anyone can assign these codes privately for their own characters and symbols or use them with specialized fonts. There are 6,400 private-use code points on the BMP and another 131,068 supplementary private-use code points elsewhere in the codespace.

Version 3.2 of Unicode specifies codes for 95,221 characters from the world's alphabets, ideograph sets, and symbol collections. The current (late 2007) version is 5.0.0.

The method described in this section is due to [Wolf et al. 00]. It is a standard compression scheme for Unicode, abbreviated SCSU. It compresses strings of code points. Like any compression method, it works by removing redundancy from the original data. The redundancy in Unicode stems from the fact that typical text in Unicode tends to have characters located in the same region in the Unicode codespace. Thus, a text using the basic Latin character set consists mostly of code points of the form U+00xx. These can be compressed to one byte each. A text in Arabic tends to use just Arabic characters, which start at U+0600. Such text can be compressed by specifying a start address and then converting each code point to its distance (or offset) from that address. This introduces the concept of a window. The distance should be just one byte because a 2-byte distance replacing a 2-byte code results in no compression. This kind of compression is called the single-byte mode. A 1-byte offset suggests a window size of 256, but we'll see why the method uses windows of half that size. In practice, there may be complications, as the following three examples demonstrate:

1. A string of text in a certain script may have punctuation marks embedded in it, and these have code points in a different region. A single punctuation mark inside a string can be written in raw form on the compressed file and also requires a special tag to indicate a raw code. The result is a slight expansion.

2. The script may include hundreds or even thousands of characters. At a certain point, the next character to be compressed may be too far from the start address, so a new start address (a new window) has to be specified just for the next character. This is done by a nonlocking-shift tag.

3. Similarly, at a certain point, the characters being compressed may all be in a different window, so a locking-shift tag has to be inserted, to indicate the start address of the new window.

As a result, the method employs tags, implying that a tag has to be at least a few bits, which raises the question of how the decoder distinguishes tags from compressed characters. The solution is to limit the window size to 128. There are 8 static and 8 dynamic windows (Tables 7.8 and 7.9, respectively, where CJK stands for Chinese, Japanese, and Korean). The start positions of the latter can be changed by tags.

SCSU employs the following conventions:

1. Each tag is a byte in the interval [0x00,0x1F], except that the ASCII codes for CR (0x0D), LF (0x0A), and TAB (or HT 0x09) are not used for tags. There can therefore be $32 - 3 = 29$ tags (but we'll see that more values are reserved for tags in the Unicode mode). The tags are used to indicate a switch to another window, a repositioning of a window, or an escape to an uncompressed (raw) mode called the Unicode mode.

2. A code in the range U+0020 through U+007F is compressed by eliminating its most-significant eight zeros. It becomes a single byte.

3. Any other codes are compressed to a byte in the range 0x80 through 0xFF. These indicate offsets in the range 0x00 through 0xEF (0 through 127) in the current window.

Example: The string 041C, 043E, 0441, 002D, 043A, 0562, and 000D is compressed to the bytes 12, 9C, BE, C1, 2D, BA, 1A, 02, E2, and 0D. The tag byte 12 indicates the window from 0x0400 to 0x047F. Code 041C is at offset 1C from the start of that window, so it is compressed to the byte 1C + 80 = 9C. Code 043E is at offset 3E, so it is compressed to 3E + 80 = BE. Code 0441 is similarly compressed to C1. Code 002D

n	Start	Major area
0	0000	Quoting tags in single-byte mode
1	0080	Latin1 supplement
2	0100	Latin Extended-A
3	0300	Combining diacritical marks
4	2000	General punctuation marks
5	2080	Currency symbols
6	2100	Letterlike symbols and number forms
7	3000	CJK symbols and punctuation

Table 7.8: Static Windows.

n	Start	Major area
0	0080	Latin1 supplement
1	00C0	Latin1 supp. + Latin Extended-A
2	0400	Cyrillic
3	0600	Arabic
4	0900	Devanagari
5	3040	Hiragana
6	30A0	Katakana
7	FF00	Fullwidth ASCII

Table 7.9: Dynamic Windows (Default Positions).

(the ASCII code of a hyphen) is compressed (without any tags) to its least-significant 8 bits 2D. (This is less than 0x80, so the decoder does not get confused.) Code 043A is compressed in the current window to BA, but compressing code 0562 must be done in window [0x0500,0x057F] and must therefore be preceded by tag 1A (followed by index 02) which selects this window. The offset of code 0562 in the new window is 62, so it is compressed to byte E2. Finally, code 000D (CR) is compressed to its eight least-significant bits 0D without an additional tag.

Tag 12 is called SC2. It indicates a locking shift to dynamic window 2, which starts at 0x0400 by default. Tag 1A is called SD2 and indicates a repositioning of window 2. The byte 02 that follows 1A is an index to Table 7.10 and changes the window's start position by $2 \times 80_{16} = 100_{16}$, so the window moves from the original 0x0400 to 0x0500.

We start with the details of the single-byte mode. This mode is the one in effect when the SCSU encoder starts. Each 16-bit code is compressed in this mode to a single byte. Tags are needed from time to time and may be followed by up to two arguments, each a byte. This mode continues until one of the following is encountered: (1) end-of-input, (2) an SCU tag, or (3) an SQU tag. Six types of tags (for a total of 27 different tags) are used in this mode as follows.

1. SQU (0E). This tag (termed quote Unicode) is a temporary (nonlocking) shift to Unicode mode. This tag is followed by the two bytes of a raw code.

2. SCU (0F). This tag (change to Unicode) is a permanent (locking) shift to Unicode mode. This is used for a string of consecutive characters that belong to different scripts and are therefore in different windows.

X	Offset[X]	Comments
00	reserved	for internal use
01–67	$X \times 80$	half-blocks from U+0080 to U+3380
68–A7	$X \times 80 + AC00$	half-blocks from U+E000 to U+FF80
A8–F8		reserved for future use
F9	00C0	Latin1 characters + half of Extended-A
FA	0250	IPA extensions
FB	0370	Greek
FC	0530	Armenian
FD	3040	Hiragana
FE	30A0	Katakana
FF	FF60	Halfwidth Katakana

Table 7.10: Window Offsets.

3. SQn (01–08). This tag (quote from window n) is a nonlocking shift to window n. It quotes (i.e., writes in raw format) the next code, so there is no compression. The value of n (between 0 and 7) is determined by the tag (between 1 and 8). This tag must be followed by a byte used as an offset to the selected window. If the byte is in the interval 00 to 7F, static window n should be selected. If it is in the range 80 to FF, dynamic window n should be selected. This tag quotes one code, then switches back to the single-byte mode. For example, SQ3 followed by 14 selects offset 14 in static window 3, so it quotes code $0300 + 14 = 0314$. Another example is SQ4 followed by 8A. This selects offset $8A - 80 = 0A$ in dynamic window 4 (which normally starts at 0900, but could be repositioned), so it quotes code $0900 + 0A = 090A$.

4. SCn (10–17). This tag (change to window n) is a locking shift to window n.

5. SDn (18–1F). This tag (define window n) repositions window n and makes it the current window. The tag is followed by a one-byte index to Table 7.10 that indicates the new start address of window n.

6. SDX (0B). This is the "define extended" tag. It is followed by two bytes denoted by H and L. The three most-significant bits of H determine the static window to be selected, and the remaining 13 bits of H and L become one integer N that determines the start address of the window as $10000 + 80 \times N$ (hexadecimal).

Tag SQ0 is important. It is used to flag code points whose most-significant byte may be confused with a tag (i.e., it is in the range 00 through 1F). When encountering such a byte, the decoder should be able to tell whether it is a tag or the start of a raw code. As a result, when the encoder inputs a code that starts with such a byte, it writes it on the output in raw format (quoted), preceded by an SQ0 tag.

Next comes the Unicode mode. Each character is written in this mode in raw form, so there is no compression (there is even slight expansion due to the tags required). Once this mode is selected by an SCU tag, it stays in effect until the end of the input or until a tag that selects an active window is encountered. Four types of tags are used in this mode as follows:

1. UQU (F0). This tag quotes a Unicode character. The two bytes following the tag are written on the output in raw format.

2. UCn (E0–E7). This tag is a locking shift to single-byte mode and it also selects window n.

3. UDn (E8–EF). Define window n. This tag is followed by a single-byte index. It selects window n and repositions it according to the start positions of Table 7.10.

4. UDX (F1). Define extended window. This tag (similar to SDX) is followed by two bytes denoted by H and L. The three most-significant bits of H determine the dynamic window to be selected, and the remaining 13 bits of H and L become an integer N that determines the start address of the window by $10000 + 80 \times N$ (hexadecimal).

The four types of tags require 18 tag values, but almost all the possible 29 tag values are used by the single-byte mode. As a result, the Unicode mode uses tag values that are valid code points. Byte E0, for example, is tag UC0, but is also the most-significant half of a valid code point (in fact, it is the most-significant half of 256 valid code points). The encoder therefore reserves these 18 values (plus a few more for future use) for tags. When the encoder encounters any character whose code starts with one of those values, the character is written in raw format (preceded by a UQU tag). Such cases are not common because the reserved values are taken from the private-use area of Unicode, and this area is rarely used.

SCSU also specifies ways to compress Unicode surrogates. With 16-bit codes, there can be 65,536 codes. However, $800_{16} = 2048_{10}$ 16-bit codes have been reserved for an extension of Unicode to 32-bit codes. The 400_{16} codes U+D800 through U+DBFF are reserved as high surrogates, and the 400_{16} codes U+DC00 through U+DFFF are reserved as low surrogates. This allows for an additional $400 \times 400 = 100,000_{16}$ 32-bit codes. A 32-bit code is known as a surrogate pair and can be encoded in SCSU in one of several ways, three of which are shown here:

1. In Unicode mode, in raw format (four bytes).

2. In single-byte mode, with each half quoted. Thus, SQU, H1, L1, SQU, H2, L2.

3. Also in single-byte mode, as a single byte, by setting a dynamic window to the appropriate position with an SDX or UDX tag.

The 2-code sequence U+FEFF (or its reversed counterpart U+FFFE) occurs very rarely in text files, so it serves as a signature, to identify text files in Unicode. This sequence is known as a *byte order mark* or BOM. SCSU recommends several ways of compressing this signature, and an encoder can select any of those.

7.3.1 BOCU-1: Unicode Compression

The acronym BOCU stands for binary-ordered compression for Unicode. BOCU is a simple compression method for Unicode-based files [BOCU 01]. Its main feature is preserving the binary sort order of the code points being compressed. Thus, if two code points x and y are compressed to a and b and if $x < y$, then $a < b$.

The basic BOCU method is based on differencing. The previous code point is subtracted from the current code point to yield a difference value. Consecutive code points in a document are normally similar, so most differences are small and fit in a single byte. However, because a code point in Unicode 2.0 (published in 1996) is in the range U+000000 to U+10FFFF (21-bit codes), the differences can, in principle, be any numbers in the interval $[-10FFFF, 10FFFF]$ and may require up to three bytes each. This basic method is enhanced in two ways.

The first enhancement improves compression in small alphabets. In Unicode, most small alphabets start on a 128-byte boundary, although the alphabet size may be more than 128 symbols. This suggests that a difference be computed not between the current and previous code values but between the current code value and the value in the middle of the 128-byte segment where the previous code value is located. Specifically, the difference is computed by subtracting a *base value* from the current code point. The base value is obtained from the previous code point as follows. If the previous code value is in the interval xxxx00 to xxxx7F (i.e., its seven LSBs are 0 to 127), the base value is set to xxxx40 (the seven LSBs are 64), and if the previous code point is in the range xxxx80 to xxxxFF (i.e., its seven least-significant bits are 128 to 255), the base value is set to xxxxC0 (the seven LSBs are 192). This way, if the current code point is within 128 positions of the base value, the difference is in the range $[-128, +127]$ which makes it fit in one byte.

The second enhancement has to do with remote symbols. A document in a non-Latin alphabet (where the code points are very different from the ASCII codes) may use spaces between words. The code point for a space is the ASCII code 20_{16}, so any pair of code points that includes a space results in a large difference. BOCU therefore computes a difference by first computing the base values of the three previous code points, and then subtracting the smallest base value from the current code point.

BOCU-1 is the version of BOCU that's commonly used in practice [BOCU-1 02]. It differs from the original BOCU method by using a different set of byte value ranges and by encoding the ASCII control characters U+0000 through U+0020 with byte values 0 through 20_{16}, respectively. These features make BOCU-1 suitable for compressing input files that are MIME (text) media types.

Il faut avoir beaucoup étudié pour savoir peu (it is necessary to study much in order to know little).

—Montesquieu (Charles de Secondat), *Pensées diverses*

Chapter Summary

This chapter is devoted to data compression methods and techniques that are not based on the approaches discussed elsewhere in this book. The following algorithms illustrate some of these original techniques:

- The Burrows–Wheeler method (Section 7.1) starts with a string S of n symbols and scrambles (i.e., permutes) them into another string L that satisfies two conditions: (1) Any area of L will tend to have a concentration of just a few symbols. (2) It is possible to reconstruct the original string S from L. Since its inception in the early 1990s, this unexpected method has been the subject of much research.

- The technique of symbol ranking (Section 7.2) uses context, rather than probabilities, to rank symbols.

- Sections 7.3 and 7.3.1 describe two algorithms, SCSU and BOCU-1, for the compression of Unicode-based documents.

Chapter 8 of [Salomon 07] discusses other methods, techniques, and approaches to data compression.

Self-Assessment Questions

1. The term "fractals" appears early in this chapter. One of the applications of fractals is to compress images, and it is the purpose of this note to encourage the reader to search for material on fractal compression and study it.

2. The Burrows–Wheeler method has been the subject of much research and attempts to speed up its decoding and improve it. Using the paper at [JuergenAbel 07] as your starting point, try to gain a deeper understanding of this interesting method.

3. The term "lexicographic order" appears in Section 7.1. This is an important term in computer science in general, and the conscientious reader should make sure this term is fully understood.

4. Most Unicodes are 16 bits long, but this standard has provisions for longer codes. Use [Unicode 07] as a starting point to learn more about Unicode and how codes longer than 16 bits are structured.

In comedy, as a matter of fact, a greater variety of methods were discovered and employed than in tragedy.

—T. S. Eliot, *The Sacred Wood* (1920)

Bibliography

Ahmed, N., T. Natarajan, and R. K. Rao (1974) "Discrete Cosine Transform," *IEEE Transactions on Computers*, **C-23**:90–93.

Bell, Timothy C., John G. Cleary, and Ian H. Witten (1990) *Text Compression*, Englewood Cliffs, Prentice Hall.

BOCU (2001) is `http://oss.software.ibm.com/icu/docs/papers/binary_ordered_compression_for_unicode.html`.

BOCU-1 (2002) is `http://www.unicode.org/notes/tn6/`.

Bookstein, Abraham and S. T. Klein (1993) "Is Huffman Coding Dead?" *Proceedings of the 16th Annual International ACM SIGIR Conference on Research and Development in Information Retrieval*, pp. 80–87. Also published in *Computing*, **50**(4):279–296, 1993, and in *Proceedings of the Data Compression Conference, 1993*, Snowbird, UT. p. 464.

Bradley, Jonathan N., Christopher M. Brislawn, and Tom Hopper (1993) "The FBI Wavelet/Scalar Quantization Standard for Grayscale Fingerprint Image Compression," *Proceedings of Visual Information Processing II*, Orlando, FL, SPIE vol. 1961, pp. 293–304, April.

Brandenburg, Karlheinz, and Gerhard Stoll (1994) "ISO-MPEG-1 Audio: A Generic Standard for Coding of High-Quality Digital Audio," *Journal of the Audio Engineering Society*, **42**(10):780–792, October.

brucelindbloom (2007) is `http://www.brucelindbloom.com/` (click on "info").

Burrows, Michael, and D. J. Wheeler (1994) *A Block-Sorting Lossless Data Compression Algorithm*, Digital Systems Research Center Report 124, Palo Alto, CA, May 10.

Calude, Cristian and Tudor Zamfirescu (1998) "The Typical Number is a Lexicon," *New Zealand Journal of Mathematics*, **27**:7–13.

Campos, Arturo San Emeterio (2006) *Range coder*, in `http://www.arturocampos.com/ac_range.html`.

Carpentieri, B., M. J. Weinberger, and G. Seroussi (2000) "Lossless Compression of Continuous-Tone Images," *Proceedings of the IEEE*, **88**(11):1797–1809, November.

Chaitin (2007) is `http://www.cs.auckland.ac.nz/CDMTCS/chaitin/sciamer3.html`.

Choueka Y., Shmuel T. Klein, and Y. Perl (1985) "Efficient Variants of Huffman Codes in High Level Languages," *Proceedings of the 8th ACM-SIGIR Conference*, Montreal, pp. 122–130.

Deflate (2003) is `http://www.gzip.org/zlib/`.

Elias, P. (1975) "Universal Codeword Sets and Representations of the Integers," *IEEE Transactions on Information Theory*, **21**(2):194–203, March.

Faller N. (1973) "An Adaptive System for Data Compression," in *Record of the 7th Asilomar Conference on Circuits, Systems, and Computers*, pp. 593–597.

Fano, R. M. (1949) "The Transmission of Information," Research Laboratory for Electronics, MIT, Tech Rep. No. 65.

Federal Bureau of Investigation (1993) *WSQ Grayscale Fingerprint Image Compression Specification, ver. 2.0*, Document #IAFIS-IC-0110v2, Criminal Justice Information Services, February.

Feldspar (2003) is `http://www.zlib.org/feldspar.html`.

Fenwick, Peter (1996a) "Punctured Elias Codes for Variable-Length Coding of the Integers," Technical Report 137, Department of Computer Science, University of Auckland, December. This is also available online.

Fenwick, P. (1996b) *Symbol Ranking Text Compression*, Tech. Rep. 132, Dept. of Computer Science, University of Auckland, New Zealand, June.

Fraenkel, Aviezri S. and Shmuel T. Klein (1996) "Robust Universal Complete Codes for Transmission and Compression," *Discrete Applied Mathematics*, **64**(1):31–55, January.

funet (2007) is `ftp://nic.funet.fi/pub/graphics/misc/test-images/`.

G.711 (1972) is `http://en.wikipedia.org/wiki/G.711`.

Gallager, Robert G. (1978) "Variations on a Theme by Huffman," *IEEE Transactions on Information Theory*, **24**(6):668–674, November.

Gardner, Martin (1972) "Mathematical Games," *Scientific American*, **227**(2):106, August.

Gemstar (2007) is `http://www.gemstartvguide.com`.

Gilbert, E. N. and E. F. Moore (1959) "Variable Length Binary Encodings," *Bell System Technical Journal*, **38**:933–967.

Gray, Frank (1953) "Pulse Code Communication," United States Patent 2,632,058, March 17.

Haar, A. (1910) "Zur Theorie der Orthogonalen Funktionensysteme," *Mathematische Annalen* first part **69**:331–371, second part **71**:38–53, 1912.

Heath, F. G. (1972) "Origins of the Binary Code," *Scientific American*, **227**(2):76, August.

Hecht, S., S. Schlaer, and M. H. Pirenne (1942) "Energy, Quanta and Vision," *Journal of the Optical Society of America*, **38**:196–208.

hffax (2007) is `http://www.hffax.de/html/hauptteil_faxhistory.htm`.

Hilbert, D. (1891) "Ueber stetige Abbildung einer Linie auf ein Flächenstück," *Math. Annalen*, **38**:459–460.

Hirschberg, D., and D. Lelewer (1990) "Efficient Decoding of Prefix Codes," *Communications of the ACM*, **33**(4):449–459.

Holzmann, Gerard J. and Björn Pehrson (1995) *The Early History of Data Networks*, Los Alamitos, CA, IEEE Computer Society Press. This is available online at `http://labit501.upct.es/ips/libros/TEHODN/ch-2-5.3.html`.

Huffman, David (1952) "A Method for the Construction of Minimum Redundancy Codes," *Proceedings of the IRE*, **40**(9):1098–1101.

incredible (2007) is `http://datacompression.info/IncredibleClaims.shtml`.

ITU-T (1989) CCITT Recommendation G.711: "Pulse Code Modulation (PCM) of Voice Frequencies."

JuergenAbel (2007) is file `Preprint_After_BWT_Stages.pdf` in `http://www.data-compression.info/JuergenAbel/Preprints/`.

Karp, R. S. (1961) "Minimum-Redundancy Coding for the Discrete Noiseless Channel," *Transactions of the IRE*, **7**:27–38.

Knuth, Donald E. (1985) "Dynamic Huffman Coding," *Journal of Algorithms*, **6**:163–180.

Kraft, L. G. (1949) *A Device for Quantizing, Grouping, and Coding Amplitude Modulated Pulses*, Master's Thesis, Department of Electrical Engineering, MIT, Cambridge, MA.

Linde, Y., A. Buzo, and R. M. Gray (1980) "An Algorithm for Vector Quantization Design," *IEEE Transactions on Communications*, **COM-28**:84–95, January.

Lloyd, S. P. (1982) "Least Squares Quantization in PCM," *IEEE Transactions on Information Theory*, **IT-28**:129–137, March.

Manber, U., and E. W. Myers (1993) "Suffix Arrays: A New Method for On-Line String Searches," *SIAM Journal on Computing*, **22**(5):935–948, October.

Max, Joel (1960) "Quantizing for minimum distortion," *IRE Transactions on Information Theory*, **IT-6**:7–12, March.

McCreight, E. M (1976) "A Space Economical Suffix Tree Construction Algorithm," *Journal of the ACM*, **32**(2):262–272, April.

McMillan, Brockway (1956) "Two Inequalities Implied by Unique Decipherability," *IEEE Transactions on Information Theory*, **2**(4):115–116, December.

MNG (2003) is `http://www.libpng.org/pub/mng/spec/`.

Moffat, Alistair, Radford Neal, and Ian H. Witten (1998) "Arithmetic Coding Revisited," *ACM Transactions on Information Systems*, **16**(3):256–294, July.

Motil, John (2007) Private communication.

Mulcahy, Colm (1996) "Plotting and Scheming with Wavelets," *Mathematics Magazine*, **69**(5):323–343, December. See also `http://www.spelman.edu/~colm/csam.ps`.

Mulcahy, Colm (1997) "Image Compression Using the Haar Wavelet Transform," *Spelman College Science and Mathematics Journal*, **1**(1):22–31, April. Also available at URL `http://www.spelman.edu/~colm/wav.ps`. (It has been claimed that any smart 15-year-old could follow this introduction to wavelets.)

Osterberg, G. (1935) "Topography of the Layer of Rods and Cones in the Human Retina," *Acta Ophthalmologica*, (suppl. 6):1–103.

Paez, M. D. and T. H. Glisson (1972) "Minimum Mean Squared Error Quantization in Speech PCM and DPCM Systems," *IEEE Transactions on Communications*, **COM-20**(2):225–230,

patents (2007) is `http://www.datacompression.info/patents.shtml`.

PDF (2001) *Adobe Portable Document Format Version 1.4*, 3rd ed., Reading, MA, Addison-Wesley, December.

Pennebaker, William B., and Joan L. Mitchell (1992) *JPEG Still Image Data Compression Standard*, New York, Van Nostrand Reinhold.

Phillips, Dwayne (1992) "LZW Data Compression," *The Computer Application Journal* Circuit Cellar Inc., **27**:36–48, June/July.

PKWare (2003) is `http://www.pkware.com`.

PNG (2003) is `http://www.libpng.org/pub/png/`.

RFC1945 (1996) *Hypertext Transfer Protocol—HTTP/1.0*, available at URL `http://www.faqs.org/rfcs/rfc1945.html`.

RFC1950 (1996) *ZLIB Compressed Data Format Specification version 3.3*, is `http://www.ietf.org/rfc/rfc1950`.

RFC1951 (1996) *DEFLATE Compressed Data Format Specification version 1.3*, is `http://www.ietf.org/rfc/rfc1951`.

RFC1952 (1996) *GZIP File Format Specification Version 4.3*. Available in PDF format at URL `http://www.gzip.org/zlib/rfc-gzip.html`.

RFC1962 (1996) *The PPP Compression Control Protocol (CCP)*, available from many sources.

RFC1979 (1996) *PPP Deflate Protocol*, is `http://www.faqs.org/rfcs/rfc1979.html`.

RFC2616 (1999) *Hypertext Transfer Protocol – HTTP/1.1*. Available in PDF format at URL `http://www.faqs.org/rfcs/rfc2616.html`.

Rice, Robert F. (1979) "Some Practical Universal Noiseless Coding Techniques," Jet Propulsion Laboratory, JPL Publication 79-22, Pasadena, CA, March.

Rice, Robert F. (1991) "Some Practical Universal Noiseless Coding Techniques—Part III. Module PSI14.K," Jet Propulsion Laboratory, JPL Publication 91-3, Pasadena, CA, November.

Robinson, Tony (1994) "Simple Lossless and Near-Lossless Waveform Compression," Technical Report CUED/F-INFENG/TR.156, Cambridge University, December. Available at `http://citeseer.nj.nec.com/robinson94shorten.html`.

Salomon, David (1999) *Computer Graphics and Geometric Modeling*, New York, Springer.

Salomon, David (2006) *Curves and Surfaces for Computer Graphics*, New York, Springer.

Salomon, D. (2007) *Data Compression: The Complete Reference*, London, Springer Verlag.

Schindler, Michael (1998) "A Fast Renormalisation for Arithmetic Coding," a poster in the Data Compression Conference, 1998, available at URL `http://www.compressconsult.com/rangecoder/`.

Shannon, Claude E. (1948), "A Mathematical Theory of Communication," *Bell System Technical Journal*, **27**:379–423 and 623–656, July and October,

Shannon, Claude (1951) "Prediction and Entropy of Printed English," *Bell System Technical Journal*, **30**(1):50–64, January.

Shenoi, Kishan (1995) *Digital Signal Processing in Telecommunications*, Upper Saddle River, NJ, Prentice Hall.

Sieminski, A. (1988) "Fast Decoding of the Huffman Codes," *Information Processing Letters*, **26**(5):237–241.

Softsound (2007) is `http://mi.eng.cam.ac.uk/reports/ajr/TR156/tr156.html`.

Strang, Gilbert, and Truong Nguyen (1996) *Wavelets and Filter Banks*, Wellesley, MA, Wellesley-Cambridge Press.

technikum29 (2007) is `http://www.technikum29.de/en/communication/fax.shtm`.

Tetrachromat (2007) is `http://en.wikipedia.org/wiki/Tetrachromat`.

Unicode (2007) is `http://unicode.org/`.

Vitter, Jeffrey S. (1987) "Design and Analysis of Dynamic Huffman Codes," *Journal of the ACM*, **34**(4):825–845, October.

Wallace, Gregory K. (1991) "The JPEG Still Image Compression Standard," *Communications of the ACM*, **34**(4):30–44, April.

Watson, Andrew (1994) "Image Compression Using the Discrete Cosine Transform," *Mathematica Journal*, **4**(1):81–88.

Weisstein-pickin (2007) is Weisstein, Eric W. "Real Number Picking." From MathWorld, A Wolfram web resource. `http://mathworld.wolfram.com/RealNumberPicking.html`.

Welch, T. A. (1984) "A Technique for High-Performance Data Compression," *IEEE Computer*, **17**(6):8–19, June.

Wirth, N. (1976) *Algorithms + Data Structures = Programs*, 2nd ed., Englewood Cliffs, NJ, Prentice-Hall.

Witten, Ian H., Radford M. Neal, and John G. Cleary (1987) "Arithmetic Coding for Data Compression," *Communications of the ACM*, **30**(6):520–540.

Wolf, Misha et al. (2000) "A Standard Compression Scheme for Unicode," Unicode Technical Report #6, available at `http://unicode.org/unicode/reports/tr6/index.html`.

Zhang, Manyun (1990) *The JPEG and Image Data Compression Algorithms* (dissertation).

Ziv, Jacob, and A. Lempel (1977) "A Universal Algorithm for Sequential Data Compression," *IEEE Transactions on Information Theory*, **IT-23**(3):337–343.

Ziv, Jacob and A. Lempel (1978) "Compression of Individual Sequences via Variable-Rate Coding," *IEEE Transactions on Information Theory*, **IT-24**(5):530–536.

zlib (2003) is `http://www.zlib.org/zlib_tech.html`.

> A literary critic is a person who finds meaning in literature that the author didn't know was there.
>
> —Anonymous

Glossary

A glossary is a list of terms in a particular domain of knowledge with the definitions for those terms. Traditionally, a glossary appears at the end of a book and includes terms within that book which are either newly introduced or at least uncommon.

In a more general sense, a glossary contains explanations of concepts relevant to a certain field of study or action. In this sense, the term is contemporaneously related to ontology.

—From `Wikipedia.com`

Adaptive Compression. A compression method that modifies its operations and/or its parameters in response to new data read from the input. Examples are the adaptive Huffman method of Section 2.3 and the dictionary-based methods of Chapter 3. (See also Semiadaptive Compression.)

Alphabet. The set of all possible symbols in the input. In text compression, the alphabet is normally the set of 128 ASCII codes. In image compression, it is the set of values a pixel can take (2, 16, 256, or anything else). (See also Symbol.)

Arithmetic Coding. A statistical compression method (Chapter 4) that assigns one (normally long) code to the entire input file, instead of assigning codes to the individual symbols. The method reads the input symbol by symbol and appends more bits to the code each time a symbol is input and processed. Arithmetic coding is slow, but it compresses at or close to the entropy, even when the symbol probabilities are skewed. (See also Model of Compression, Statistical Methods.)

ASCII Code. The standard character code on all modern computers (although Unicode is fast becoming a serious competitor). ASCII stands for American Standard Code for Information Interchange. It is a $(1+7)$-bit code, with one parity bit and seven data bits per symbol. As a result, 128 symbols can be coded. They include the uppercase and lowercase letters, the ten digits, some punctuation marks, and control characters. (See also Unicode.)

Bark. Unit of critical band rate. Named after Heinrich Georg Barkhausen and used in audio applications. The Bark scale is a nonlinear mapping of the frequency scale over the audio range, a mapping that matches the frequency selectivity of the human ear.

Bi-level Image. An image whose pixels have two different colors. The colors are normally referred to as black and white, "foreground" and "background," or 1 and 0. (See also Bitplane.)

Bitplane. Each pixel in a digital image is represented by several bits. The set of all the kth bits of all the pixels in the image is the kth bitplane of the image. A bi-level image, for example, consists of one bitplane. (See also Bi-level Image.)

Bitrate. In general, the term "bitrate" refers to both bpb and bpc. However, in audio compression, this term is used to indicate the rate at which the compressed file is read by the decoder. This rate depends on where the file comes from (such as disk, communications channel, memory). If the bitrate of an MPEG audio file is, e.g., 128 Kbps, then the encoder will convert each second of audio into 128 K bits of compressed data, and the decoder will convert each group of 128 K bits of compressed data into one second of sound. Lower bitrates mean smaller file sizes. However, as the bitrate decreases, the encoder must compress more audio data into fewer bits, eventually resulting in a noticeable loss of audio quality. For CD-quality audio, experience indicates that the best bitrates are in the range of 112 Kbps to 160 Kbps. (See also Bits/Char.)

Bits/Char. Bits per character (bpc). A measure of the performance in text compression. Also a measure of entropy. (See also Bitrate, Entropy.)

Bits/Symbol. Bits per symbol. A general measure of compression performance.

Block Coding. A general term for image compression methods that work by breaking the image into small blocks of pixels, and encoding each block separately. JPEG (Section 5.6) is a good example, because it processes blocks of 8×8 pixels.

Burrows–Wheeler Method. This method (Section 7.1) prepares a string of data for later compression. The compression itself is done with the move-to-front method (see item in this glossary), perhaps in combination with RLE. The BW method converts a string S to another string L that satisfies two conditions:

1. Any region of L will tend to have a concentration of just a few symbols.

2. It is possible to reconstruct the original string S from L (a little more data may be needed for the reconstruction, in addition to L, but not much).

CCITT. The International Telegraph and Telephone Consultative Committee (Comité Consultatif International Télégraphique et Téléphonique), the old name of the ITU, the International Telecommunications Union. The ITU is a United Nations organization responsible for developing and recommending standards for data communications (not just compression). (See also ITU.)

CIE. CIE is an abbreviation for Commission Internationale de l'Éclairage (International Committee on Illumination). This is the main international organization devoted to light and color. It is responsible for developing standards and definitions in this area. (See also Luminance.)

Circular Queue. A basic data structure (see the last paragraph of Section 1.3.1) that moves data along an array in circular fashion, updating two pointers to point to the start and end of the data in the array.

Codec. A term that refers to both encoder and decoder.

Codes. A code is a symbol that stands for another symbol. In computer and telecommunications applications, codes are virtually always binary numbers. The ASCII code is the defacto standard, although the new Unicode is used on several new computers and the older EBCDIC is still used on some old IBM computers. In addition to these fixed-size codes there are many variable-length codes used in data compression and there are the all-important error-control codes for added robustness (See also ASCII, Unicode.)

Compression Factor. The inverse of compression ratio. It is defined as

$$\text{compression factor} = \frac{\text{size of the input file}}{\text{size of the output file}}.$$

Values greater than 1 indicate compression, and values less than 1 imply expansion. (See also Compression Ratio.)

Compression Gain. This measure is defined as

$$100 \log_e \frac{\text{reference size}}{\text{compressed size}},$$

where the reference size is either the size of the input file or the size of the compressed file produced by some standard lossless compression method.

Compression Ratio. One of several measures that are commonly used to express the efficiency of a compression method. It is the ratio

$$\text{compression ratio} = \frac{\text{size of the output file}}{\text{size of the input file}}.$$

A value of 0.6 indicates that the data occupies 60% of its original size after compression. Values greater than 1 mean an output file bigger than the input file (negative compression).

Sometimes the quantity $100 \times (1 - \text{compression ratio})$ is used to express the quality of compression. A value of 60 means that the output file occupies 40% of its original size (or that the compression has resulted in a savings of 60%). (See also Compression Factor.)

Continuous-Tone Image. A digital image with a large number of colors, such that adjacent image areas with colors that differ by just one unit appear to the eye as having continuously varying colors. An example is an image with 256 grayscale values. When adjacent pixels in such an image have consecutive gray levels, they appear to the eye as a continuous variation of the gray level. (See also Bi-level image, Discrete-Tone Image, Grayscale Image.)

Decoder. A program, an algorithm, or a piece of hardware for decompressing data.

Deflate. A popular lossless compression algorithm (Section 3.3) used by Zip and gzip. Deflate employs a variant of LZ77 combined with static Huffman coding. It uses a 32-Kb-long sliding dictionary and a look-ahead buffer of 258 bytes. When a string is not found in the dictionary, its first symbol is emitted as a literal byte. (See also Zip.)

Dictionary-Based Compression. Compression methods (Chapter 3) that save pieces of the data in a "dictionary" data structure. If a string of new data is identical to a piece that is already saved in the dictionary, a pointer to that piece is output to the compressed file. (See also LZ Methods.)

Discrete Cosine Transform. A variant of the discrete Fourier transform (DFT) that produces just real numbers. The DCT (Sections 5.5 and 5.6.2) transforms a set of numbers by combining n numbers to become an n-dimensional point and rotating it in n dimensions such that the first coordinate becomes dominant. The DCT and its inverse, the IDCT, are used in JPEG (Section 5.6) to compress an image with acceptable loss, by isolating the high-frequency components of an image, so that they can later be quantized. (See also Fourier Transform, Transform.)

Discrete-Tone Image. A discrete-tone image may be bi-level, grayscale, or color. Such images are (with some exceptions) artificial, having been obtained by scanning a document, or capturing a computer screen. The pixel colors of such an image do not vary continuously or smoothly, but have a small set of values, such that adjacent pixels may differ much in intensity or color. (See also Continuous-Tone Image.)

Discrete Wavelet Transform. The discrete version of the continuous wavelet transform. A wavelet is represented by means of several filter coefficients, and the transform is carried out by matrix multiplication (or a simpler version thereof) instead of by calculating an integral.

Encoder. A program, algorithm, or hardware circuit for compressing data.

Entropy. The entropy of a single symbol a_i is defined as $-P_i \log_2 P_i$, where P_i is the probability of occurrence of a_i in the data. The entropy of a_i is the smallest number of bits needed, on average, to represent symbol a_i. Claude Shannon, the creator of information theory, coined the term *entropy* in 1948, because this term is used in thermodynamics to indicate the amount of disorder in a physical system. (See also Entropy Encoding, Information Theory.)

Entropy Encoding. A lossless compression method where data can be compressed such that the average number of bits/symbol approaches the entropy of the input symbols. (See also Entropy.)

Facsimile Compression. Transferring a typical page between two fax machines can take up to 10–11 minutes without compression. This is why the ITU has developed several standards for compression of facsimile data. The current standards (Section 2.4) are T4 and T6, also called Group 3 and Group 4, respectively. (See also ITU.)

Fourier Transform. A mathematical transformation that produces the frequency components of a function. The Fourier transform represents a periodic function as the sum of sines and cosines, thereby indicating explicitly the frequencies "hidden" in the original representation of the function. (See also Discrete Cosine Transform, Transform.)

Gaussian Distribution. (See Normal Distribution.)

Golomb Codes. The Golomb codes consist of an infinite set of parametrized prefix codes. They are the best variable-length codes for the compression of data items that are distributed geometrically. (See also Unary Code.)

Gray Codes. Gray codes are binary codes for the integers, where the codes of consecutive integers differ by one bit only. Such codes are used when a grayscale image is separated into bitplanes, each a bi-level image. (See also Grayscale Image,)

Grayscale Image. A continuous-tone image with shades of a single color. (See also Continuous-Tone Image.)

Huffman Coding. A popular method for data compression (Chapter 2). It assigns a set of "best" variable-length codes to a set of symbols based on their probabilities. It serves as the basis for several popular programs used on personal computers. Some of them use just the Huffman method, while others use it as one step in a multistep compression process. The Huffman method is somewhat similar to the Shannon–Fano method. It generally produces better codes, and like the Shannon–Fano method, it produces best code when the probabilities of the symbols are negative powers of 2. The main difference between the two methods is that Shannon–Fano constructs its codes top to bottom (from the leftmost to the rightmost bits), while Huffman constructs a code tree from the bottom up (builds the codes from right to left). (See also Shannon–Fano Coding, Statistical Methods.)

Information Theory. A mathematical theory that quantifies information. It shows how to measure information, so that one can answer the question, how much information is included in a given piece of data? with a precise number! Information theory is the creation, in 1948, of Claude Shannon of Bell Labs. (See also Entropy.)

ITU. The International Telecommunications Union, the new name of the CCITT, is a United Nations organization responsible for developing and recommending standards for data communications (not just compression). (See also CCITT.)

JFIF. The full name of this method (Section 5.6.7) is JPEG File Interchange Format. It is a graphics file format that makes it possible to exchange JPEG-compressed images between different computers. The main features of JFIF are the use of the YCbCr triple-component color space for color images (only one component for grayscale images) and the use of a marker to specify features missing from JPEG, such as image resolution, aspect ratio, and features that are application-specific.

JPEG. A sophisticated lossy compression method (Section 5.6) for color or grayscale still images (not video). It works best on continuous-tone images, where adjacent pixels have similar colors. One advantage of JPEG is the use of many parameters, allowing the user to adjust the amount of data loss (and thereby also the compression ratio) over a very wide range. There are two main modes, lossy (also called baseline) and lossless (which typically yields a 2:1 compression ratio). Most implementations support just the lossy mode. This mode includes progressive and hierarchical coding.

The main idea behind JPEG is that an image exists for people to look at, so when the image is compressed, it is acceptable to lose image features to which the human eye is not sensitive.

The name JPEG is an acronym that stands for Joint Photographic Experts Group. This was a joint effort by the CCITT and the ISO that started in June 1987. The JPEG standard has proved successful and has become widely used for image presentation, especially in web pages.

Kraft–McMillan Inequality. A relation that says something about unambiguous variable-length codes. Its first part states: Given an unambiguous variable-size code, with n codes of sizes L_i, then

$$\sum_{i=1}^{n} 2^{-L_i} \leq 1.$$

[This is Equation (1.4).] The second part states the opposite, namely, given a set of n positive integers $(L_1, L_2, \ldots, L_n)$ that satisfy Equation (1.4), there exists an unambiguous variable-size code such that L_i are the sizes of its individual codes. Together, both parts state that a code is unambiguous if and only if it satisfies relation (1.4).

Laplace Distribution. A probability distribution similar to the normal (Gaussian) distribution, but narrower and sharply peaked. The general Laplace distribution with variance V and mean m is given by

$$L(V, x) = \frac{1}{\sqrt{2V}} \exp\left(-\sqrt{\frac{2}{V}} |x - m|\right).$$

Experience seems to suggest that the values of the residues computed by many image compression algorithms are Laplace distributed, which is why this distribution is employed by those compression methods, most notably MLP. (See also Normal Distribution.)

Lossless Compression. A compression method where the output of the decoder is identical to the original data compressed by the encoder. (See also Lossy Compression.)

Lossy Compression. A compression method where the output of the decoder is different from the original data compressed by the encoder, but is nevertheless acceptable to a user. Such methods are common in image and audio compression, but not in text compression, where the loss of even one character may result in wrong, ambiguous, or incomprehensible text. (See also Lossless Compression.)

Luminance. This quantity is defined by the CIE (Section 5.6.1) as radiant power weighted by a spectral sensitivity function that is characteristic of vision. (See also CIE.)

LZ Methods. All dictionary-based compression methods are based on the work of J. Ziv and A. Lempel, published in 1977 and 1978. Today, these are called LZ77 and LZ78 methods, respectively. Their ideas have been a source of inspiration to many researchers, who generalized, improved, and combined them with RLE and statistical methods to form many commonly used adaptive compression methods, for text, images, and audio. (See also Dictionary-Based Compression, Sliding-Window Compression.)

LZW. This is a popular variant (Section 3.2) of LZ78, originated by Terry Welch in 1984. Its main feature is eliminating the second field of a token. An LZW token consists of just a pointer to the dictionary. As a result, such a token always encodes a string of more than one symbol. (See also Patents.)

Model of Compression. A model is a method to "predict" (to assign probabilities to) the data to be compressed. This concept is important in statistical data compression. When a statistical method is used, a model for the data has to be constructed before compression can begin. A simple model can be built by reading the entire input, counting the number of times each symbol appears (its frequency of occurrence), and computing the probability of occurrence of each symbol. The data is then input again, symbol by symbol, and is compressed using the information in the probability model. (See also Statistical Methods.)

One feature of arithmetic coding is that it is easy to separate the statistical model (the table with frequencies and probabilities) from the encoding and decoding operations. It is easy to encode, for example, the first half of a data using one model, and the second half using another model.

Move-to-Front Coding. The basic idea behind this method is to maintain the alphabet A of symbols as a list where frequently occurring symbols are located near the front. A symbol s is encoded as the number of symbols that precede it in this list. After symbol s is encoded, it is moved to the front of list A.

Normal Distribution. A probability distribution with the well-known bell shape. It occurs often in theoretical models and real-life situations. The normal distribution with mean m and standard deviation s is defined by

$$f(x) = \frac{1}{s\sqrt{2\pi}} \exp\left\{-\frac{1}{2}\left(\frac{x-m}{s}\right)^2\right\}.$$

Patents. A mathematical algorithm can be patented if it is intimately associated with software or firmware implementing it. Several compression methods, most notably LZW, have been patented, creating difficulties for software developers who work with GIF, UNIX `compress`, or any other system that uses LZW. (See also LZW.)

Pel. The smallest unit of a facsimile image; a dot. (See also Pixel.)

Pixel. The smallest unit of a digital image; a dot. (See also Pel.)

PKZip. A compression program developed and implemented by Phil Katz for the old MS/DOS operating system. Katz then founded the PKWare company which also markets the PKunzip, PKlite, and PKArc software (`http://www.pkware.com`).

Prediction. Assigning probabilities to symbols.

Prefix Property. One of the principles of variable-length codes. It states that once a certain bit pattern has been assigned as the code of a symbol, no other codes should start with that pattern (the pattern cannot be the prefix of any other code). Once the string 1, for example, is assigned as the code of a_1, no other codes should start with 1 (i.e., they all have to start with 0). Once 01, for example, is assigned as the code of a_2, no other codes can start with 01 (they all should start with 00). (See also Variable-Length Codes, Statistical Methods.)

Psychoacoustic Model. A mathematical model of the sound-masking properties of the human auditory (ear–brain) system.

Rice Codes. A special case of the Golomb code. (See also Golomb Codes.)

RLE. A general name for methods that compress data by replacing a run of identical symbols with one code, or token, containing the symbol and the length of the run. RLE sometimes serves as one step in a multistep statistical or dictionary-based method.

Scalar Quantization. The dictionary definition of the term "quantization" is "to restrict a variable quantity to discrete values rather than to a continuous set of values." If the data to be compressed is in the form of large numbers, quantization is used to convert them to small numbers. This results in (lossy) compression. If the data to be compressed is analog (e.g., a voltage that varies with time), quantization is used to digitize it into small numbers. This aspect of quantization is used by several audio compression methods. (See also Vector Quantization.)

Semiadaptive Compression. A compression method that uses a two-pass algorithm, where the first pass reads the input to collect statistics on the data to be compressed, and the second pass performs the actual compression. The statistics (model) are included in the compressed file. (See also Adaptive Compression.)

Shannon–Fano Coding. An early algorithm for finding a minimum-length variable-size code given the probabilities of all the symbols in the data. This method was later superseded by the Huffman method. (See also Statistical Methods, Huffman Coding.)

Shorten. A simple compression algorithm for waveform data in general and for speech in particular (Section 6.5). Shorten employs linear prediction to compute residues (of audio samples) which it encodes by means of Rice codes. (See also Rice Codes.)

Sliding-Window Compression. The LZ77 method (Section 1.3.1) uses part of the already-seen input as the dictionary. The encoder maintains a window to the input file, and shifts the input in that window from right to left as strings of symbols are being encoded. The method is therefore based on a sliding window. (See also LZ Methods.)

Space-Filling Curves. A space-filling curve is a function $\mathbf{P}(t)$ that goes through every point in a given two-dimensional region, normally the unit square, as t varies from 0 to 1. Such curves are defined recursively and are used in image compression.

Statistical Methods. Statistical data compression methods work by assigning variable-length codes to symbols in the data, with the shorter codes assigned to symbols or groups of symbols that appear more often in the data (have a higher probability of occurrence). (See also Variable-Length Codes, Prefix Property, Shannon–Fano Coding, Huffman Coding, and Arithmetic Coding.)

Symbol. The smallest unit of the data to be compressed. A symbol is often a byte but may also be a bit, a trit $\{0, 1, 2\}$, or anything else. (See also Alphabet.)

Token. A unit of data written on the compressed file by some compression algorithms. A token consists of several fields that may have either fixed or variable sizes.

Transform. An image can be compressed by transforming its pixels (which are correlated) to a representation where they are decorrelated. Compression is achieved if the new values are smaller, on average, than the original ones. Lossy compression can be achieved by quantizing the transformed values. The decoder inputs the transformed values from the compressed file and reconstructs the (precise or approximate) original data by applying the opposite transform. (See also Discrete Cosine Transform, Discrete Wavelet Transform, Fourier Transform.)

Unary Code. A simple variable-size code for the integers that can be constructed in one step. The unary code of the nonnegative integer n is defined (Section 1.1.1) as $n - 1$ 1's followed by a single 0 (Table 1.2). There is also a general unary code. (See also Golomb Code.)

Unicode. A new international standard code, the Unicode, has been proposed, and is being developed by the international Unicode organization (www.unicode.org). Unicode specifies 16-bit codes for its characters, so it provides for $2^{16} = 64K = 65,536$ codes. (Notice that doubling the size of a code much more than doubles the number of possible codes. In fact, it squares the number of codes.) Unicode includes all the ASCII codes in addition to codes for characters in foreign languages (including complete sets of Korean, Japanese, and Chinese characters) and many mathematical and other symbols. Currently, about 39,000 out of the 65,536 possible codes have been assigned, so there is room for adding more symbols in the future. (See also ASCII, Codes.)

Variable-Length Codes. These codes are employed by statistical methods. Most variable-length codes are prefix codes (page 28) and should be assigned to symbols based on their probabilities. (See also Prefix Property, Statistical Methods.)

Vector Quantization. Vector quantization is a generalization of the scalar quantization method. It is used in both image and audio compression. In practice, vector quantization is commonly used to compress data that has been digitized from an analog source, such as sampled sound and scanned images (drawings or photographs). Such data is called digitally sampled analog data (DSAD). (See also Scalar Quantization.)

Voronoi Diagrams. Imagine a petri dish ready for growing bacteria. Four bacteria of different types are simultaneously placed in it at different points and immediately start multiplying. We assume that their colonies grow at the same rate. Initially, each colony consists of a growing circle around one of the starting points. After a while some of them meet and stop growing in the meeting area due to lack of food. The final result is that the entire dish gets divided into four areas, one around each of the four starting points, such that all the points within area i are closer to starting point i than to any other start point. Such areas are called Voronoi regions or Dirichlet tessellations.

Wavelets.   (See Discrete-Wavelet Transform.)

Zip. Popular software that implements the Deflate algorithm (Section 3.3) that uses a variant of LZ77 combined with static Huffman coding. It uses a 32-Kb-long sliding dictionary and a look-ahead buffer of 258 bytes. When a string is not found in the dictionary, its first symbol is emitted as a literal byte. (See also Deflate.)

Glossary (noun). An alphabetical list of technical terms in some specialized field of knowledge; usually published as an appendix to a text on that field.

—A typical dictionary definition

Solutions to Puzzles

Page 30. The diagram shows how easy it is.

Page 47. No, because each rectangle on the chess board covers one white and one black square, but the two squares that we have removed have the same color.

Page 67. The next two integers are 28 and 102. The rule is simple but elusive. Start with (almost) any positive 2-digit integer (we somewhat arbitrarily selected 38). Multiply the two digits to obtain $3 \times 8 = 24$, then add $38 + 24$ to generate the third integer 62. Now multiply $6 \times 2 = 12$ and add $62 + 12 = 74$. Similar multiplication and addition produce the next two integers 28 and 102.

Page 76. Just me. All the others were going in the opposite direction.

Page 98. Each win increases the mount in Mr Ambler's pocket from m to $1.5m$ and each loss reduces it from n to $0.5n$. In order for him to win half the time, g, the number of games, has to be even and we denote $i = g/2$. We start with the simple case $g = 2$, where there are two possible game sequences, namely WL and LW. In the first sequence, the amount in Mr Ambler's pocket varies from a to $\frac{3}{2}a$ to $\frac{1}{2}\frac{3}{2}a$ and in the second sequence it varies from a to $\frac{1}{2}a$ to $\frac{3}{2}\frac{1}{2}a$. It is now obvious that the amount left in his pocket after i wins and i losses does not depend on the precise sequence of winnings and losses and is always $\left(\frac{1}{2}\right)^i \left(\frac{3}{2}\right)^i a = \left(\frac{3}{4}\right)^i a$. This amount is less than a, so Ambler's chance of net winning is zero.

Page 107. The schedule of the London underground is such that a Brixton-bound train always arrives at Oxford circus a minute or two after a train to Maida Vale has departed. Anyone planning to complain to London Regional Transport, should do so at http://www.tfl.gov.uk/home.aspx.

Page 110. The next integer is 3. The first integer of each pair is random, and the second one is the number of letters in the English name of the integer.

Page 132. Three socks.

Page 151. When each is preceded by BREAK it has a different meaning.

Page 179. Consider the state of the game when there are five matches left. The player whose turn it is will lose, because regardless of the number of matches he removes (between 1 and 4), his opponent will be able to remove the last match. A similar situation exists when there are 10 matches left because the player whose turn it is can remove five and leave five matches. The same argument applies to the point in the game when 15 matches are left. Thus, he who plays the first move has a simple winning strategy; remove two matches.

Page 209. This is easy. Draw two squares with a common side (five lines), and then draw a diagonal of each square.

Page 231. When fully spelled in English, the only vowel they contain is E.

Page 238. The letters NIL can be made with six matches.

Page 253. It is 265. Each integer is the sum of two consecutive squares. Thus, $1^2 + 2^2 = 5$, $3^2 + 4^2 = 25$, and so on.

Page 257. FLOUR, FLOOR, FLOOD, BLOOD, BROOD, BROAD, BREAD.

Who in the world am I? Ah, that's the great puzzle.

—Lewis Carroll

Answers to Exercises

> A bird does not sing because he has an answer, he sings because he has a song.
> —Chinese Proverb

Intro.1. When a software maker has a popular product it tends to come up with new versions. Typically, a user downloads the update off the maker's site anonymously. Over time, the updates become bigger and may take too long to download. This is why such updates should be supplied in compressed format. This is an example of data that is compressed once, at the source, and is decompressed once by each user downloading it. Obviously, the speed of encoder and decoder is uncritical, but efficient compression is important.

1.1. We can assume that each image row starts with a white pixel. If a row starts with, say, seven black pixels, we can prepare the run lengths 0, 7, ... and the compressor will simply ignore the run of zero white pixels.

1.2. "Cook what the cat dragged in," "my ears are turning," "sad egg," "a real hooker," "my brother's beeper," and "put all your eggs in one casket."

1.3. The following list summarizes the advantages and downsides of each approach:

■   Two-passes: slow, not online, may require memory to store result of the first pass, on the other hand it achieves best possible compression.

■   Training: sensitive to the choice of training documents (which may or may not reflect the characteristics of the data being compressed). Fast, because all the data symbols have been assigned variable-length codes even before the encoder starts. General purpose (this has been proved by the fax compression standard). Good performance if the training data is statistically relevant.

■   Adaptive: adapts while reading and compressing the data, which is why it performs poorly on small input files. Online, generally faster than the other two methods.

1.4. 6,8,0,1,3,1,4,1,3,1,4,1,3,1,4,1,3,1,2,2,2,2,6,1,1. The first two are the bitmap resolution (6×8). The original image occupies either 48 bits, so compression will be achieved if the resulting 25 runs can be encoded in fewer than 48 bits. Like most compression methods, RLE does not work well for small data files.

1.5. RLE of images is based on the idea that adjacent pixels tend to be identical. The last pixel of a row, however, has no reason to be identical to the first pixel of the next row.

1.6. It is not necessary if the width of a row is known a priori. For example, if image dimensions are contained in the header of the compressed image. If the eol is sent for the first row, there is no need to signal the end of a line again, since the decoder can infer the line width after decoding the first line and split the runs into lines by counting the pixels. It is possible to signal the end of a scan line without using any special symbol. The end of a line could be signalled by inserting two consecutive zeros. Since it is not possible to have two consecutive runs of zero length, the decoder may interpret two consecutive zeros as the end of a scan line.

1.7. Method (b) has two advantages as follows:

1. The paragraph following Equation (5.6) shows that a block of DCT coefficients (Section 5.5) has one large element (the DC) at its top-left corner and smaller elements (AC) elsewhere. The AC coefficients generally become smaller as we move from the top-left to the bottom-right corner and are largest on the top row and the leftmost column. Thus, scanning a block of DCT coefficients in zigzag order collects the large elements first. Notice that this order collects all the coefficients of the top row and leftmost column before it even starts collecting the elements in the bottom-right half of the block. Thus, this scan order, which is used in JPEG, transforms a two-dimensional block of DCT coefficients into a one-dimensional sequence where numbers, especially after quantization, become smaller and smaller, and include runs of zeros. Such a sequence is easy to compress with variable-length codes and RLE, which is why a zigzag scan is a key to effective lossy compression of images.

2. In a zigzag scan, every pair of pixels are near neighbors. When scanning by rows, the last element of a row is not correlated with the first element of the next row. Thus, we have to make sure that each row has an even number of elements (otherwise, the last column must be duplicated and temporarily appended to the image being scanned). The same problem exists when scanning by columns or as shown in Figure 1.12c.

Method (b) also has its own downside. It is easy to see, from Figure 1.12 or any similar grid, that the distance between diagonally-adjacent pixels is slightly larger than the distance between near neighbors on the same row or on the same column. Thus, if the distance between the centers of pixels on the same row is 1, then the distance between the centers of neighbors on a diagonal is $\sqrt{2}$, about 41% greater. If we assume that correlation is inversely proportional to distance, then a 41% greater distance translates to 41% weaker correlation and therefore worse compression.

1.8. Each of the first four rows yields the eight runs 1,1,1,2,1,1,1,eol. Rows 6 and 8 yield the four runs 0,7,1,eol each. Rows 5 and 7 yield the two runs 8,eol each. The total number of runs (including the eol's) is therefore 44.

When compressing by columns, columns 1, 3, and 6 yield the five runs 5,1,1,1,eol each. Columns 2, 4, 5, and 7 yield the six runs 0,5,1,1,1,eol each. Column 8 gives 4,4,eol, for a total of 42 runs. We conclude that this image is "balanced" with respect to rows and columns.

1.9. The straightforward answer is that the decoder doesn't know but it does not need to know. The decoder simply reads tokens and uses each offset to locate a string of text without having to know whether the string was a first or a last match.

1.10. Imagine a history book divided into chapters. One chapter may commonly employ words such as "Greek," "Athens," and "Troy," while the following chapter may have a preponderance of "Roman," "empire," and "legion." In such a document, we can expect to find more matches in the newer (recent) part of the search buffer. Now imagine a very long poem or hymn, organized in long stanzas, each followed by the same chorus. When trying to match pieces of the current chorus, the best matches may be found in the previous chorus, which may be located in the older part of the search buffer. Thus, the distribution of matches depends heavily on the type of data that is being compressed.

1.11. The next step matches the space and encodes the string ⊔e.

sir⊔sid⊔eastman⊔easily⊔	⇒ (4,1,e)
sir⊔sid⊔e astman⊔easily⊔te	⇒ (0,0,a)

and the next one matches nothing and encodes the a.

1.12. Any two correlated pixels a and b are similar (this is what being correlated means). Thus, if the pair (a, b) is considered a point, it will be located in the xy plane on or near the 45° line $x = y$. After the rotation, the point will end up on or near the x axis, where it will have a small y coordinate, while its x coordinate will not change much (Figure 5.4). We say that the rotation squeezes the range of one of the two dimensions and slightly increases the range of the other.

1.13. This transform, like anything else in life, does not come "free" and involves a subtle cost. The original numbers were correlated, but the transform coefficients are not. The statistical cross-correlation of a set of pairs (x_i, y_i) is the sum $\sum_i x_i y_i$, and it is easy to see that the cross-correlation of our five pairs has dropped from 1729.72 before the transform to -23.0846 after it. A significant reduction!

2.1. Figure Ans.1a,b,c shows the three trees. The codes sizes for the trees are

$$(5 + 5 + 5 + 5 \cdot 2 + 3 \cdot 3 + 3 \cdot 5 + 3 \cdot 5 + 12)/30 = 76/30,$$
$$(5 + 5 + 4 + 4 \cdot 2 + 4 \cdot 3 + 3 \cdot 5 + 3 \cdot 5 + 12)/30 = 76/30,$$
$$(6 + 6 + 5 + 4 \cdot 2 + 3 \cdot 3 + 3 \cdot 5 + 3 \cdot 5 + 12)/30 = 76/30.$$

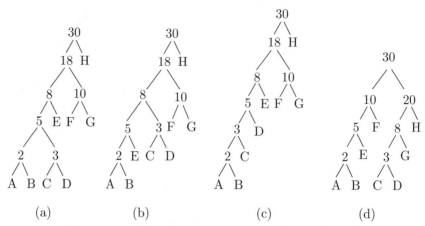

Figure Ans.1: Three Huffman Trees for Eight Symbols.

2.2. After adding symbols A, B, C, D, E, F, and G to the tree, we were left with the three symbols ABEF (with probability 10/30), CDG (with probability 8/30), and H (with probability 12/30). The two symbols with lowest probabilities were ABEF and CDG, so they had to be merged. Instead, symbols CDG and H were merged, creating a non-Huffman tree.

2.3. The second row of Table 2.2 (due to Guy Blelloch) shows a symbol whose Huffman code is three bits long, but for which $\lceil -\log_2 0.3 \rceil = \lceil 1.737 \rceil = 2$.

2.4. The explanation is simple. Imagine a large alphabet where all the symbols have (about) the same probability. Since the alphabet is large, that probability will be small, resulting in long codes. Imagine the other extreme case, where certain symbols have high probabilities (and, therefore, short codes). Since the probabilities have to add up to 1, the rest of the symbols will have low probabilities (and, therefore, long codes). We therefore see that the size of a code depends on the probability, but is indirectly affected by the size of the alphabet.

2.5. Figure Ans.2 shows Huffman codes for 5, 6, 7, and 8 symbols with equal probabilities. In the case where n is a power of 2, the codes are simply the fixed-sized ones. In other cases the codes are very close to fixed-size. This shows that symbols with equal probabilities do not benefit from variable-length codes. (This is another way of saying that random text cannot be compressed.) Table Ans.3 shows the codes, their average sizes and variances.

2.6. It increases exponentially from 2^s to $2^{s+n} = 2^s \times 2^n$.

2.7. The binary value of 127 is 01111111 and that of 128 is 10000000. Half the pixels in each bitplane will therefore be 0 and the other half, 1. In the worst case, each bitplane will be a checkerboard, i.e., will have many runs of size one. In such a case, each run requires a 1-bit code, leading to one codebit per pixel per bitplane, or eight codebits per

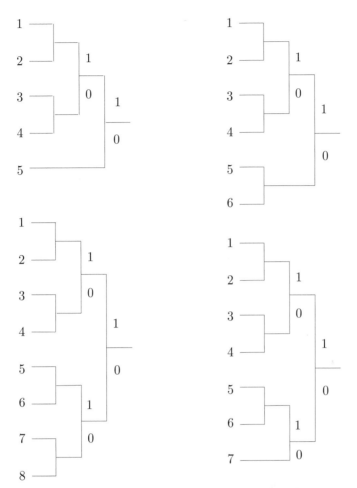

Figure Ans.2: Huffman Codes for Equal Probabilities.

n	p	a_1	a_2	a_3	a_4	a_5	a_6	a_7	a_8	Avg. size	Var.
5	0.200	111	110	101	100	0				2.6	0.64
6	0.167	111	110	101	100	01	00			2.672	0.2227
7	0.143	111	110	101	100	011	010	00		2.86	0.1226
8	0.125	111	110	101	100	011	010	001	000	3	0

Table Ans.3: Huffman Codes for 5–8 Symbols.

pixel for the entire image, resulting in no compression at all. In comparison, a Huffman code for such an image requires just two codes (since there are just two pixel values) and they can be one bit each. This leads to one codebit per pixel, or a compression factor of eight.

2.8. The two trees are shown in Figure 2.13c,d. The average code size for the binary Huffman tree is

$$1 \times 0.49 + 2 \times 0.25 + 5 \times 0.02 + 5 \times 0.03 + 5 \times .04 + 5 \times 0.04 + 3 \times 0.12 = 2 \, \text{bits/symbol},$$

and that of the ternary tree is

$$1 \times 0.26 + 3 \times 0.02 + 3 \times 0.03 + 3 \times 0.04 + 2 \times 0.04 + 2 \times 0.12 + 1 \times 0.49 = 1.34 \, \text{trits/symbol}.$$

2.9. A symbol with high frequency of occurrence should be assigned a shorter code. Therefore, it has to appear high in the tree. The requirement that at each level the frequencies be sorted from left to right is artificial. In principle, it is not necessary, but it simplifies the process of updating the tree.

2.10. Figure Ans.4 shows the initial tree and how it is updated in the 11 steps (a) through (k). Notice how the *esc* symbol gets assigned different codes all the time, and how the different symbols move about in the tree and change their codes. Code 10, e.g., is the code of symbol "i" in steps (f) and (i), but is the code of "s" in steps (e) and (j). The code of a blank space is 011 in step (h), but 00 in step (k).

The final output is: "s0i00r100␣1010000d011101000". A total of $5 \times 8 + 22 = 62$ bits. The compression ratio is thus $62/88 \approx 0.7$.

2.11. Because a typical fax machine scans lines that are about 8.2 inches wide ($\approx$ 208 mm), so a blank scan line produces 1,664 consecutive white pels.

2.12. These codes are needed for cases such as example 4, where the run length is 64, 128, or any length for which a make-up code has been assigned.

2.13. There may be fax machines (now or in the future) built for wider paper, so the Group 3 code was designed to accommodate them.

2.14. Each scan line starts with a white pel, so when the decoder inputs the next code it knows whether it is for a run of white or black pels. This is why the codes of Table 2.22 have to satisfy the prefix property in each column but not between the columns.

2.15. Imagine a scan line where all runs have length one (strictly alternating pels). It's easy to see that this case results in expansion. The code of a run length of one white pel is 000111, and that of one black pel is 010. Two consecutive pels of different colors are thus coded into nine bits. Since the uncoded data requires just two bits (01 or 10), the compression ratio is $9/2 = 4.5$ (the compressed data is 4.5 times bigger than the original data; a significant expansion).

Initial tree

(a). Input: s. Output: 's'.
$esc\, s_1$

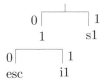

(b). Input: i. Output: 0'i'.
$esc\, i_1\, 1\, s_1$

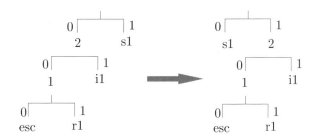

(c). Input: r. Output: 00'r'.
$esc\, r_1\, 1\, i_1\, 2\, s_1 \to$
$esc\, r_1\, 1\, i_1\, s_1\, 2$

(d). Input: ␣. Output: 100'␣'.
$esc_{␣1}\, 1\, r_1\, 2\, i_1\, s_1\, 3 \to$
$esc_{␣1}\, 1\, r_1\, s_1\, i_1\, 2\, 2$

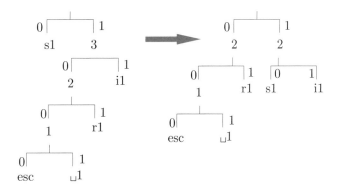

Figure Ans.4: Exercise 2.10. Part I.

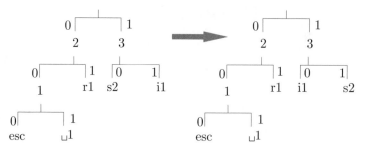

(e). Input: s. Output: 10.

$esc_{\sqcup 1} 1\, r_1\, s_2\, i_1\, 2\, 3 \rightarrow$

$esc_{\sqcup 1} 1\, r_1\, i_1\, s_2\, 2\, 3$

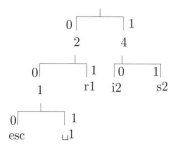

(f). Input: i. Output: 10.

$esc_{\sqcup 1} 1\, r_1\, i_2\, s_2\, 2\, 4$

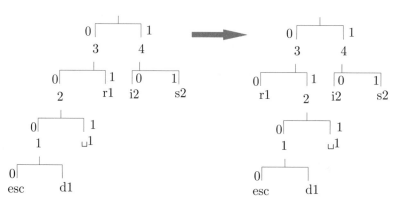

(g). Input: d. Output: 000'd'.

$esc\, d_1\, 1_{\sqcup 1}\, 2\, r_1\, i_2\, s_2\, 3\, 4 \rightarrow$

$esc\, d_1\, 1_{\sqcup 1}\, r_1\, 2\, i_2\, s_2\, 3\, 4$

Figure Ans.4: Exercise 2.10. Part II.

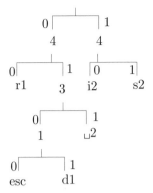 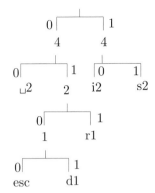

(h). Input: ␣. Output: 011.
$esc\, d_1\, 1\,{}_{\sqcup 2}\, r_1\, 3\, i_2\, s_2\, 4\, 4 \rightarrow$
$esc\, d_1\, 1\, r_1\, {}_{\sqcup 2}\, 2\, i_2\, s_2\, 4\, 4$

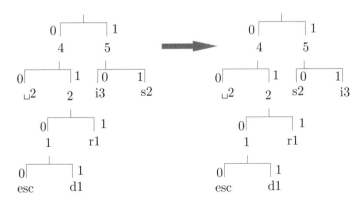

(i). Input: i. Output: 10.
$esc\, d_1\, 1\, r_1\, {}_{\sqcup 2}\, 2\, i_3\, s_2\, 4\, 5 \rightarrow$
$esc\, d_1\, 1\, r_1\, {}_{\sqcup 2}\, 2\, s_2\, i_3\, 4\, 5$

Figure Ans.4: Exercise 2.10. Part III.

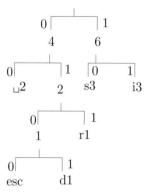

(j). Input: s. Output: 10.
$esc\,d_1\,1\,r_1\,{\sqcup}2\,2\,s_3\,i_3\,4\,6$

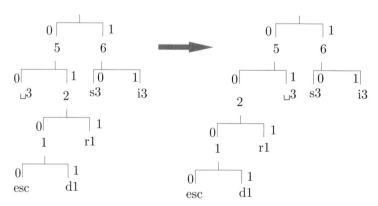

(k). Input: ⊔. Output: 00.
$esc\,d_1\,1\,r_1\,{\sqcup}3\,2\,s_3\,i_3\,5\,6 \rightarrow$
$esc\,d_1\,1\,r_1\,2\,{\sqcup}3\,s_3\,i_3\,5\,6$

Figure Ans.4: Exercise 2.10. Part IV.

3.1.   (1) The size of the output is $N[48 - 28P] = N[48 - 25.2] = 22.8N$. The size of the input is, as before, $40N$. The compression factor is therefore $40/22.8 \approx 1.75$. (2) Maximum compression is obtained when the output size $N[48 - 28P]$, is minimum, which occurs when $P = 1$. The compression factor in this case is $40N/N[48 - 28P] = 2$.

3.2.   This is straightforward. The remaining steps are listed in Table Ans.5

Dictionary		Token		Dictionary		Token
15	␣t	(4, t)		21	␣si	(19,i)
16	e	(0, e)		22	c	(0, c)
17	as	(8, s)		23	k	(0, k)
18	es	(16,s)		24	␣se	(19,e)
19	␣s	(4, s)		25	al	(8, 1)
20	ea	(4, a)		26	s(eof)	(1, (eof))

Table Ans.5: Next 12 Encoding Steps in the LZ78 Example.

3.3.   Table Ans.6 summarizes the steps. The output emitted by the encoder is

97 (a), 108 (1), 102 (f), 32 (␣), 101 (e), 97 (a), 116 (t), 115 (s), 32 (␣), 256 (al), 102 (f), 265 (alf), 97 (a),

and the following new entries are added to the dictionary

(256: al), (257: lf), (258: f), (259: ␣e), (260: ea), (261: at), (262: ts), (263: s), (264: ␣a), (265: alf), (266: fa), (267: alfa).

I	In dict?	New entry	Output		I	In dict?	New entry	Output
a	Y				s	N	263-s	115 (s)
al	N	256-al	97 (a)		␣	Y		
1	Y				␣a	N	264-␣a	32 (␣)
lf	N	257-lf	108 (1)		a	Y		
f	Y				al	Y		
f	N	258-f	102 (f)		alf	N	265-alf	256 (al)
␣	Y				f	Y		
␣e	N	259-␣e	32 (w)		fa	N	266-fa	102 (f)
e	Y				a	Y		
ea	N	260-ea	101 (e)		al	Y		
a	Y				alf	Y		
at	N	261-at	97 (a)		alfa	N	267-alfa	265 (alf)
t	Y				a	Y		
ts	N	262-ts	116 (t)		a,eof	N		97 (a)
s	Y							

Table Ans.6: LZW Encoding of alf eats alfalfa.

3.4. The encoder inputs the first a into I, searches and finds a in the dictionary. It inputs the next a but finds that Ix, which is now aa, is not in the dictionary. The encoder thus adds string aa to the dictionary as entry 256 and outputs the token 97 (a). Variable I is initialized to the second a. The third a is input, so Ix is the string aa, which is now in the dictionary. I becomes this string, and the fourth a is input. Ix is now aaa which is not in the dictionary. The encoder thus adds string aaa to the dictionary as entry 257 and outputs 256 (aa). I is initialized to the fourth a. Continuing this process is straightforward.

The result is that strings aa, aaa, aaaa, ... are added to the dictionary as entries 256, 257, 258, ..., and the output is

$$97 \text{ (a)}, 256 \text{ (aa)}, 257 \text{ (aaa)}, 258 \text{ (aaaa)}, \ldots$$

The output consists of pointers pointing to longer and longer strings of a's. The first k pointers thus point at strings whose total length is $1 + 2 + \cdots + k = (k + k^2)/2$.

Assuming input data that consists of one million a's, we can find the size of the compressed output stream by solving the quadratic equation $(k + k^2)/2 = 1,000,000$ for the unknown k. The solution is $k \approx 1,414$. The original, 8-million bit input is thus compressed into 1,414 pointers, each at least 9-bit (and in practice, probably 16-bit) long. The compression factor is thus either $8M/(1414 \times 9) \approx 628.6$ or $8M/(1414 \times 16) \approx 353.6$.

This is an impressive result but such input files are rare (notice that this particular input can best be compressed by generating an output file containing just "1,000,000 a", and without using LZW).

3.5. We simply follow the decoding steps described in the text. The results are:
1. Input 97. This is in the dictionary so set I=a and output a. String ax needs to be saved in the dictionary but x is still unknown.
2. Input 108. This is in the dictionary so set J=l and output l. Save al in entry 256. Set I=l.
3. Input 102. This is in the dictionary so set J=f and output f. Save lf in entry 257. Set I=f.
4. Input 32. This is in the dictionary so set J=␣ and output ␣. Save f␣ in entry 258. Set I=␣.
5. Input 101. This is in the dictionary so set J=e and output e. Save ␣e in entry 259. Set I=e.
6. Input 97. This is in the dictionary so set J=a and output a. Save ea in entry 260. Set I=a.
7. Input 116. This is in the dictionary so set J=t and output t. Save at in entry 261. Set I=t.
8. Input 115. This is in the dictionary so set J=s and output s. Save ts in entry 262. Set I=t.
9. Input 32. This is in the dictionary so set J=␣ and output ␣. Save s␣ in entry 263. Set I=␣.
10. Input 256. This is in the dictionary so set J=al and output al. Save ␣a in entry 264. Set I=al.
11. Input 102. This is in the dictionary so set J=f and output f. Save alf in entry 265. Set I=f.

12. Input 265. This has just been saved in the dictionary so set J=alf and output alf. Save fa in dictionary entry 266. Set I=alf.
13. Input 97. This is in the dictionary so set J=a and output a. Save alfa in entry 267 (even though it will never be used). Set I=a.
14. Read eof. Stop.

3.6. Assume that the dictionary is initialized to just the two entries (1: a) and (2: b). The encoder outputs

1 (a), 2 (b), 3 (ab), 5 (aba), 4 (ba), 7 (bab), 6 (abab), 9 (ababa), 8 (baba), ...

and adds the new entries (3: ab), (4: ba), (5: aba), (6: abab), (7: bab), (8: baba), (9: ababa), (10: ababab), (11: babab), ... to the dictionary. This regular behavior can be analyzed and the kth output pointer and dictionary entry predicted, but the effort is probably not worth it.

3.7. The answer to Exercise 3.4 shows the relation between the size of the compressed file and the size of the largest dictionary string for the "worst case" situation (input that creates the longest strings). For a 1 Mbyte input file, there will be 1,414 strings in the dictionary, the largest of which is 1,414 symbols long.

3.8. A simple alternative it to store the 256 8-bit values in the first (rightmost) 256 bytes of the sliding window and keep these locations fixed whenever the window is shifted.

3.9. No. Besides the slowdown caused by evaluating a much larger number of matching candidates, sending the offset of a match is expensive and matches of length shorter than 3 would probably increase the size of the compressed file.

4.1. Table Ans.7 shows the steps of encoding the string $a_2a_2a_2a_2$. Because of the high probability of a_2 the low and high variables start at very different values and approach each other slowly.

a_2 $\quad\quad\quad\quad$ $0.0 + (1.0 - 0.0) \times 0.023162 = 0.023162$
$\quad\quad\quad\quad\quad\quad$ $0.0 + (1.0 - 0.0) \times 0.998162 = 0.998162$
a_2 $\quad\quad\quad\quad$ $0.023162 + 0.975 \times 0.023162 = 0.04574495$
$\quad\quad\quad\quad\quad\quad$ $0.023162 + 0.975 \times 0.998162 = 0.99636995$
a_2 $\quad\quad\quad$ $0.04574495 + 0.950625 \times 0.023162 = 0.06776322625$
$\quad\quad\quad\quad\quad$ $0.04574495 + 0.950625 \times 0.998162 = 0.99462270125$
a_2 $\quad$ $0.06776322625 + 0.926859375 \times 0.023162 = 0.08923124309375$
$\quad\quad$ $0.06776322625 + 0.926859375 \times 0.998162 = 0.99291913371875$

Table Ans.7: Encoding the String $a_2a_2a_2a_2$.

4.2. It can be written either as $0.1000\ldots$ or $0.0111\ldots$.

4.3. In practice, the eof symbol has to be included in the original table of frequencies and probabilities. This symbol is the last to be encoded, and the decoder stops when it detects an eof.

4.4. The encoding steps are simple (see first example on page 124). We start with the interval $[0, 1)$. The first symbol a_2 reduces the interval to $[0.4, 0.9)$. The second one, to $[0.6, 0.85)$, the third one to $[0.7, 0.825)$ and the eof symbol to $[0.8125, 0.8250)$. The approximate binary values of the last interval are 0.1101000000 and 0.1101001100, so we select the 7-bit number 1101000 as our code.

The probability of $a_2 a_2 a_2$eof is $(0.5)^3 \times 0.1 = 0.0125$, but since $-\log_2 0.0125 \approx 6.322$ it follows that the practical minimum code size is 7 bits.

5.1. An image with no redundancy is not always random. The definition of redundancy tells us that an image where each color appears with the same frequency has no redundancy (statistically) yet it is not necessarily random and may even be interesting and/or useful.

5.2. The results are shown in Table Ans.8 together with the Matlab code used to calculate it.

43210	Gray	43210	Gray	43210	Gray	43210	Gray
00000	00000	01000	01100	10000	11000	11000	10100
00001	00001	01001	01101	10001	11001	11001	10101
00010	00011	01010	01111	10010	11011	11010	10111
00011	00010	01011	01110	10011	11010	11011	10110
00100	00110	01100	01010	10100	11110	11100	10010
00101	00111	01101	01011	10101	11111	11101	10011
00110	00101	01110	01001	10110	11101	11110	10001
00111	00100	01111	01000	10111	11100	11111	10000

Table Ans.8: First 32 Binary and Gray Codes.

```
a=linspace(0,31,32); b=bitshift(a,-1);
b=bitxor(a,b); dec2bin(b)
```

Code for Table Ans.8.

5.3. The code of Figure Ans.9 yields the coordinates of the rotated points

$$(7.071, 0), (9.19, 0.7071), (17.9, 0.78), (33.9, 1.41), (43.13, -2.12)$$

(notice how all the y coordinates are small numbers) and shows that the cross-correlation drops from 1729.72 before the rotation to -23.0846 after it. A significant reduction!

5.4. Numerical precision aside, the resulting quantization errors (Table Ans.10) computed in (1) and (2) should be the same (approximately 0.011 for the finest quantization, 1.1778 for the second best, and 1.244 for the coarsest). This feature is a useful consequence of the linearity of the IDCT and it can be used to estimate the quantization error in the quantized data without having to perform an IDCT.

```
p={{5,5},{6, 7},{12.1,13.2},{23,25},{32,29}};
rot={{0.7071,-0.7071},{0.7071,0.7071}};
Sum[p[[i,1]]p[[i,2]], {i,5}]
q=p.rot
Sum[q[[i,1]]q[[i,2]], {i,5}]
```

Figure Ans.9: Code for Rotating Five Points.

Items	12.000000	10.000000	8.000000	10.000000	12.000000	10.000000	8.000000	11.000000	
DCT	28.637500	0.571202	0.461940	1.757000	3.181960	-1.729560	0.191342	-0.308709	
Q1	28.600000	0.600000	0.500000	1.800000	3.200000	-1.800000	0.200000	-0.300000	
Q2	28.000000	1.000000	1.000000	2.000000	3.000000	-2.000000	0.000000	0.000000	
Q3	28.000000	0.000000	0.000000	2.000000	3.000000	-2.000000	0.000000	0.000000	
E1	0.0014062	0.0008293	0.0014486	0.0018490	0.0003254	0.0049618	0.0000750	0.0000758	0.0109712
E2	0.4064062	0.1838677	0.2895086	0.0590490	0.0331094	0.0731378	0.0366118	0.0953012	1.1769918
E3	0.4064062	0.3262717	0.2133886	0.0590490	0.0331094	0.0731378	0.0366118	0.0953012	1.2432758
IDCT1	12.025400	10.023300	7.960540	9.930970	12.016400	9.993210	7.943540	10.998900	
IDCT2	12.188300	10.231500	7.749310	9.208630	11.787600	9.545490	7.828650	10.655700	
IDCT3	11.236000	9.624430	7.662860	9.573020	12.347100	10.014600	8.053040	10.684200	
E1	0.0006452	0.0005429	0.0015571	0.0047651	0.0002690	0.0000461	0.0031877	0.0000012	0.0110143
E2	0.0354569	0.0535923	0.0628455	0.6262665	0.0451138	0.2065793	0.0293608	0.1185425	1.1777575
E3	0.5836960	0.1410528	0.1136634	0.1823119	0.1204784	0.0002132	0.0028132	0.0997296	1.2439586

Table Ans.10: Results of a DCT Quantization Error Experiment.

5.5. The *Mathematica* code of Figure 5.7 produces the eight coefficients 140, −71, 0, −7, 0, −2, 0, and 0. We now quantize this set coarsely by clearing the last two nonzero weights −7 and −2, When the IDCT is applied to the sequence 140, −71, 0, 0, 0, 0, 0, 0, it produces 15, 20, 30, 43, 56, 69, 79, and 84. These are not identical to the original values, but the maximum difference is only 4; an excellent result considering that only two of the eight DCT coefficients are nonzero.

5.6. The eight values in the top row are very similar (the differences between them are either 2 or 3). Each of the other rows is obtained as a right-circular shift of the preceding row.

5.7. It is obvious that such a block can be represented as a linear combination of the patterns in the leftmost column of Figure 5.24. The actual calculation yields the eight weights 4, 0.72, 0, 0.85, 0, 1.27, 0, and 3.62 for the patterns of this column. The other 56 weights are zero or very close to zero.

5.8. First figure out the zigzag path manually, then record it in an array zz of structures, where each structure contains a pair of coordinates for the path as shown, e.g., in Figure Ans.11.

    If the two components of a structure are zz.r and zz.c, then the zigzag traversal can be done by a loop of the form:

```
for (i=0; i<64; i++){
```

$$
\begin{array}{cccccccc}
(0,0) & (0,1) & (1,0) & (2,0) & (1,1) & (0,2) & (0,3) & (1,2) \\
(2,1) & (3,0) & (4,0) & (3,1) & (2,2) & (1,3) & (0,4) & (0,5) \\
(1,4) & (2,3) & (3,2) & (4,1) & (5,0) & (6,0) & (5,1) & (4,2) \\
(3,3) & (2,4) & (1,5) & (0,6) & (0,7) & (1,6) & (2,5) & (3,4) \\
(4,3) & (5,2) & (6,1) & (7,0) & (7,1) & (6,2) & (5,3) & (4,4) \\
(3,5) & (2,6) & (1,7) & (2,7) & (3,6) & (4,5) & (5,4) & (6,3) \\
(7,2) & (7,3) & (6,4) & (5,5) & (4,6) & (3,7) & (4,7) & (5,6) \\
(6,5) & (7,4) & (7,5) & (6,6) & (5,7) & (6,7) & (7,6) & (7,7)
\end{array}
$$

Figure Ans.11: Coordinates for the Zigzag Path.

```
row:=zz[i].r; col:=zz[i].c
...data_unit[row][col]...}
```

5.9. The third DC difference, 5, is located in row 3 column 5, so it is encoded as 1110|101.

5.10. Thirteen consecutive zeros precede this coefficient, so $Z = 13$. The coefficient itself is found in Table 5.32 in row 1, column 0, so $R = 1$ and $C = 0$. Assuming that the Huffman code in position $(R, Z) = (1, 13)$ of Table 5.33 is 1110101, the final code emitted for 1 is 1110101|0.

5.11. Figure Ans.12a shows a simple, 8×8 image with one diagonal line above the main diagonal. Figure Ans.12b,c shows the first two steps in its pyramid decomposition. It is obvious that the transform coefficients in the bottom-right subband (HH) indicate a diagonal artifact located above the main diagonal. It is also easy to see that subband LL is a low-resolution version of the original image.

```
12 16 12 12 12 12 12 12        14 12 12 12│4 0 0 0        13 13 12 12│2 2 0 0
12 12 16 12 12 12 12 12        12 14 12 12│0 4 0 0        12 13 13 12│0 2 2 0
12 12 12 16 12 12 12 12        12 14 12 12│0 4 0 0        12 12 13 13│0 0 2 2
12 12 12 12 16 12 12 12        12 12 14 12│0 0 4 0        12 12 12 13│0 0 0 2
12 12 12 12 12 16 12 12        12 12 14 12│0 0 4 0         2  2  0  0│4 4 0 0
12 12 12 12 12 12 16 12        12 12 12 14│0 0 0 4         0  2  2  0│0 4 4 0
12 12 12 12 12 12 12 16        12 12 12 14│0 0 0 4         0  0  2  2│0 0 4 4
12 12 12 12 12 12 12 12        12 12 12 12│0 0 0 0         0  0  0  2│0 0 0 4
          (a)                          (b)                        (c)
```

Figure Ans.12: The Subband Decomposition of a Diagonal Line.

5.12. The average can easily be calculated. It turns out to be 131.375, which is exactly 1/8 of 1051. The reason the top-left transform coefficient is eight times the average is that the Matlab code that did the calculations uses $\sqrt{2}$ instead of 2 (see function `individ(n)` in Figure 5.51).

5.13. Figure Ans.13a–c shows the results of reconstruction from 3277, 1639, and 820 coefficients, respectively. Despite the heavy loss of wavelet coefficients, only a very small loss of image quality is noticeable. The number of wavelet coefficients is, of course, the same as the image resolution $128 \times 128 = 16,384$. Using 820 out of 16,384 coefficients corresponds to discarding 95% of the smallest of the transform coefficients (notice, however, that some of the coefficients were originally zero, so the actual loss may amount to less than 95%).

5.14. The Matlab code of Figure Ans.14 calculates W as the product of the three matrices A_1, A_2, and A_3 and computes the 8×8 matrix of transform coefficients. Notice that the top-left value 131.375 is the average of all the 64 image pixels.

```
clear
a1=[1/2 1/2 0 0 0 0 0 0; 0 0 1/2 1/2 0 0 0 0;
 0 0 0 0 1/2 1/2 0 0; 0 0 0 0 0 0 1/2 1/2;
 1/2 -1/2 0 0 0 0 0 0; 0 0 1/2 -1/2 0 0 0 0;
 0 0 0 0 1/2 -1/2 0 0; 0 0 0 0 0 0 1/2 -1/2];
% a1*[255; 224; 192; 159; 127; 95; 63; 32];
a2=[1/2 1/2 0 0 0 0 0 0; 0 0 1/2 1/2 0 0 0 0;
 1/2 -1/2 0 0 0 0 0 0; 0 0 1/2 -1/2 0 0 0 0;
 0 0 0 0 1 0 0 0; 0 0 0 0 0 1 0 0;
 0 0 0 0 0 0 1 0; 0 0 0 0 0 0 0 1];
a3=[1/2 1/2 0 0 0 0 0 0; 1/2 -1/2 0 0 0 0 0 0;
 0 0 1 0 0 0 0 0; 0 0 0 1 0 0 0 0;
 0 0 0 0 1 0 0 0; 0 0 0 0 0 1 0 0;
 0 0 0 0 0 0 1 0; 0 0 0 0 0 0 0 1];
w=a3*a2*a1;
dim=8; fid=fopen('8x8','r');
img=fread(fid,[dim,dim])'; fclose(fid);
w*img*w' % Result of the transform
```

131.375	4.250	−7.875	−0.125	−0.25	−15.5	0	−0.25
0	0	0	0	0	0	0	0
0	0	0	0	0	0	0	0
0	0	0	0	0	0	0	0
12.000	59.875	39.875	31.875	15.75	32.0	16	15.75
12.000	59.875	39.875	31.875	15.75	32.0	16	15.75
12.000	59.875	39.875	31.875	15.75	32.0	16	15.75
12.000	59.875	39.875	31.875	15.75	32.0	16	15.75

Figure Ans.14: Code and Results for the Calculation of Matrix W and Transform $W \cdot I \cdot W^T$.

5.15. Figure Ans.15 lists the Matlab code of the inverse wavelet transform function iwt1(wc,coarse,filter) and a test.

5.16. The simple equation $10 \times 2^{20} \times 8 = (500x) \times (500x) \times 8$ is solved to yield $x^2 = 40$ square inches. If the card is square, it is approximately 6.32 inches on a side. Such

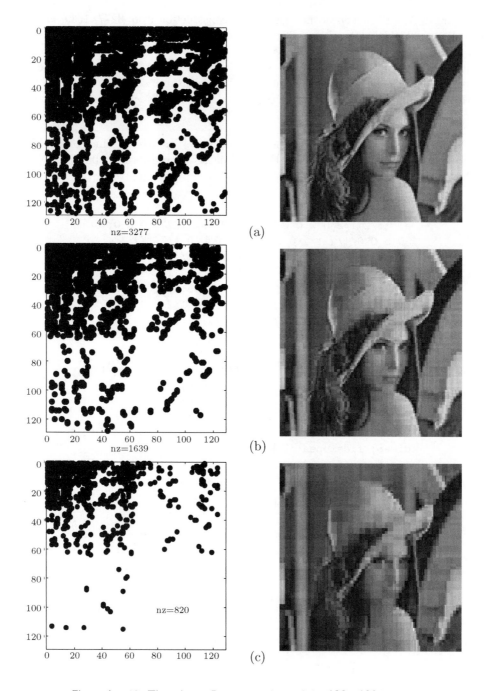

Figure Ans.13: Three Lossy Reconstructions of the 128×128 Lena Image.

```
function dat=iwt1(wc,coarse,filter)
% Inverse Discrete Wavelet Transform
dat=wc(1:2^coarse);
n=length(wc); j=log2(n);
for i=coarse:j-1
 dat=ILoPass(dat,filter)+ ...
  IHiPass(wc((2^(i)+1):(2^(i+1))),filter);
end

function f=ILoPass(dt,filter)
f=iconv(filter,AltrntZro(dt));

function f=IHiPass(dt,filter)
f=aconv(mirror(filter),rshift(AltrntZro(dt)));

function sgn=mirror(filt)
% return filter coefficients with alternating signs
sgn=-((-1).^(1:length(filt))).*filt;

function f=AltrntZro(dt)
% returns a vector of length 2*n with zeros
% placed between consecutive values
n =length(dt)*2; f =zeros(1,n);
f(1:2:(n-1))=dt;
```

A simple test of iwt1 is

```
n=16; t=(1:n)./n;
dat=sin(2*pi*t)
filt=[0.4830 0.8365 0.2241 -0.1294];
wc=fwt1(dat,1,filt)
rec=iwt1(wc,1,filt)
```

Figure Ans.15: Code for the 1D Inverse Discrete Wavelet Transform.

a card has 10 rolled impressions (about 1.5×1.5 each), two plain impressions of the thumbs (about 0.875×1.875 each), and simultaneous impressions of both hands (about 3.125×1.875 each). All the dimensions are in inches.

6.1. An average book may have 60 characters per line, 45 lines per page, and 400 pages. This comes to $60 \times 45 \times 400 = 1,080,000$ characters, requiring one byte of storage each.

6.2. Audio samples are normally 16-bit unsigned integers, so they are in the interval $[1, 2^{16} - 1]$. The residuals tend to be small numbers, but can also be large. In principle, a residual can be as large as 2^{16} and as small as -2^{16}. Thus, enough variable-length codes are needed to encode all the residuals. The first audio sample of an input file is not subtracted from anything but is encoded with the same variable-length code used to encode the residuals and such codes exist even for the largest samples because they are needed for the residuals.

6.3. Such an experiment should be repeated with several persons, preferably of different ages. The person should be placed in a sound insulated chamber, and a pure tone of frequency f should be played. The amplitude of the tone should be gradually increased from zero until the person can just barely hear it. If this happens at a decibel value d, point (d, f) should be plotted. This should be repeated for many frequencies until a graph similar to Figure 6.2a is obtained.

6.4. We first select identical items. If all $s(t - i)$ equal s, Equation (6.5) yields the same s. Next, we select values on a straight line. Given the four values a, $a + 2$, $a + 4$, and $a + 6$, Equation (6.5) yields $a + 8$, the next linear value. Finally, we select values roughly equally-spaced on a circle. The y coordinates of points on the first quadrant of a circle can be computed by $y = \sqrt{r^2 - x^2}$. We select the four points with x coordinates 0, $0.08r$, $0.16r$, and $0.24r$, compute their y coordinates for $r = 10$, and substitute them in Equation (6.5). The result is 9.96926, compared to the actual y coordinate for $x = 0.32r$ which is $\sqrt{r^2 - (0.32r)^2} = 9.47418$, a difference of about 5%. The code that did the computations is shown in Figure Ans.16.

```
(* Points on a circle. Used in exercise to check
 4th-order prediction in FLAC *)
r = 10;
ci[x_] := Sqrt[100 - x^2];
ci[0.32r]
4ci[0] - 6ci[0.08r] + 4ci[0.16r] - ci[0.24r]
```

Figure Ans.16: Code for Checking Fourth-Order Prediction.

7.1. Because the original string S can be reconstructed from L but not from F.

7.2. A direct application of Equation (7.1) eight more times produces:

$$\text{S}[10-1-2]=\text{L}[T^2[I]]=\text{L}[T[T^1[I]]]=\text{L}[T[7]]=\text{L}[6]=\text{i};$$
$$\text{S}[10-1-3]=\text{L}[T^3[I]]=\text{L}[T[T^2[I]]]=\text{L}[T[6]]=\text{L}[2]=\text{m};$$
$$\text{S}[10-1-4]=\text{L}[T^4[I]]=\text{L}[T[T^3[I]]]=\text{L}[T[2]]=\text{L}[3]=\text{\textvisiblespace};$$
$$\text{S}[10-1-5]=\text{L}[T^5[I]]=\text{L}[T[T^4[I]]]=\text{L}[T[3]]=\text{L}[0]=\text{s};$$
$$\text{S}[10-1-6]=\text{L}[T^6[I]]=\text{L}[T[T^5[I]]]=\text{L}[T[0]]=\text{L}[4]=\text{s};$$
$$\text{S}[10-1-7]=\text{L}[T^7[I]]=\text{L}[T[T^6[I]]]=\text{L}[T[4]]=\text{L}[5]=\text{i};$$
$$\text{S}[10-1-8]=\text{L}[T^8[I]]=\text{L}[T[T^7[I]]]=\text{L}[T[5]]=\text{L}[1]=\text{w};$$
$$\text{S}[10-1-9]=\text{L}[T^9[I]]=\text{L}[T[T^8[I]]]=\text{L}[T[1]]=\text{L}[9]=\text{s};$$

The original string swiss␣miss is indeed reproduced in S from right to left.

7.3. Figure Ans.17 shows the rotations of S and the sorted matrix. The last column, L of Ans.17b happens to be identical to S, so S=L=sssssssssh. Since A=(s,h), a move-to-front compression of L yields $C = (1, 0, 0, 0, 0, 0, 0, 0, 0, 1)$. Since C contains just the two values 0 and 1, they can serve as their own Huffman codes, so the final result is 1000000001, 1 bit per character!

```
sssssssssh          hsssssssss
sssssssshs          shssssssss
ssssssshss          sshsssssss
ssssssshss          ssshssssss
sssshsssss          sssshsssss
sssshsssss          ssssshssss
ssshssssss          sssssshsss
sshsssssss          ssssssshss
shssssssss          sssssssshs
hsssssssss          sssssssssh
```

(a)   (b)

Figure Ans.17: Permutations of "sssssssssh".

7.4. The encoder starts at T[0], which contains 5. The first element of L is thus the last symbol of permutation 5. This permutation starts at position 5 of S, so its last element is in position 4. The encoder thus has to go through symbols S[T[i − 1]] for $i = 0, \dots, n-1$, where the notation $i-1$ should be interpreted cyclically (i.e., $0-1$ should be $n-1$). As each symbol S[T[i − 1]] is found, it is compressed using move-to-front. The value of I is the position where T contains 0. In our example, T[8]=0, so I=8.

I don't have any solution, but I certainly admire the problem.
—Ashleigh Brilliant

Index

The index caters to those who have already read the book and want to locate a familiar item, as well as to those new to the book who are looking for a particular topic. I have included any terms that may occur to a reader interested in any of the topics discussed in the book (even topics that are just mentioned in passing). As a result, even a quick glance over the index gives the reader an idea of the terms and topics included in the book. Notice that the index items "data compression" and "image compression" are very general.

I have attempted to make the index items as complete as possible, including middle names and dates. Any errors and omissions brought to my attention are welcome. They will be added to the errata list and will be included in any future editions.

2-pass compression, 14, 26, 57, 76, 90, 278

A-law companding, 238–244
adaptive arithmetic coding, 137–140
adaptive compression, 14, 27, 58
adaptive Huffman coding, 76–83, 271
Adler, Mark (1959–), 108
algorithmic encoder, 16
alphabet (definition of), 10, 271
analog data, 278
Aristotle (384–322) B.C., 115
arithmetic coding, 123–141, 271
  adaptive, 137–140
  in JPEG, 181, 191
  QM coder, 181
ASCII, 271, 273
asymmetric compression, 15, 16, 49, 55
audio compression, 15, 227–245
  μ-law, 238–244
  A-law, 238–244

frequency masking, 233–234
temporal masking, 233–235

background pixel (white), 272
Bain, Alexander (1811–1877), 83
Bakewell, Frederick Collier, 83
Bandura, Albert (1925–), xiii
Bark (unit of critical band rate), 234, 272
Barkhausen, Heinrich Georg (1881–1956), 234, 272
  and critical bands, 234
Baudot code, 151
Baudot, Jean Maurice Emile (1845–1903), 151
Belin, Edouard (1876–1963), 84
Bell, Alexander Graham (1847–1922), 83, 84
Benedetto, John J., 201
beta code, 29, 31
bi-level image, 65, 143, 272
bijection, 29

Billings, Josh (1818–1885), 117
bitplane, 272
bitplane (definition of), 143
bitrate (definition of), 16, 272
bits/char (bpc), 16, 272
bits/symbol, 272
bitstream (definition of), 14
Blake, William (1757–1827), ix
Blelloch, Guy, 65
block coding, 272
block mode, 16
BOCU-1 (Unicode compression), ix, 121,
    247, 262–263
bpb (bit per bit), 16
bpc (bits per character), 16, 272
bpp (bits per pixel), 17
Bradshaw, Naomi, 91
Braille code (as example of compression), 2
Braille, Louis (1809–1852), 2
Brett, Catherine, ix
Brislawn, Christopher M., 220
Burrows–Wheeler method, ix, 16, 121,
    247–252, 263, 264, 272

canonical Huffman codes, 75–76, 113
Cantor, Georg Ferdinand Ludwig Philipp
    (1845–1918), 135
Carroll, Lewis (1832–1898), 189, 257, 282
cartoon-like image, 144
CCITT, 85, 272
Cervantes, Miguel Saavedra de (1547–1616),
    v
Chaitin, Gregory John (1947–), 136
Chambord (Château, 1526), 178
channel coding, viii, 10
Christie Mallowan, Dame Agatha Mary
    Clarissa (Miller 1890–1976), 83
chromaticity diagram, 184
CIE, 184, 272
  color diagram, 184
circular queue, 273
Clancy, Thomas Leo (1947–), 225
codec, 14, 273
codes
  ASCII, 273
  definition of, 273
  EBCDIC, 273
  phased-in binary, 78
  Rice, 278

Unicode, 273
  variable-length
    unambiguous, 39, 276
codes for the integers, 28–38
  Fibonacci, 253
color
  cool, 185
  warm, 185
color images (and grayscale compression),
    43
color space, 184
companding, 14
companding (audio compression), 229–231
compression factor, 17, 273
compression gain, 17, 273
compression performance measures, 16–17
compression ratio, 16, 273
compressor (definition of), 14
continuous-tone image, 143, 144, 273
cool colors, 185
correlation between pixels, 8, 22, 65

da Vinci, Leonardo (1452–1519), 178
data compression (approaches to), 21–58
data hiding (steganography), viii
data structures, ix, 81, 273
Daubechies, Ingrid (1954–), 199
decoder, 274
  definition of, 14
  deterministic, 16
decompressor (definition of), 14
decorrelated pixels, 152
definition (definition of), 18
Deflate, 50, 108–119, 274
delta code (Elias), 32–35
deterministic decoder, 16
Deutsch, Peter, 114
dictionary-based compression, 47–50, 93–119
dictionary-based methods, 274
discrete cosine transform, 159–174, 187, 274
discrete wavelet transform (DWT), 274
discrete-tone image, 143, 274
distributions
  Gaussian, 275
  Laplace, 276
  normal, 277
downsampling, 180
Dudeney, Henry Ernest (1857–1930), 30

EBCDIC, 273
Elias codes, 30–36
Elias, Peter (1923–2001), 30, 32, 124
Eliot, George (1819–1880), 208
Eliot, Thomas Stearns (1888–1965), 264
encoder, 274
  algorithmic, 16
  definition of, 14
entropy, 10–14, 40, 65
  definition of, 274
Erdős–Kac theorem, 179
escape code in adaptive Huffman, 77
eye (and brightness sensitivity), 146

facsimile compression, 85–90, 146, 274
  1D, 85–89
  2D, 89–90
factor of compression, 17, 273
Fano, Robert Mario (1917–), 61, 62
Favors, Donna A. (1955–), 226
Fibonacci code, 253
Fibonacci numbers (and height of Huffman
  trees), 74
Fibonacci, Leonardo Pisano (1170–1250),
  253
file differencing, 16
filter banks, 216–218
fingerprint compression, ix, 121, 218–225
finite-state machines, 65
foreground pixel (black), 272
Fourier transform, 275
Fourier, Jean Baptiste Joseph (1768–1830),
  198, 275
Frazier, Michael W., 201
frequencies of symbols, 78, 79
frequency domain, 233
frequency masking, 233–234

Gailly, Jean-Loup, 108
gain of compression, 17, 273
Gallager, Robert Gray (1931–), 61
gamma code (Elias), 31–32
gas molecules (and normal distribution), 178
Gauss, Carl Friedrich (1777–1855), 178
Gaussian distribution, 178–179, 275
Golomb code, 275
Gordon, Charles, 24
Gray codes, 149–151
Gray, Elisha (1835–1901), 84

Gray, Frank, 151
grayscale image, 143, 275
grayscale image compression (extended to
  color images), 43
group 3 fax compression, 85, 274
group 4 fax compression, 85, 274
Gzip, 274

Haar transform, 199–215
Haar, Alfred (1885–1933), 199, 200
Hardy, Thomas (1840–1928), 140
Hartley (information unit), 10
Hawthorne, Nathaniel (1804–1864), 120
hearing (properties of), 231–235
Hell, Rudolf (1901–2002), 84
hierarchical image compression, 182
Hilbert curve, 46–47
Hilbert, David (1862–1943), 46
Huffman coding, 61–83, 89, 275
  adaptive, 76–83, 271
  canonical, 75–76
  code size, 70–71
  decoding, 67–69
  in JPEG, 189
  not unique, 63
  number of codes, 71–72
  ternary, 72
  2-symbol alphabet, 65
  variance, 64
Huffman, David Albert (1925–1999), 61, 62
human hearing, 231–235
human voice (range of), 231
Hummel, Ernest A., 84

i.i.d., *see also* memoryless
i.i.d. (independent and identically
  distributed), 53
image
  bi-level, 65, 272
  bitplane, 272
  continuous-tone, 273
  discrete-tone, 274
  grayscale, 275
  interlaced, 44
  resolution of, 143
  types of, 143–144
image compression, 143–226
  bi-level (extended to grayscale), 150

principle of, 146
image transforms, 152–174, 279
information theory, 10–14, 275
instantaneous codes, 28
interlacing scan lines, 44
ITU, 272, 274, 275
ITU-T, 85
  recommendation T.4, 85
  recommendation T.6, 85

JFIF, 197, 275
JPEG, 179–195, 272, 275
  blocking artifacts, 181, 226
  lossless mode, 194
JPEG-LS, 194

Katz, Philip Walter (1962–2000), 108, 117, 119, 277
Knuth, Donald Ervin (1938–), 310, (Colophon)
Korn, Arthur (1870–1945), 84
Kraft–McMillan inequality, 39–41, 276
  and Huffman codes, 65

Laplace distribution, 37, 148, 179, 276
Lempel, Abraham (1936–), 47, 98, 277
linear prediction (in audio compression), 235–238
  in shorten, 244
lockstep, 77
logarithm (as the information function), 12
lossless compression, 15, 276
lossy compression, 15, 276
luminance component of color, 180, 181, 184–186, 208
LZ77 method, 48–50, 278
LZ78, 95–97
LZW, 98–107, 277
  decoding, 102

Manfred, Eigen (1927–), 125
mean square error (MSE), 17
memoryless, *see* i.i.d., 11
midriser quantization, 242
midtread quantization, 241
minimal binary codes, *see* phased-in binary codes
MLP, 276
MMR coding, 89

model (in data compression), 17, 277
modem, 85
Montesquieu, (Charles de Secondat, 1689–1755), 263
Morse code, 25
  as compression, 2
Morse, Samuel Finley Breese (1791–1872), 25
Motil, John Michael (1938–), ix, 71
Motta, Giovanni (1965–), ix
move-to-front method, 272, 277
μ-law companding, 238–244
Muirhead, Alexander, 85

nat (information unit), 10
Nelson, Mark, 18
Newton, Isaac (1643–1727), 134
Nin, Anais (1903–1977), (Colophon)
nonadaptive compression, 14
normal distribution, 178–179, 277
Nyquist, Harry (1889–1976), 9, 228

Occam's razor, 2
omega code (Elias), 35–36
optimal compression method, 16

patents of algorithms, 277
peak signal-to-noise ratio (PSNR), 17
Peano curve, 46
pel (in fax compression), 85
perceptive compression, 15
Perkins, Dexter, 19
phased-in binary codes, 78
Picasso, Pablo Ruiz (1881–1973), 177, 186
pixels
  background, 272
  decorrelated, 152
  definition of, 143, 277
  foreground, 272
PKArc, 277
PKlite, 277
PKunzip, 277
PKWare, 277
PKzip, 277
power law distribution of probabilities, 31
prediction, 278
prefix property, 28, 278
prime factors (and normal distribution), 179
probability model, 17

progressive image compression, 149
Prowse, David (Darth Vader, 1935–), 77
psychoacoustic model, 278
psychoacoustics, 231–235
pyramid (wavelet image decomposition), 201

QM coder, 181, 191
quadrature mirror filters, 217
quantization, 24
    definition of, 51
    image transform, 152
    in JPEG, 187–189
    midriser, 242
    midtread, 241
    scalar, 51–55, 278
    vector, 55–58, 279
queue (data structure), 273

random data, 65
range encoding, 140–141
Ranger, Richard H., 84
ratio of compression, 273
redundancy, 10–14
    definition of, 12–13
reflected Gray codes, 149–151, 275
Resnikoff, Howard L., 215
Reynolds, Paul, 95
RGB (reasons for using), 184
Rice codes, 36–38, 278
    for audio compression, 229
Rice, Robert F. (Rice codes developer), 36
RLE, 278
Robinson, Tony (Shorten developer), 38
run-length encoding (RLE), 22, 41–46
    and BW method, 248, 250

Sagan, Carl Edward (1934–1996), 52
scalar quantization, 51–55, 278
Schopenhauer, Arthur (1788–1860), 142
SCSU (Unicode compression), ix, 121, 247,
    258–263
semiadaptive compression, 15
Shannon, Claude Elwood (1916–2001), 10,
    11, 13, 61, 62, 254, 274, 275
Shannon–Fano method, 61–62, 275, 278
Shorten (audio compression), 38, 244–245,
    278
sibling property, 78, 79
Sierpiński curve, 46

sliding window compression, 48–50, 278
source (of data), 10
source coding, vii, 10
space-filling curves, 46–47, 278
sparseness ratio, 209
standard (wavelet image decomposition),
    201
statistical methods, 279
stone-age binary (unary code), 2, 30
streaming mode, 16
subband transform, 152, 201–218
symbol ranking, ix, 121, 247, 254–257, 263
symmetric (wavelet image decomposition),
    220
symmetric compression, 15

taboo code, 59
taps (wavelet filter coefficients), 220
temporal masking, 233–235
text
    files, 15
    random, 65
token (definition of), 279
training (in data compression), 86
training documents (used in compression),
    27
transforms, 23–24, 50–51
    discrete cosine, 274
    Haar, 199–215
    images, 279
    subband, 201–218
    wavelet, 198–218
tree
    adaptive Huffman, 77–79
    Huffman, 63, 77–79
        height of, 73–75
trie (definition of), 97
trit (ternary digit), 10, 72, 279
two-pass compression, 14, 26, 57, 76, 90, 278

unary code, 30, 279
    general, 279
Unicode, 273, 279
Unicode compression, 258–263
uniquely decodable (UD) codes, 22
    not prefix codes, 28
universal compression method, 16
Updike, John Hoyer (1932–), 15

Vail, Alfred (1807–1859), 25
variable-length codes, 21–22, 25–38, 253, 279
  unambiguous, 39, 276
variance of Huffman codes, 64
vector quantization, 55–58, 279
Voronoi diagrams, 279
Voronoi regions, 57

warm colors, 185
wavelet image decomposition
  pyramid, 201
  standard, 201
  symmetric, 220
wavelet transform, 198–218
wavelets
  discrete transform, 274
  filter banks, 216–218
  quadrature mirror filters, 217
wavelets (Daubechies D4), 216

wavelets scalar quantization (WSQ),
  218–225
Welch, Terry A., 98, 277
Wells, Raymond O'Neil, 215
Wheeler, John Archibald (1911–), 12
Wheeler, Wayne, ix
Wilde, Erik, 198
William of Ockham, 2

Xenophon (431–350) B.C., 246

YCbCr color space, 146, 185, 186, 197
YIQ color model, 208

zigzag sequence
  in JPEG, 189
  in RLE, 45
Zip (compression software), 108, 274, 280
Ziv, Jacob (1931–), 47, 98, 277

Any inaccuracies in this index may be explained by the
fact that it has been sorted with the help of a computer.

—D. Knuth

Colophon

This book was written during the short period February through September 2007. The book was designed by the author and was typeset by him with the TeX typesetting system developed by Donald Knuth. The text and the tables were done with Textures, a TeX implementation for the Macintosh. The figures were generated in Adobe Illustrator, also on the Macintosh. Figures with calculations were computed first in *Mathematica* or Matlab, and then "polished" in Illustrator.

The CM set of fonts consists of 75 fonts that are described in Knuth's *Computer Modern Typefaces* (Volume E of the Computers and Typesetting series) as well as the "line," "circle," and symbol fonts associated with LaTeX.

Knuth started his research in computerized typesetting in 1975 and developed the fonts as part of the huge TeX project. The fonts were initially called AM (American Modern) and were later improved, to become the familiar CM fonts, released in 1985.

The Type 1 versions of the Computer Modern fonts (1990) and AMSFonts (1992) were produced by Blue Sky Research and Y&Y, who published the fonts as part of their implementations of TeX.

Character outlines for the CM fonts were derived from high-resolution METAFONT-generated character bitmaps by *ScanLab* from Projective Solutions, applied and corrected by Blue Sky Research. The outlines for the AMS Euler fonts were derived algorithmically from METAFONT code using tools developed by Y&Y. Character- and font-level hints were programmed using software from Y&Y, with extensive manual labor by programmers from both companies.

In 1988, Blue Sky Research released the PostScript Type 3 versions of the CM fonts.

The CMMI* fonts were revised in 1996 to conform to Knuth's changes to the Greek delta and arrow characters.

In 1997, the type-1 CM fonts became public domain.

Life shrinks or expands in proportion to one's courage.

—Anais Nin